GENDER IN HISTORY

Series editors:
Lynn Abrams, Cordelia Beattie, Julie Hardwick and Penny Summerfield

The expansion of research into the history of women and gender since the 1970s has changed the face of history. Using the insights of feminist theory and of historians of women, gender historians have explored the configuration in the past of gender identities and relations between the sexes. They have also investigated the history of sexuality and family relations, and analysed ideas and ideals of masculinity and femininity. Yet gender history has not abandoned the original, inspirational project of women's history: to recover and reveal the lived experience of women in the past and the present.

The series Gender in History provides a forum for these developments. Its historical coverage extends from the medieval to the modern periods, and its geographical scope encompasses not only Europe and North America but all corners of the globe. The series aims to investigate the social and cultural constructions of gender in historical sources, as well as the gendering of historical discourse itself. It embraces both detailed case studies of specific regions or periods, and broader treatments of major themes. Gender in History titles are designed to meet the needs of both scholars and students working in this dynamic area of historical research.

Taking travel home

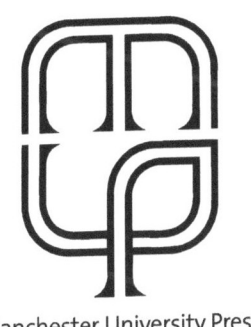

Manchester University Press

OTHER RECENT BOOKS
IN THE SERIES

The state as master: Gender, state formation and commercialisation in urban Sweden, 1650–1780   Maria Ågren

Love, intimacy and power: Marriage and patriarchy in Scotland, 1650–1850   Katie Barclay (Winner of the 2012 Women's History Network Book Prize)

Men on trial: Performing emotion, embodiment and identity in Ireland, 1800–45   Katie Barclay

Modern women on trial: Sexual transgression in the age of the flapper   Lucy Bland

The Women's Liberation Movement in Scotland   Sarah Browne

Modern motherhood: Women and family in England, c. 1945–2000   Angela Davis

Women against cruelty: Protection of animals in nineteenth-century Britain   Diana Donald

Gender, rhetoric and regulation: Women's work in the civil service and the London County Council, 1900–55   Helen Glew

Jewish women in Europe in the Middle Ages: A quiet revolution   Simha Goldin

Women of letters: Gender, writing and the life of the mind in early modern England   Leonie Hannan

Women and museums 1850–1914: Modernity and the gendering of knowledge   Kate Hill

The shadow of marriage: Singleness in England, 1914–60   Katherine Holden

Women, dowries and agency: Marriage in fifteenth-century Valencia   Dana Wessell Lightfoot

Catholic nuns and sisters in a secular age: Britain 1945–90   Carmen Mangion

Out of his mind: Masculinity and mental illness in Victorian Britain   Amy Milne-Smith

Medieval women and urban justice: Commerce, crime and community in England, 1300–1500   Teresa Phipps

Women, travel and identity: Journeys by rail and sea, 1870–1940   Emma Robinson-Tomsett

Imagining Caribbean womanhood: Race, nation and beauty contests, 1929–70   Rochelle Rowe

Infidel feminism: Secularism, religion and women's emancipation, England 1830–1914   Laura Schwartz

Women, credit and debt in early modern Scotland   Cathryn Spence

Being boys: Youth, leisure and identity in the inter-war years   Melanie Tebbutt

Women art workers and the Arts and Crafts movement   Zoë Thomas

Queen and country: Same-sex desire in the British Armed Forces, 1939–45   Emma Vickers

The 'perpetual fair': Gender, disorder and urban amusement in eighteenth-century London   Anne Wohlcke

TAKING TRAVEL HOME

THE SOUVENIR CULTURE OF BRITISH WOMEN TOURISTS, 1750–1830

Emma Gleadhill

MANCHESTER UNIVERSITY PRESS

Copyright © Emma Gleadhill 2022

The right of Emma Gleadhill to be identified as the author of this work has been asserted by them in accordance with the Copyright, Designs and Patents Act 1988.

Published by Manchester University Press
Oxford Road, Manchester M13 9PL

www.manchesteruniversitypress.co.uk

British Library Cataloguing-in-Publication Data
A catalogue record for this book is available from the British Library

ISBN 978 1 5261 5527 6 hardback
ISBN 978 1 5261 9161 8 paperback

First published 2022
Paperback published 2025

The publisher has no responsibility for the persistence or accuracy of URLs for any external or third-party internet websites referred to in this book, and does not guarantee that any content on such websites is, or will remain, accurate or appropriate.

EU authorised representative for GPSR:
Easy Access System Europe – Mustamäe tee 50,
10621 Tallinn, Estonia
gpsr.requests@easproject.com

Typeset
by New Best-set Typesetters Ltd

To Shane, David, Jessica and Chelsea, 'I am so grateful that if all my souvenirs were marked with cups, there would be many more than mile stones from hence to Ampthill'.[1]

Le Souvenir
I have sometimes sung praises to glory,
More often I have sung praises to love:
The daughters of memory guided me to them,
First one then the other.
Destroying everything on his way,
The god who banishes pleasures,
Warns me that I should at my age
Sing praises only to *souvenir*.

Souvenir, the heavenly present,
The shadow of good things we no longer have,
It still is a pleasure that remains,
After all those we have lost.
Of the errors of youth,
Time, seeking to cure us,
Brings us experience,
On the wings of *souvenir*.

Love, which in changing heart, we offend,
Complains of this forgetfulness of the heart:
It is right, because it is constancy
That is the *souvenir* of happiness.
Through it the past begins again;
It enriches our future,
And sweet gratitude
Is the daughter of *souvenir*.

1 Letter from Horace Walpole to Anne Fitzpatrick, Countess of Upper Ossery, 1775, in Horace Walpole, *The Yale Edition of Horace Walpole's Correspondence*, ed. W. S. Lewis (New Haven: Yale University Press, 1965), vol. 34, 278.

One views with pleasure the image
Of the peril that we have faced;
We like to paint the storm
At the port where we have already arrived.
There are sorrows in life
That a tender heart likes to feel.
It savours in its melancholy
The pleasure of *souvenir*.

I do not really know what to believe
Neither in hell, nor in heavens;
But I know that our memory
Proves the justice of the gods.
If a wicked soul gives way to
Remorse that he cannot flee,
For the just man the Elysium
Of life is the *souvenir*.

How many beautiful days our youth
Has seen quickly pass away!
Sometimes, in our old age,
Happiness can call them back.
Treasures which Flora has given us
We cannot enjoy for long;
But the smell of autumnal fruits
Is of springtime a *souvenir*.[2]

---

[2] Translated from the French as it appears in the Royal Irish Academy, Wilmot Papers, 12 L 25, Martha Bradford (née Wilmot) and Princess Ekaterina Romanovna Daskova, 'Poems and Miscellaneous Notes', early nineteenth century. The poem is a copy of 'Les souvenirs' by Louis-Philippe de Ségur, *Oeuvres complètes de M. le comte de Ségur* (Paris: Alexis Eymery, 1825), 387–8.

Contents

List of plates and figures	page viii
Acknowledgements	xiii
Map of the central women travellers' residences in England, Wales and Ireland	xvi
Introduction: remembering travel	1

Part I: Gendering connoisseurship

1 The Grand Tour: a masculine legacy of taste	33
2 Shopping for souvenirs	56
3 Creating their own cultural capital: Lady Anna Miller and Hester Lynch Piozzi	77

Part II: Gendering science

4 Every fair Columbus	107
5 Dorothy Richardson's extensive knowledge	123
6 Lady Elizabeth Holland, the social orchestrator of science	142

Part III: Gendering friendship

7 From diplomatic gift to trifle from Tunbridge Wells	175
8 A snuff-box and other Napoleonic keepsakes	202
9 Princess Ekaterina Dashkova's gifts to Martha Wilmot	226
Conclusion: remembering the souvenir	252
Bibliography	254
Index	280

Plates and figures

Plates

1 Johan Zoffany, *The Tribuna degli Uffizi*, 1772–78/9, 123.5 cm × 155 cm, oil on canvas. (Royal Collection Trust/© Her Majesty Queen Elizabeth II, 2021)
2 W. Chambers, *The Townley Collection in the Dining Room at Park Street, Westminster*, 1794–95, 390 mm × 540 mm, watercolour on paper. (© Trustees of the British Museum)
3 Pietro Fabris, *Kenneth Mackenzie, First Earl of Seaforth 1744–81, at Home in Naples: Concert Party*, 1771, 355 mm × 476 mm, oil on canvas. (© National Galleries Scotland)
4 Pietro Fabris, *Kenneth Mackenzie, First Earl of Seaforth 1744–81, at Home in Naples: Fencing Scene*, 1771, 355 mm × 476 mm, oil on canvas. (© National Galleries Scotland)
5 Sir Nathaniel Dance-Holland, *Portrait of Olive Craster*, 1762, 72.39 cm × 60.17 cm, oil on canvas. (By permission of Minneapolis Institute of Art)
6 Grand Tour fan, 1780, 275 mm (guardstick), leather (kid) leaf, ivory guards and sticks. (Royal Collection Trust/© Her Majesty Queen Elizabeth II 2021)
7 Lady Miller's monument, Bath Abbey. (Photographed by Alan Morley, by permission of Anna Riggs)
8 Lady Miller's monument, Bath Abbey, detail. (Photographed by Alan Morley, by permission of Anna Riggs)
9 Unknown Italian artist, *Hester Lynch Piozzi (née Salusbury, later Mrs Thrale)*, 1785–86, 756 mm × 629 mm, oil on canvas. (© National Portrait Gallery, London)

Plates and figures ix

10 Felice Fontana, *Wooden Man*, 1799, 160 cm (height), wood and paper mache. (Photographed by Thierry Ollivier, by permission of Musée de l'Histoire de la Médecine, Université René Descartes)
11 Felice Fontana, *Wooden Man* (head detail), 1799, 160 cm (height), wood and paper mache. (Photographed by Thierry Ollivier, by permission of Musée de l'Histoire de la Médecine, Université René Descartes)
12 John Wykeham Archer, *Holland House*, 1857, 270 mm × 372 mm, watercolour over graphite. (© Trustees of the British Museum)
13 Green leather case containing pencil and dance card, given by Queen Maria Carolina to Caroline Swinburne (front view). (By permission of Sir Brooke Boothby, image courtesy of Anne French)
14 Adrien Jean Maximilien Vachette, box; cameo, 1797–1815, 72 mm × 52 mm × 20 mm, gold and agate (front view). (© Trustees of the British Museum)
15 Grigory Ugryumov, *Tsar Ivan IV Conquering Kazan in 1552*, 1799–1800, 1,075 cm × 875 cm, oil on canvas. (© National Art Museum of Belorussian Republik, Minsk/Alamy).

Figures

Front matter Map of the central women travellers' residences in England, Wales and Ireland. (Drawn by Marley Slade) *page* xvi
1.1 William Say (after Sir Joshua Reynolds), *Members of the Society of Dilettanti*, 1812–16, 580 mm × 418 mm, mezzotint. (© Trustees of the British Museum) 35
1.2 Philip Dawe, *The Macaroni, a Real Character at the Late Masquerade*, 1773, 351 mm × 250 mm, mezzotint. (© Trustees of the British Museum) 37
1.3 Pompeo Batoni, *Sir Thomas Gascoigne, Eighth Baronet*, 1779, 248.9 cm × 172.7 cm, oil on canvas. (© Leeds Museums and Galleries/Bridgeman Images) 38
1.4 Giuseppe Cades, *Gavin Hamilton Leading a Party of Grand Tourists to the Archaeological Site at*

	Gabii, 1793, 449 mm × 583 mm, ink and wash over pencil. (© The National Galleries of Scotland)	43
1.5	Henry Tresham, *Grand Tourists Purchasing Antiquities*, 1790, 330 mm × 483 mm, pen and ink grey wash. (Private collection)	43
1.6	William Russell Birch (after Richard Cooper II), *Saltram, Devonshire*, 1790, 150 mm × 178 mm, stipple and etching. (© Trustees of the British Museum)	49
2.1	Hair comb, England, nineteenth century. (© Pitt Rivers Museum, University of Oxford)	65
2.2	Jane and Mary Parminter, bricolaged specimen table, 1790s, shells, polished marble, lapis lazuli, micromosaics, plaster casts and a mourning plaque, A la Ronde, Devon. (National Trust, image courtesy of Freya Gowrley)	68
3.1	Map of Hester Lynch Piozzi and Lady Anna Miller's Grand Tours. (Drawn by Marley Slade)	78
3.2	John Chessell Buckler, *Batheaston Villa from the S. E.*, 1825. (© Victoria Art Gallery Bath & North East Somerset Council/Bridgeman Images)	80
3.3	The Batheaston Vase adorned with myrtle, 144 mm × 89 mm, etching, William Hibbert (author), Printed by R. Cruttwell for L. Bull, in Bath, and sold, in London, by Hawes, Clarke, and Collins, 1775. (Topographical Collection/Alamy)	82
3.4	J. Baker, *Brynbella, the Seat of G. Piozzi Esqr*, 1795, 110 mm × 164 mm, aquatint. (By permission of Llyfrgell Genedlaethol Cymru/The National Library of Wales)	95
5.1	'Halifax Gibbet', in John Rylands Library, Dorothy Richardson Papers, GB 133 Eng MS 1125, Dorothy Richardson, 'Travel Journal Yorkshire (North Riding) and Lancashire', 1779, fol. 250. (Image courtesy of the John Rylands Research Institute and Library, University of Manchester)	128
5.2	Francesco Bartolozzi (after Giovanni Battista Cipriani), *A View of the Indians of Terra del Fuego in Their Hut*, 1773, 208 mm × 280 mm, engraving.	

	(Image courtesy of the National Library of Australia)	136
6.1	Map of Lady Elizabeth Holland's Grand Tour, 1791–96. (Drawn by Marley Slade)	145
6.2	'Anatomical Venus', wax model with human hair and pearls in rosewood and Venetian glass case, 'La Specola' (Museo di Storia Naturale), Florence, Italy; probably modelled by Clemente Susini, around 1790. (© Joanna Ebenstein)	148
6.3	Charles Henry Jeens, after Robert Fagan, *Elizabeth Vassall Fox (née Vassall), Lady Holland (formerly Webster)*, 1874, 146 mm × 94 mm, line engraving. (© National Portrait Gallery, London)	155
7.1	Leather case containing pencil and dance card, given by Queen Maria Carolina to Caroline Swinburne (back view). (By permission of Sir Brooke Boothby, image courtesy of Anne French)	188
7.2	Early wooden container for carrying ink, with a compartment for sand, stamped 'A trifle from Tunbridge Wells', eighteenth century. (Image courtesy of the Amelia)	192
7.3	Pincushion, 'A trifle from Brighton'. (Image courtesy of the Amelia)	193
7.4	Tunbridge-ware sewing clamp in the form of a castle, eighteenth century. (Image courtesy of the Amelia)	194
8.1	James Gillray, Introduction of Citizen Volpone and his suite, at Paris, 1802, 265 mm × 368 mm, hand-coloured etching. (© National Portrait Gallery, London)	204
8.2	George Cruikshank, *The Head of the Great Nation in a Queer Situation*, 1813, 250 mm × 350 mm, hand-coloured etching. (© Trustees of the British Museum)	206
8.3	James Gillray, *Maniac-Ravings – or – Little Boney in a Strong Fit –*, 1803, 262 mm × 353 mm, hand-coloured etching. (© National Portrait Gallery, London)	206
8.4	William Holland, *An Attempt to Swallow the World!!*, 1803, 327 mm × 250 mm, etching. (© Trustees of the British Museum)	209

8.5	Holland House, Dutch Garden, bust of Napoleon, reimagined by Gibon, classic art with a modern twist reimagined, 1889. (Gibon Art/Alamy)	212
8.6	*Il famoso Satyro colla Capra*, 1761, 138 mm × 126 mm, etching. (© Trustees of the British Museum)	215
8.7	Adrien Jean Maximilien Vachette, box; cameo, 1797–1815, 72 mm × 52 mm × 20 mm, gold and agate (verso card insert). (© Trustees of the British Museum)	216
8.8	Adrien Jean Maximilien Vachette, box; cameo, 1797–1815, 72 mm × 52 mm × 20 mm, gold and agate (recto card insert). (© Trustees of the British Museum)	217
8.9	Samuel de Wilde, *Sketch for a Prime Minister or How to Purchase a Peace*, 1811, 235 mm × 195 mm, etching and aquatint. (© Trustees of the British Museum)	221
9.1	Dimitry Grigorievich Levitsky, *Portrait of Yekaterina Vorontsova-Dashkova*, 1784, 59.6 cm × 49.5 cm, oil on canvas. (© Hillwood Estate, Museum and Gardens, photographed by Edward Owen)	232
9.2	Portrait of Martha Wilmot, in *The Russian Journals of Martha and Katherine Wilmot 1803–1808*, ed. The Marchioness of Londonderry and H. M. Hyde (London: Macmillan and Co., 1934) (inside front cover).	235
9.3	Fireplace, *c.*1800, Russian Imperial Arms Factory, Tula, forged, blued and cut steel with facetted steel and gilt brass ornaments. (©Victoria and Albert Museum, London).	241
9.4	'Eine Finnin im Feyertags Kleide', in Royal Irish Academy, Wilmot Papers, 12 L 26–8, *Description de toutes les nations de l'Empire de Russie*, St. Petersbourg, 1776–7, vol. 1, 17.	243

Acknowledgements

This book is a souvenir of the people who have inspired and encouraged me over the years it has taken for it to come to fruition.

David Garrioch, you scattered the seeds of thought from which this book has grown. I cannot thank you enough for shaping my practice as a historian and for your gentle nudges to always look harder and think deeper. Jessica O'Leary, thank you for pushing me to fully explicate my thoughts in my writing. Our monthly meetings online inspired major turning points in the writing of this book. Your rigorous critique helped me to realise the clarity of expression that I needed and wanted to explain why the souvenir and the women who created it were, and are, significant and worthy of study. Chelsea Barnett, thank you for always encouraging me throughout this whole, sometimes very difficult process, for listening and patiently pointing out where I might pull threads together, especially when I could not tell the warp from the weft. I am not certain that I would have continued to persist with academia or this book without your enthusiasm for this project and for myself as an academic. And Shane, what can I say to thank you enough? You tended and watered the seeds of this project from when David first scattered them by reviewing multiple versions of my writing and by listening and offering up perceptive responses to my many musings on walks, over dinner, on the couch. It is only with your love, support and conversation every day in every shape and form that I have written this. The book is dedicated to the four of you.

Many others have helped along the way by hearing or reading different iterations of this material and generously offering their thoughts and suggestions. A particular thank you to Rosemary Sweet, Mary Spongberg, Jennifer Milam, Richard White, Kate Fullagar,

Clare Monagle and Sarah Bendall for taking the time to read earlier versions of parts of this book and for offering advice at key points. I have presented on this topic at conferences and seminars organised by the Australian and New Zealand Society for Eighteenth-Century Studies, the Sydney Feminist History group, the Sydney Intellectual History Network, the Romantic Studies Association of Australasia, the Australian Historical Association, the Art Association of Australia and New Zealand, the Professional Historians Association of Victoria and the Royal Historical Association of Victoria. Thank you to the members of these groups who attended my presentations for your early engagement and encouragement. I am most grateful to Jessica Sun and the members of the eighteenth-century studies reading group; Helen Bones and the members of the Sydney history writing group; and Jeannine Baker, Justine Lloyd, Nicole Matthews and the members of the gender studies reading group for your very helpful comments on draft sections of this book or related articles and presentations. And lastly, thank you to the Awards Committee of the Australian Academy of the Humanities for granting me a Publication Subsidy to assist with the publication of this book, specifically the inclusion of the beautiful colour plates at its centre. I am lucky to have such a supportive network of scholars and groups to draw from in Sydney and Melbourne.

Sections of the gift analysis in Chapter 9 appeared in my co-authored article with Ekaterina Heath, 'Giving women history: a history of Ekaterina Dashkova through her gifts to Catherine the Great and others', in *Women's History Review* (19 April 2021). The Napoleonic memorabilia explored in Chapter 8 has formed inspiration for Katja and my new project Souvenirs *and the Death of Celebrity*, which will provide a gender history of the visual and material culture of Napoleon, Rousseau and other political and cultural figures of the eighteenth century. Katja, it is an absolute pleasure to work with you and I look forward to uncovering a different aspect of souvenir culture with you in our new project. Part II of this book investigates the agency of British women tourists who were active in the scientific realm. My article '"For I asked him men's questions": late eighteenth-century British women tourists' contributions to scientific inquiry' in *Eighteenth-Century Life* (2021) established that women tourists were indeed present in that realm. The articles 'Improving upon birth, marriage and divorce: the cultural

Acknowledgements

capital of three late eighteenth-century female Grand Tourists' in *The Journal of Tourism History* (2018) and 'Collecting cosmopolitan credentials: Lady Holland's Grand Tour souvenirs and the "House of all Europe"' in *eMaj* (2017) similarly showed women's presence as Grand Tour collectors, while this book examines their agency. Thank you to the editors and reviewers of all of these journals for their valuable comments on my manuscripts.

This book could not have been written without the guidance of the anonymous peer reviewers and my editor at Manchester University Press, Meredith Carroll. Every piece of criticism and advice I received came at just the right time in the process and helped me to find the book's final shape and form. This book also would not have been written without the cultural institutions from which I have drawn my source material. I have particularly benefitted from the assistance of the librarians, archivists and curators at the British Library, the John Rylands Library, the Royal Irish Academy, the Amelia and Bath Abbey. Especial thanks to Ian Beavis, Research Curator at the Amelia, for your expertise on Tunbridge-ware; to Anna Riggs, Bath Abbey Archivist (and Lady Anna Riggs Miller's namesake) for your generous assistance with researching her vase and dedication; and to Sonja Poncet ('Handywoman'), Musée d'Histoire de la Médecine, for introducing me to photographer Thierry Ollivier's beautiful images of Fontana's *Wooden Man*.

Finally, an enormous thank you to my friends, my family – Robyn, Phil, Peter and Verona – and my colleagues in research support at Macquarie University – especially Robert, Jan, Christine, Jo, Anu and Roberta – who have shared my excitement with new finds and discoveries as this book as developed. I hope that you will enjoy the result.

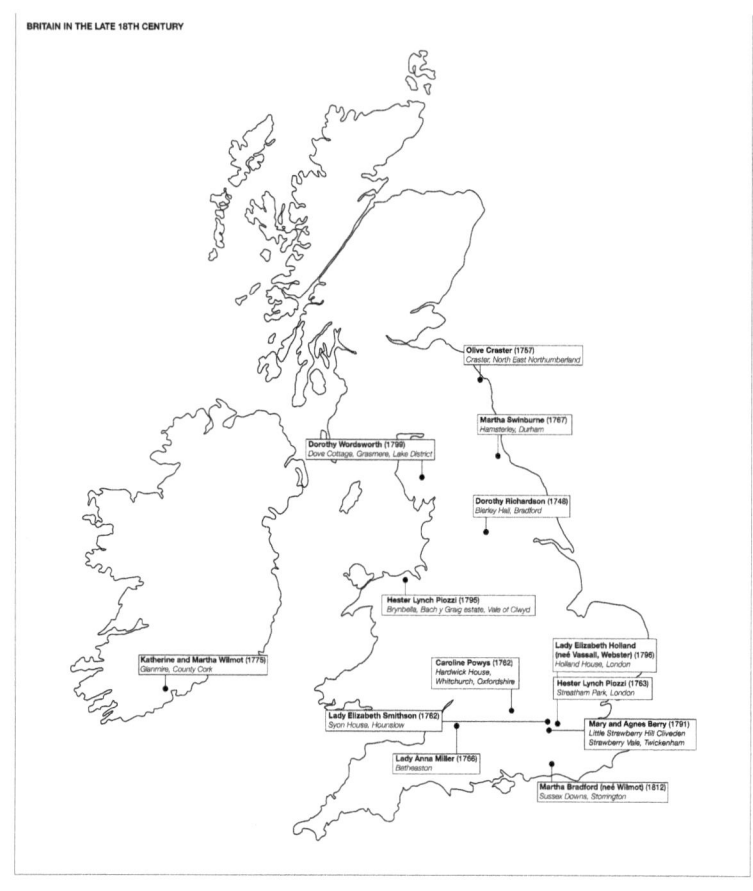

(front matter) Map of the central women travellers' residences in England, Wales and Ireland.

Introduction: remembering travel

'Having spent some time in viewing this magnificent wonder', Caroline Powys wrote of her visit to Stonehenge in 1759, 'we endeavoured with some tools our servants had, to carry some pieces of it with us'.[1] Not without difficulty the future mistress of Hardwick House accomplished this feat and proudly polished her small sandstones and bluestones to display her special connection to the sarsen circle. Caroline was not the only pillager of the past. Ten years later, Lady Anna Miller fretted that her 'collection of fossils, if they augment in proportion to what they have hitherto done, may endanger the bottoms of our trunks'.[2] The author of *Letters from Italy* had good reason to worry about accommodating her growing travel collection; she would return from her Grand Tour with an Etruscan vase from Cicero's villa, several prints of Rome by Piranesi and a case of mosaic pieces she had collected on a beach near Naples.[3] She displayed these and other souvenirs to guests visiting her poetry salon near Bath.

From 1750 to 1830 British women were active tourists, and they sought to find new ways to memorialise their travel experiences. Some brought great monuments home to represent great deeds, but more often they took home small objects to represent something of themselves and how they perceived the world. Some published accounts, but many more did not and their memories were instead captured in their journals and letters. The primary purpose of *Taking Travel Home* is to view the souvenir through a gendered lens. Using an interdisciplinary framework which is informed by literary and design theory – including the influential work of thinkers like Walter Benjamin and Susan Stewart – art history, material culture studies and tourism studies, this book asks: what motivated women to collect objects from their travels? How did they acquire and display them? What meanings did they have for individual women and how did these change over their lifetimes? On a broader comparative level it asks: how did women's material representations of travel relate to those of their male counterparts? And what roles did other factors like status, regionality and personality play in the meanings of the objects they brought home? Answering these questions allows the historian to unpack the systems of social and cultural value that developed around travel during this period of flux when rising incomes, cheaper, more reliable transport and changes to the political landscape opened Britain and the Continent up to a larger cohort than ever before. *Taking Travel Home* is invested in exploring how British women tourists challenged and subverted gender norms in pursuit of their own subjectivity and the role they played in shaping the precursor to the mass tourism of today.

Over the course of three parts, *Taking Travel Home* applies a gendered analysis to three overlapping arenas for representing travel in the eighteenth century: connoisseurship, science and friendship. Within each arena, I provide an overview of how men established practices to constitute and reinforce their power and analyse how women enlisted material culture to negotiate the barriers that were raised against their participation. I then assess the efforts of particular women who exemplified these negotiations, weighing up the roles that gender, status, regionality and personality played in their success.

I argue that women, finding themselves variously excluded from connoisseurship, science and politics, found the souvenir a particularly useful mechanism to negotiate meaning and value. By the 'souvenir', I mean an object that a traveller takes home from the travel environment to serve as a memento, or evidence that they were *there*. A souvenir can be given, bought, found or created by the traveller themselves and can act as a reminder of anything from within the travel environment: a past event, place, condition, an absent person or something that once existed. As an object whose purpose was to act as a proxy, or a stand-in for one's travels – that is, something that materially manifested an aspect or experience of travel – the souvenir required little financial outlay (if any). However, the object had a potentially very high associational value, one that went beyond prestige or money, if a woman attached an empowering travel narrative to it. These objects could be transferred from the travel environment to Britain, inviting commentary and prompting women to reveal the experiences they had while travelling.

Ultimately, I argue that souvenirs are representative of female agency during this period. For elite women, revelling in the independence and identity formation of travel, but hampered by polite models of femininity and reliant on their menfolk, the creation of souvenirs provided a socially acceptable way to physically prove their contentious claims to the authority of the travelling subject.

The women tourists

Taking Travel Home focuses on the elite British women who undertook Grand Tours, other forms of Continental tour and domestic tours of Britain in the second half of the eighteenth century and first three decades of the nineteenth century. The pervading travel culture for Britain's social elite was the culture of the Grand Tour. Roman Catholic priest and tutor Richard Lassels is known to have first introduced the term 'Grand Tour' into the English language in 1670: 'no man understands Livy and Caesar, Guicciardini and Monluc, like him, who hath made exactly the Grand Tour of France, and the Giro of Italy', Richard advised the classically educated sons of the British nobility and gentry who were his charges.[4] By the early eighteenth century the wealthy British nation had formed a sizeable social elite with both the money and the leisure to travel. This group of nobles and landed gentry idealised the Grand Tour as a rite of passage for their young men.[5] An extended journey to the principal cities of Europe that generally took travellers through France or the Netherlands, Switzerland, Austria and the German princely states, but centred upon Italy, and above all Rome, the Tour was understood to provide the final education to the British male patrician. In practice, however, there was a wider range of travellers undertaking these Continental journeys, including elite women. 'It is now all the fashion for the ladies to travel', Grand Tourist Joseph Spence observed to his mother as early as 1733, after seeing a surprising number of Englishwomen in Florence.[6] Professionals, including diplomats, artists and musicians (some of them women), also undertook Grand Tours, as did the tutors and servants who catered to the Grand Tourists' needs. The social elite (including its women) did not stay static but expanded as the century progressed and nouveau riche merchant and colliery families – particularly from the north of England, which experienced great prosperity through agriculture, lead-mining and the coal trade – keen to cement their newly landed status, undertook their own Grand Tours, often together as a family, or sent their sons and daughters to the Continent.

Looking back at the Grand Tour, Bruce Redford has divided it into the following four generally accepted phases: 'a period of growing popularity, from about 1670 to 1700; a heyday extending from about 1700 to 1760; a period of gradual decline, approximately 1760 to 1790; and a restricted revival, 1815 to about 1835'.[7] He and others cite the conclusion of the Grand Tour as the 1830s with the development of steam travel and package tourism for middle-class clientele. From the 1760s, rising incomes and more reliable transport led to a demographic shift from landed to middle class tourists, and also to family groups of men, women and children outnumbering tutors and their pupils.[8] The prosperity enjoyed by Britain's merchant and colliery families generated more opportunities for women travellers and this is reflected by their writing. Prior to 1770, just two travelogues were published by women – Elizabeth Justice's *Voyage to Russia* (1739) and Lady Mary Wortley Montagu's *Embassy Letters* (1763) – but between 1770 and 1800 over twenty were published, with many more unpublished manuscripts circulated among friends and family.[9] Thus, the period of decline of the elite male Grand Tourist was the heyday of the woman Grand Tourist.

Whether they wrote their own accounts or not, women tourists travelling in the latter part of the century were inspired by the distinctive female voice of Lady Mary Wortley Montagu's highly popular *Embassy Letters*, published soon after her death following her stay in Constantinople from 1716 to 1718 as wife of the British ambassador, and her letters from other travels in Europe. Mary claimed an authoritative female perspective, due to her ability to access private homes and female-only spaces. In comparison she dismissed male Grand Tourists for providing 'many wrong notions of Italy', advising Mary Stuart, the Countess of Bute, in a letter from Genoa in 1739 that:

> they return no more instructed than they might have been at home, by the help of a map. The boys only remember where they met with

the best wine or the prettiest women; and the governors (I speak of the most learned amongst them) have only remarked situations and distances, or, at most, statues and edifices.[10]

According to Mary, she brought to travel a better on-the-ground understanding of the details of social life and the spaces in which it took place than her male counterparts. While many other scholars have already explored the ways in which the rituals of society and domesticity generally assumed greater importance in women's daily lives and how they brought associated values to what they saw and did, here I analyse the gendered values they brought to what they bought and collected.

From 1789 to 1815 the French Revolution and Napoleonic Wars made the traditional Grand Tour route difficult for British men and women alike. According to Linda Colley, under these restrictions 'Continental Europe was more a cockpit for battle, and a landscape of revolutionary subversion, than a fashionable playground and cultural shrine'.[11] A patriotic exploration of one's own country was recommended instead and so domestic tours, already undertaken in preparation for longer tours of the Continent or as cheaper alternatives, were increasingly promoted. The ruins of the British Isles now filled in for the ruins of Rome, the health and pleasure-giving properties of Bath and Tunbridge Wells took the place of Aix-en-Provence, and tourists flocked to paint picturesque views of the Lake District, witness the impressive industrial growth of the Peak District and take advantage of the commercial expansion of London.

Women Grand and domestic tourists travelled for a greater diversity of reasons than the idealised young elite male Grand Tourist; whether as companions, for education, for their health, to economise or to escape domestic embarrassment. They travelled at a range of ages, with everyone from children to elderly widows taking to the road. Some undertook just one tour while others set out on multiple journeys throughout their lives. Daughters accompanied their parents on the Grand Tour to learn Italian and French and acquire social polish. At the ages of twenty and twenty-one, Mary and Agnes Berry travelled with their widower father, Robert, to the Continent, where they were educated from 1783 to 1785. It was also not uncommon for newly married women to travel to Italy for an extended honeymoon. Olive Craster made a wedding Tour in 1760–63 with her husband George, a wealthy northern landowner. In 1784, at forty-three years of age, Hester Lynch Piozzi went on a somewhat unconventional honeymoon with her second husband, Gabriel. The couple's three-year tour of the Continent, undertaken just after their wedding, was also a flight from scandal, for Gabriel was Hester's daughters' Italian music teacher. Other couples travelled later in their marriages. This was the case for thirty-one-year-old Lady Anna Miller and her husband, John, who travelled to Italy in 1770 to economise while they built a house at extravagant cost near Bath.

Other women travelled as companions to older husbands returning to Italy later in life, only to have their own youthful Grand Tour experiences. Martha and her husband, Henry, of the Swinburne Baronetcy of Capheaton, Northumberland, went on multiple tours of the Courts of Europe and post-revolution France following their marriage in 1767. When she was twenty-one, Lady Elizabeth Holland (née Vassall), the supreme travel collector of this book, managed to set out on a Grand Tour with one husband only to return with another. As the sole heir of three Jamaican sugar plantations, she was born into excessive slave-based wealth and so already had a degree of agency unimagined by most women before she accompanied her first husband, Sir Godfrey Webster (who was thirty years her senior), on a tour of Italy in 1791. In 1795 she refused to return to England with him and would instead come back the following year with Henry Richard Fox, third Baron Holland. Three months later, Godfrey changed his name to Vassall and succeeded to his father-in-law's West Indian estates. When he then divorced Elizabeth, Godfrey was able to revert to his previous surname and retain her West Indian fortune of £7,000 per annum.[12] Thankfully, Elizabeth's second husband supported her desire to travel (in part because it contributed to his career, as the nephew of the Whig politician Charles James Fox). The Hollands would go on to visit many more countries, including Scotland in 1798, Germany in 1800, Paris in 1802, Spain in 1805 and 1808–9, and Italy in 1815.

Women domestic tourists included the likes of forty-six-year-old Mary, who in 1791 travelled to Milford Haven in Pembrokeshire, Wales, with her husband, the Reverend Caesar Morgan. For many years Mary had looked forward to this journey to her husband's home district, 'with the most ardent expectation'.[13] In 1796, ten years after her naval captain husband's death, fifty-two-year-old Sarah Murray set out on a five-month tour of Scotland accompanied by two servants. Some brave women still managed to undertake Continental tours during this period but found themselves caught in the Napoleonic Wars. Katherine Wilmot of Glanmire, County Cork, accompanied her neighbours Stephen Moore, the second Earl of Mount Cashell, his wife, Margaret, and six 'Irish adventurers' on a Grand Tour in 1801. During her travels Katherine met Napoleon, made friends with the famed Austrian painter Angelica Kauffman and had an audience with Pope Pius VI, but quickly returned home when England and France resumed hostilities in 1803.

Most single women travelled accompanied by immediate family members. Some, like Harriet Carr of Dunston Hill, Durham, went to Italy with a brother.[14] There are occasional accounts of women who travelled alone, with only a female servant, but these are rare. Lady Elizabeth Percy, Duchess of Northumberland, spent unusually long periods away from her 'Soul's best Joy' – as she called her husband, Hugh. Her immense wealth as the heiress to the Percy estates and supportive husband gave her the independence to travel to the Low Countries and Germany from 1766 to 1770 and France and Switzerland in 1772 with only her drawing master, Jean Vilet, performing the role of *valet de chambre*.[15] From the ages of thirteen to fifty-two Dorothy Richardson, the unmarried daughter of a rector, visited Yorkshire, Lancashire, Derbyshire, Nottinghamshire, Oxford, Bath and London with her parents, uncles, brothers and brother-in-law. A mixed group usually set out by chaise, but the actual exploration of sites was often undertaken by Dorothy and a male companion on foot or horseback. In 1801, with four decades of travelling experience behind her, she finally set out on her first solo journey to the East Riding of Yorkshire, with only her maid. This, however, obliged her to hold the company (and pace) of other women, which she found vexing. When Dorothy wanted to visit a lighthouse recommended by the artist William Gilpin, for instance, she bridled at having her request barred by a Mrs Smythe, who 'put an absolute negative saying that the walk was too long for a hot day'.[16]

The fact that these women were able to undertake leisured travels, write and acquire souvenirs reveals their social status; they were clearly not poor, but rather came from noble, landed gentry or wealthy nouveau riche merchant and colliery families. Within these ranks, however, there was significant variation that impacted upon the journeys the women were able to undertake and the types of objects they acquired. Lady Elizabeth Holland and Lady Elizabeth Percy were both of a level of independent wealth that was extraordinary, and especially so for a woman. The former was the universal heiress of Richard Vassall (of one of the chief plantar families in the Caribbean); the latter was the grand-daughter of the sixth Duke of Somerset and inherited the vast Percy estates following the death of her brother on a Grand Tour in 1744. These women's travels to Italy and elsewhere offered them the chance to become collectors and patrons of the arts. Elizabeth Holland bought classical sculptures, antique gems and Renaissance or seventeenth-century pictures, together with contemporary paintings, sculptures, porcelain, natural specimens and furniture on her various travels to grace the halls of her Whig political salon, Holland House. An aficionado of Murillo's expressive depictions of women, she commissioned an 'admirable sketch in crayons' of his fresco *Death of Saint Clare* (1646) after seeing it in Spain in 1805.[17] As a fan of Napoleon, in 1815 she commissioned a bust of the French leader from Canova in Rome.[18] These are just two souvenirs from Lady Elizabeth Holland's vast collection. Lady Elizabeth Percy was an even more avid collector: she drew up lists in an effort to itemise her collection into antiquities, books, bronzes, drawings, Japan work, marbles, medals, paintings, pastels, porcelain, prints and specimens of wood, which have subsequently been bound into eight volumes of museum catalogues.[19]

Harriet Carr and her brother came from a nouveau riche Newcastle merchant family. Their father, Ralph, made his own tour of the commercial capitals of Europe in 1737–38 for business, rather than education or pleasure. He established his family's wealth through a range of activities, including coal-mining, banking, underwriting, ship-owning and the import and export of goods to Europe and the Americas. Harriet and Henry's Grand Tour of 1791–94 formed part of the family's larger claim to gentry through the purchase of country seats at Dunston and Hedgeley in Northumberland and a townhouse in Charlotte Square. Harriet's chief souvenirs were her records in watercolour of the Old Master paintings and landscapes she saw in Italy, and of her circle of friends in Florence. Her father was impressed by her artistic talents that were honed on the Grand Tour, affectionately calling his daughter 'one of my richest jewels'.[20]

Similarly, Mary and Agnes Berry were the daughters of Robert Berry, the nephew of a successful Scottish merchant. While Robert was taken into his uncle's business, he was more interested in literature than commerce and married a distant cousin, Elizabeth Seaton, who was without portion. When Robert's uncle died in 1781, he left the bulk of his fortune and estate to Robert's brother William, who established an annuity for Robert of £1,000 per year. The sisters were not of a status or wealth to become patrons of the arts and collectors, but they enjoyed making purchases at Italy's manufactories, including 'a piece of crape … at two paoli and a half the braccia, about two shillings the English yard' and two fans depicting 'the ruins of Rome for a sequin apiece'.[21] By then in his dotage, Horace Walpole, the fourth Earl of Orford, was impressed by the returned sisters' refinement, describing them as 'the best informed and the most perfect creatures I ever saw at their age'.[22] He patronised the women and installed them at his property, Little Strawberry Hill.

Domestic traveller Dorothy Richardson was the third child of Reverend Henry Richardson, rector of Thornton-in-Craven. Her grandfather Richard Richardson had trained at Oxford and Leiden to become a doctor. He was an antiquarian, member of the Royal Society and close friend of the Anglo-Irish physician, naturalist and collector Hans Sloane. Dorothy was able to spend much of her life undertaking small tours of the English countryside to follow her own natural history and antiquarian pursuits because she was unmarried and of a well-off and locally prominent academic family that esteemed intellectual endeavour. Between tours she spent a great deal of time at the family library at Bierley Hall, just outside Bradford, which is regarded as one of the great eighteenth-century libraries.

I am concerned with the whole gamut of objects that these women and others brought or sent home and the travel narratives they attached to them. These objects include cheap, mass-produced purchases, like the two painted fans Agnes and Mary Berry bought 'of the ruins of Rome for a sequin apiece', or the 'charming Aeolian harps, sold for five shillings each' that Sarah Murray saw at the Crosthwaite Museum in the Lake District.[23] They also include expensive commissions, like the Grand Tour portrait that Lady Elizabeth Holland had painted in 1793. I am interested in those objects that were made to be worn on the body, like the 'very rich stuffs for furniture and very fine embroidery' the Berry sisters saw in Italy's manufactories and the comb 'incrusted with gold, to imitate an Etruscan border, copied from an antique vase' that Lady Anna Miller had custom-made in Florence.[24] Natural specimens collected on the road, like the 'variety of sea weeds' that Dorothy Richardson gathered on a beach in Heysham, Lancashire, are also examined, as are gifts, like the 'bless'd beads, made of agate and jasper encased in gold' that Katherine Wilmot received during her audience with the Pope.[25]

Outlined above are the women who are central to this book, but many others make short appearances throughout. Whether single or married, of excessive or more moderate wealth, all of these travellers found themselves dependent, to varying degrees, on the men in their lives; those who were single relied on the support of their fathers and brothers, while under the law of coverture those who were married relied on the generosity of their husbands, even when they brought significant wealth to the marriage. These women delighted in the independent identity formation of travel but, as we will see, impossible ideals of femininity and reliance on their menfolk restricted them in a multitude of ways. The souvenir offered them a platform to take home (and show off) independent identities reflective of the female experience of travel.

Gendering eighteenth-century travel

Analysing the rise of the souvenir reveals that women formed spaces in which they could create and control their own travel narratives and produce their own understandings of gendered phenomena like connoisseurship, science and friendship. Yet, this significant site of contestation over the legitimacy of the male and female experience has been largely overlooked by scholarship that has dismissed the souvenir as a trivial and inauthentic object. I argue instead that the souvenir is a significant object of particular use to the historian, in that it is redolent of the struggle between the sexes and the classes to control the meanings of travel. We can use the souvenir to access how women carved out a space of their own in the contested space of travel and the cultural cache it imparted.

Introduction: remembering travel 11

Since the 1980s, literary scholars and historians have worked hard to uncover and write more nuanced histories of eighteenth-century travellers – where they came from, where they went and why they went there – that challenge the dominance of the homogenous young patrician male Grand Tour narrative. As the scholarship on travel in the late eighteenth and early nineteenth centuries increases, more nuanced terms, categories and cultures of travel are being brought forward pertaining to the distinct and overlapping cultures of different nations, regions and social groups. In 2017 this culminated in Rosemary Sweet, Gerrit Verhoeven and Sarah Goldsmith's *Beyond the Grand Tour: Northern Metropolises and Early Modern Travel Behaviour*.[26] Leading the way to resituate the Grand Tour as part of a wider context of travel and topographical writing, the authors took a fresh approach by focusing on practices of travel in northern and western Europe, particularly Britain, the Low Countries and Germany. My aim here has been to offer a deep analysis of how those British women of the social elite who left behind rich and accessible written records (more on this later) constructed their subjectivities through the object-associated travel narratives they brought home. My geographic and demographic scope is therefore limited to these select women who left behind written and material records. In response to Sweet, Verhoeven and Goldsmith's call to pay closer attention to the relationship between foreign and domestic travel, my focus does extend to women travelling to other destinations on the Continent and domestically within Britain, with several participating in multiple journeys throughout their lives; indeed, the elite were defined by their mobility. While the first chapter on the cultural capital of connoisseurship centres on the Grand Tour as a pivotal experience in many elite women's lives, the other chapters are not restricted to an exclusive focus on domestic or foreign travel.

Regarding the scholarship on women travellers, in the late twentieth century Mary Russell and Jane Robinson produced three anthologies.[27] Brian Dolan and Kathryn Walchester have since brought attention to the experiences of some of those women who undertook Grand Tours.[28] Since the 1990s, scholars have acknowledged not just the need to bring women into the historical record but also to uncover the historically contingent gendered meanings through which male and female travel subjects were produced. Michèle Cohen has led the way when it comes to masculinity and national identity.[29] Elizabeth Bohls, Chloe Chard and Katherine Turner have examined the gendered literary strategies women and men used in their travel writings.[30] Yet, although scholars have worked hard to uncover the gendered meanings through which subjects and their experiences were produced in travel writings, they have yet to consider how they were produced in the objects travellers brought home. There have been a wealth of art histories of Grand Tour collecting and connoisseurship, but scholars have only just started to take a gender lens to the material culture of travel.[31] Rosemary Sweet and Isabelle Baudino have looked at male and female experiences of cities on the Grand Tour.[32] In reference to domestic travel, in the second half of the twentieth century, Esther Moir and Ian Ousby first drew attention to the development of Britain's tourist industry.[33] Since then, Tim Youngs has explored how the new gendered meanings that familiar goods obtained in the travel environment challenged travellers' understandings of themselves as British subjects, while Zoë Kinsley has considered how women constructed their identities by writing about commodities in their travel journals.[34] But a gender lens has not been taken to examine the memorabilia of travel.[35]

This book joins the aforementioned scholarship invested in historicising masculinity and femininity by drawing attention, for the first time, to the ways in which contingent meanings of femininity emerged and gained legitimacy through women tourists' combined textual and material efforts to represent their travel experiences and the ensuing rise of the souvenir. My focus is on, for the first time, gendering the souvenir. I recognise that women and men of different life stages and from different social classes, from various countries and regions within countries, travelled alone or in groups to a wide range of locations for a diversity of reasons. I do not, however, engage with the full range or diversity of travelling cultures during the period, or even the full range of regional cultural variance within the female travelling cohort of Britain. I hope that other scholars will both deepen and broaden the scope of the gendered souvenir culture I expose here.

Gendering the souvenir poses two interrelated sets of challenges. The first is theoretical and concerns determining how women related to the objects they brought home. The second is methodological and concerns interpreting both the objects themselves and how they were represented in text. I will start by addressing the theoretical challenge of the souvenir.

Gendering the souvenir

Today souvenirs are thought of almost entirely as objects gathered in the course of travel. They serve as reminders of places visited and more generally of experiences associated with travel. But the connection of the French origin word *souvenir* with travel is relatively new. Its first recorded appearance in the English language is in 1775 in correspondence between Horace Walpole and Anne Fitzpatrick, Countess of Upper Ossery: 'You have always been so good to me, Madam', Horace wrote in a note attached to a fine cup, 'and I am so grateful that if all my *souvenirs* were marked with cups, there would be many more than mile stones from hence to Ampthill'.[36] Throughout the following decades a souvenir meant a keepsake, more often a reminder of a person than of a place visited. It was generally a gift that recalled a special relationship. In the nineteenth century, 'souvenir' continued to be used in English in its etymological sense of 'memory', often connected to travel.

The souvenir was first theorised in the 1930s by Walter Benjamin as a memento, not necessarily related to travel. Benjamin drew from Marx's idea of commodity fetishism (where, under capitalism, objects are abstracted from the history of their production and instead filled with consumer fantasies) to conceive it as a symptom of the rapid industrialisation and the move towards a consumer culture.[37] According to Benjamin, as an object manufactured for the purposes of continuous reflection, the souvenir formed part of capitalism's larger assault on memory. Benjamin's examination of how transformations in capital, and the organisation of the relations of production, distribution and consumption altered people's relations to objects in the eighteenth century is essential to understanding the rise of the souvenir. Yet, Benjamin theoretically positioned the souvenir in a negative relationship with the decreasing meaning of labour and the distinction of the workers from the product of that labour. This framework understood the needs and desires of the consumer to be misplaced.

In the second half of the twentieth century design theorists and anthropologists drew from Benjamin to associate the souvenir with bad taste, the unoriginal, the affected and the superficial, terming it 'memory fetish' or a 'debased tourist artform'.[38] An association was established between the souvenir and the trivial, so that it sat within a culturally produced hierarchy of objects, with art and high design at its apex and the kitsch and mass-produced at its base. This 'anti-consumerism' and 'anti-tourism' discourse, however, was as illusory as the efforts of travellers in the nineteenth century to identify themselves as 'travellers', rather than 'tourists', and reflected the same class distinctions. These scholars failed to recognise that socioeconomic systems do not completely saturate and determine human relations to the material world.

In 1984 Susan Stewart instead productively combined Benjamin's interpretation with the psychoanalyses of Jacques Lacan and Julia Kristeva, to open up new and poetic ways of talking about the souvenir's nostalgic role as a possession that people use to form a self-identity and autobiography from fragmented experiences. According to Stewart, 'We do not desire souvenirs of events that are repeatable'; instead, 'we need and desire souvenirs of events that are reportable, events whose materiality has escaped us'.[39] Unable to 'entirely recoup' the initial event through our souvenirs, we supplement them with a 'narrative' (or a 'myth') of our own 'interiority and authenticity'.[40]

Two years after Stewart, Beverly Gordon theoretically positioned the travel souvenir in relation to Nelson Graburn and Erik Cohen's structural analyses of tourism as a socio-psychological contrast, where the tourist moves from an ordinary or mundane state at home to an extraordinary or sacred state when travelling.[41] According to Gordon:

> The tourist is concerned with a pursuit of experience distinct from and in [structural] opposition to everyday or ordinary life. People feel a need to bring objects home from the sacred, extraordinary time or space, as home is equated with the ordinary, mundane time and space. They can't hold on to the non-ordinary experience, for it is by nature ephemeral, but they can hold on to a tangible piece of it, an object that came from it. Western culture tends to define reality as 'that which you can put your hands on'. When one puts his hands on a souvenir, he is not only remembering he was there, but 'proving' it.[42]

Stewart's theorisation of the souvenir as a locus for nostalgic identity formation and Gordon's positioning of it in relation to the extraordinary space of travel is crucial to understanding the souvenir as a tool of female agency.

While they provide a framework through which to understand the souvenir, theorists Stewart and Gordon necessarily consider relations between people and souvenirs in the abstract. As a cultural historian, I shift our understanding of the souvenir from a concept to a cultural practice to uncover how women engaged in the production, representation and circulation of gendered meanings when they created souvenirs. I draw from Stewart and Gordon's work to argue that women travellers of the late eighteenth and early nineteenth centuries valued the objects they brought home because they had made contact with their bodies in an extraordinary space and had survived the ravages of the journey home. By touching an object she had personally taken home from the travel environment, a woman could remember her experiences there and narrate them to others. Her narrative could take whatever form she wanted and could be adjusted over time for different audiences; her narrative could be empowering.

Reflecting on the souvenir

It is through a multidimensional analysis of the women's own written reflections on the objects they collected and (where they exist) the objects themselves or visual representations of them, foregrounded in the social and cultural realities of the eighteenth century, that I uncover the hidden operations of gender in the souvenir. The women's travel accounts, journals and correspondence provide me with indications about how and why they acquired their souvenirs (whether they were bought, found, exchanged or gifted) and what they meant to them over time.[43] Some objects, for example, were cherished for their rarity and associations with the ancients, while others were important as reminders of a first encounter with a new experience or as presents from a new acquaintance. I have drawn from well-known editions of published travel accounts and correspondence – such as Hester Piozzi's *Observations and Reflections*, table talk diary, *Thraliana* and letters – but also lesser-known manuscript diaries and personal correspondence held in institutional archives, such as the Holland House papers, Dorothy Richardson papers and Wilmot papers. The accounts of guests to the women's homes and critiques from the periodical press are also valuable sources for interpreting their material strategies in light of contemporary debates about the value of travel.

Scattered through my deep analysis of the sources several elite women have left behind are hints at many other elite women's souvenir narratives which I have carefully drawn out from catalogues, anthologies and art histories.[44] My deep analysis of the published and archival sources of particular women provides insight into the meanings a particular object held to them (for this is the essence of the souvenir). Together with the fragments of information about other women, I paint broader picture of late eighteenth- and early nineteenth-century British women's souvenir culture. My research has been restricted to those travel accounts and personal correspondence easily accessible from my location in Australia and the few research trips to the UK and Europe I have had the capacity to undertake. The published and archival sources I have chosen to focus on are travel accounts, personal correspondence and some household catalogues. There is much more work to be done by delving into more personal diaries and letters and other underutilised archival sources, such as lists of travel expenses, scrapbooks, the printed ephemera of the early modern travel industry and, of course, by reading the material culture of the souvenir objects themselves (more on this shortly).[45]

Engaging with written sources has required careful reflection on the relationship between texts and objects. In this domain, literary methodologies have provided the most assistance. I draw from thing theory, which has been used to explain the development of an eighteenth-century literary phenomenon by which John Locke's empirical conception of body parts as carriers of personhood worked in combination with the century's expanding market culture to inform the development of 'part objects'.[46] These include the 'keepsakes that clutter sentimental fiction (the lockets that protagonists wear next to their hearts; the sleeve buttons or snuffboxes that pairs of characters exchange to memorialise their first meeting or last, teary-eyed party)'.[47] Thing theory informs my analysis of how the women travellers represented their object worlds in writing or used textual invocations of objects.

Reconstructing British women travellers' engagement with the actual physical objects they brought home some two hundred years ago is not without its problems. I consider both the objects themselves and visual representations of them (paintings, drawings, engravings, inventories, catalogues and advertisements). I use the latter to trace those objects that no longer exist or, when an object survives, find out about its relationship to other objects. My methodology to interpret the objects and pictorial renderings of them chiefly draws from art and design studies. Art historians have done a great deal of work establishing the gendered meanings of aesthetics and art objects in the eighteenth and nineteenth centuries. Viccy Coltman has analysed the 'packaging and repackaging' of ancient artefacts by British collectors, engravers and manufacturers and patrons to uncover how neo-classicism was fabricated as part of the process of establishing an elite male British national identity.[48] Marcia Pointon, meanwhile, has examined the affective and imaginative aspects of women's acts of representation in the mediums of portraiture, drawing and antiquarianism.[49] I borrow from these scholars sophisticated strategies for analysing aesthetically inflected objects, like antiquities and Grand Tour portraits, to bring out the associational values that souvenirs held for women travellers.

While art and design methodologies are helpful for analysing women's self-representation through their souvenirs, a material culture approach offers the fresh and exciting perspective of the objects themselves as historical actors.[50] According to Giorgio Riello and Leora Auslander, there are three ways in which a material culture approach can enrich history. First, people have always used all five of their senses (sight, hearing, touch, taste and smell) in their intellectual, affective, expressive and communicative practices. A material culture approach allows for an exploration of these aspects of human expression not reducible to words. Second, by reconceptualising objects as active agents in history (rather than simply products of history) that structure people's perceptions of the world, a material culture approach allows historians to ask new questions. Third, most people for most of human history have not used written language as their major form of expression. A material culture approach draws attention to the other ways in which people have created meaning (for example, through textiles, wood, metal, music and dance).[51] I have, accordingly, sought to enrich my study by bringing to life the past material world of the women travellers.

The purpose of this book is to broadly expose the rise of a souvenir culture through a deep analysis of how elite British women travellers of the late eighteenth and early nineteenth centuries developed that culture. It is important to note that, while I have made an effort to engage with the material culture approach, the women's own writings have provided the starting point for this study, not the objects themselves. The elite status of the women this study concerns allowed them to leave behind a rich assortment of reflective accounts about their souvenirs. My focus has been to shed light on these women's reflections on the objects they brought home. This is not something that has been considered as yet in the scholarship, but it is my hope that other scholars will follow my efforts, particularly with studies grounded in a material culture approach that tell us more about the involvement of other actors in the rise, expansion and fall of the gendered souvenir culture this book has exposed. There is much work to be done in mapping the shape and form of the gendered culture of the souvenir, taking into consideration different travelling cultures. I draw from the knowledge bases and techniques of these disciplines to make a cultural historian's contribution to the growing interdisciplinary reflection on the souvenir. I am interested in the specific relation between the general and the particular, and with souvenirs we are really talking about a particular object.

Taking Travel Home is not a national survey of every British woman who toured Britain and Europe and returned home with souvenirs from 1750 to 1830. Rather, it is a deep cultural history of several women – some whom will be very familiar to readers and others less so – who have left behind the most extensive and accessible published and manuscript accounts of their souvenirs. The women central to this book inhabited different positions within the social elite and returned home to a range of primary residences located across England, Wales and Ireland (see map in front matter).[52] It is my hope that this study will establish the role that a growing collection of elite British women played in the development of the culture of the souvenir in the late eighteenth and early nineteenth centuries and that others will adopt and adapt this framework to provide a more comprehensive and diverse coverage of other facets of this gendered culture.

My cultural history of the relationship between women and the rise of the souvenir also makes an important contribution to scholarship on the souvenir more generally, which thus far has been driven by tourism and consumer behaviour studies.[53] While these scholars have demonstrated how social and cultural context influences the meaning of a souvenir, they have not considered how historical context has the same effect. Anderson and Littrell, and later Wilkins, for instance, found that 'women tend to purchase souvenirs more frequently than men' and that they place more importance on the role of the souvenir as an 'aide memoire', but they attribute this to some intrinsic difference between the male and female experience without recognising that this behaviour has been socially and culturally constructed over two centuries.[54] In 2000, Mars and Mars examined the motivations and attitudes of the working-class British women who brought mass-produced ceramic ornaments home from the seaside holiday spot of Blackpool, Lancashire, from 1880 to 1960. They argued that these objects helped working-class women to 'short circuit' male control over household spending and consolidated links between generations of women.[55] This article hints at the important role the souvenir has played in gender negotiations. My work shows that women tourists did not simply return from their travels to resume their previous lives; they brought objects back as a means of using their empowering travel experiences to build upon the already considerable power that they wielded in the social and domestic realm.

Travel had the potential to be empowering for women tourists for the same reasons that it was empowering for the male political elite: a way to familiarise themselves with Britain's classical cultural heritage; a means of gaining knowledge through experience and; an opportunity to network. Women, therefore, sought to enlist the objects they brought home as proxies for the empowering experience of travel and by such means assert their own legitimacy and agency. However, by the late eighteenth century the meaning of travel was shifting. For one thing, the usual itinerary was in flux, with the Revolutionary and Napoleonic Wars suspending the Grand Tour for the last two decades of the 1700s. For another, the objects that were brought home from travel were changing, with factory production from the 1770s leading to uniform pre-emptive souvenirs, like wooden Tunbridge-ware boxes and printed fans. Women were both the agents and the targets of this early tourism industry.

The first part of the book concerns those women who went on Grand Tours to Italy in search of cultural capital in the second half of the eighteenth century. They especially valued souvenirs for physical proof of their invisible claims to a heightened taste and connoisseurship acquired through Continental travel. These objects could be transferred from Italy to the women's homes in Britain, inviting commentary and prompting their owners to reveal the knowledge they had acquired. The souvenirs thus gave women a platform to perform cultural capital for which they were well received, often leading to the establishment of salons and similar settings in which men and women could mingle and discuss experiences to which only the elite were privy. Souvenirs, therefore, were representative of female agency during this period. Elite women chose to conduct the Grand Tour and to feminise elements of its practices to better suit the female experience during this time. Analysing the rise of the souvenir reveals that women sought to find spaces in which they could create and control their own travel narratives and produce their own understandings of taste, virtue and connoisseurship.

I perform three distinct tasks in Part I. In Chapter 1, I explore the literature and art that contributed to the construction of an exclusive, classical, elite male Grand Tour narrative. In Chapter 2, I show how women, by returning home with souvenirs, challenged the foundations on which this narrative functioned. In Chapter 3, I conduct an in-depth analysis of the ways in which two different women used their souvenirs to respond to and mount a challenge to the major claims that circulated in the dominant elite male Grand Tourist narrative. I argue that these women and others contributed to a reshaping of the Grand Tour, from a male exercise in classical connoisseurship to a far wider practice that was equally the imaginary property of both men and women.

The second part of *Taking Travel Home* is about the knowledge-finding and knowledge-making narratives women created while collecting objects abroad. Women interacted with objects, which we might today call specimens, in an experiential way that gave them a unique, first-hand understanding of the natural and man-made worlds. Bruno Latour has explored the way in which scientific knowledge about the world is 'packed' and circulated by means of material culture ('circulating references') from the field to 'calculation centres' (including laboratories, archives and offices).[56] Collecting objects to demonstrate their knowledge of the natural and man-made worlds provided an opening for women travellers to take part in this packaging and circulation of scientific knowledge. When we consider women's engagement with science, Latour's concept of material circulating references interlinks too with the concept of the 'social circulation' of knowledge. For the period with which this book is concerned (1750–1830) was just prior to the professionalisation of science, marked by the coinage of the term 'scientist' by William Whewell in 1833 to replace 'natural philosopher'. During this time, the collection of minerals, fossils, plants and other samples was not a discrete scientific endeavour, but was motivated and shaped by sociability, taste and aestheticised forms of curiosity. The women valued these objects (usually gathered or gifted) for their typically low (if any) financial outlay and physical proof of their invisible claims to an authoritative eyewitness understanding of natural and man-made phenomena. They could be transferred from the travel environment to the women's homes, prompting their owners to reveal the eyewitness knowledge they had acquired. One's travel memories were thus central to the meanings of these objects, which were a sort of hybrid of the seventeenth-century 'curiosity', the nineteenth-century 'specimen' and the souvenir – standing in as proxy for one's empirical engagement with the extraordinary environment of travel.

Although scholars have recognised individual women for their contributions to science during the period, few historians have explored the ways in which understandings of masculinity and femininity have informed the historical development of the practice of scientific collecting and tourism.[57] In Chapter 4, I look more closely at the multiple visions for scientific travelling and collecting during the period and how they unfolded in the cultural world through specific modes of masculinity and femininity. In Chapter 5, I analyse how one woman, with a level of scientific education unusual for her sex, negotiated these visions during her investigative explorations of different parts of Britain over a period of forty years. Chapter 6 is about the curiosity cabinet of the supreme traveller of this book, Lady Elizabeth Holland. Elizabeth used her cabinet in the context of the salon to test the limits of 'polite conversation', in much the same manner as the women in the previous chapter used their souvenirs to lay claim to the Grand Tour's cultural capital. I alternate in these chapters between labelling the objects the women collected as curiosities, specimens and souvenirs. I give them these alternating labels because of the nebulous way in which the women conceived the objects themselves and in which science was understood by their contemporaries during the period. The relationship of these objects to science was a result of the women's wishes to evoke memories and create narratives of their own engagement with this developing discipline. To only call the objects 'specimens' and use them to measure each woman's contribution to science as we conceive it today would be to follow a modern conception of what was valuable work during the period and override the agency of the women. If we instead consider the different and competing understandings of science that intermingled during the period, a more complex image of scientific collecting and of women's role in this cultural practice begins to emerge – one that extends beyond the simple story of progression from the early modern curiosity cabinet to the modern museum.

The final part of *Taking Travel Home* is concerned with women's sentimentalisation of people and relationships through travel souvenirs. In the eighteenth and early nineteenth centuries femininity was both shaping and being shaped by a culture of sensibility. I argue that by the end of the eighteenth century, the values that women travellers placed on small tokens from the travel environment had gained social traction. Keen to take advantage of society's privileging of sensibility, women and men alike then magnified and formalised these values as 'sentimental' and the objects themselves as 'keepsakes' or '*souvenirs*'. Seeing an opportunity for profit, publishers and traders marketed sentimental value to ever-growing numbers of tourists in the form of sentimental literature and mass-produced knick-knacks.

In Chapter 7 I trace the transformation of the cultural meanings of the travel souvenir from gift to keepsake. I argue that women exchanged keepsakes with each other to solidify and amplify friendships that transcended their lower status within the patriarchy. These friendships found their richest expression in travel because an object representing a friendship gains significance when that friendship is threatened by physical distance. In Chapter 8 I analyse how the Anglo-Irish traveller Katherine Wilmot and Lady Elizabeth Holland engaged with Napoleon through keepsakes. While both women had similarly disappointing first impressions of Napoleon, Katherine rejected his keepsakes to condemn him. Conversely, Elizabeth used them to project an image of an extraordinary friendship with the Emperor. In Chapter 9 I turn to consider the material development of a powerful friendship between Katherine's younger sister Martha, and Princess Ekaterina Romanovna Dashkova. Teasing out the complexities of these women's material sentimentalisation of friendships reveals the keepsake as a powerful narrative instrument that women travellers used to defy their inferior economic, social, cultural and political value in Britain during this period.

By closely examining the diverse networks of social and cultural meanings in which individual women tourist's souvenirs were embedded, this book allows us to better answer familiar questions about women's identities during this period and changes the nature of the questions we can ask. It brings us closer to women of the past by giving us access to new dimensions of their experience, so recovering the range and complexity of meanings that have been historically associated with having travelled.

Notes

1 British Library (hereafter BL), Powys Diaries, Add. MS 42164, Caroline Lybbe Powys (née Girle), 'Journal of a Tour to Oxford, Blenheim, &c.', 1759, fol. 22r°.
2 Anna Riggs Miller, *Letters from Italy, Describing the Manners, Customs, Antiquities, Paintings, &c. of that Country, in the Years MDCCLXX and MDCCLXXI, to a Friend Residing in France* (Dublin: W. Watson, 1776), vol. 1, 359.
3 Miller, *Letters from Italy*, vol. 2, 131 and 57.
4 Richard Lassels, 'A preface to the reader concerning travelling', in *The Voyage of Italy, or a Compleat Journey through Italy. In Two Parts.* (London: John Starkey, 1670).
5 There is a great deal of academic literature on the Grand Tour, including, but not limited to, Jeremy Black, *The British Abroad: The Grand Tour in the Eighteenth Century* (New York: St. Martin's Press, 1992); Jeremy

Black, *Italy and the Grand Tour* (New Haven: Yale University Press, 2003); Edward Chaney, *The Evolution of the Grand Tour: Anglo-Italian Cultural Relations since the Renaissance* (London: Frank Cass, 1998); Chloe Chard, *Pleasure and Guilt on the Grand Tour: Travel Writing and Imaginative Geography, 1600–1830* (Manchester: Manchester University Press, 1999); Christopher Hibbert, *The Grand Tour* (London: Hamlyn Publishing Group, 1974); Clare Hornsby, *The Impact of Italy: The Grand Tour and Beyond* (London: British School at Rome, 2000); Rosemary Sweet, *Cities and the Grand Tour: The British in Italy, c.1690–1820* (Cambridge: Cambridge University Press, 2012); Andrew Wilton and Ilaria Bignamini, *Grand Tour: The Lure of Italy in the Eighteenth Century* (London: Tate Gallery Publishing, 1996); Lynne Withey, *Grand Tours and Cooks' Tours: A History of Leisure Travel, 1750–1915*, 1st edn (New York: W. Morrow, 1997). The Tour is also synopsised in larger studies of tourism, for example James Buzard, 'The Grand Tour and after (1660–1840)', in *The Cambridge Companion to Travel Writing*, ed. Peter Hulme and Tim Youngs (Cambridge: Cambridge University Press, 2002); Eric Zuelow, *A History of Modern Tourism* (London and New York: Palgrave Macmillan, 2015).

6 Joseph Spence, *Joseph Spence: Letters from the Grand Tour*, ed. Slava Klima (Montreal and London: McGill-Queen's University Press, 1975), 138.

7 Bruce Redford, *Venice and the Grand Tour* (New Haven: Yale University Press, 1996), 11. Redford attributes the decline of the Tour to a revival of Britain's public schools and universities accompanied by new strategies for cementing patrician authority (including 'the consolidation of estates and the promulgation of a specifically British cultural identity to replace the cosmopolitan ideal').

8 Towner, John. "The Grand Tour: A Key Phase in the History of Tourism." *Annals of Tourism Research*, 12 (1985): 297–333, 312.

9 Katherine Turner, *British Travel Writers in Europe, 1750–1800: Authorship, Gender, and National Identity* (Aldershot and Burlington: Ashgate, 2001), 25–6.

10 Lady Mary Wortley Montagu, *Lady M. W. Montagu's Letters from France and Italy*, The British Prose Writers, vol. 8 (London: John Sharpe, 1821), 120.

11 Linda Colley, *Britons: Forging the Nation, 1707–1837* (New Haven and London: Yale University Press, 1992), 167.

12 C. J. Wright, 'Fox, Elizabeth Vassall [née Elizabeth Vassall], Lady Holland [other married name Elizabeth Vassall Webster, Lady Webster] (1771?–1845)', *Oxford Dictionary of National Biography*, last updated 3 January 2008, https://doi.org/10.1093/ref:odnb/10028.

13 Mary Morgan, *A Tour to Milford Haven, in the Year 1791* (London: John Stockdale, 1795), 1.
14 A. W. Purdue, 'John and Harriet Carr: a brother and sister from the north-east on a Grand Tour', *Northern History* 30 (1994): 122–38.
15 Anne French, *Art Treasures in the North: Northern Families on the Grand Tour* (Norwich: Unicorn Press, 2009), 69.
16 Quoted in Marcia Pointon, *Strategies for Showing: Women, Possession, and Representation in English Visual Culture, 1665–1800* (Oxford and New York: Oxford University Press, 1997), 100.
17 Elizabeth Vassall Fox Holland, *The Spanish Journal of Elizabeth Lady Holland*, ed. Giles Stephen Fox-Strangways Ilchester (London: Longmans, Green, 1910), 279; T. Faulkner and B. West, *History and Antiquities of Kensington* (London: T. Egerton, 1820), 119.
18 Wright, 'Fox, Elizabeth Vassall'.
19 These are held in the Archives of the Duke of Northumberland at Alnwick Castle. For a description of their contents, see Appendix 2 in French, *Art Treasures in the North*, 276–81.
20 French, *Art Treasures in the North*, 132.
21 Mary Berry, *Extracts from the Journals and Correspondence of Miss Berry: From the Year 1783 to 1852*, ed. Lady Theresa Lewis (London: Longmans Green, 1865), vol. 1, 52, 71.
22 Horace Walpole, *The Yale Edition of Horace Walpole's Correspondence*, ed. W. S. Lewis (New Haven: Yale University Press, 1965), vol. 34, 24.
23 Berry, *Extracts from the Journals and Correspondence*, vol. 1, 71; Sarah Murray, *A Companion, and Useful Guide to the Beauties of Scotland* (London: George Nicol, 1799), 25. From 1781, Peter Crosthwaite sold these souvenirs to tourists after they enjoyed the mournful whistling of his own Aeolian harp, which rested on a windowsill in his museum.
24 Berry, *Extracts from the Journals and Correspondence*, vol. 1, 135; Miller, *Letters from Italy*, vol. 2, 57.
25 John Rylands Library (hereafter JRL), Dorothy Richardson Papers, GB 133 Eng MS 1122, Dorothy Richardson 'Yorkshire (West Riding), Derbyshire, Nottinghamshire and Lancashire', 1761–75, fol. 266; Katherine Wilmot, *The Grand Tours of Katherine Wilmot*, ed. Elizabeth Mavor (London: Weidenfeld and Nicolson, 1992), 82.
26 Rosemary Sweet, Gerrit Verhoeven and Sarah Goldsmith, *Beyond the Grand Tour: Northern Metropolises and Early Modern Travel Behaviour* (London and New York: Routledge, 2017). Their introduction includes an excellent breakdown of the growing diversity of scholarship.
27 Mary Russell, *The Blessings of a Good Thick Skirt* (London: Collins, 1986); Jane Robinson, *Wayward Women: A Guide to Women Travellers*

(New York: Oxford University Press, 1990); Jane Robinson, *Unsuitable for Ladies: An Anthology of Women Travellers* (Oxford and New York: Oxford University Press, 1994).

28 Brian Dolan, *Ladies of the Grand Tour* (London: HarperCollins, 2001); Kathryn Walchester, *Our Own Fair Italy: Nineteenth Century Women's Travel Writing and Italy 1800–1844* (Oxford: Peter Lang, 2007).

29 Michèle Cohen, 'The Grand Tour: constructing the English gentleman in eighteenth-century France', *History of Education* 21, no. 3 (1992); Michèle Cohen, 'Manliness, effeminacy and the French: gender and the construction of national character in eighteenth-century England', in *English Masculinities, 1660–1800*, ed. Tim Hitchcock and Michèle Cohen (London: Longman, 1999); Michèle Cohen, 'The Grand Tour: language, national identity and masculinity', *Changing English* 8, no. 2 (2001); Michèle Cohen, '"Manners" make the man: politeness, chivalry, and the construction of masculinity, 1750–1830', *Journal of British Studies* 44, no. 2 (2005).

30 Elizabeth A. Bohls, *Women Travel Writers and the Language of Aesthetics, 1716–1818* (Cambridge: Cambridge University Press, 1995); Chard, *Pleasure and Guilt*; Turner, *British Travel Writers in Europe*.

31 Including, but not limited to, Ilaria Bignamini and Clare Hornsby, *Digging and Dealing in Eighteenth-Century Rome*, vol. 1 (New Haven: Yale University Press, 2010); Viccy Coltman, *Classical Sculpture and the Culture of Collecting in Britain since 1760* (Oxford and New York: Oxford University Press, 2009); French, *Art Treasures in the North*; David Ryley Marshall, Susan May Russell and Karin Elizabeth Wolfe, *Roma Britannica: Art Patronage and Cultural Exchange in Eighteenth-Century Rome* (London: British School at Rome, 2011); Jonathan Scott, *The Pleasures of Antiquity: British Collectors of Greece and Rome* (New Haven: Yale University Press, 2003). For a comprehensive breakdown of the scholarship on connoisseurship and collecting, see footnotes 7 and 8 in the Introduction to Sweet, Verhoeven and Goldsmith, *Beyond the Grand Tour*, 18–19.

32 Sweet, *Cities and the Grand Tour*, 23–64; Isabelle Baudino, *Les voyageuses britanniques au XVIIIe siècle: L'étape lyonnaise dans l'itinéraire du Grand Tour* (Paris: L'Harmattan, 2015).

33 Esther Moir, *The Discovery of Britain: The English Tourists 1540–1840* (London: Routledge, 1964); Ian Ousby, *The Englishman's England: Taste, Travel and the Rise of Tourism* (Cambridge: Cambridge University Press, 1990).

34 Tim Youngs, 'Buttons and souls: some thoughts on commodities and identity in women's travel writing', *Studies in Travel Writing* 1 (1997): 117–40; Zoë Kinsley, 'Travel and material culture: commodity, currency,

and destabilised meaning in women's home tour writing', *Studies in Travel Writing* 10 (2006): 101–22.
35 With the exception of Freya Gowrley, 'Craft(ing) narratives', *Eighteenth-Century Fiction* 31, no. 1 (2018): 77–97. On memorabilia in the domestic space, see Freya Gowrley, *Domestic Space in Britain, 1750–1840: Materiality, Sociability and Emotion* (London: Bloomsbury, 2022).
36 Walpole, *Correspondence*, vol. 34, 278.
37 *Walter Benjamin: Selected Writings, 1938–1940*, ed. Michael William Jennings and Howard Eiland, vol. 4 (Cambridge, MA, and London: Belknap Press of Harvard University Press, 2003), 182–3 and 190.
38 Ludwig Giesz, *Phänomenologie des Kitsches: ein Beitrag zur anthropologischen Ästhetik* (Heidelberg: Rothe, 1960); Nelson Graburn, *Ethnic and Tourist Arts: Cultural Expressions from the Fourth World* (Berkeley: University of California Press, 1976), 6; Gillo Dorfles and John McHale, *Kitsch: An Anthology of Bad Taste* (London: Studio Vista, 1969).
39 Susan Stewart, *On Longing: Narratives of the Miniature, the Gigantic, the Souvenir, the Collection* (Baltimore: Johns Hopkins University Press, 1984), 135–6.
40 Stewart, *On Longing*, 135–6.
41 Nelson H. H. Graburn, 'Tourism: the sacred journey', in *Hosts and Guests: The Anthropology of Tourism*, ed. Valene L. Smith (Philadelphia: University of Pennsylvania Press, 1989), 17–31; Erik Cohen, 'A phenomenology of tourist experiences', *Sociology* 13 (1979): 179–201.
42 Beverly Gordon, 'The souvenir: messenger of the extraordinary', *Journal of Popular Culture* 20, no. 3 (1986): 136.
43 On late eighteenth-century British women's travel writing itself as a souvenir or memory-holder, see Emma Gleadhill, '"Let her now set her thoughts down as she can recollect them": late eighteenth-century British women tourist's literary souvenirs', in *Microtravel: Confinement, Deceleration, Proximity*, edited by Charles Forsdick, Zoë Kinsley and Kate Walchester (New York: Anthem Press, forthcoming 2022).
44 See especially Brinsley Ford and John Ingamells, *A Dictionary of British and Irish Travellers in Italy, 1701–1800* (New Haven: Yale University Press, 1997); French, *Art Treasures in the North*; Wilton and Bignamini, *Grand Tour*.
45 I know of women travellers' journals and personal correspondence in the Bedfordshire Record Office, Devon Archives, Durham County Record Office, Essex Record Office, Flintshire Record Office, Leigh Archives, National Library of Scotland, Northumberland County Record Office, Shropshire Archives, University of Glasgow and University of Southampton and other institutional archives which I have not had

the capacity to consult. There are also the private archives consulted by the authors referenced above in note 44. While it is outside of the scope of this study, Pauline Trevelyan's forty-four-volume diary held in the Kenneth Spencer Research Library, University of Kansas, and 'Sketches in Greece in 1842 by Lady Trevalyan' promise to be valuable for researching British women's souvenir culture post-1830.

46 Deidre Lynch, 'Personal effects and sentimental fictions', *Eighteenth-Century Fiction* 12, no. 2–3 (2000): 345–68; Mark Blackwell, *The Secret Life of Things: Animals, Objects and It-Narratives in Eighteenth-Century England* (Lewisburg: Bucknell University Press, 2007); Julie Park, *The Self and It: Novel Objects in Eighteenth-Century England* (Stanford: Stanford University Press, 2010); Ileana Baird and Christina Ionescu, *Eighteenth-Century Thing Theory in a Global Context* (Farnham and Burlington: Ashgate, 2014).

47 Lynch, 'Personal effects and sentimental fictions', 345.

48 Viccy Coltman, *Fabricating the Antique: Neoclassicism in Britain, 1760–1800*, 1st edn (Chicago and London: University of Chicago Press, 2006). See also Coltman, *Classical Sculpture*.

49 Pointon, *Strategies for Showing*. See also Marcia Pointon, 'Women and their jewels', in *Women and Material Culture, 1660–1830*, ed. Jennie Batchelor and Cora Kaplan (Basingstoke: Palgrave Macmillan, 2007).

50 Anne Gerritsen and Giorgio Riello, *Writing Material Culture History* (London: Bloomsbury, 2014), 1. See also, Victor Buchli, *The Material Culture Reader* (Oxford and New York: Berg, 2002); Paula Findlen, *Early Modern Things: Objects and Their Histories, 1500–1800* (London and New York: Routledge, 2012); Karen Harvey, *History and Material Culture: A Student's Guide to Approaching Alternative Sources* (London and New York: Routledge, 2013); Tara Hamling and Catherine Richardson, *Everyday Objects: Medieval and Early Modern Material Culture and Its Meanings* (London: Routledge, 2016); Stephanie Downes, Sally Holloway and Sarah Randles, *Feeling Things: Objects and Emotions Through History* (Oxford: Oxford University Press, 2018).

51 Gerritsen and Riello, *Writing Material Culture History*, 3; Leora Auslander, 'Beyond words', *American Historical Review* 110, no. 4 (2005): 1015–45.

52 Scottish artist Anne Forbes studied in Italy, but I have not delved into her art as a Grand Tour souvenir. There have been some excellent recent studies of tourism in Scotland, for example Elizabeth Hagglund, 'Tourists and Travellers: Women's Non-Fictional Writing about Scotland 1770–1830' (PhD thesis, University of Birmingham, 2000); Katherine Haldane Grenier, *Tourism and Identity in Scotland, 1770–1914: Creating Caledonia* (Aldershot: Ashgate, 2005). Little, however, has been

written on women Scottish tourists. Chapter 6, titled 'Travel, tourism and place', in Katharine Glover, *Elite Women and Polite Society in Eighteenth-Century Scotland* (Woodbridge: Boydell Press, 2011), 139–65, indicates that Scottish women's travel and souvenir culture would be a fruitful avenue of research.

53 Few historians have looked at travel souvenirs and this is the first gender history of souvenir culture. There are some antiquarian studies of objects sold to tourists and excellent work on particular categories of objects, such as trench art from the First World War battlefields, for instance, Brian Austen, *Tunbridge Ware and Related European Decorative Woodwares: Killarney, Spa, Sorrento* (London: W. Foulsham Company, 1992); Nicholas Saunders, *Trench Art: Materialities and Memories of War* (Oxford: Berg Publishers, 2003).

54 Luella F. Anderson and Mary A. Littrell, 'Souvenir-purchase behavior of women tourists', *Annals of Tourism Research* 22, no. 2 (1995): 328–48; Luella F. Anderson and Mary A. Littrell, 'Group profiles of women as tourists and purchasers of souvenirs', *Family and Consumer Sciences Research Journal* 25, no. 1 (1996): 28–56; Hugh Wilkins, 'Souvenirs: what and why we buy', *Journal of Travel Research* 50, no. 3 (2010): 239–47.

55 Gerald Mars and Valerie Mars, '"Souvenir-gifts" as tokens of filial esteem: the meanings of Blackpool souvenirs', in *Souvenirs: The Material Culture of Tourism*, ed. Michael Hitchcock and Ken Teague (Aldershot: Ashgate, 2000), 91–111.

56 Latour, Bruno. *Pandora's Hope: Essays on the Reality of Science Studies*. Cambridge; London: Harvard University Press, 1999.

57 For more on eighteenth-century women tourist's involvement in science, see Emma Gleadhill, '"For I asked him men's questions": late eighteenth-century British women tourists' contributions to scientific inquiry', *Eighteenth-Century Life* 45, no. 3 (2021): 158–77, https://doi.org/10.1215/00982601-9273034.

Part I

Gendering connoisseurship

1

The Grand Tour: a masculine legacy of taste

In the late seventeenth century, the Grand Tour became established as a rite of passage for noble and gentry men. Narrowly defined as a period of Continental travel undertaken by an elite young man of rank after school or university, just prior to entering adult society, the Tour was a significant marker of distinction between adolescence and adulthood in the eighteenth century.[1] The ideal Grand Tourist was expected to spend time in France to perfect his manners and conversation by socialising with the beau monde, before travelling to Italy to experience the ruins and art of classical civilisations that had been the subject of his humanist education based on Latin and Greek models.[2] As their empire expanded, Britain's elite drew parallels between their nation's political virtue and that of ancient Rome, positioning the classics at the apex of their cultural heritage. 'A man who has not been in Italy', Samuel Johnson observed in 1776, 'is always conscious of an inferiority,- from his not having seen what it is expected a man should see'. According to Johnson, this was because 'All our religion, almost all our law, almost all our arts, almost all that sets us above the savages, has come to us from the shores of the Mediterranean'.[3]

The Grand Tour was an opportunity for the Augustan-styled elite young man to rid himself of the two main markers of adolescence – a lack of control over one's emotions and bachelorhood. In order to return home a man, he was expected to engage in drinking, gambling and sexual exploits while safely 'out of sight and out of mind'.[4] These independent activities and the self-reliance wrought by travel were expected to 'wean him from the dangerous fondness of his mother' and imbue him with the adult characteristics of courage, honour, self-control and a stoic endurance of hardship.[5]

At the same time, through a standard curriculum of mixing with polite society, acquiring accomplishments (such as the French language, dancing and swordsmanship), viewing churches, colleges, libraries and ruins, and taking note of trade, government, architecture and artworks, the Grand Tourist would gain a formal and experiential education in politics, statecraft and antiquity. Ideally, he returned home accomplished and experienced, a patrician man. A collection of antiquities and artworks attained in Italy would support his social status when displayed appropriately in the neo-classical interior of a Palladian-style estate, like that of politician Richard Child, first Earl of Tylney's Wanstead House, for example, with its six Corinthian columns, or banker Henry Hoare I's Stourhead, with its temples to Ceres, Hercules and Apollo.

This development of cultural capital through a humanist education, a carefree, youthful romp, the building of a collection and institutional affiliation was something from which women were excluded. Paintings of the Tour, like Johan Zoffany's *The Tribuna degli Uffizi* (1772) and Joshua Reynolds's portrait of *Members of the Dilettanti Society* (1777–79), show that the exclusive homosocial comradery developed on the Tour continued to shape elite men's lives long after. These paintings depict groups of men socialising and exclude women, except as objects of masculine desire. The only women in Zoffany's painting of the central room of Francesco de Medici's gallery are the paintings and sculptures of Venus, Madonna, Cleopatra and Charity, which are surrounded by gawking male Grand Tourists, art dealers and collectors (see plate 1). The commissioner, Queen Charlotte, was clearly unimpressed to receive this male group portrait. It was reported that the King 'expressed wonder at Zoffany having done so improper a thing as to introduce the portraits of Sir Horace Man – Patch, & others. – He sd. The Queen wd. not suffer the picture to be placed in any of her apartments'.[6] Membership of the Society of Dilettanti was a function of Continental travel experience, status and simply being a man.[7] According to Horace Walpole, 'The nominal qualification [for membership] is having been to Italy, and the real one, being drunk'.[8] In the Dilettanti group portrait Sir John Taylor, first Baronet, delicately pinches a woman's garter between his forefingers as he gazes out at the viewer with a twinkle in his eye, while Sir William Hamilton (whose inauguration the painting commemorates) and the others compare an ancient vase to their

1.1 William Say (after Sir Joshua Reynolds), *Members of the Society of Dilettanti*, 1812–16, 580 mm × 418 mm, mezzotint.

wine glasses (figure 1.1).[9] Thus, the antiquities that elite men brought home from their Grand Tours continued to connect them over the years as they became politicians and leaders through fond memories of shared adolescent debauchery that matched that of the ancient

Romans and could only be undertaken in the extraordinary space of travel.

The ideal of the classically educated elite male Grand Tourist, however, was not stable and uncontested. From the two decades prior to the outbreak of the French Revolutionary Wars (1792–1802), British manhood was increasingly defined against a foreign and effeminate other.[10] Discussions of the 'Macaroni phenomenon' reflect the increasing concern that foreign travel compromised the masculinity of British youth by promoting habits of effeminacy.[11] From the 1760s, returned Grand Tourists joined the Macaroni club, which ostensibly formed the standard of taste in fashion as well as in polite learning. In the succeeding decades, however, the macaroni grew into an excessive and inauthentic effeminate figure symbolising the foreign contagion of luxurious consumption, with the *Oxford Magazine* reporting in 1770 of

> a kind of animal, neither male nor female, a thing of the neuter gender, latterly started up amongst us. *It* is called a *Macaroni. It* talks without meaning, *it* smiles without pleasantry, *it* eats without appetite, *it* rides without exercise, *it* wenches without passion.[12]

The popular press derided the unpatriotic and narcissistic macaroni 'Conceived in the Courts of France and Italy', whose main concern was to decorate himself and most important accessory was a mirror (figure 1.2).[13]

At the same time as the esteem in which the classically educated male cosmopolite was held declined, the social elite expanded to include nouveau riche merchant and colliery families and the 'millocracy'. These groups saw the Grand Tour as a form of social investment that would set the seal on their newly landed status. Whereas the earlier Tour was dominated by young men and their tutors with a smattering of couples on wedding tours and invalids, in the last two decades of the century it was dominated by family groups and mixed parties of men and women travelling together for education and for recreation.[14] A portrait of Sir Thomas Gascoigne, eighth Baronet, by the most renowned Grand Tour portrait painter Pompeo Batoni forms a nice illustration of a woman edging her way into the Tour's visual culture (figure 1.3). Batoni was known for his 'swagger portraits' of young British men in red brocade proudly standing in front of classical Rome. We instead find Sir

The Grand Tour: a masculine legacy of taste 37

1.2 Philip Dawe, *The Macaroni, a Real Character at the Late Masquerade*, 1773, 351 mm × 250 mm, mezzotint.

Thomas in a library surrounded by the spoils of his travels. Among these are two classical sculptures and, rather than representing the ancient Romans, they are portrait busts of Sir Thomas's two travel companions, Martha and Henry Swinburne. The daughter of a

1.3 Pompeo Batoni, *Sir Thomas Gascoigne, Eighth Baronet*, 1779, 248.9 cm × 172.7 cm, oil on canvas.

Protestant barrister from Chichester, Martha Swinburne (née Baker) was raised in her mother's Catholic faith in Ursuline convents in Lille and Paris. In 1764 Henry met Martha on his return from a Grand Tour and they were married three years later. Martha brought immense wealth to the marriage from the West Indies property she inherited from her father John, Solicitor General of the Leeward Islands.[15] The couple proceeded to divide their lives between Henry's estate of Hamsterley in County Durham and the Continent, travelling frequently throughout their long marriage together with their growing family. Educated in Greek and Latin, Martha is said to have provided companionship and art expertise to Sir Thomas. The busts depicted in the painting were likely copied from those modelled in Rome for the Swinburnes by the Irish sculptor Christopher Hewetson.[16] The portrait of Sir Thomas, then, has quite a different tone from that of the previous Tour paintings. It is a tribute to a friendship between a man and a couple. Sir Thomas's worldly gaze is mirrored by that of Martha behind him. She returns the gaze of her husband over a globe of the world that that reflects the couple's cosmopolitanism and global reach. Martha is portrayed as herself, rather than in the guise of a goddess or muse, but she remains an object in the background of a painting, rather than the central figure.[17]

Women had a more complex range of motives for travel than their male counterparts. In combination with their femininity, these ambitions threatened to further undermine the ideal of the Augustan-styled elite male Grand Tourist. Married women travelling as companions sought to refine their language skills and musicianship. Margaret Earle, the wife of Giles of Eastcourt, Wiltshire (son of the captain and politician of the same name), for instance, hoped to improve her talents on the harpsicord. Writing of the Earles in 1771, art dealer James Byres remarked that Giles had 'prolonged his stay in Rome purely to oblige Mrs Earle', who 'applies to her music most assiduously ... from a Tom-tit she is become very near a nightingale'.[18] Margaret may have been inspired by Charles Burney's *The Present State of Music in France and Italy*, published in the same year, which presented Italy as a feast for the ears.[19] Some widowed matriarchs travelled to Italy with their daughters, in the hope of not only finishing off the girls' education but also finding them suitable husbands. This was the case for Baroness Anna Berwick, who travelled to Italy in 1792 with her three daughters. She was pleased when her eldest, Henrietta, married Charles Brudenell-Bruce, the Marquess of Ailesbury, only one year in. She had less luck, however, with her two younger daughters, who remained unmarried despite Anna's efforts with the recently divorced Sir Richard Worsley, who she thought 'wd just do for A[nne] as she loves Venice so much & he is rather old than young'.[20]

Other women sought a more frugal lifestyle in Italy or removed themselves to the warmer climate of southern Europe to recover their strength. Finding herself left without a pension after the death of her Royal Navy officer husband, Admiral Joseph Knight, in 1778, Lady Phillipina Knight and her nineteen-year-old daughter hoped to economise by spending time in 'the cheapest city in the world and the most beautiful'.[21] They would remain in Rome for eleven years. In 1787 the painter Georgiana Hare-Naylor and her witty but insolvent historian husband, Francis, also sought financial stability offshore.[22] At the doctor's orders, the widow Elizabeth Somerset, Duchess of Beaufort, spent a mild winter in Nice in 1770–71 with her daughter and grand-daughter.[23] Sarah Bentham, widowed for a second time after the death of husband, Jeremiah (father of the philosopher, Jeremy Bentham), travelled to Italy with her son John and sick daughter-in-law, Mary.[24] Sadly, their quest to improve Mary's ailing health was unsuccessful and her body was shipped back to England for burial in Westminster Abbey within five weeks.

Just as young men were expected to 'run after women and bad company' during their Grand Tours so that they could 'begin at home a new man', some British women suffering from disrepute fled to the safely of the Continent.[25] Georgiana Cavendish, Duchess of Devonshire, was temporarily banished to Italy by her husband, both for her extravagance and because she was with child by future prime minister Charles Grey.[26] For the sake of appearance, Georgiana announced that she was escorting her invalid sister abroad. One year later, having given birth to her daughter, she would return to England at her husband's request. While the opera singer Elizabeth Billington officially went to Naples in 1794 to 'improve her taste', her departure was encouraged by the appearance of James Ridgeway's scurrilous *Memoirs of Mrs Billington*, which purported to reveal her many affairs.[27] In Italy she pursued her career unperturbed. An eruption of Vesuvius would be attributed to her magnificent performance at the Teatro S. Carlo of an opera specially composed for her by Giuseppe Francesco Bianchi.[28]

Elizabeth was not the only professional woman to advance her career on the Continent. In 1767 twenty-two-year-old Anne Forbes went to Italy accompanied by her mother.[29] Her travels were sponsored by her grandfather, the Scottish portraitist William Aikman, and Sir Lawrence Dundas, the Scottish politician and collector of art. Under the tutorship of Gavin Hamilton, she learnt from the works of Italy's greatest painters, including Correggio, Titian, Guido Reni, Baldassare Franceschini and Benedetto Luti, and sold the results to Charles Francis Greville and Henry, eighth Baron Arundell of Wardour. While Anne's society friends shunned her for going into business, other women followed. Anne Seymour Damer undertook three tours of Italy between 1778 and 1786 to establish herself as a sculptor.[30] She succeeded, exhibiting regularly in the Royal Academy for close to forty years.

Whether travelling as companions, for education, health, to cut costs, to escape scandal or to expand their careers, women Grand Tourists subscribed to the same canons of taste that made Italy such an important destination for patrician men. 'I love the notion of seeing all the places one has read of in Roman history, where great men have been and great things done', Lady Caroline Fox told her sister as she prepared for her Grand Tour in 1766.[31] One of the four daughters of Charles Lennox, second Duke of Richmond, Caroline benefitted from a fine education. Elizabeth Somerset, Duchess of Beaufort, was educated alongside her brothers in Latin, Italian, French and history, but unlike them, did not get to undertake a Grand Tour until later in life after her husband's death.[32] While women were not usually educated in Latin, knowledge of the language was not necessary to establish an understanding of ancient Rome; indeed, engaging English and French translations of Roman poets, such as Virgil, were widely available.[33] Women had also long played the role of 'armchair travellers', reading the accounts and viewing the collections of their male counterparts. 'You may from the commonest print, form a very good idea' of Rome, Lady Anna Miller noted when she arrived in the city in 1773.[34] 'Its size, though I had seen models and views of it, and expected it great', Mary Berry proclaimed of the colosseum, 'surprised me – one can easily conceive it holding "uncrowded nations in its womb"'.[35] No matter their reason for travel, all elite women thus expected to gain valuable first-hand knowledge of the Roman history that formed the bedrock of the British nation by treading on classic ground.

Having this expectation, upon arriving in Italy most women sought to develop connoisseurship by studying the architecture, antiquities and artworks of the ancients. Sir Horace Mann observed that Anne Pitt, daughter of the politician Robert Pitt, was 'more active in running after curiosities than any of the young men' on her Grand Tour in 1774.[36] This was also true for Lady Harriet Malmesbury: 'I think it very ingenious of me to bring him to a country which furnished nothing but the things he detests – antiques, cameos and intaglios', she gleefully remarked of her husband James Harris, Earl of Malmesbury, in Rome in 1791.[37] Harriet left James to his own devices while she undertook a course in antiquities with Princess Marie-Louise Thérèse of Savoy-Carignan. Henry Swinburne enjoyed having his wife, Martha (whose bust made an appearance in the Batoni portrait discussed earlier in this chapter), as a travelling companion: 'except in taking views [sketching]', he remarked, 'my wife has the same propensities as myself for antiquities, and our mode of life is so pleasant in this delicious climate, where no impediment of weather prevents our daily journeys of discovery'.[38] As is the case today, it seems that Grand Tourists, male and female alike, were driven in a large part by their own talents and inclinations when it came to engaging with antiquity, although elite men's education and social roles meant that there were higher expectations for them to make a performance of their connoisseurship.

Sketches from the last decade of the century support these statements about women's interest and involvement in studying the remains of the ancients. Giuseppe Cades's *Gavin Hamilton Leading a Party of Grand Tourists to the Archaeological Site at Gabii* (1793) depicts a heterosocial group of Grand Tourists being led to a newly discovered archaeological site (figure 1.4). Henry Tresham's *Grand Tourists Purchasing Antiquities* (1790) similarly portrays both sexes grouped around a table examining the various busts, vases, bronzes, lamps and tripods that have been brought to them by excavators (figure 1.5). After a few months in Italy, some women considered their connoisseurship advanced enough to pass judgement on antiquity. Elizabeth Somerset, Duchess of Beaufort, found herself disappointed by Pompeii's columns when she visited the city in 1772: 'none ... are of good architecture', she lamented, because they were made of 'brick cover'd with plaister and fluted'.[39] In 1794 Lady Elizabeth Holland similarly dismissed the Doric pillars at Paestum as 'too uneven ... squat and clumsy'.[40] Women Grand Tourists clearly subscribed to the same canons of taste as their male counterparts

The Grand Tour: a masculine legacy of taste   43

1.4 Giuseppe Cades, *Gavin Hamilton Leading a Party of Grand Tourists to the Archaeological Site at Gabii*, 1793, 449 mm × 583 mm, ink and wash over pencil.

1.5 Henry Tresham, *Grand Tourists Purchasing Antiquities*, 1790, 330 mm × 483 mm, pen and ink grey wash.

and were very much involved in 'discovering' and appraising the visual and material legacy of the ancients.

Women, however, encountered a barrier when they attempted to display their cultural capital because, on several levels, connoisseurship was considered unfeminine and therefore undesirable. Much of this criticism lay in the idea that a purposeful, rational expertise in naked bodies (the subject matter of much of antiquity) was considered quite unacceptable for a lady. In 1781 the Scottish physician John Moore announced:

> Ladies, who have remained some time at Rome and Florence, particularly those who affect a taste for virtù, acquire an intrepidity and a cool minuteness, in examining and criticising naked figures, which is unknown to those who have never passed the alps.[41]

This comment is symptomatic of a wider unease about British women perusing naked male bodies during the period. Female nudes, like the *Venus de' Medici*, did not provoke concern, but phallic objects, such as the Lion's Priapus in the ducal galleries at Florence, and sexual scenes, such as the painting of *Leda and the Swan* in the Palazzo Bovi in Bologna, were removed from women's sight.[42] Ostensibly, it was the prudery of British women in the face of such imagery that separated their character from that of French or Italian women, as historian and pamphleteer John Andrews explained:

> A man must be endued with a very extraordinary share of firmness and constancy, in his preference for the less shining qualities of candour, discretion, modesty, and the other countless ornaments of an English woman's character to oppose them effectually, and while operating only through the force of remembrance, to the more splendid, though less amiable qualities of wit, vivacity, and sprightliness of humour and deportment, that embellish the whole system of so many French ladies, and render them completely irresistible in their attempts to subdue the hearts of pliant, inexperienced youth.[43]

As noted earlier, as part of their rite of passage, elite young male Grand Tourists were expected to partake in a homosocial libertine culture that embraced foreign women and sculptures like the statue of the goat and the satyr at Portici ('Go several times to the Museum of Portici. You *cannot* see it all at once or twice. Mind you have an order to see the satyr fucking the Goat', the Earl of Pembroke instructed his son[44]), before returning home to settle down with a morally upright wife. The woman British Grand Tourist, however, was expected to do the exact opposite. She needed to exercise discretion so that she could remain the modest and unworldly woman that she (preferably) had been before she set out. If British women Grand Tourists became worldly connoisseurs able to properly appreciate the aesthetic qualities of works of art, the *raison d'être* of the Grand Tour would be no more.

If they were not criticised for the unfeminine artifice of viewing antiquity in the objective fashion of a man, women were criticised for the culpable feminine attribute of viewing it in the subjective fashion of a woman. Upon seeing the *Farnese Hercules* in 1771, Lady Anna Miller observed that, although it 'may be very beautiful, and the most perfect model of a man in the world ... if all mankind were so proportioned, I should think them very disagreeable and odious'.[45] In response, John Moore implied that women were incapable of distinguishing between the charms demanded of a sculpture and those demanded of men by reflecting that 'the women in particular find something unsatisfactory and even odious in this figure' because they could not believe 'a man so formed could ever have been the reliever of distressed damsels'.[46] This idea of a culpable feminine want of seriousness was not restricted to nude sculptures. In 1780 Mrs Betty Coutts was mocked by several of her male counterparts for purportedly remarking of the Colosseum: 'When furnished and whitewashed it would be a very pretty building'.[47] A serving-maid from Lancashire, Betty had risen in society after 'marrying up' to the banking magnate Thomas Coutts. Similarly, though the architect Sir John Soane had a high enough opinion of Lady Anna Miller's *Letters from Italy* to take them on his own Grand Tour, he carefully underlined and corrected every mistake in measurement or observation the 'authoress' made.[48] Sir John replaced Anna's note that Pompeii was sixteen miles from Naples with twelve and also replaced her note that the Royal Palace in Naples contained twenty-two front windows with twenty-one.[49] Unimpressed with her observation that Rome's Arch of Constantine contained 'not the smallest vestige remaining of any metal', he instead observed that 'the Cornice round the Aperture is all of Bronze & part of the gilding remains'.[50] These pedantic amendments were peppered with mocking exclamations at Anna's ignorance, such as, 'surely, Lady M is here much deceived'.[51]

Such critiques of British women Grand Tourists' unfeminine accuracy on the one hand (that is, the 'intrepidity and cool minuteness') and their culpable feminine inaccuracy on the other (that is, their likelihood to be 'much deceived') effectively worked to prevent those women who offered their views on art and architecture from threatening elite male knowledge and the patriarchy. These critiques, along with an education that, while sometimes extensive, rarely included Latin, Greek, surveying or mathematics, made many women reluctant to venture their opinions at all.[52] They deferred instead to the greater learning of their husbands, brothers and *ciceroni*. 'I hope by my industry to be able soon to accompany M— [my husband]', Lady Anna Miller noted in Naples in 1771, 'in the researches after antiquity, without being an interruption to him'.[53] Yet, even when women attempted to remove themselves from viewing statues and paintings that were considered inappropriate for their sex, they found themselves criticised for their overly scrupulous female British attitude. In 1750, for instance, Horace Mann jokingly wrote of Miss Bruce, who

> was sent to Italy some years ago to learn painting, and could not bear the filthy figures in the gallery. She was even offended at the two little naked angels with I had got copied from a picture of Raphael, who were learning their halleluh, because both hands were employed in holding the scroll. 'The pecture may be gud', said she, 'but in troth, it makes one seck to see such endecencies'.[54]

He went on to laugh that this 'virgin of about 30' happily 'went from hence to Rome and married a great Irishman to remove all her scruples at once'.[55] Here Horace critiqued Miss Bruce for her British prudery – that self-same attribute that ostensibly set British women apart from their carefree and corporeal Continental equivalents. But he went on to characterise her as a backward and unbridled Catholic peasant because she had married an Irishman – a common quip the English used to defend their rule over Ireland. It seems that according to ideals of British femininity, it was simply impossible for women to attain or sustain connoisseurship. And critiques of British women were compounded by an elite male desire to create exclusivity as merchant, colliery and 'millocracy' families from across England, Wales, Scotland and Ireland vied with each other for the Tour's cultural capital in the second half of the century.

Yet, as competition for the cultural capital of the Grand Tour increased among an expanding social elite, women often reframed their exclusion from connoisseurship as a strength of their sex, rather than a weakness. Instead of seeking to judge an impossible aesthetic, they drew from their gendered roles as hostesses and social facilitators to look past the common conception of Italy's classical past as active, to instead view it as a misguided preoccupation that overshadowed a true understanding of contemporary Italy: 'The first and strongest sensation one feels on entering Italy', Lady Elizabeth Holland observed in 1795 after spending some time in Florence,

> is the recollection of those historical events that from childhood are impressed upon the mind, and those classical sentiments that one strives both from vanity and taste to bring back to memory; but when the turbulence of the imagination subsides, and a long residence in the country familiarises one with objects so attractive, modern Italy, her poets, historians, and artists, attest the attention very justly by the admiration to which they are entitled.[56]

Like the idealised patrician male Grand Tourist, Elizabeth here drew from a shared classical past, but then problematised the authenticity of this commonly made link by revealing the ways in which it was culturally constructed for the purposes of 'vanity and taste'. Her interests in 'modern Italy' reflect those of the widening demographic of both men and women from the social elite in the latter part of the century, who were coming to appreciate Italian writers, like Tasso and Ariosto, and British playwrights, like Otway and Shakespeare: 'My head ran more on Romeo than on Virgil at Mantua and Verona', Hester Piozzi confessed in a letter to her daughter in 1785.[57]

The women's comments when visiting the great estates of elite male Grand Tourists following their return home indicate their sense that they had gone quite beyond the model of the classically educated elite male Grand Tourist. Collecting classical sculptures 'is not that a true Italian idea', Hester Piozzi remarked after visiting Charles Townley's Park Street Gallery in 1788.[58] The gallery, located in Westminster, was one of the sights of London, complete with its own guidebook.⁵⁹ It displayed the extensive collection of classical sculptures, vases, coins, manuscripts, and Old Master drawings and paintings that Townley had amassed across three Grand Tours. A 1794 watercolour by William Chambers depicts the sculptures in the Park Street Gallery dining room (see plate 2). At its centre stands Townley's last major purchase, the renowned *Discobolus*. Beneath his downturned gaze, a gentleman assists a lady with her drawing.⁶⁰ Following her own Grand Tour, Hester Piozzi clearly felt that she did not require a man's assistance to draw or observe antiquity, for she had her own, more authoritative, understanding of the people who had originally developed these collections from spending time in Italy with her Italian husband (more on this in Chapter 3).⁶¹

When Lady Elizabeth Holland visited Saltram House in Devon in 1799, she acknowledged that the apartments were 'excellent', because they boasted several fine pictures and a pleasing outlook, but regretted that 'Switzerland, Italy, the Tyrol, and Nice have rendered me difficult about picturesque and grand views, therefore I am less inclined to be enthusiastic than most people'.⁶² The seat of John Parker, Earl of Morley, Saltram House was designed by the most fashionable architect of the day, Robert Adam. It contained a suite of neo-classical rooms, decorated with paintings by John's close friend and the head of the Royal Academy, Joshua Reynolds. At the time of Elizabeth's visit, John had just had a parkland planted to complement his impressive view of a triumphal Doric arch (figure 1.6). But it seems Elizabeth was left unimpressed; she had, after all, visited Emperor Hadrian's freshly excavated colossal sculpture of Antinous among many other ancient treasures.⁶³ Little wonder an English garden folly now did little to whet her appetite.

Elite women thus sought a different set of experiences in Italy to those of their male counterparts and returned home with different narratives to perpetuate. This was also true of the expanding range of men from different backgrounds and life stages who undertook Grand Tours in the latter part of the century. Their lower investment in the Grand Tour as a rite of passage, however, gave women a greater autonomy to disregard its conventions than any man enjoyed. The activities the women engaged in, and the objects they brought home to remember them, will be the subject of the next two chapters. It is through these souvenirs that elite women shifted the narrative of the Grand Tour.

The Grand Tour: a masculine legacy of taste

1.6 William Russell Birch (after Richard Cooper II), *Saltram, Devonshire*, 1790, 150 mm × 178 mm, stipple and etching.

Conclusion

In the late seventeenth and early eighteenth centuries, the Grand Tour came to be culturally understood as both a literal and figurative voyage from adolescence to adulthood. During their adolescent sojourn, elite young men were expected to be sexually voracious and make poor decisions, driven by emotion. The Tour offered them a way to shake off adolescent debauchery and the energy of youth. These characteristics could then be put to one side when the men returned home, married and became respectable adults, only to be taken out on occasion during homosocial society meetings with other men who had been part of the same rite of passage. Women were not entitled to this behaviour – in effect missing out on a carefree adolescence. However, they did discover themselves and engage in identity formation during their travels. While the exercise of connoisseurship was typically described as an elite masculine trait, in practice most women expected to appreciate the antiquities of ancient Rome and sought to lay claim to taste and virtue. Yet, the critiques of women Grand Tourists show that they balanced between the display of an unfeminine level of antiquarian learning, and gaining and demonstrating a sufficient knowledge of history and ancient literature to legitimately show off the cultural capital they had gained on their travels.[64] Rather than attempting to walk this tightrope, many women, like Lady Elizabeth Holland, exploited their exclusion from the classics to instead promote their lived experiences of contemporary Italy (its 'poets, historians and artists') as the 'real deal'. In the process they exposed the artifice of the traditional elite male Grand Tourist's focus on the past, rather than the present. This served to deepen the multiple cracks that already existed between the Grand Tourist ideal and the conflicting meanings of what it meant to be a Grand Tourist (and to be a man) that were circulating in the cultural landscape in the second half of the eighteenth century as the Tour opened up to a larger and more diverse social elite. In the next chapter, I analyse the sorts of objects that women acquired and the meanings they gave them. I argue that they actively sought souvenirs that would provide evidence of their unique and authentic engagement with contemporary Italy.

Notes

1 For surveys of scholarship on the Grand Tour, see Barbara Ann Naddeo, 'Cultural capitals and cosmopolitanism in eighteenth-century Italy: the historiography of Italy and the Grand Tour', *Journal of Modern Italian Studies* 10, no. 2 (2005); John Wilton-Ely, 'Classic Ground: Britain, Italy, and the Grand Tour' (book review), *Eighteenth-Century Life* 28, no. 1 (2004).

2 On the Grand Tour and elite male education, see Michèle Cohen, 'The Grand Tour: constructing the English gentleman in eighteenth-century France', *History of Education* 21, no. 3 (1992); Michèle Cohen, 'The Grand Tour: language, national identity and masculinity', *Changing English* 8, no. 2 (2001); Michèle Cohen, '"Manners" make the man:

politeness, chivalry, and the construction of masculinity, 1750–1830', *Journal of British Studies* 44, no. 2 (2005); Henry French and Mark Rothery, '"Upon your entry into the world": masculine values and the threshold of adulthood among landed elites in England, 1680–1800', *Social History* 33, no. 4 (2008); Jennifer Mori, 'Hosting the Grand Tour: civility, enlightenment and culture, c.1740–1790', in *Educating the Child in Enlightenment Britain: Beliefs, Cultures, Practices*, ed. Jill Shefrin and Mary Hilton (London: Routledge, 2016); Sarah Goldsmith, 'Nostalgia, homesickness and emotional formation on the eighteenth-century Grand Tour', *Cultural and Social History* 15, no. 3 (2018).

3 James Boswell, *The Life of Samuel Johnson* (London: Henry Baldwin and Charles Dilly, 1791), vol. 2, 61.

4 According to Samuel Johnson, 'if a young man is wild, and must run after women and bad company, it is better this should be done abroad, as, on his return, he can break off such connections and begin at home a new man' (Boswell, *The Life of Samuel Johnson*, vol. 1, 170).

5 Richard Lassels, 'A preface to the reader concerning travelling', in *The Voyage of Italy, or a Compleat Journey through Italy. In Two Parts* (London: John Starkey, 1670). On the Tour's toughening role, see Sarah Goldsmith, *Masculinity on the Grand Tour* (London: University of London Press, 2020); Cohen, 'The Grand Tour: constructing the English gentleman in eighteenth-century France', 249–51.

6 Joseph Farington, *The Farington Diary*, vol. 3, ed. James Greig (London: Hutchinson, 1924), 35.

7 The Society of Dilettanti was a metropolitan fraternity founded in 1732 that sponsored research and publications into aspects of classical culture. Members included noted collectors like Charles Townley, the British ambassador in Naples Sir William Hamilton and the archaeologist Richard Payne Knight. On the Society of Dilettanti, see Jason M. Kelly, *The Society of Dilettanti: Archaeology and Identity in the British Enlightenment* (New Haven: Yale University Press, 2009).

8 Horace Walpole, *The Yale Edition of Horace Walpole's Correspondence*, ed. W. S. Lewis (New Haven: Yale University Press, 1954), vol. 18, 211.

9 Viccy Coltman, *Classical Sculpture and the Culture of Collecting in Britain since 1760* (Oxford; New York: Oxford University Press, 2009), 175.

10 See Gerald Newman, *The Rise of English Nationalism: A Cultural History 1740–1830* (New York: St. Martin's Press, 1987), 80–1; Michèle Cohen, 'Manliness, effeminacy and the French: gender and the construction of national character in eighteenth-century England', in *English Masculinities, 1660–1800*, ed. Tim Hitchcock and Michèle

Cohen, 44–62 (London: Longman, 1999); Michèle Cohen, *Fashioning Masculinity: National Identity and Language in the Eighteenth Century* (London: Routledge, 1996).

11 See Amelia Rauser, 'Hair, authenticity, and the self-made macaroni', *Eighteenth-Century Studies* 38, no. 1 (2004); Harry Mount, 'The monkey with the magnifying glass: constructions of the connoisseur in eighteenth-century Britain', *Oxford Art Journal* 29, no. 2 (2006).

12 Members of the University of Oxford, *The Oxford Magazine: Or, Universal Museum*, vol. 4 (London, Cambridge, Dublin and York: Bladon, Coote, Fletcher, Hodson, Smith and Etherington, 1770), 228.

13 Cohen, "The Grand Tour: constructing the English gentleman in eighteenth-century France," 253; Cohen, *Fashioning Masculinity*, 132–3.

14 Anne French, *Art Treasures in the North: Northern Families on the Grand Tour* (Norwich: Unicorn Press, 2009), 24.

15 J. E. Thurgood, 'Swinburne, Henry (1743–1803)', *Oxford Dictionary of National Biography*, last updated 3 October 2013, https://doi.org/10.1093/ref:odnb/26837.

16 French, *Art Treasures in the North*, 49.

17 Pompeo Batoni did paint a portrait of Martha Swinburne in 1779, intended to hang as a pendant together with a portrait of her husband. The pendant portraits are bust length, unlike the portrait of Sir Thomas Gascoigne, and the background is a simple dark green oval. Anne French notes that Martha's features and expression are standardised. In comparison, the portrait of Henry Swinburne shows a 'sensitive understanding of character' (French, *Art Treasures in the North*, 49).

18 Quoted in Brinsley Ford and John Ingamells, *A Dictionary of British and Irish Travellers in Italy, 1701–1800* (New Haven: Yale University Press, 1997), 327.

19 Charles Burney, *The Present State of Music in France and Italy: Or, The Journal of a Tour Through Those Countries, Undertaken to Collect Materials for a General History of Music*, vol. 1 (London: T. Becket, 1771).

20 'Berwick, Anna (Vernon) (1748–1797)', 11 December 1795, in Ford and Ingamells, *A Dictionary*, 86–7.

21 'Knight, Lady Phillipina (Deane) (1726–1799)', in Ford and Ingamells, *A Dictionary*, 581–3.

22 'Hare-Naylor, Mrs Georgiana (Shipley) (*c*.1755–1806)', in Ford and Ingamells, *A Dictionary*, 465–6.

23 'Beaufort, Duchess Elizabeth (Berkeley) (1713–1799)', in Ford and Ingamells, *A Dictionary*, 66–7.

24 'Bentham, Mrs Sarah (Farr) (d.1809) (mother of the philosopher Jeremy Bentham)', in Ford and Ingamells, *A Dictionary*, 77–8.

25 Boswell, *The Life of Samuel Johnson*, vol. 1, 170.
26 'Devonshire, Duchess Georgiana (Spencer) (1757–1806)', in Ford and Ingamells, *A Dictionary*, 295–6.
27 Elizabeth Billington, *Memoirs of Mrs. Billington, from Her Birth: Containing a Variety of Matter, Ludicrous, Theatrical, Musical, and with Copies of Several Original Letters, Now in the Possession of the Publisher, Written by Mrs. Billington, to Her Mother, the Late Mrs. Weichsel* (London: James Ridgway, 1792).
28 'Billington, Mrs Elizabeth (1765/8–1818)', in Ford and Ingamells, *A Dictionary*, 90–1.
29 See entry for 'Forbes, Anne (1745–1840)', in Ford and Ingamells, *A Dictionary*, 367.
30 'Damer, Anne (Seymour Conway) (1748–1828)', in Ford and Ingamells, *A Dictionary*, 270.
31 Stella Tillyard, *Aristocrats: Caroline, Emily, Louisa and Sarah Lennox 1740–1832* (London: Vintage, 1995), 252.
32 Rosemary Sweet, *Cities and the Grand Tour: The British in Italy, c.1690–1820* (Cambridge: Cambridge University Press, 2012), 31.
33 On women's reading, see Susan Staves, '"Books without which I cannot write": how did eighteenth-century women writers get the books they read?', in *Women and Material Culture, 1660–1830*, ed. Jennie Batchelor and Cora Kaplan (Basingstoke and New York: Palgrave Macmillan, 2007); Amanda Vickery, *The Gentleman's Daughter: Women's Lives in Georgian England* (New Haven: Yale University Press, 1998), 259.
34 Anna Riggs Miller, *Letters from Italy, Describing the Manners, Customs, Antiquities, Paintings, &c. of that Country, in the Years MDCCLXX and MDCCLXXI, to a Friend Residing in France* (Dublin: W. Watson, 1776), vol. 2, 22.
35 Mary Berry, *Extracts from the journals and correspondence of Miss Berry: From the Year 1783 to 1852*, ed. Lady Theresa Lewis (London: Longmans Green, 1865), vol. 1, 64.
36 'Pitt, Anne (1712–1781)', in Ford and Ingamells, *A Dictionary*, 772.
37 'Malmesbury, Lady Harriet Maria (Amyand) (1761–1830)', in Ford and Ingamells, *A Dictionary*, 630–1.
38 Quoted in French, *Art Treasures in the North*, 45.
39 Quoted in Ford and Ingamells, *A Dictionary*, 66.
40 Elizabeth Vassall Fox Holland, *The Journal of Elizabeth Lady Holland (1791–1811)*, ed. Giles Stephen Fox-Strangways Ilchester (London: Longmans Green, 1908), vol. 1, 128.
41 John Moore, *A View of Society and Manners in Italy: With Anecdotes Relating to Some Eminent Characters*, vol. 2 (London: A. Strahan and T. Cadell, 1781), 424–5.

42 Sweet, *Cities and the Grand Tour*, 55–6.
43 John Andrews, *Remarks on the French and English Ladies* (Dublin: Walker, Beatty, Burton, White and Doyle, 1783), 59.
44 Henry Herbert Pembroke, *Henry, Elizabeth and George (1734–80): Letters and Diaries of Henry, Tenth Earl of Pembroke, and His Circle*, ed. Sidney Charles Herbert (London: J. Cape, 1939), 197.
45 Miller, *Letters from Italy*, vol. 2, 230.
46 Moore, *A View of Society and Manners in Italy*, 10–11.
47 M. W. Patterson, *Sir Francis Burdett and His Times (1770–1844)* (London: Macmillan, 1931), 17.
48 On Soane's use of Miller's *Letters*, see Pierre de la Ruffinière du Prey, *John Soane: The Making of an Architect* (Chicago: University of Chicago Press, 1982), 132–44.
49 Sir John Soane's Museum Library and Archive, Anna Riggs Miller, *Letters from Italy, Describing the Manners, Customs, Antiquities, Paintings, &c. of that Country, in the Years MDCCLXX and MDCCLXXI*, vol. 2 (London: Edward and Charles Dilly, 1777), annotated by Sir John Soane During his Travels, 89 and 138.
50 Miller, *Letters from Italy*, annotated by Sir John Soane, 193.
51 Miller, *Letters from Italy*, annotated by Sir John Soane, 125. Soane's Tour was also informed by Lassels, 'A preface to the reader concerning travelling'; Frédéric-Samuel Ostervald, *Description des montagnes et des vallées qui font partie de la Principauté de Neuchatel et Valangin* (Neuchatel: Samuel Fauche, 1766); Pompeo Sarnelli, *La guida de' forestieri curiosi di vedere, e di riconoscere le cose più memorabili di Pozzuoli, Baja, Cuma, Miseno, Gaeta, ed altri luoghi circonvicini* (Naples: Saverio Rossi, 1768). Soane did not annotate these other travel accounts.
52 Rosemary Sweet, 'Antiquaries and antiquities in eighteenth-century England', *Eighteenth-Century Studies* 34, no. 2 (Winter 2001): 71.
53 Miller, *Letters from Italy*, vol. 2, 48.
54 Quoted in the entry for 'Bruce, Miss (b.c.1715)', in Ford and Ingamells, *A Dictionary*, 147.
55 Ford and Ingamells, *A Dictionary*, 147.
56 Holland, *Journal*, vol. 1, 135–6.
57 Hester Lynch Piozzi, *The Piozzi Letters: Correspondence of Hester Lynch Piozzi (Formerly Mrs. Thrale)*, ed. Edward A. Bloom and Lillian D. Bloom, vol. 1, *1784–1791* (London: Associated University Presses, 1989), 14.
58 Piozzi, *The Piozzi Letters*, vol. 1, 270.
59 On Townley's Park Street collection, see Viccy Coltman, 'Representation, replication and collecting in Charles Townley's late eighteenth-century

library', *Art History* 29, no. 2 (2006): 10; Viccy Coltman, 'The cream of antiquity: Charles Townley and his august family of ancient marbles', in *Fabricating the Antique: Neoclassicism in Britain, 1760–1800*, 1st edn (Chicago and London: University of Chicago Press, 2006); Mary Bryant, *The Museum by the Park: 14 Queen Anne's Gate from Charles Townley to Axel Johnson* (London: Paul Holberton Publishing, 2017).

60 A Graeco-Roman copy of a fifth-century bc bronze statue, the *Discobolus* was excavated at Hadrian's villa at Tivoli in 1791. After restoration by Carlo Albacini, Charles Townley purchased it for £400. The statue's head was wrongly restored and should have been turned to watch the discus. See Nicolas Barker, Mark Jones and P. T. Craddock, *Fake?: The Art of Deception* (Berkeley: University of California Press, 1990), 140–1.

61 Hester Lynch Piozzi, *Streatham Park, Surrey: A Catalogue of the Excellent and Genuine Household Furniture* (London: Mr. Squibb, 1816), 28–9.

62 Holland, *Journal*, vol. 2, 19.

63 Holland, *Journal*, vol. 1, 141.

64 Sweet, *Cities and the Grand Tour*, 27.

2

Shopping for souvenirs

Two paintings commissioned by Kenneth Mackenzie, Earl of Seaforth, during his stay in Naples in 1771 best illustrate the types of objects that the ideal elite male Grand Tourist was expected to take home. These paintings are of two sides of a room in Kenneth's apartment in Naples. In the first, the Earl and the British ambassador to Naples, Sir William Hamilton, enjoy a performance by Leopold Mozart and his son Wolfgang (see plate 3). In the second, the Earl busily sharpens his fencing talents (see plate 4). In both, Kenneth is surrounded by his collection of Renaissance paintings, replicas of frescos from Pompeii and Herculaneum, an Etruscan vase and everyday objects from antiquity (including bronze figures, lamps, candlesticks and stirrups). A display case contains coral and rock specimens. Susan Lamb notes that these canvases portray the 'very best of tourists' who patronised local luminaries, exercised gentlemanly accomplishments and collected the finest examples from art, antiquity and nature.[1] The portraits themselves also contributed to the Earl's travel collection, suggesting that all the things the Tour stood for would remain a permanent part of his repertoire. Indeed, at the time of his Tour, Kenneth was already a member of the Society of Dilettanti and he would become a fellow of the Society of Antiquaries upon his return home.[2]

Patrons in their own right, aristocratic women Grand Tourists returned home with some of the same sorts of objects as Kenneth. Elizabeth Somerset, Duchess of Beaufort, for example, commissioned two views of Florence from Thomas Patch and copies of Raphael and Guido Reni's works from William Parry during her Tour from 1771 to 1774. James Byres also designed a chimney piece for the

Duchess, his original design having been shown to her by German painter Anton Raphael Mengs in Florence. Elizabeth had these, and many other prints, casts and marble-topped tables, shipped back to England.[3] Georgiana Spencer, Duchess of Devonshire, spent her time in Rome 'closely employed … in the usual course of viewing & describing the Antiquities' under the tutelage of James Byres's nephew Patrick Moir.[4] She had her portrait painted by Hugh Robinson and received an antique stag's head from King Charles III when she visited the Royal Palace at Caserta. Georgiana's close friend (and supplanter) Elizabeth Christiana Cavendish even undertook excavations of the base of the columns of Phocas in the Forum in 1813.[5] Marble-topped tables or recently excavated antiquities could thus announce the wealth of a returned Grand Tourist, whether male or female. But, as we saw in Chapter 1, models of femininity made connoisseurship appear inauthentic when it was displayed by women. This, combined with women's social positioning as hostesses and social facilitators, led them to take a greater interest in contemporary Italy.

If we turn to consider more generally the consumption patterns of elite women while on Tour, their travel accounts, correspondence and purchase records suggest a correlation with the trends Amanda Vickery and other historians have noted when the British were *not* travelling; that is, while female consumption was small and predominantly mundane, male consumption was 'occasional and impulsive, or expensive and dynastic'.[6] Women's accounts and correspondence show the men they accompanied generally held the authority to make extraordinary purchases requiring considerable capital. When 'fortune' threw in Lady Anna Miller's way 'a few excellent pictures', for instance, it was her husband who did not 'let slip the opportunity to make the purchase'.[7] Nonetheless, while women were typically excluded from purchasing 'big ticket' items, they enjoyed recognised independence as shoppers for clothing, accoutrements and small household goods. I argue that on the Grand Tour this translated into considerable power in the developing tourist market, for – unlike at home – women had the option to turn the small objects they bought into souvenirs, thus shifting the mundane into something extraordinary. And all women, no matter their status or wealth, had access to the creative potential of the objects that they encountered in the travel environment. In the following pages I will begin by discussing the range of shops that women visited and objects that they bought on their Grand Tours. I will then turn to consider the range of meanings that these objects embodied as souvenirs.

The sheer amount of consumer detail in women's travel accounts and correspondence suggests that the management of consumption (during travel, as at home) was their domain. Although she acknowledged that 'One comes to Italy to see churches and pictures', when she visited Venice in 1784, Hester Piozzi's interest was quickly taken up by shops and produce:

> one ought to have seen this lovely city: every shop adorned with its own peculiar produce, disposed in a manner so luxuriant and at the same time so tasteful, there is no telling of it. Milliners crowning the new made dignatorys picture with flowers, canopys, feathers, columns of ribbon, gauze &c made an elegant appearance. The furrier formed his thing into representations of the animals, to whom they once belonged, the poulterers and fruiterers were by many thought more beautiful shops than any other, and I admired at the truly Italian ingenuity of a gunsmith, who had turned his instruments of destruction into objects of delight, and by the pleasing and judicious disposition of them. Every shop was illuminated with a large glass chandelier before it, besides the wax candles or coloured lamps interspersed among the ornaments within.[8]

Hester's delightedly detailed description of the array of stores and produce in Venice is typical of women Grand Tourists who transposed the leisure practice of shopping to the French and Italian urban environments and viewed it as central to the experience of travel in a way that male Grand Tourists did not. In comparison, men rarely described manufactories, shops or what they purchased, nor did they refer to 'going shopping' as an activity; shops and manufactories were only helpful references when they sought to itemise the antiquities, paintings, or prints and books they had shipped back to Britain.[9]

The shopping behaviour of women Grand Tourists matches a pattern historians and sociologists have identified more generally – that is, while purchase of goods is carried out equally by both sexes, as a pastime it is particularly associated with women.[10] If we turn to the travel journal of twenty-something Mary Berry, who toured Italy with her sister and widower father from 1783 to 1785, and the record books of Olive Craster, who undertook a wedding tour with her husband George in 1760–63, we can get a sense of the types of objects women typically bought as souvenirs and the female experience of shopping on Tour.

For most women, visiting artists' studios, markets and manufactories was a communal excursion, undertaken accompanied by others of their own sex. In the British trading outpost of Livorno, Mary accompanied Mrs Franc (the wife of a banker she had just dined with) to a coral manufactory. 'This is a great business at Leghorn', she observed,

> carried on by the Jews, who work, cut, and polish the coral, and send it to England and other places to go to the East Indies; saw some beautiful natural specimens as it comes out of the water. The price enormous when cut and polished and made into beads. We saw a long string of large beads, which they said was worth more than 1,200l. sterling.[11]

At the time of Mary's travels, Livorno was the centre for coral manufacture, with the shops of the Sephardi Jewish Attias and Franco families the most highly reputed. Only found in the western Mediterranean, the red quality of the Livorno coral was in great demand and beads were traded with India for diamonds, hence Mary's surprise at their high price.[12]

Mary and her sister's itinerary of art studio visits is also typical; they visited the two Scottish neo-classical history and landscape painters Gavin Hamilton and Jacob More, the English copyist and history painter James Durno and the Irish history painter Henry Tresham.[13] Contemporary art was an area in which women could express their taste without fear of derision because paintings were generally displayed in an acceptable mixed-sex social setting and understanding their aesthetics depended only on one's authority as an eyewitness. Renaissance paintings were less accessible conceptually due to the barrier of connoisseurship outlined in Chapter 1 and practically due to where they were displayed. 'My disappointment was so great', Hester cried from St George's Church in Venice in 1785, where she missed out on seeing 'a famous picture painted by Paul Veronese, of the marriage at Canna in Galilee', because 'the picture was kept in a refectory belonging to friars'. 'Everyone said it was my own fault', she lamented, 'for I might put on men's clothes and see it whenever I pleased'.[14]

Most women took care to keep tallies of goods purchased in their travel journals or account books; for instance, Olive Craster's *Memorandum Book* and *Account of Antiques & Curiosities* meticulously records a string of purchases made during her Grand Tour with her husband. The daughter of Solicitor of the Treasury John Sharpe, Olive was an heiress to a £30,000 fortune. In 1757 she married George, the only surviving son of Northumbrian London-based lawyer John Craster and Catherine (née Villiers), a descendant of the Duke of Buckingham. From 1760 to 1763 Olive and George travelled through France and Italy spending their combined family fortunes lavishly. In the South of France, Olive noted the purchase of brushes and combs, corsets, dress fabric, fans, feathers, flower egrets, gauze mittens, gloves, handkerchiefs, lace, petticoats, slippers and silk stockings. At the milliner's she had her dress fabrics made into gowns. In Naples she bought snuff and bon-bon boxes, combs pins and needles.[15] Her *Account of Antiques & Curiosities* records the purchase of gems: 'an intallio of Tullys Head' and 'two small heads' of members of the Roman imperial family. In Rome Olive recorded purchasing more of these, including 'an agatte of Hercules Mistress' (3 scudi) and a 'blue onix of Cupid who has rob'd Mercury of his purse & Caduceus, set in a gold ring' (3 scudi, 8 paoli).[16] It was here that George had his portrait painted by Batoni and Olive had hers painted by his young English protégée Nathaniel Dance-Holland. The focus of Olive's portrait is her clothes, rather than the treasures of ancient Rome (see plate 5). Her rococo costume covered in extravagant frills and furbelows is likely the 'blue & silver Negligee' Olive bought for 159 ducats in Naples, while her hair is decorated with the flowers she is known to have bought from Italian convents as hair ornaments.[17] A pet squirrel on a delicate silver chain sits on Olive's wrist. Anne French has labelled this 'an English portrait painted abroad'. In many ways it is, but it is also a reflection of Olive's activities and experiences on Tour as a wealthy woman.[18]

Mary Berry did not enjoy Olive's excessive wealth, but she also took care to note the quality and price of the goods she purchased in her travel journal, and took a particular interest in how they had been made. In 'the Pope's manufactory of printed linen', Mary Berry found 'the patterns, particularly those for furniture, taken from the Arabesques, very elegant'; they were sold at 'five shillings a yard'.[19] Clement XIV had established the calico works at the Baths of

Diocletian ten years prior to Mary's visit in an effort to stimulate the manufacturing economy, but according to her this venture had been unsuccessful: 'they cannot make it answer, and they say it must be given up', she observed.[20] Mary's interest in the Pope's efforts to stimulate the economy and relieve poverty is unseen in male-authored travel accounts, perhaps because they were invested in maintaining the view that the city survived on their patronage alone.[21]

What the wider array of women travelling in the latter part of the century offered, then, was a new perspective on cities and towns, a perspective that took into account the people they saw, and sometimes extended to their wages and the conditions that they worked under. At the Villa Negroni in the Rione de Monti, Mary took careful note of the workers 'digging for antiquities'. 'The whole soil, at about ten or twelve feet deep, is a mass of old materials and buildings', she observed. 'They have got out a number of broken columns, pieces of marble, and some medals ... The sale of the old bricks they find, in all these adventures, pays the charge of digging'.[22] Every visit to a silk, velvet or lace mill was marked by similar attention to those who produced the object Mary brought home. On Monday, 16 July 1784 (she always marked the exact date), for example, Mary noted in her journal that she had gone 'to see cut velvet wove – the most complicated of all the looms'. Here she found

> A weaver working assiduously from 5 in the morning to 9 at night cannot make above half a yard and a quarter a day of a stuff for which they are paid by the mercers eight livres a yard. A weaver of brocaded gold-stuff, working the same number of hours, cannot make more than half a yard, and the payment uncertain. All these weavers, lodged up in the fourth and fifth stories of dirty stinking houses, surprised me by the propriety and civility of their manner, and their readiness to satisfy our questions.[23]

The next morning she continued her investigations at different manufactories:

> To a weaver of gold-lace. Or a lace about two inches broad, a person working well can make about two yards or two yards and a half a day, for which they are paid eight or ten Louis a yard by the merchant who gives them the gold to work. To a great manufacturer of gauze. There are two horses up in the fifth story of the houses, turning silk mills, which wind I know not how many bobbins at once. The women who watch these, to arrange them, and take up the threads that break, are there from 5 in the morning till 9 at night for twelve sous.[24]

Such attention to the practicalities and conditions of manufacture shows that women's shopping on Tour cannot be restricted to the category of leisure. As far as Mary was concerned, shopping was a form of employment to be taken seriously and one that was her responsibility as a woman.

A female investment in mealtime ceremony and domestic sociability is reflected by the particular care women took to ensure the quality of their purchases of porcelain. While Mary found 'the painting of the china ... neatly executed' at 'Ginori's china manufactory, about five miles from Florence', she regretted that she was 'not in general happy in their patterns'. 'The clay, too, is heavy', she complained.[25] Founded in 1737 by Marchese Carlo Ginori, the Doccia factory was the first porcelain manufactory to be established in the city. The local clay, kaolin, was far from the pure white of the Saxon clay used at the famous Meissen porcelain manufactory. Ginori experimented with formulas, but his porcelain, known as *masso bastardo*, was, with few exceptions, crude, heavy and grey in colour because of the quality of the clay.[26] This is probably why Mary was left unimpressed and did not make any purchases that day.

The large-scale excavation of Herculaneum from 1738 allowed women the opportunity to apply their interest in consumption to the classical past by revealing the everyday objects of the ancients, including wine, bread, cloth, ink, lamps, furniture and kitchen equipment.[27] When she wrote of visiting the museum in Portici which displayed these finds, in 1771, Lady Anna Miller showed a strong interest in all of the 'domestic utensils', including 'moulds for ices', 'a great variety of strainers' and other household objects 'in all shapes and sizes'.[28] While she took care to note her intention to proceed onto the 'more extensive objects', Anna could not help observing that 'a kind of portable kitchen ... would be a most convenient machine' for those who 'like to eat in parks'.[29] This reinterpretation of the classical past through the lens of consumption offered women the opportunity to imagine themselves as domestic managers through history, with an important role to play that complimented the public roles of the male political orators and military heroes who were typically prioritised by elite male Grand Tourists visiting Rome.

Women also projected consumption practices onto the travel environment itself by purchasing landscape paintings of sites they had visited. During her tour in 1770–71, Mrs Margaret Earle was typical in acquiring a set of views of Naples by Pietro Antoniani, who was esteemed for his exotic depictions of Vesuvius, and by Solomon Delane, known for his views of Tivoli at night.[30] Landscapes were not, however, always affordable: 'I long to have a thousand views', Lady Harriet Maria Malmesbury despaired in 1792, 'but drawings are so dear ... [artists] make no scruple in asking you twenty-five or thirty guineas for a landscape in water-colours. Everything in the way of art here is much dearer than in England, as there are few very good artists'.[31] But this was not a problem for accomplished women who could take ownership of the landscape by viewing it through the painter's eyes. In April 1785, as she gazed at the island of San Giorgio Maggiore, Hester Piozzi expressed a 'longing for a pencil to repeat what has been so often exquisitely painted by Canaletti'.[32] Upon seeing the ruins of two castles in Nassau in December 1793, Lady Holland declared, 'How I longed for a pencil to sketch their mouldering walls ere the rude blast of winter shall destroy their antique forms!'[33] However, some women did come prepared with art supplies and crammed their portfolios with drawings of favourite spots on the tourist trail to be perused and finished in adventurous new watercolour techniques at home. Lady Mary Coke made some sketches during a voyage upon the Rhine in 1767, which she intended to 'have drawings taken from when I return to England'.[34] From 1780 to 1800, William Gilpin's guidebooks showed women exactly how to view and draw the landscape. Gilpin encouraged his pupils to 'take up a tree here, and plant it there ... pare a knoll, or make an addition to it ... remove a piece of paling – a cottage – a wall – or any movable object which I dislike'.[35] To achieve this, women carried drawing aids like the Claude glass, which allowed them to view and sketch their own miniaturised and softened versions of the landscape as reflected in a small convex mirror.[36] By using a Claude glass to bring some elements of the landscape into focus and obscure others, the women manipulated the scene to suit their own desires without altering their actual surrounds. When the women painted the scene up according to this vision, they formed their own souvenirs, mementos of their romanticised visions of the travel location.

This demonstration of female authority over the travel landscape did not go unchallenged. Satires were raised against the female artist consumer. James Plumptre's comic opera *The Lakers* (1798), for example, introduced Miss Beccabunga Veronique, who reflected on a finished sketch which failed to depict anything approaching the scene before her: 'If it is not like what is, it is what it ought to be. I have only made it picturesque'.[37] This critique of a flawed female gaze shows a concern with women tourists' exertion of authority as aesthetic subjects (rather than objects of the male gaze) who could manipulate a scene to suit their own desires and then take possession of it in the form of a souvenir sketch or painting. Such satires were created to deflect the challenge this posed to the elite male claim to a monopoly on the visual possession of the travel landscape.

Women not only viewed the classical past through the lens of consumption, they transcribed the antique onto accoutrements and domestic vessels to craft distinctive souvenirs that reflected their identity and taste. 'This city is famous for a manufacture in tortoiseshell which they inlay curiously with gold, and are very ingenious at representing any object you choose', Lady Anna Miller wrote to her mother from Bologna in 1771. She continued:

> I have had a comb made for my chignon incrusted with gold, to imitate an Etruscan border, copied from an antique vase, which is so well done that we have bespoke several other articles: you are not forgot; I shall send you **** by the first opportunity, with some other trifles.[38]

When translated onto a small fashion accessory, the antique could form a potent extension of one's body and identity. Anna's comb, with its inlaid gold, was likely made using the art of piqué, which found its apogee in Naples between 1720 and 1760.[39] By having a craftsman combine the shell of the hawksbill sea turtle, gold and mother-of-pearl to create this bespoke piece, Anna combined the latest fashion with ancient Roman style – ornamental back combs with long teeth and decorative headings were all the rage at the time, while Etruscan borders had once decorated the tunics and togas of the ancient Romans (figure 2.1). This combination of modern fashion and ancient style was a method Anna used to negotiate her femininity with the connoisseurship expected of the Grand Tour.

Other women had imposing ancient structures scaled down and fashioned onto fans and micro mosaic jewellery in an effective

2.1 Hair comb, England, nineteenth century. Although this is a nineteenth-century comb, it provides an idea of Lady Anna Miller's purchase.

inversion of the Grand Tour's monumental classical objects into an expression of fashion and sociability. Many thousands of fan leaves were made for women, both mounted and unmounted, showing the power of their consumption to develop a market. In Rome in 1784, Mary Berry visited 'a painter of fans' from whom she bought 'two of the ruins of Rome for a sequin apiece'.[40] It is likely that the fans depicted one or more of the ancient Roman sites that appear on a painted Grand Tour fan belonging to Princess Augusta, the second daughter of George III and Queen Charlotte (see plate 6). In the central oval of the fan is the Pantheon; to its left are the three columns of the Temple of the Dioscuri, and to its right is the Basilica of Maxentius. In the smaller fields appear the tombs of Cecilia Metella, the Horatii and the Curiatii, the Temple of Vesta and a fragment of a Corinthian cornice.

Women also chose to decorate their fans with antique designs connected to powerful women of the past: 'The baths of Livia [Drusilla, wife and adviser of the Roman emperor Augustus] are still elegantly designed round her small apartments', Hester Piozzi commented on her Tour, 'and one has copies sold of them upon fans; the curiosity of the original is to see how well the gilding stands; in many places it appears just finished'.[41] The 'original' Hester referred to was one of the well-preserved frescos or mosaic floors in Livia Drusilla's house on the Palatine Hill. By noting 'how well the gilding stands' on the original, Hester drew attention to the fact that she herself had visited the home of this famous female figure.

When they returned home and held their souvenir fans, women Grand Tourists not only protected their creamy white complexions from the heat of a home hearth, but also materially enlisted the ancient ruins they had visited in Rome to decorate their persons, direct conversations and perhaps flirt. Such multiple possibilities are indicated by this poem that appeared in the *Gentleman's Magazine* in 1764:

> *On a Fan*
> For various uses serves the fan,
> As thus – a decent blind,
> Between the Sticks to peep at man,
> Not yet betray your mind
>
> Each action has a meaning plain,
> Resentment's in the snap,
> A flirt expresses strong disdain,
> Consent a gentle tap.
>
> All passions will the fan disclose,
> All modes of female art,
> And to advantage sweetly shews
> The hand, if not the heart.
>
> 'Tis folly's scepter, first design'd
> By love's capricious boy,
> Who knows how lightly all mankind
> Are govern'd by a toy.[42]

This poem demonstrates the power that women held as directors of conversation and they enlisted the antiquities of the Grand Tour to support this. To accord with the use of fans as playful conversation pieces, the commanding structures of ancient Rome were usually displayed on their front leaves to create a polite yet simultaneously boastful boundary, while festoons of open and inviting flowers decorated their interiors.[43]

Although, under the laws of coverture, ultimate control of financial resources in a marriage belonged to the husband, there is no evidence that women felt financially constrained when it came to making smaller purchases that required the outlay of considerably less capital than a recently excavated Roman bust or large Renaissance painting. While women tended to defer to their husbands when it came to extraordinary purchases, the purchase of small objects and accoutrements intended for household and personal consumption was their domain. In Genoa, for instance, Anna bought some 'gold filigree perfect, and executed in an exceedingly good taste'.[44] 'I have purchased some of the best of their productions in this workmanship', she proudly announced in her travel account, using the first-person pronoun 'I' to take full ownership of the intricate gold and silver metalwork jewellery, hand crafted using pliers (*bruxelle*).

The Millers also returned home with paintings bought in Parma, but Anna credited her husband with purchasing these and used asterisks to conceal the identities of the sellers, artists and pictures:

> We have not yet quitted Parma, owing to a most agreeable accident, I assure you. Fortune has thrown in our way a few excellent pictures. M—has not let slip this opportunity to make the purchase, though most unexpected, as well as the manner we came by them. Here are the subjects and the painters names ***** The genteel and honourable conduct of the gentleman from whom he has bought them, will appear strongly in the following anecdotes of him and his family, and the reasons for his disposing of them. ******[45]

It is unclear why the details of these paintings were obscured in Anna's published travel account; perhaps she did this to maintain her guise of anonymity, or to foster a sense of intrigue in her readers, who might have guessed that the Millers had fallen upon a valuable collection of paintings by the 'favourite sons' of Parma, the sixteenth-century mannerists Correggio and Parmigianino. Despite Anna's care to note the 'genteel and honourable conduct' of the seller, it is also possible that the Millers had attained the paintings by dishonest means: 'Some we steal, some we buy, and our court is much adorned with them', the politician John Bacon Sawrey Morritt remarked of his own Grand Tour, referring to the common British practice of pillaging antiquities and artwork from Italy.[46]

There are indications that women brought home some of the same smaller antique objects as elite male Grand Tourists but imbued them with more sentimental and talismanic associations than their male counterparts. During their Grand Tour from 1784 to 1791, Jane and Elizabeth Parminter, the daughters of a wealthy merchant family in Devon, and their cousin Mary acquired a selection of micro mosaic urns, intaglio gemstones and plaster casts of antique cameos. When they returned home, Jane and Mary combined these with several shells and pebbles collected from the shores of local beaches to decorate a small octagonal rosewood worktable. At the centre of the collage a plaque depicting a vestal virgin read 'LIFE SHALL TRIUMPH OVER DEATH' (figure 2.2). Elite male Grand Tourists often returned home with specimen tables containing such antique fragments, arranged in a rigid, geometric format, with each specimen assigned an individual number.[47] Jane and Mary's table was instead decorated in a seemingly eclectic fashion that reflected its personal and familial purpose. Elizabeth passed away shortly after the trio returned from their tour. It is likely, therefore, that the central plaque served to communicate Jane and Mary's bereavement at losing their travelling companion, while the plaster casts, intaglios, micro mosaics, shells and pebbles that surrounded it commemorated the group's experiences together in Italy and Devon.[48]

2.2 Jane and Mary Parminter, bricolaged specimen table, 1790s, shells, polished marble, lapis lazuli, micromosaics, plaster casts and a mourning plaque, A la Ronde, Devon.

When self-consciously writing about how they acquired some of their souvenirs in their travel journals, women dwelt at length on their associations with people met and experiences had. In this way, even the most seemingly small and inconsequential objects could testify to their knowledge and experience as travellers. Lady Anna Miller drew a link between the shells and coral that she brought home from Naples and her own intimate insider knowledge of the Italian lower classes who dove for and sold them:

> The Lazzaroni, as they are here called, are the lowest rank amongst the people. They are, in general, bred to no other business than that of fishing and carrying burdens, and are of a different character to the other Neapolitans. Being a very extraordinary people, I assure you, they govern themselves by a point of honour, which is strictly observed ... We are very fond of conversing with this people, and have often gone into their houses, which are not dirty, but closely ornamented with bad pictures of saints, looking-glasses, some good shells, and fine coral, which they dive for, and find in great abundance near the coast, particularly on the side towards Sicily. We have bought several articles of various sorts from them, and never found one amongst them inclined to knavery or imposition. They declare themselves the descendants of the ancient inhabitants of Naples and its neighbourhood. They are extremely sensible and entertaining in conversation, and when they have brought me shells, &c. to purchase, I used to make them sit down on the floor (which is a great favour here) in order to hear their legendary accounts of themselves and country. They are the only Neapolitans whose features resemble the bustos and statues found at Herculaneum and Pompeia.[49]

Here Anna set a new Grand Tour agenda by drawing from the popularity of conjectural history in the second half of the century to highlight her understanding of the manners and customs of real Italian men, over the 'bustos and statues' of the Romans.

Some antique fragments Anna acquired in Sibyl's Cave, near Puzzoli, Naples, testified to her independence and intrepidity in acquiring them. Here Anna's description of crawling along the floor of the cave and digging her treasures out of the dirt shows the value she placed on the experience of scavenging for her own pieces of history:

> The entrance of Sibyl's Cave is by a broad and flat arch; and is so filled up with earth, as to prevent your penetrating it farther than

about twenty paces without difficulty ... We entered the cave a few paces, but the arch and the ground were so near, that it soon became necessary to get upon our hands and knees ... I filled my pockets with some handfuls of earth, amongst which there are abundance of antique bits of mosaic, broken agate, &c.: and upon examination, found one intaglio of jasper; it represents the sign Scorpion, holding a crescent between the fore-claws, and has a star placed near the tail; it is perfect, but I was sorry it was not upon a fine gem. I have packed a couple of deal-boxes, which contain some antiques and articles of natural history: they are to go to England by sea the first opportunity.[50]

By collecting the intaglio, Anna formed a site for women's souvenir-making associated with symbols of mythical figures of antiquity. The scorpion that decorated Anna's most important find, the 'jasper intaglio', appears frequently in Mesopotamian art, often accompanied by the crescents and stars that she observed, and was identified with Išbara, the goddess of oaths.[51] According to Virgil's *Aeneid*, the Cumaean Sibyl (stemming from the ancient Greek word *sibylla*, meaning prophetess) had once inhabited the cave Anna visited and here had prophesied by 'singing the fates' and writing on oak leaves, which she arranged inside its entrance.[52] In 1818 Mary Shelley, the author of *Frankenstein*, would declare that she had discovered a collection of the Sibyl's prophetic leaves in the very same cave, by then a popular tourist spot. She claimed to have brought these home with her from her own travels and then edited them to form her apocalyptic novel *The Last Man* (1826).[53] Thus, with the right travel narrative attached, even the most seemingly insignificant or mundane objects could, in the hands of a woman traveller, become repositories of memories of experiences encountered in the extraordinary space of travel.

While a comparative study of elite men and women's travel collections themselves remains to be done, the extensive collection developed by Lady Elizabeth Percy, first Duchess of Northumberland, also displays a souvenir culture that differed from the classical paradigm followed by her male contemporaries, including her own husband. After her brother died on his own Grand Tour in 1744 and her father, Algernon Seymour, seventh Duke of Somerset, died six years later, Elizabeth inherited the vast Percy estates in Northumberland. She and her husband, Hugh Smithson, first Duke of Northumberland – a commoner, who inherited a Yorkshire baronetcy from his grandfather – were propelled to the centre of politics and culture.[54] Elizabeth divided her time between Alnwick Castle and Syon House, and the Continent, where she developed the collections they would house. From 1766 to 1774 she went on many tours of the Austrian Netherlands, France, Germany and Switzerland. Notably, Elizabeth only travelled to Italy once, when she visited Milan in 1774.

While her husband's tastes and collecting habits were shaped by his youthful Grand Tour, which he undertook at the age of nineteen, Elizabeth's were embedded in her varied travel experiences later in life between the ages of fifty and fifty-eight. She drew up lists to itemise her collection, which have since been bound into eight volumes of museum catalogues, housed in the archives at Alnwick castle.[55] Both the collection itself and the lists reflect Elizabeth's travels and her enthusiasm for every aspect of contemporary life in the places she visited. Like a contemporary photograph album, watercolours by her drawing master and *valet de chambre*, Jean Vilet, provide a visual record of the locations Elizabeth visited. But her chief interest was in cabinet-sized Dutch and Flemish genre paintings and prints depicting social scenes from her travels. Studies of 'Dutch trades', 'German dresses on cards' and 'Feasts given at Strasbourg to Louis XV' display the same fascination with Continental tradesmen, armies, costumes, feasts, art galleries and artists as Elizabeth's travel diaries.[56] She collected portraits and prints of those people she met on her travels, including a set of waxes of the Hesse-Cassel family and of the Elector of Cologne, prints of Frederick II, King of Prussia and Voltaire, who she visited at Ferney.[57] Elizabeth took care in her lists to record the details of those objects she had collected or received as gifts, including 'Two Landskips in Marble' won in a lottery at Bonn and an alabaster 'Bas relief of Augustus and Livia given me by Sir Thomas Robinson'.[58]

In his *Memoirs*, Louis Dutens, Elizabeth's son's Grand Tour tutor, wrote condescendingly that Elizabeth 'amused herself by collecting prints and medals, and by making other collections of different sorts', but this was not the purpose of her Grand Tour collection.[59] 'We cannot be proud of someone else's souvenir', Susan Stewart notes in her reflections on the souvenir and the collection, 'unless the narrative is extended to include our relationship with the object's owner or unless we transform the souvenir into the collection'.[60]

Elizabeth did not want to transform her souvenirs into a collection. She wanted them to remain samples of her own unique travels, rather than examples; she wanted them to remain a metonymy rather than a metaphor. The purpose of Elizabeth's collection was to lend authenticity to her past travel experiences, not to perform the self-enclosed ahistoricism of a collection. The individual narratives that lay behind the objects in Elizabeth's collection superseded the spatial whole of the collection itself. The collection of this woman traveller, then, was a souvenir. The validity of such a collection (or a 'curiosity cabinet') was increasingly put into question with the development of the museum, something that is further explored in Chapter 4.

Conclusion

In this chapter I have drawn attention to some of the objects that women bought, found or created on their Grand Tours and the complex meanings they attached to them to prove the worth of their travel experiences to both themselves and to others. In some cases, women put the objects towards a feminine reinterpretation of elite male Grand Tour practices. In others, they used them to prompt the remembrance of particular people or travel experiences and to express their individuality.

While only further investigation into male consumption practices on the Grand Tour and a comparison of male and female travel collections will reveal to what extent the material values outlined in this chapter can be seen as distinctly female, the evidence here suggests there were marked gender differences in attitudes between male and female Grand Tourists. Women's journals and letters home consistently reveal an enjoyment of the social practice of shopping as a pastime central to their travel experiences and a more mindful and emotional engagement with the small objects they bought or collected during their travels.[61] Denied access to connoisseurship and unable to pass on the invisible mysteries of institutional power through learned societies, like the Society of the Dilettanti or the Society of Antiquaries, women turned to household and personal artefacts to convey their cultural capital. These consumption practices contributed to a gradual recreation of the meanings of the Tour itself, through physically leading to changes in the travel environment as industries (such as the souvenir fan industry) developed to meet demand and through culturally leading to changes in how the experience of the Grand Tour was conceived and understood. But a genuine effort to explore women's relationships with their souvenirs must move beyond the moment of purchase, for these objects were bought to be taken home from the travel environment as material representations of it. The next chapter will explore the meanings that two women's souvenirs accrued according to use and context following their return home.

Notes

1 Susan Lamb, *Bringing Travel Home to England: Tourism, Gender, and Imaginative Literature in the Eighteenth Century* (Newark, DE: University of Delaware Press, 2009), 116.
2 The Society of Antiquaries was founded in 1707 for the study and collection of British manuscripts, paintings and artefacts; see Susan Pearce, *Visions of Antiquity: The Society of Antiquaries of London 1707–2007* (London: Society of Antiquaries of London, 2007).
3 Brinsley Ford and John Ingamells, *A Dictionary of British and Irish Travellers in Italy, 1701–1800* (New Haven: Yale University Press, 1997), 66.
4 Ford and Ingamells, *A Dictionary*, 295.
5 'Foster, Lady Elizabeth (Hervey) (1758–1824)', in Ford and Ingamells, *A Dictionary*, 375.
6 Amanda Vickery, *The Gentleman's Daughter: Women's Lives in Georgian England* (New Haven: Yale University Press, 1998), 168.
7 Anna Riggs Miller, *Letters from Italy, Describing the Manners, Customs, Antiquities, Paintings, &C. Of That Country, in the Years MDCCLXX and MDCCLXXI, to a Friend Residing in France* (Dublin: W. Watson, 1776), vol. 1, 282.
8 JRL, Thrale-Piozzi Papers, GB 133 Eng MS 618, Hester Lynch Piozzi, 'Journals: Travels in Italy and Germany', 1784–1787, vol. 1, fol. 31r°.
9 Rosemary Sweet, *Cities and the Grand Tour: The British in Italy, c.1690–1820* (Cambridge: Cambridge University Press, 2012), 43.
10 Helen Berry, 'Polite consumption: shopping in eighteenth-century England', *Transactions of the Royal Historical Society* 12 (2002): 375–94; Margot Finn, 'Men's things: masculine possession in the consumer revolution', *Social History* 25, no. 2 (2000): 133–55; Amanda

Vickery, 'His and hers: gender consumption and household accounting in eighteenth-century England', *Past and Present* Supplement 1 (2006).

11 Mary Berry, *Extracts from the Journals and Correspondence of Miss Berry: From the Year 1783 to 1852*, ed. Lady Theresa Lewis (London: Longmans Green, 1865), vol. 1, 123.

12 Francesca Trivellato, 'The exchange of Mediterranean coral and Indian diamonds', in *The Familiarity of Strangers: The Sephardic Diaspora, Livorno, and Cross-Cultural Trade in the Early Modern Period* (New Haven: Yale University Press, 2009), 224–50.

13 Berry, *Extracts from the Journals and Correspondence*, vol. 1, 61, 71, 103.

14 Hester Lynch Piozzi, *Observations and Reflections Made in the Course of a Journey through France, Italy, and Germany* (London: A. Strahan and T. Cadell, 1789), vol. 1, 172.

15 Anne French, *Art Treasures in the North: Northern Families on the Grand Tour* (Norwich: Unicorn Press, 2009), 93.

16 French, *Art Treasures in the North*.

17 French, *Art Treasures in the North*.

18 French, *Art Treasures in the North*, 93.

19 Berry, *Extracts from the Journals and Correspondence*, vol. 1, 111.

20 Sweet, *Cities and the Grand Tour*, 136.

21 Sweet, *Cities and the Grand Tour*, 136.

22 Berry, *Extracts from the Journals and Correspondence*, vol. 1, 95.

23 Berry, *Extracts from the Journals and Correspondence*, vol. 1, 135.

24 Berry, *Extracts from the Journals and Correspondence*, vol. 1, 135.

25 Berry, *Extracts from the Journals and Correspondence*, vol. 1, 121.

26 Clare Le Corbeiller, *Eighteenth-Century Italian Porcelain* (New York: Metropolitan Museum of Art, 1985), 12–19.

27 Charlotte Roberts, 'Living with the ancient Romans: past and present in eighteenth-century encounters with Herculaneum and Pompeii', *Huntington Library Quarterly* 78, no. 1 (2015): 61–85.

28 Miller, *Letters from Italy*, vol. 2, 260.

29 Miller, *Letters from Italy*, vol. 2, 261.

30 Ford and Ingamells, *A Dictionary*, 327.

31 Ford and Ingamells, *A Dictionary*, 630–1.

32 Piozzi, *Observations and Reflections*, vol. 1, 171.

33 Elizabeth Vassall Fox Holland, *The Journal of Elizabeth Lady Holland (1791–1811)*, ed. Giles Stephen Fox-Strangways Ilchester (London: Longmans Green, 1908), vol. 1, 107.

34 Mary Coke, *The Letters and Journals of Lady Mary Coke*, vol. 2, ed. James Archibald Home (Bath: Kingsmead Bookshops, 1970), 83.

35 William Gilpin, *Observations on the River Wye and Several Parts of South Wales Relative Chiefly to Picturesque Beauty Made in the Summer of the Year of 1770* (London: R. Blamire, 1789), 68.
36 John Brewer, *The Pleasures of the Imagination: English Culture in the Eighteenth Century* (London: HarperCollins, 1997), 501.
37 James Plumptre, *The Lakers: A Comic Opera, in Three Acts* (London: W. Clarke, 1798), 44.
38 Miller, *Letters from Italy*, vol. 2, 57.
39 Alexis Kugel, *Piqué: Gold, Tortoiseshell and Mother-of-Pearl at the Court of Naples* (Paris: Milano Mondadori Electa, 2018); Susan Moore, 'The virtuosic tortoiseshell workers of 18th-century Naples', *Apollo: The International Art Magazine*, 11 September 2018, accessed 21 January 2020, www.apollo-magazine.com/the-virtuosic-tortoiseshell-workers-of-18th-century-naples/.
40 Berry, *Extracts from the Journals and Correspondence*, vol. 1, 71.
41 Piozzi, *Observations and Reflections*, vol. 1, 393.
42 Sylvanus Urban, 'Poetical Essays; December 1764', in *The Gentleman's Magazine and Historical Chronicle* (London: D. Henry and R. Cave, 1764), 594.
43 Helene Alexander, *Fans* (Oxford: Shire Publications, 2002), 17–19.
44 Miller, *Letters from Italy*, vol. 1, 218.
45 Miller, *Letters from Italy*, vol. 1, 282.
46 John Bacon Sawrey Morritt, *The Letters of John B. S. Morritt of Rokeby Descriptive of Journeys in Europe and Asia Minor in the Years 1794–1796* (London: John Murray, 1914), 179.
47 Freya Gowrley, 'Craft(ing) narratives', *Eighteenth-Century Fiction* 31, no. 1 (2018): 83.
48 Gowrley, 'Craft(ing) narratives', 94–5.
49 Miller, *Letters from Italy*, vol. 2, 154.
50 Miller, *Letters from Italy*, vol. 2, 131.
51 E. Douglas Van Buren, 'The scorpion in Mesopotamian art and religion', *Archiv für Orientforschung* 12 (1937): 1–28.
52 'Cumae (Napoli, Italy)', in *International Dictionary of Historic Places: Southern Europe*, ed. Adele Hast et al. (Chicago and London: Fitzroy Dearborn, 1994), 176–9.
53 Mary Wollstonecraft Shelley, *The Last Man*, vol. 1 (Philadelphia: Carey, Lea and Blanchard, 1833), iii–viii.
54 Hugh Smithson's son James is known for having provided the founding bequest to the Smithsonian Institution in Washington, DC.
55 See 'Appendix 2: The 1st Duchess of Northumberland's "Museum Catalogues" or "Lists"', in French, *Art Treasures in the North*, 276–81.
56 French, *Art Treasures in the North*, 68.

57 French, *Art Treasures in the North*, 278.
58 French, *Art Treasures in the North*, 277.
59 Louis Dutens, *Memoirs of a Traveller, Now in Retirement*. 5 vols. Vol. 2 (London: R. Phillips), 1806, 100–1.
60 Susan Stewart, *On Longing: Narratives of the Miniature, the Gigantic, the Souvenir, the Collection* (Baltimore: Johns Hopkins University Press, 1984), 137.
61 This has also been noted of women at home; see Vickery, *The Gentleman's Daughter*.

3

Creating their own cultural capital: Lady Anna Miller and Hester Lynch Piozzi

The Grand Tour acted as a catalyst for change for returned women travellers. Some became prominent patrons of the arts, others renovated or rebuilt their family houses in the years following their Tours. Some women flawlessly fulfilled the social positions they had left behind, while others gained a promotion to a higher social group on their return from Italy. Harnessing the cultural capital of a masculinised institution, however, did not come without its obstacles. In this chapter I analyse how two women used their travel collections to establish successful salons that resembled the French salons and Italian *conversazioni*. Susan Schmid has described British salons as 'both places and non-places ... defined not through stable architectural surroundings but through accessibility and visibility in which performances of the self took place'.[1] Salon hostesses, however, combined household architecture and souvenirs to form real places that were central to their performances of the cultural capital they had gained on their Tours.

Lady Anna Miller (1741–81) and Hester Lynch Piozzi (1741–1821) each held an insecure social position, the former through social status and the latter through marriage, and each sought to exploit the prestige of having undertaken a tour of Italy to establish herself more firmly in society upon her return home. While they travelled a decade apart, in 1771 and 1782, both women followed much the same route (figure 3.1), demonstrating the long-standing popularity of the Grand Tour. Taking a closer look at how these women established the villas of Batheaston, near Bath, and Brynbella, in Wales, tells us something of the gendered performance of the Tour at home and how it intersected with social status, regionality and personality among other factors.

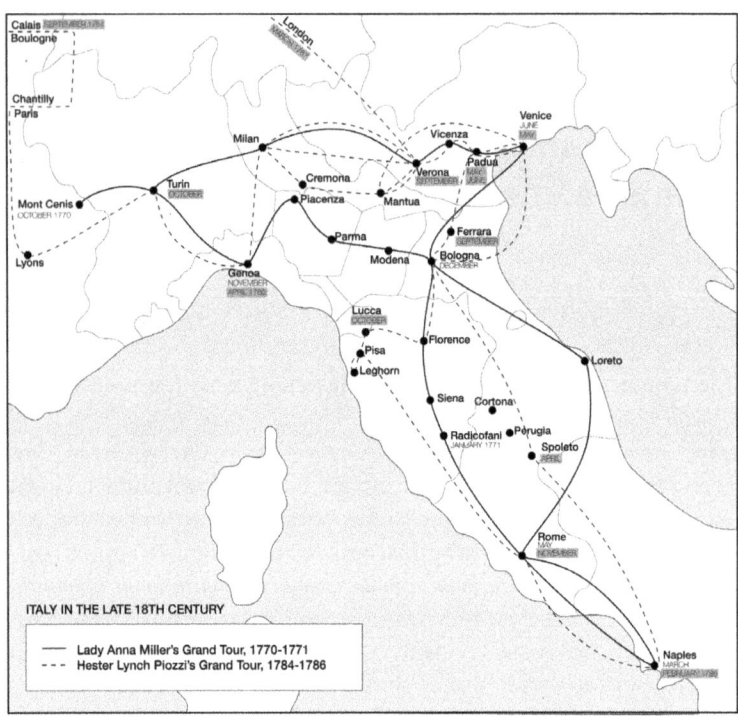

3.1 Map of Hester Lynch Piozzi and Lady Anna Miller's Grand Tours.

Lady Anna Miller and Batheaston

Anna was not born a Lady. The daughter of London customs official Edward Riggs and his wife, Margaret (née Pigott), of the ancient house of Chetwynd, Shropshire, she inherited a considerable fortune from her grandfather, Edward Riggs of Riggsdale, Cork, a privy councillor and member of the Irish House of Commons.[2] In 1765 Anna married Sir John Miller. Sir John came from a poor family seated at Ballicasey, Clarecame, but was proclaimed an Irish baronet in 1778 for his services during the Seven Years' War (1756–63). Anna's title accompanied this honour.[3] In 1770–71 the couple undertook an eight-month Grand Tour. The time spent living frugally in Italy was intended to reduce living costs while they had an expensive Italianate villa built near Bath.

Five years after her travels, Anna became the first woman to publish a Grand Tour account. To appropriately fit the eighteenth-century topos of British female modesty, she published anonymously and framed *Letters from Italy* as a form of personal correspondence to her mother, making sure to note that 'we travel merely for our own amusement' and 'write for yours only'.[4] In the latter part of the eighteenth century the familiar letter was widely regarded as a genre women excelled at and letter-writing had come to represent femininity.[5] This format then formed an appropriately demure framework for Anna's account. She nonetheless authoritatively assessed Italy's art market for a female audience, insisting that her views were superior to those of Joseph Addison, the established authority on the Grand Tour.[6] She confidently advised her readers to 'turn over a few pages' if they were 'unacquainted with the merits of painting' and drew their attention to those painters and portraitists that were 'reasonable in their prices'.[7] Despite her book being officially anonymous, Anna was soon recognised in several Bath guides, including Genius Loci's *Bath Anecdotes and Characters* (1782), where she was described as 'That lady in pink satin ... whom you must have heard of as the writer of some agreeable letters from Italy'.[8]

Others have fruitfully analysed Anna's self-presentation in *Letters from Italy*, which represented an important attempt by a woman from an undistinguished background to assert her own aesthetic judgement in a sphere of largely male authorship.[9] But it was not only her commercialisation of letter-writing that allowed Anna to direct Bath's emerging literary culture; her material enlistment of the Tour's cultural capital was key to her success.

In 1766 Horace Walpole flatteringly described the newly-wed couple's 'small new-built house with a bow-window',

> directly opposite to which the Avon falls in a wide cascade, a church behind it in a vale, into which two mountains descend, leaving an opening into the distant country. Their garden is little, but pretty, and watered with several small rivulets among the bushes.[10]

Following their Tour, the Millers' introduced Continental embellishments, including a magnificent studded front door, like that of an Italian palazzo, and mirrored shutters. 'Near Bath is erected a new Parnassus', Horace less kindly quipped of the renovated villa in 1775,

3.2 John Chessell Buckler, *Batheaston Villa from the S. E.*, 1825.

'composed of three laurels, a myrtle-tree, a weeping-willow, and a view of the Avon, which has been new christened Helicon'.[11] Sir John invited his guests 'to walk round the house, and see his green-house, &c'.[12] From here they could admire its curving castellated facade (figure 3.2) and the view of the north bank of the River Avon as it cut a deep trench through the southern end of the Cotswold Hills.

To finish the scene, Anna commissioned a copy of the Temple of Clitumnus at Foligno from the architect Sir John Soane (the Grand Tourist who was not impressed with Anna's feminine inaccuracies in Chapter 1). She described the 'beautiful little temple' in some detail when she visited Foligno in May 1771:

> it is called the Temple of Clitumnus, supposed to have been dedicated to that river god. The plan is an oblong square, it has four columns, and two Corinthian pilasters; the portico is vaulted within; and the friezes are *basso relievos*, representing olive branches, grapes, and leaves finely executed. The two centre pillars of the four are sculpted from top to bottom, describing laurel leaves, placed in alternate rows, the other two are fluted and in spiral lines; the pediment they support is beautifully proportioned. Its two entrances, which were at each end, are quite in ruins. The little room in the interior of the temple, measures only ten feet by eight: this small edifice is built of an iron-grey marble, which appears to have been highly polished.[13]

The architectural detail of her description suggests that Anna was already considering having her own copy of the temple made as a garden feature at the time of her travels.

As well as publishing her account, Anna established a literary salon that attracted provincial gentry and clergy, including Elizabeth Percy, Duchess of Northumberland; Frederick Howard, fifth Earl of Carlisle; Henry John Temple, third Viscount Palmerston (who twice served as prime minister); and Thomas Sedgwick Whalley (described by one of his contemporaries as 'a sensible, well-informed and educated, polished, old well-beneficed, nobleman's and gentleman's house-frequenting, literary and chess-playing divine'[14]). It also drew together celebrated and up-and-coming writers, such as the poet Christopher Anstey, the novelist Frances Burney, liberal writer Edward Jermingham, biographer William Mason, actor and playwright David Garrick and Anna Seward, the 'Swan of Lichfield'.

The Millers' literary soirees were held once a fortnight during the Bath season. 'The room into which we were conducted was so much crowded we could hardly make our way', Fanny Burney recalled of her visit.[15] Among candle-niches carved from Carrara marble, quarried in Tuscany, Anna presented her guests with silver spoons and delicate porcelain dishes holding 'a profusion of jellies, sweetmeats, ice creams'.[16] Anna also had her many souvenirs on display, including the mosaic pieces and intaglio of jasper depicting the sign of the Scorpion she had discovered in Sibil's cave; the 'good shells and fine coral' she had personally acquired from Naples' Lazzaroni; the gold filigree jewellery she had purchased in Genoa; and the tortoiseshell comb with a Etruscan border she had commissioned in Rome (see Chapter 2).[17] Anna returned home too with etchings by Giovanni Battista Piranesi. While she found his 'prints of the ruins of Rome ... too confused to give a clear idea of them', this did not prevent her from purchasing some because it was the fashion:

> he is so ridiculously exact in trifles, as to have injured the fine proportions of the portico to the pantheon, by inserting, in his gravings, the papers stuck on them, such as advertisements, &c. Many other silly particulars of this nature have confused his designes; yet they are esteemed the best here; and we have made of an ample collection of the most valuable them.[18]

Anna's most significant souvenir, however, was an Etruscan vase (figure 3.3) from Frascati, the country seat of Cicero. Etruscan vases

3.3 The Batheaston Vase adorned with myrtle, 1775, 144 mm × 89 mm, etching.

had long been popular objects for Grand Tourists to take home; they evoked the birth of European civilisation and had an aura of timeless serenity later celebrated by Keats. Anna presented hers as 'Old Tully's Vase' (as though she was on first-name terms with the celebrated Roman orator) and exhibited it in the bay window of her drawing room.[19] Salon attendees would place poems composed around rhyming words or subjects like fashion, dancing or society into the vessel.[20] Following this, a gentleman was appointed to 'read them aloud and judge of their rival merits without knowledge of the authors', and upon the reveal, the best were awarded myrtle wreaths and published.[21] Along with the vase, Anna returned to Bath with two social practices: *bouts-rimés* (poetry as a parlour game) was an amusement she had adopted from France, while the idea of awarding myrtle wreaths was drawn from Rome's Academy of Arcadia, where intellectual exercises won crowns of laurel and myrtle in the late seventeenth century.[22]

Anna so combined her Etruscan vase, the literary productions of her visitors and her myrtle wreaths to astutely form a 'brand' of literary patronage intimately linked to her Grand Tour experiences. She encouraged guests to write poems that celebrated 'The second Time of opening of the Tusculum Vase' or lamented the 'the closing of the Vase for this Season', and it became common for visitors to note the appearance and location of the vase; on her visit in 1780, Fanny Burney was disappointed to find 'the place appropriated for the vase, but at this time it was removed'.[23] When David Garrick passed away in 1779, the (then up-and-coming) poet Anna Seward wrote a 'Monody' that opened with a vignette of the Millers' mourning over their 'damp vase', 'scattered myrtles' lying unattended at their feet.[24] The myrtle wreaths in turn became souvenirs for Anna's female guests, who showed off their inclusion in her circle and loyalty to her by pinning them to their dresses when they attended Bath's many balls.[25] In 1781 Elizabeth Hayley was ecstatic to receive a wreath after copying a poem written by her husband, the celebrated writer William Hayley. 'A prize! a prize! my dearest Hotspur! And the very first!' she exclaimed in a letter. 'I was so complimented at your expense, that I did not get home to dinner till after five; for I called to shew my elegant wreath (which was pinned into my hair by the beautiful Miss Wraughton)'.[26] William assured his wife that he had placed her wreath on her 'favourite little horse of bronze on the chimney-piece', a location where souvenirs are still so often displayed.[27]

Between 1775 and 1781 over two hundred of the poems created at Anna's literary gatherings were published nationally in four sold-out volumes, modestly titled *Poetical Amusements at a Villa Near Bath*. The proceeds from these sales linked pleasure to utility by funding Bath's pauper charity and hospital, which Sir John Miller presided over as president.[28] Like the Bluestocking salons, the Batheaston assemblies gave women writers, including Anna Seward and the poets and essayists Jane Bowdler and Mary Alcock, the opportunity to perform and receive feedback from polite company. When Anna chose a verse to be published, it had passed the test of polite taste and aesthetic decorum, so allowing women contributors safe access to the marketplace and a share in public discourse.[29] Indeed, in his biography of Anna Seward, Walter Scott credited Lady Anna Miller with initiating the poet's career, for it was at Batheaston that the celebrated *Elegy on Captain Cook* (1780) and *Mondody on Major Andre* (1781) were first read and approved.[30]

Not surprisingly, Anna's social and commercial success excited sarcasm and derision from London's more established (and largely male) literary coterie. Their commentary indicates a resistance to the hostess as an upstart woman whose enlistment of the Tour's cultural capital represented a larger shift that threatened to reduce the capacity of connoisseurship to produce social distinction. 'Alas!' Horace Walpole despaired in 1775, in a letter to his cousin, Field Marshall Henry Seymour Conway,

> Mrs. Miller is returned a beauty, a genius, a Sappho, a tenth Muse, as romantic as Mademoiselle Scudéri, and as sophisticated as Mrs. Vesey. The Captain's fingers are loaded with cameos, his tongue runs over with virtu, and that both may contribute to the improvement of their own country, they have introduced bouts-rimés as a new discovery. They hold a Parnassus fair every Thursday, give out rhymes and themes, and all the flux of quality at Bath contend for prizes.[31]

Here Horace likened Anna to the seventeenth-century French novelist Madeleine de Scudéry, whose philosophical works were about improving the condition of women. Madeleine also held renowned Saturday salons. Her critics labelled these gatherings amateurish and claimed that her philosophical ideas were derivative and confused.[32]

Horace also linked Anna to the wealthy Irish intellectual Elizabeth Vesey, who was credited for fostering the Bluestocking Society in England in the 1750s. For Horace, the combination of Anna's showy erudition and her husband's excessive finery suggested that Anna had tried to spend her way into the Tour's legacy of taste as a means of joining the Bluestocking circle but was intellectually incapable of the subtleties of choice a true Bluestocking possessed. However, I argue that the inability to make these choices was less a result of Anna's level of intelligence than it was of her social status.

While their provincial locale allowed the Millers to achieve a level of fame and social standing unachievable in a large established city like London, their restriction to the developing Romanesque spa town opened the couple up to derision on regional lines. Periodical attacks of the 'Batheaston follies' corresponded with Anna's chosen fortnightly poetry subjects and drew a distinction between the sophisticated metropolitans of London and the ignorant provincials of Bath, where it was said 'every upstart of fortune, harnessed to the trappings of the mode, presents himself'.[33] In 1781, for instance, *The Hibernian Magazine* published a 'copy of a Doggerel Letter to a Friend from Bath' on the subject of 'fun':

> Now scampering away to Bath-Easton we run,
> And the Old and the Young shew they can't write- for fun;
> You must famish and fume to hear rickety versus,
> And their dull authors bray 'em, which exceedingly worse is.
> For though earthquakes and hurricanes ravage the earth,
> Such incidents only to humour give birth.[34]

Domestic tourist Ellen Wilson reflected a common view when she observed that Bath was a 'retreat of widows & unmarried ladies' that allowed 'those whose fortunes … are sufficient to enable them to live in genteel life' to 'live in that rank of society cheaper than elsewhere'.[35] In comparison to Anna's single place of residence in Bath, the respected 'Queen of the Blues', Elizabeth Montagu, regularly moved between her three different estates in London, Denton and Sandleford. Elizabeth Egar has suggested that it was this ability to shift properties that allowed Elizabeth to geographically demarcate the different spheres of culture, commerce, intellect and pleasure that she used to maintain 'a reputation for virtue and economy at the same time as she indulged in a talent for lavish display'.[36] Anna could ill-afford such a level of geographical mobility.

The most extensive mockery, however, targeted Anna's Etruscan vase. This mockery demonstrates how London's literary elite were able to question the sartorial motivations of those they disliked more largely to question their authenticity and intelligence. Objects like Anna's Etruscan vase, which demonstrated dignity, civility and elegance in the hands of an elite male Grand Tourist could, in the hands of a woman, just as easily represent foolish pretension. The following poem published in the *Gentleman's Magazine* in 1778 put the authenticity of Anna's Grand Tour experience into question by indicating that she had fallen into the classic feminine trap of being seduced by the superficial artifice of ornaments rather than understanding the principles of correct classical form:

> *The Wreath of Fashion*
> On a spruce pedestal of Wedgwood ware,
> Where motley forms, and tawdry emblems glare,
> Behold she consecrates to cold applause,
> A Petrifaction, work'd into a Vase:
> The Vase of Sentiment!— to this impart
> Thy kindred coldness, and congenial art.
> Here (as in humbler scenes, from Cards and Gout,
> Miller convenes her literary Rout)
> With votive song, and tributary verse,
> Fashion's gay train her gentle rites rehearse.
> What soft poetic incense breaths around!
> What soothing hymns from Adulation found![37]

Here Richard Tickell invoked the myth and design formula that classicism was strictly masculine and diversions were feminine by drawing attention to Anna's ill-conceived decoration of her vase with pink ribbons and myrtle wreaths ('motley forms, and tawdry emblems') and her fashionable repurposing of it for sentiment. At the same time, the reference to consumer culture ('Wedgwood') indicated that it was not only Anna's gender but also her social status that limited her ability to properly understand antiquity. In the second half of the eighteenth century a 'vase mania' descended on Britain as Josiah Wedgwood and other manufacturers offset their elite trade by creating replicas of Roman urns for 'the Middling Class of People' who bought 'quantities of them at a reduced price'.[38]

While Anna reinterpreted her Etruscan vase by using it as a vessel for poetry, her neighbours houses were furnished with British-made neo-classical vases whose functions had been extended beyond ornamentation; with the addition of metal branches some became candelabras and candle holders, while perforated lids transformed others into perfume burners, ice pails or tea urns.[39] Although Anna's Etruscan vase was a genuine souvenir from her time in Italy, equating it with these common household decorations undermined her claim to the Tour's legacy of taste and the threat to Britain's male political elite. Over the years, this commercialised and inauthentic version of Anna's vase was likened to her very person. In 1780 Fanny Burney described an acquaintance mocking the vase 'without mercy' at a public breakfast to which Anna's friend Mrs Whalley, 'grew quite enraged, reasoning upon the wickedness of laughing at her good friends'.[40] Tellingly, the acquaintance eventually apologised by claiming that his intention had been 'to ridicule the vase, not the Millers'.[41]

On 24 June 1781, at forty-one years of age, Anna died suddenly at the Hotwells, Bristol. She was buried near Bath Abbey. Her Etruscan vase is now lost, but it was drawn by the sculptor Thomas Parsons in his pocketbook and is the central feature of a grand memorial her husband commissioned from the famed sculptor John Bacon the Younger for the north wall of the sanctuary of the Bath Abbey church (see plate 7). Beneath the large relief of the vase, sits Anna's portrait surrounded by a myrtle wreath and framed by two muses in flowing Grecian gowns who decorate the vase with laurel branches (see plate 8). The epitaph by Anna Seward reads:

> Devoted stone! Amidst the wrecks of time
> Uninjured bear thy MILLER'S spotless name:
> The virtues of her youth and ripen'd prime,
> The tender thought, th' enduring record claim.
>
> When closed the numerous eyes that round this bier
> Have wept the loss of wide extended worth,
> O gentle stranger, may one generous tear
> Drop as thou bendest o'er this hallowed earth?
>
> Are truth and genius, love and pity thine,
> With liberal charity and faith sincere?
> Then rest thy wandering step beneath this shrine,
> And greet a kindred spirit hovering near.[42]

Here the poet wittily urged the marble panel itself ('Devoted stone!') to preserve 'MILLER'S spotless name' without injury, unlike the short-lived perishable paper satires of London's literary elite.[43] Seward listed the hostess's virtues, among them 'truth and genius', followed by 'love and pity', then 'liberal charity and faith' – the same qualities that she extoled in a longer elegy *Poem to the Memory of Lady Miller* (1782).[44] Nonetheless, despite the efforts of Anna's supporters to memorialise her as a patron of the arts who promoted encouragement over criticism, her gender, social status and regionality continued to contribute to the jibes of her detractors long after her death. In 1805 Richard Graves provided a satirical account of the 'trifling exhibition' of Lady Miller's regular morning assemblies in *The Triflers*.[45] And scholarship continued to court parody into the twentieth century, with Anna's only biographer to date, Ruth Hesselgrave, opening her 1927 publication with a caricature of Charles Dickens's fictional literary hostess Mrs Leo Hunter, author of an 'Ode to an Expiring Frog'.[46] She concluded that the Batheaston salon was a 'mediocre institution ... interesting only as a manifestation of the literary aspirations of society toward the end of the eighteenth century'.[47]

This enduring caricature of Anna, along with that of Mrs Betty Coutts, who sought to 'pretty up' the Colosseum, and Miss Bruce, who concerned herself with the 'endecencies' of two naked angels (see Chapter 1), point to the expansion of the social elite in the late eighteenth century and the ensuing ridicule of women as men from the nobility, gentry and the nouveau riche landholders competed with one another for social status. They point to the existential threat that an opening up of the Grand Tour's cultural capital posed to the male patrician's classical paradigm derived from the masculine traditions of civic humanism. When it came to her own souvenirs, Anna's professions of personal value and associations were lofty and sentimental. Members of her literary circle adopted these meanings and circulated them more widely. Accusations of materialism, pretension and covetousness, however, provided useful ammunition for critics of this woman and, by extension, of other women seeking to commercialise their travels. And so the Tour's legacy of taste continued to elude Anna even long after her death, as 'good taste confirmed the good breeding of the elite, who themselves set the canons of good taste'.[48] We will now turn to another literary hostess who in 1784, fourteen years after the Millers' Grand Tour, extended upon Anna's attempts to challenge an archaic agenda and set a new one.

Hester Lynch Piozzi and Brynbella

Hester Lynch Piozzi (unlike Lady Anna Miller) was born into a family of powerful oligarchs. Her parents – the co-founder of Halifax, Nova Scotia, Sir John Salusbury, and his wife, Hester Maria, of Bachygraig, Flintshire – were cousins and descendants of Catrin of Berain, 'Mam Cymru' ('Mother of Wales').[49] Hester, as an only child and thus the sole focus of their attention, received an outstanding education: '*I* was their Joynt Play Thyng', she later recalled, '& although Education was a Word then unknown, as applied to Females; They had taught me to read, & speak, & think, & translate from the French, till I was half a Prodigy'.[50] The fortunes of the Salusburys were low, however, and Hester was heavily reliant on her childless uncle, Sir Robert Cotton of Lleweni Hall, Denbighshire. In 1763, at twenty-two years of age, and one year after the death of her father, she was wedded to the wealthy London brewer Henry Thrale. From 1764 to 1778 Hester bore twelve children, only four of whom survived to maturity, while her husband retained his bachelor lifestyle. Although unhappy in her imposed marriage, as the hostess of Streatham Park estate Hester revelled in forming a Bluestocking salon around the celebrated writer Samuel Johnson. She also did some travelling during this time. Ever drawn to the beauties of her homeland, in 1774 she encouraged her husband to accompany her on a tour of Wales and went to France the following year with Italian scholar Joseph Baretti and a maidservant. It was once Henry Thrale died from a series of strokes in 1781, however, that Hester gained the independent wealth to fulfil her long-standing ambition to undertake a Grand Tour.

In 1784, after selling her late husband's brewery for £135,000, Hester made a love match, marrying her daughter Queeny's music teacher, Gabriel Piozzi. Born at Guinzano, Venice, in 1740, Gabriel had emigrated to London in 1776 and here thrived as a concert pianist and music teacher. This second marriage to a professional class Roman Catholic, and the death in the same year of Samuel

Johnson (who it was generally assumed Hester would marry), led her daughters and the Bluestocking circle to shun her. 'Mrs Thrale's imprudent marriage shortened [Samuel Johnson's] life', Elizabeth Montagu regretted. She went on, 'Her letters to her friends from abroad were full of her felicity, it is said accounts are now come that she is confined in a convent at Milan'.[51] Hurt by this tale of her confinement, Hester lamented the circle's 'ill Treatment of me, & my Resentment towards *them*' in her diary, and regretted that it would 'make it difficult for me ever to live happily in England any more'.[52] In the face of this social exclusion, the couple set out on a four-year honeymoon in Italy from 1784 to 1787. Following her return, Hester fashioned a new identity for herself as a 'demi-naturalised' Welsh-Italian traveller that was based on both her Grand Tour experience and her Welsh ancestry, of which she was immensely proud.[53] This dual identity served a social purpose by defending her marriage choice, and an intellectual one by allowing her to separate her travel experiences from those of the elite male Grand Tourists who came before her.

Like Anna, Hester began her transformation by publishing an account of her Tour two years after she returned home. Prior to *Observations and Reflections*, the only travel accounts to be published by women followed Anna's lead by taking the form of personal correspondence. 'For the book – I have not thrown my thoughts into the form of private letters', Hester explained in her preface, 'because a work of which truth is the best recommendation, should not above all others begin with a lie'.[54] As implied by its title, *Observations and Reflections* was ostensibly a direct account of Hester's journey through Italy. She strengthened this impression with the literary trope of 'on-the-spot composition'.[55] 'But hark! While I am writing this peevish reflection in my room, I hear some voices under my window answering each other upon the Grand Canal', Hester exclaimed in one passage, after idly wondering if the rumour that Venetian gondoliers sang parts of Tasso and Ariosto while they rowed was true. 'It is, it *is* the gondolieri sure enough; they are at this moment singing to an odd sort of tune, but in no unmusical manner, the flight of Erminia from Tasso's Jerusalem'.[56] She used such passages to authenticate her account as a true souvenir of her travels, rich with memory, that surpassed the mere description of the typical male Grand Tourist's account. By contrast, she as the author was *present* and instantaneously reacting to travel experiences as they occurred.

However, far from being the impromptu in-the-moment jotting suggested by such literary tropes, *Observations and Reflections* was a deliberate performance.[57] Two folio notebooks and Hester's diary, *Thraliana*, formed the foundations for her published account. She developed these into a rough draft of seven notebooks during a two-month stay in Exmouth in 1788.[58] 'Mean Time I do not labour so as to hurt myself I assure you', Hester wrote to her friend Sophia Byron during these difficult months, 'ten pages o'Day of long folio paper is all I pretend to, and on Sundays *you see how I rest my weary fingers*'.[59] She also used her time in Exmouth study travel literature and verify her facts: 'Tell me if you recollect the name of the very very old church at Padua, whose Walls were covered with Cimabue's Pictures', Hester wrote to her travelling companion, Reverend Leonard Chappelow, 'And do tell me if it's true that the Harebell, that red Weed which grows in all our Hedges, is peculiar to England or no; and whether you think there was ever a Weeping Willow on the Banks of the Brenta- I say there was none'.[60] Leonard agreed that there were no willows on the banks of the Brenta and Hester shaped a passage in *Observations and Reflections* around this absence, using it to express the salient characteristics of the Venetians: 'I longed to see the weeping willow planted along this elegant stream; but the Venetians like to see nothing weep I fancy'.[61]

The breadth of commentary we see from Hester's literary process seen in her personal correspondence is unparalleled among surviving Grand Tour accounts – male or female. This, in combination with Hester's folio notebooks and diary, offers a rare look into how she reshaped her travel narrative over time to more accurately reflect the identity she wanted to assume as a result of her travels. A comparison of the same section of text in the different drafts of Hester's travel account shows that she developed a demi-naturalised part-Italian persona following her return home, despite feeling out of place when she was in Italy. In *Observations and Reflections*, Hester celebrated her 'insight into every day behaviour, and common occurrences, which can alone be called knowing something of a country', in comparison to the limited vision of elite male Grand Tourists who, she lamented, 'run from town to town, with no impression made but on their bones'.[62] 'I ought to learn that which before us lies in daily life, if proper use were made of my *deminaturalisation*', she went on to remark.[63] This self-identifier is, however, missing from the same section of text in Hester's original folio notebook. Here, she instead regretted her status as a 'Foreigner' and inability to judge 'eloquence in any language but my own'.[64] The development of this demi-naturalised personality shows more broadly that the meanings women attached to their travel experiences were not rigid, but changed over time depending on the identity they sought to foster.

Hester's gradual creation of a demi-naturalised identity is also reflected in the Grand Tour portraits she chose to take home. During her stay in Rome, from November 1785 to April 1786, Hester sat for two painted portraits.[65] She unflatteringly described her appearance in one of these in letter to her eldest daughter as 'a Red-haired old Hag in a white Bedgown ... neither "Ornamento" of *one* country, nor "Grazia" of *another*', and hoped to have it 'burned'.[66] Nonetheless, in the same letter Hester enjoyed creating a far more nuanced written self-portrait that showcased her adoption of contemporary Italian fashions:

> I was looking at myself the other day, & thought I wd tell you what a motley Creature I was become: for my Riding Habit was bought at Rome I recollected; my Hat & Shirt at Naples; my Shoes at Padua, my Stockings at Brescia, my Ruffles at Genoa, one of my Petticoats at Milan, & the rest of my dress in England.[67]

While Grand Tour portraits typically demonstrated a British appropriation of Rome's classical past through the male sitter's interaction with faux-marble ancients, *objets d'art*, books or classical views, the preferred second portrait (see plate 9) that Hester chose to return home with, like this written self-portrait, showcased her engagement with both contemporary Italian and British fashion.[68] Here the black neck ribbon and stiffened silk gauze collar, with the tippet crossed over the bosom à la Medici, showed Hester's preference for the revivalist Renaissance style popular in the 1780s, while the striped pattern and large bows that cover her dress, and her puffed indoors cap were all the rage in London at the time.[69]

When Hester and Gabriel returned to Streatham Park in 1790, they found that much damage had been done by renters over the preceding seven and a half years. In the course of their restoration, they fitted it out in Italianate splendour that reflected their Grand Tour. 'My poor Piozzi laid out £2,000 on the furniture', Hester later recalled, and 'hung up some very valuable pictures'.[70] These pictures included the head of St Cecilia, the patron saint of music, by the Bolognese Baroque painter Domenico Zampieri; a portrait of the Quietist priest Don Giuseppe Beccarelli by Murillo; another portrait of the sixteenth-century Italian poet Tasso by Titian; and the head of a colossal female by Cipriani.[71] The couple also decorated their house with Italian landscapes, including two drawings of Venice by the etcher Giovanni Vitalba.[72] Hester proudly displayed her 'Prints from Roman Antiquities brought over by myself from *Rome*', including seven prints of the interior of the Vatican by the Rome-based Austrian artist Anton von Maron.[73] These sat alongside six prints after the artist John Collins's stage designs for Tasso's epic poem *Jerusalem Delivered*. Against the backdrop of these paintings and prints stood two antique Etruscan vases, found in the ruins of Cicero's villa in Tusculum; two alabaster vases; a bronze of the *gladiator repellens*, or fighting gladiator; a bronze group of the rape of Dejanira, wife of Hercules, by the centaur Nessus; and a bronze of Zeus and his consort, the Phoenician princess Europa.[74] Such Italianate classical souvenirs required a fitting context, so Hester and Gabriel installed neo-classical fittings, including a 'fine chimney-piece' by the Viennese sculptor and woodworker Giovanni Battista Locatelli.[75] We can see here that Hester's independent wealth following the death of her first husband and marriage to a foreigner meant that she was able to build a far larger collection than that of Lady Anna Miller. For this reason, she did not need, or desire, to frame one of her two Etruscan vases as a unique souvenir from her travels and make it the centrepiece of her home. Rather, she followed the more typical elite male Grand Tour practice of including the vase as part and parcel of a larger collection shared with her husband.

To mark their seventh wedding anniversary and the Italianate transformation of Streatham Park, Hester and Gabriel threw a grand party in 1790. 'We have kept our seventh Wedding Day, and celebrated our Return to this House with prodigius Splendor and Gayety', Hester noted in *Thraliana*:

> Seventy People eat at our Expence, Thirty six of which dined at an immensely long Table in the Library —The Plate so fine too, the

China so showy, all so magnificent, and at the Time of Dinner Horns Clarin &c wch afterwards performed upon the Water in our new Boat that makes such a beautiful, such an elegant Figure. Never was a pleasanter Day seen, nor Weather half as favourable: the Setting Sun, the full moon rising, were wonderfully happy Additions; and at Night the Trees & Front of the House were illuminated with Colour'd Lamps, that called forth our Neighbours from all the adjacent Villages to admire & enjoy such Diversion. Many Friends swear that not less than a Thousand Men Women & Children might have been counted in the House & Grounds, where tho' all were admitted, nothing was stolen, lost, broken, or even damaged—a Circumstance almost incredible; & which gave Mr Piozzi a high Opinion of English Gratitude and respectful Attachment.[76]

Here, among her Grand Tour collection, Hester was able to welcome a new literary coterie to her new home that included loyal friends from former days, Continental guests like the Veronese poet Ippolito Pindemonte, and fresh acquaintances like the poet Samuel Rogers, the controversial dissenter and supporter of the French Revolution Helen Maria Williams, the novelist sisters Harriet and Sophia Lee and the religious poet and playwright Hannah Moore.[77]

Hester's demi-naturalised persona, however, remained incomplete at Streatham Park, which remained, despite the couple's alterations, the home that she had once reluctantly shared with her first husband and later with Samuel Johnson. As early as 1788, Hester had confided a hope to return to Wales: 'Were some great Windfall to drop in', she mused in *Thraliana*, 'I would coax my Husband to buy a House in London, & build a cottage on Dymerchion Hill: the Situation is demidivine, and it would be *his own*'.[78] 'After half a century spent in the empty yet bustling world – here am I like a hare ending at the place I set out from', Hester was finally able to write to Queeny in the Autumn of 1794, from lodgings in Denbigh, Wales, where the couple were staying to supervise the build of a new house on the family's Bachygraig estate, in the hillside in the Vale of Clwyd. One year (and £20,000) later, they were in residence.

Brynbella (part Welsh and part Italian, meaning 'Beautiful Hill'), like its name, was both Welsh and Italian in design. The dominant central core with supporting side wings was reminiscent of a Palladian villa, but double bows rendered it a more localised Georgian appearance (figure 3.4).[79] In the centre sat Gabriel's music

3.4 J. Baker, *Brynbella, the Seat of G. Piozzi Esqr*, 1795, 110 mm × 164 mm, aquatint.

room, where a special recess with carved musical instruments was made for his chamber organ. Inside the double Georgian wings, mahogany doors separated the principal rooms, which contained exquisite marble chimney pieces designed by Clement Mead (the same surveyor who designed the house) and Benjamin Bromfield of Liverpool.[80] The walls were adorned with pictures purchased in Venice during the couple's Grand Tour, including copious Old Masters by the sixteenth-century mannerist painter Jacopo Bassano (known for his depictions of animals and nocturnal scenes) and the Baroque painters Guido Reni and Domenico Zampieri.[81] Hester's favourite artist, the popular painter and printmaker Canaletto, graced many a wall at Brynbella.[82] Hester adored Canaletto's *vedute* of Venice because she loved the city and admired the artist's esteemed accuracy (likely gained through using a *camera lucida* to create an optical overlay of the viewing subject upon the surface of his canvas). In a letter to her friend Samuel Lysons during her Grand Tour in 1785, Hester promised not to 'teize' him 'with Descriptions that every

Venezia illustrate can produce', but still asked him to cast his 'Eyes on Cannaletti's Views when you have a Mind of a little Chat with Mr. and Mrs. Piozzi, as they lodge upon the grand Canal a good Way below the Rialto'.[83] A few months later, she had 'bought … one Canaletti which one *must* love because tis the best Representation of *Piazza St. Marco*, which after all we have seen still holds the first Place in my heart, for Elegance and Architecture', and would acquire a further seven.[84]

It was among these cosmopolitan surrounds that Hester embarked on her most ambitious literary project, *Retrospection* (1801), the first attempt by an Englishwoman to write a history of the world.[85] 'I remember her [Hester] taking me into her bedroom to show me the floor covered with folios, quartos, and octavos, for consultation', Henry Petty-Fitzmaurice, third Marquess of Lansdowne, recollected on 18 August 1860 of his visit to Brynbella in his youth, 'and indicating the labour she had gone through in compiling an enormous volume she was then publishing, called "Retrospection"'.[86] After successfully laying claim to the Tour's legacy of taste, Hester obviously felt confident to write history, which women were expected to read but not to publish. And so it was in her 'beautiful new residence', 'white and lovely, admired by those who see it, and hid from no one', 'built for me in my own lovely country by the husband of my heart's choice' that her dual Italian-Welsh persona was fully realised.[87]

Both Lady Anna Miller and Hester Piozzi managed to exploit the cultural capital of their Tours to achieve a range of possibilities from social positions that were far from secure.[88] When examined side by side, Hester and Anna demonstrate that gender was not the only factor determining the barriers women encountered when they attempted to harness the Grand Tour's cultural capital to fulfil their ambitions: social status, location of residence and personality combined with gender to determine the success of a woman's attempts, as did where they sat in the chronology of women undertaking Grand Tours.

When displayed or worn by Anna, the Grand Tour's objects were taken to be proof of feminine conceit and inconsequence. This was not the case for Hester, who travelled a decade later and was a member of a prominent Anglo-Welsh landowning family. While Hester deferred to her husband as the ultimate provider of any extraordinary purchases that required the outlay of considerable capital, his status as a foreigner gave her the opportunity to intimately combine her Welsh heritage with his Italian background to form a powerful new demi-naturalised persona that supported her marriage choice and literary career. By contrast, Anna's marriage to a husband from a poor Irish family and commercial background as the daughter of a commissioner of customs restricted her to one chief residence, and she returned home with a smaller selection of objects. She attached individualised narratives to these objects as a means of expressing her cultural capital and it was this reinterpretation of a few traditional Grand Tour artworks and antiquities as souvenirs that attracted the criticism of London's literary coterie, keen to undermine the literary ambitions of this upstart woman who had commercialised her travel letters. Travelling ten years prior to Hester Piozzi, however, Anna was somewhat of a pioneer when it came to feminising elements of the Grand Tour to better suit her own agenda. The criticism that followed her is a reflection of the impact of her innovative new take on the Tour.

Rather than building on the performance of Lady Anna Miller and the other women who came before her, Hester made a distinct effort to separate herself from them and the criticism that they had received for seeking to harness the prestige of a male rite of passage. Others have examined how Hester separated herself from the men who came before her in the way she wrote about her travels, but how she performed them in other ways has not yet been examined, nor has her relationship to the women travellers who came before her. Here I have connected Hester's performance of her Tour to that of Lady Anna Miller, but this study points to the fruitful possibilities of tying it to other women's performances of their Grand Tours.

Conclusion

As the Grand Tour opened up to more women and the social elite expanded to include a wider demographic of people in the latter part of the eighteenth century, the classical sculptures, antique gems, Renaissance pictures, contemporary paintings, sculpture, porcelain and furniture that travellers brought home came to play an explicit role in the struggle to control its meanings. The desired quality of 'connoisseurship' was carefully regulated by elite men to prevent women and other wealthy nouveau riche merchants, colliery owners and the 'millocracy' from enlisting the cultural capital of their Grand Tours to become collectors, patrons of the arts and powerful political actors.

This first part of the book has shown that women Grand Tourists dealt with their exclusion from the Tour's legacy of taste by placing different values on the objects they brought home from those of their male counterparts based on their own gendered experiences of Italy. It is clear that women typically placed a greater emphasis on the objects they acquired as vehicles for engaging in social interactions and for remembering them. Women's lack of ready finance and roles as household managers and social facilitators also meant that they tended to shop for small consumables, rather than the 'big ticket' items of their male counterparts, which they sometimes even found or made for themselves.

By taking part in creating their own travel narratives around the objects they brought home and by taking a greater interest in smaller and more mundane objects than their male counterparts, each woman contributed towards forming a new souvenir culture that could be equally the imaginary property of both men and women.

Notes

1 Susanne Schmid, *British Literary Salons of the Late Eighteenth and Early Nineteenth Centuries* (New York: Palgrave Macmillan, 2013), 14–15.
2 Elizabeth Lee, 'Miller [née Riggs], Lady Anna (1741–1781)', revised by Rebecca Mills, *Oxford Dictionary of National Biography*, last updated 23 September 2004, https://doi.org/10.1093/ref:odnb/18720.
3 During the Seven Years' War, Sir John Miller rose from the rank of cornet in the light dragoons in 1760 to that of captain in the 113th foot, resigning the latter commission at the peace of 1763. While Anna took the title, John adopted her maiden surname before his own in 1780 due to the fortune she brought to the marriage.
4 Anna Riggs Miller, *Letters from Italy, Describing the Manners, Customs, Antiquities, Paintings, &C. Of That Country, in the Years MDCCLXX and MDCCLXXI, to a Friend Residing in France* (Dublin: W. Watson, 1776), vol. 1, 17.

5 Rebecca Earle, *Epistolary Selves: Letters and Letter-Writers, 1600–1945* (Aldershot: Ashgate, 1999), 6.
6 Miller, *Letters from Italy*, vol. 1, 218 and 416.
7 Miller, *Letters from Italy*, vol. 1, 218 and 416, Advertisement to the Reader; Miller, *Letters from Italy*, vol. 2, 283–4.
8 Genius Loci, *Bath Anecdotes and Characters* (London: Dodsley, 1782), 148. Lady Miller also appeared in Philip Thicknesse, *The New Prose Bath Guide: For the Year 1778* (London and Bath: Dodsley, Brown and Wood, 1778); *The Original Bath Guide: Considerably Enlarged and Improved; Comprehending Every Species of Information That Can Be Required by the Visitor and Inhabitant* (Bath: J. Savage, and Meyler and Son, 1811).
9 See Laura Olcelli, 'Lady Anna Riggs Miller: the "modest" selfexposure of the female grand tourist', *Studies in Travel Writing* 19, no. 4 (2015); Susan Whyman, 'Letter-writing, reading, and literary culture: the Johnson family and Anna Miller', in *The Pen and the People: English Letter Writers 1660–1800* (Oxford: Oxford University Press, 2009).
10 Horace Walpole, *The Yale Edition of Horace Walpole's Correspondence*, ed. W. S. Lewis (New Haven: Yale University Press, 1941), vol. 10, 233.
11 Horace Walpole, *The Yale Edition of Horace Walpole's Correspondence*, ed. W. S. Lewis (New Haven: Yale University Press, 1974), vol. 39, 240.
12 Fanny Burney, *Diary and Letters of Madame d'Arblay*, ed. Charlotte Barrett, vol. 1 (London: Henry Colburn, 1842), 142.
13 Miller, *Letters from Italy*, vol. 2, 298.
14 William Wilberforce (1813), quoted in Thomas Sedgewick Whalley, *Journals and Correspondence of Thomas Sedgewick Whalley, D.D.*, ed. Hill Wickham, vol. 2 (London: Richard Bentley, 1863), 39.
15 Burney, *Diary and Letters*, 142.
16 Richard Graves, *The Triflers: Consisting of Trifling Essays, Trifling Anecdotes, and a Few Poetical Trifles* (London: H. D. Symonds, 1805), 12.
17 Miller, *Letters from Italy*, vol. 2, 154.
18 Miller, *Letters from Italy*, vol. 2, 157.
19 Anna Riggs Miller, *Poetical Amusements at a Villa near Bath*, vol. 1 (London: Edward and Charles Dilly, 1776), 44.
20 Miller, *Poetical Amusements*, 46, 82, 103, 49.
21 'An impartial review of new publications: XV. A poem to the memory of Lady Miller. By Miss Seward, author of the elegy on Capt. Cook, and the monody on Major Andre', in *London Magazine: Or, Gentleman's Monthly Intelligencer*, vol. 51 (London: R. Baldwin, 1782), 139.
22 Ruth Avaline Hesselgrave, *Lady Miller and the Batheaston Literary Circle* (New Haven: Yale University Press, 1927), 17; Martin Sturge,

'Lady Miller of Batheaston' (Public lecture, University of Bath, Claverton Down, 23 November 2009).
23 Miller, *Poetical Amusements*, 89–93 and 113–14.
24 Anna Seward, *The Poetical Works of Anna Seward: With Extracts from Her Literary Correspondence*, ed. Walter Scott, vol. 2 (Edinburgh: J. Ballantyne, 1810), 15.
25 Graves, *The Triflers*, 12.
26 William Hayley, *Memoirs of the Life and Writings of William Hayley, Esq: The Friend and Biographer of Cowper*, vol. 1 (London: H. Colburn and Co., 1823), 234.
27 Hayley, *Memoirs of the Life and Writings*, 235.
28 Whyman, 'Letter-writing, reading, and literary culture', 197.
29 Claudia Kairoff, *Anna Seward and the End of the Eighteenth Century* (Baltimore: Johns Hopkins University Press, 2011), 40.
30 Walter Scott, *Complete Works: With a Biography, and His Last Additions and Illustrations* (Philadelphia: A. Hart, 1853), 24.
31 Walpole, *Correspondence*, vol. 39, 241.
32 'Madeleine de Scudéry', *Stanford Encyclopedia of Philosophy* [website], Stanford University, updated 22 August 2019, accessed 7 February 2020, https://plato.stanford.edu/entries/madeleine-scudery/.
33 Tobias Smollett, *The Miscellaneous Works of Tobias Smollett, M.D.*, vol. 6 (Edinburgh: David Ramsay, 1790), 37. See also James Walvin, *Beside the Seaside: A Social History of the Popular Seaside Holiday* (London: Penguin, 1978), 16.
34 'Copy of a Doggrel Letter to his friend from Bath', *The Hibernian Magazine, Or, Compendium of Entertaining Knowledge* (January 1781): 327.
35 Ellen Wilson, 'A Shropshire lady in Bath, 1794–1807', *Bath History* 4 (1992): 101.
36 Elizabeth Eger, 'Luxury, industry and charity: Bluestocking culture displayed', in *Luxury in the Eighteenth Century: Debates, Desires and Delectable Goods*, ed. Maxine Berg and Elizabeth Eger (New York: Palgrave Macmillan, 2003), 196.
37 Richard Tickell, *The Wreath of Fashion: Or, The Art of Sentimental Poetry* (London: T. Becket, 1778), 5.
38 Jenny Uglow, 'Vase mania', in *Luxury in the Eighteenth-Century: Debates, Desires and Delectable Goods*, ed. Maxine Berg and Elizabeth Eger (New York: Palgrave Macmillan, 2003); Richard Tames, *Josiah Wedgwood: An Illustrated Life of Josiah Wedgwood 1730–1795* (Aylesbury: Shire Publications, 1984), 26.
39 Uglow, 'Vase mania', 154.
40 Burney, *Diary and Letters*, 183–4.
41 Burney, *Diary and Letters*, 184.

42 'Lady Miller', in *The New Annual Register, Or General Repository of History, Politics, and Literature, for the Year 1785* (London: G. G. and J. Robinson, 1786), 61.
43 Kairoff, *Anna Seward*.
44 'Versus from Miss Seward's Poem to the Memory of Lady Miller' in *London Magazine: Or, Gentleman's Monthly Intelligencer*, 140.
45 Graves, *The Triflers*, 11–13.
46 Graves, *The Triflers*; Hesselgrave, *Lady Miller*, xi.
47 Hesselgrave, *Lady Miller*, 85.
48 Amanda Vickery, *Behind Closed Doors* (New Haven: Yale University Press, 2009), 144.
49 Michael J. Franklin, 'Piozzi [née Salusbury; other married name Thrale], Hester Lynch (1741–1821)', in *Oxford Dictionary of the National Biography*, last updated 23 September 2004, https://doi.org/10.1093/ref:odnb/22309.
50 Hester Lynch Piozzi, *Autobiography, Letters and Literary Remains of Mrs Piozzi (Thrale): With Notes and an Introductory Account of Her Life and Writings*, ed. Abraham Hayward, vol. 2 (Cambridge: Cambridge University Press, 2013), 10.
51 Hester Lynch Piozzi, *Thraliana: The Diary of Mrs Hester Lynch Thrale (later Mrs Piozzi), 1776–1809*, 2nd edn (Oxford: Clarendon Press, 1951), 627n2.
52 Piozzi, *Thraliana*, 627.
53 See Marianna D'Ezio, 'The advantages of "demi-naturalization": mutual perceptions of Britain and Italy in Hester Lynch Piozzi's *Observations and Reflections Made in the Course of a Journey through France, Italy and Germany*', *Journal for Eighteenth-Century Studies* 33, no. 2 (2010). Although the Welsh part of Hester's identity is not discussed in this article.
54 Hester Lynch Piozzi, *Observations and Reflections Made in the Course of a Journey through France, Italy, and Germany* (London: A. Strahan and T. Cadell, 1789), vol. 1, vi–vii.
55 D'Ezio, 'The advantages of "demi-naturalization"', 122; Chloe Chard, *Pleasure and Guilt on the Grand Tour: Travel Writing and Imaginative Geography, 1600–1830* (Manchester: Manchester University Press, 1999), 95–8.
56 Piozzi, *Observations and Reflections*, vol. 1, 175.
57 James L. Clifford and Margaret Anne Doody, *Hester Lynch Piozzi (Mrs. Thrale)*, 2nd edn. (Oxford and New York: Oxford University Press, 1986).
58 Hester Lynch Piozzi, *The Piozzi Letters: Correspondence of Hester Lynch Piozzi (Formerly Mrs. Thrale)*, ed. Edward A. Bloom and Lillian D. Bloom, vol. 1, *1784–1791* (London: Associated University Presses,

1989), 260; JRL, Thrale-Piozzi Papers, GB 133 Eng MS 619, Hester Lynch Piozzi, 'Draft: Observations and reflections collected from the diary of Hester Lynch Piozzi', *c.*1788, 7 vols; GB 133 Eng MS 620–2, Hester Lynch Piozzi, 'Hester Piozzi's final draft: Observations and reflections made in the course of a journey through France, Italy, and Germany', *c.*1788, 3 vols.

59 Piozzi, *The Piozzi Letters*, vol. 1, 264.
60 Piozzi, *The Piozzi Letters*, vol. 1, 262.
61 Piozzi, *Observations and Reflections*, vol. 2, 183.
62 Piozzi, *Observations and Reflections*, vol. 1, 67.
63 Piozzi, *Observations and Reflections*, vol. 1.
64 JRL, Thrale-Piozzi Papers, GB 133 Eng MS 618, Hester Lynch Piozzi, 'Journals: Travels in Italy and Germany', 1784–1787, vol. 1, fol. 17v°.
65 John Ingamells, *National Portrait Gallery Mid-Georgian Portraits 1760–1790* (London: National Portrait Gallery, 2004), 382.
66 Piozzi, *The Piozzi Letters*, vol. 1, 215.
67 Piozzi, *The Piozzi Letters*, vol. 1, 214–15.
68 Andrew Wilton, *The Swagger Portrait: Grand Manner Portraiture in Britain from Van Dyck to Augustus John, 1630–1930* (London: Tate Gallery, 1992), 30.
69 Aileen Ribeiro, *The Gallery of Fashion* (London: National Portrait Gallery, 2000), 144.
70 Hester Lynch Piozzi, *The Piozzi Letters: Correspondence of Hester Lynch Piozzi (Formerly Mrs. Thrale)*, ed. Edward A. Bloom and Lillian D. Bloom, vol. 5, *1811–1816* (London: Associated University Presses, 1999), 90–1.
71 Hester Lynch Piozzi, *Streatham Park, Surrey: A Catalogue of the Excellent and Genuine Household Furniture* (London: Mr. Squibb, 1816).
72 Piozzi, *Streatham Park, Surrey*.
73 Piozzi, *Streatham Park, Surrey*.
74 Piozzi, *Streatham Park, Surrey*.
75 Piozzi, *The Piozzi Letters*, vol. 5, 91–2.
76 Piozzi, *Thraliana*, 775.
77 Franklin, 'Piozzi'.
78 Piozzi, *Thraliana*, 708.
79 Charles Field Glazebrook, 'Brynbella', in *Brynbella, Tremeirchion, St. Asaph, Clwyd, the Contents Including an Important Collection of Modern British Paintings and Other British Paintings, Furniture, Clocks, Silver, Carpets, Ceramics and Glass, Works of Art, Books, Garden Statuary and Household Items* (London: Sotheby's, 1994), 10; Elizabeth Edwards, '"Place makes a great difference": Hester Piozzi's Welsh independence', *Wales Arts Review*, 28 August 2014, accessed

8 March 2020, www.walesartsreview.org/the-gregynog-papers-7-place-makes-a-great-difference-hester-piozzis-welsh-independence/.
80 Glazebrook, 'Brynbella', 10.
81 Glazebrook, 'Brynbella', 10.
82 Glazebrook, 'Brynbella', 10.
83 Piozzi, *The Piozzi Letters*, vol. 1, 139–40.
84 Piozzi, *The Piozzi Letters*, vol. 1, 195.
85 Hester Lynch Piozzi, *Retrospection: Or: A Review of the Most Striking and Important Events, Characters, Situations, and Their Consequences, which the Last Eighteen Hundred Years Have Presented to the View of Mankind* (London: J. Stockdale, 1801).
86 Hayward, Abraham. *A Selection from the Correspondence of Abraham Hayward, Q.C., from 1834 to 1884: With an Account of His Early Life*. Edited by Henry E. Carlisle. 2 vols. Vol. 2, London: John Murray, 1886, 49.
87 Piozzi, *The Piozzi Letters*, vol. 1, 186–7; quoted in Glazebrook, 'Brynbella', 10.
88 For more on Lady Miller and Hester Piozzi's Grand Tour cultural capital, and also that of Lady Elizabeth Holland, see Emma Gleadhill, 'Improving upon birth, marriage and divorce: the cultural capital of three late eighteenth-century female Grand Tourists', *Journal of Tourism History*, published online 28 March 2018, https://doi.org/10.1080/1755182X.2018.1449904.

Part II

Gendering science

4

Every fair Columbus

The eighteenth century was marked by the spread of Enlightenment classificatory schemas. These included the Swedish naturalist Carl Linnaeus's *Systema Naturae* (1735, a taxonomy designed to classify all the plant forms on the planet, known or unknown, according to their reproductive organs) and Denis Diderot and Jean le Rond d'Alembert's *Encyclopédie* (1751–66, seventeen engraved folio volumes intended to gather all the knowledge in the world).[1] Informed by the totalising view of nature that such works encouraged, Mary Louise Pratt has proposed 'the emergence of a new version of what I like to call Europe's "planetary consciousness," a version marked by an orientation toward interior explorations and the construction of global-scale meaning through the descriptive apparatuses of natural history'.[2] According to Pratt, 'the benign, decidedly literate figure of the "herborizer", armed with nothing more than a collector's bag, a notebook, and some specimen bottles', joined 'the seafarer, the conqueror, the captive, the diplomat' in a process of

> collecting plants and insects, measuring, annotating, preserving, making drawings, and trying desperately to get it all home intact. The information was written up into books; the specimens, if dead, were mounted into natural history collections which became serious hobbies for people of means all over the continent; if alive, they were planted in the botanical gardens that likewise began springing up in cities and private estates all over the continent.[3]

This travelling and collecting activity culminated in the opening of the first public national museum and library in the world in 1759. The British Museum at Montagu House contained a legacy of collections assembled by Grand Tourists and New World adventurers alike. Intended to assist the public in discerning a universal order and at the same time discover new resources to benefit mankind, the spatial organisation of the exhibits illustrated an orderly progression in nature. Under this model, the natural history specimens collected by renowned botanist Joseph Banks on Captain Cook's explorations were divided from the antiquities and literature of the arts and organised using Linnaean taxonomic methods.[4]

The 'systematising project', however, was not as systematic as it may seem in hindsight. While museums today are broadly understood as State institutions in which distinct material and forms are catalogued to build public knowledge, in the eighteenth century there was no hard and fast distinction between a museum and a 'curiosity cabinet' – a privately owned structure in which objects valued for their singularity were arranged in relation to one another. The founders of the British Museum may have sought systematisation and universality, but they relied on the practice of collecting for the museum's contents, which was culturally conceived as a private and impassioned pursuit, driven by 'curiosity' – an idea that had both positive and negative connotations linked to knowledge, intellect, desire and licentiousness. In this chapter I will explore the cultural construction of collecting as an activity pervaded by desire and how women travellers engaged in and with that construction. I argue that their collecting practices and reflections on them challenged the detached mastery over the objects and fields of knowledge that scientific institutions claimed by raising questions about the circuits of exchange and private passions involved in the attainment of the objects that made up institutional collections.

With the status of science far from settled in the eighteenth century, its practitioners sought to locate and legitimise it within polite society. This necessitated marketing natural history and natural philosophy to women. Throughout the century, public lectures, periodicals, handbooks and instruments were created to promote a familiarity with astronomy, chemistry, botany and minerology as legitimate and necessary accomplishments for women. Published for over a century from 1704, *The Ladies Diary* was distributed in the form of a compact pocketbook of twenty leaves. Editor John Tipper asked his subscribers to submit answers to his 'Enigmas' and 'Arithmetical Questions' from the privacy of their own homes. These ranged from Newtonian infinitesimal calculus, to the dates and times of the year's eclipses, of which the women were also instructed to make models.[5] Eliza Haywood's *Female Spectator* (1744–46) and George Robinson's *The Lady's Magazine* (1770–1832) soon followed.

As James Secord has shown, by mid-century an interest in science had entered the home itself to become an activity for the entire family.[6] This integration of natural history and natural philosophy into childhood education prompted a corresponding increase in female authors. In *Practical Education* (1798), Maria Edgeworth introduced families to the empiricism of John Locke and the educational pedagogy of Joseph Priestley, the scientist credited with the discovery of oxygen, to promote experiments as a means of learning.[7] In *Domestic Recreation; or, Dialogues Illustrative of Natural and Scientific Subjects* (1805), Priscilla Wakefield gave scientific instruction in the form of conversations between the fictional character Mrs Dimsdale and her daughters.[8] Mrs Dimsdale encouraged Emily and Lucy to pursue a broad range of topics including animal life ('Animalcules', 'Sea Anemonies', 'The Gnat'), human life ('Instinct', 'The Human Eye compared to those of Animals', 'The Progress of Civilisation') and space ('Solar Microscopes', 'Meteors, Light and Colours').[9]

Women-authored polite scientific texts not only encouraged women to explore the natural world but also to collect from it, with notable curiosity cabinets amassed, for example, by Sarah Sophia Banks (sister of Joseph Banks) and Margaret Cavendish Bentinck, Duchess of Portland. Margaret's estate in Buckinghamshire, Bulstrode Hall, was known in court circles as 'The Hive' for the team of botanists, entomologists and ornithologists she employed to study her shells, corals, insects, animals and porcelain.[10] Women who did not have the means to form a cabinet of curiosities on this scale were still encouraged to venture out into the world and collect specimens from it. Eliza Haywood, in her capacity as 'Philo-Naturae' of the *Female Spectator* (1748), urged her readers to venture into the countryside to gather and document natural phenomena:

> As ladies frequently walk out in the Country in little Troops, if every one of them would take with her a Magnifying Glass ... [t]hey would doubtless perceive Animals which are not to be found in the most accurate Volumes of Natural Philosophy; and the Royal Society might be indebted to every fair Columbus for a new World of Beings to employ their Speculations.[11]

Here, Haywood challenged the restriction of female scientific pursuits to the polite realm by arguing that in travelling the countryside and empirically observing it, women could render the scientific institutions from which they were excluded in their debt. Despite Haywood's encouragement, women were excluded from joining the Linnaean Society (founded in 1788) until 1904, and the Royal Society (founded in 1660) until 1945.[12] As late as 1901, a statute for the Society of Antiquaries (founded in 1707) was amended to include the phrase 'Ladies are not admitted' after the classicist Maria Lathbury Evans dared to accompany her husband, John, to Society meetings. An Oxford-educated woman with strong opinions of her own, Maria could not simply be disregarded as an appendage to her husband, yet those present voted forty-four to seven to exclude her nevertheless.[13] Thus, women were invited to accrue knowledge for the purposes of polite conversation but, as botanist Maria Elizabetha Jacson's *Botanical Dialogues* (1797) attests, simultaneously expected to 'avoid obtruding their knowledge upon the public' by lecturing or publishing their findings.[14]

Yet, in the above passage, Haywood suggested that women were capable of superseding even 'the most accurate Volumes of Natural Philosophy' produced by the gentlemen of the Royal Society.[15] While she only playfully elevated women to the comparatively great role of 'fair Columbus', according to her it was their supposed feminine aptitude for perceiving minutiae that made their observations superior to those of men. In making this proposal, Haywood indirectly drew from John Locke's influential view that ideas were formed and developed by association and cumulative, progressive empirical studies. While *Some Thoughts Concerning Education* (1693) was directed towards a young male subject, Locke's remarks made no distinction of sex.[16] In his view, eyewitness expertise was equally within the realms of both men and women. Women travellers with their polite scientific education could, then, ostensibly use their five senses and reasoning to challenge the '(lettered, male, European) eye that held the system' of science.[17]

British women travellers' journals and correspondence show that they frequently took up such calls. On this topic, the diary of Lady Anna Miller is typical of many women. In 1770, at the age of twenty-nine, Anna visited the thermal springs at Aix-en-Provence, France. Built in 1705, these springs contained the same lime and carbonic acid that first drew the Romans to Aix and prompted them to give it the name Aquae Sextiae. Here she 'made every inquiry, our time would permit of, in regard to the medicinal qualities of its waters', tested the waters and wrote down her findings:

> Lepers bath here and, we are told, some have been cured. The second spring brings down with it a kind of stuff or paste in flakes, in colour and consistence not unlike white of egg a little hardened; which flames and burns when applied to a lighted candle. Curiosity led me to taste the water, of which having drunk a glass with several flakes in it; I was almost instantaneously seized with a sickness in the stomach. It is used in consumptions, and all disorders of the breast. I folded up in a paper some of the most condensed flakes, which stuck about the spring, and put them into my pocketbook to dry; but, an hour or two after, there was not the smallest vestige of them to be seen; nothing remained but an exceedingly bad smell. However, they had covered a knife and scissors, which were near them in my pocket-book, with rust.[18]

Anna thus followed her intellectual and experiential desire ('curiosity'), to seek material evidence of the thermal springs' renowned healing properties. It sounds, however, like her experiment was almost a case of 'curiosity killed the cat', with the taste test of the water leading to a stomach ailment. A few months later, in 1771, Anna again attempted to take home and study a specimen from a miracle that she saw performed in the Vatican library:

> Opposite to this pillar is a tomb of white marble, and in it a winding sheet made of a linen which readily catches fire, but does not consume thereby. The linen is secured by iron work, and in order to prove that it stands the fire, our Ciceroni pulled one end of it through the iron, and set fire to it with a lighted Bougie. It burnt fast, and presently extinguished of its own accord. The corner which had endured the flame appeared rather cleaner and whiter than the rest of the sheet, which was all the effect the fire produced. I pulled it as hard as I could, with design to have torn and brought off a rag of it with me, but in vain; and I believe the Ciceroni suspected me, for he thrust it into its place, and so secured it from any further attempts. It is probably formed of the asbestos.[19]

The asbestos shroud Anna studied so intently had been uncovered eleven years earlier, in 1760, in a marble sarcophagus from the time of Constantine (ad 272–337).[20] Both fibrous and crystalline, elastic and brittle, asbestos was seen during the period as a wonderous 'mineralogical vegetable'. Scholars found that the Romans had woven it into cloth with vegetable fibres to wrap corpses, collect ashes and still the sound of falling trees during construction projects.[21] By empirically observing this miracle to consider the science that lay behind it, Anna demonstrated her authority as an enlightened British woman who had travelled to the very seat of the Catholic church. She also, however, displayed the morally questionable behaviour of the collector in her attempt to purloin something from a religious institution for her own private gratification.

While she failed in her attempt to take home a sample of the Vatican's asbestos, Anna would return with a 'collection of fossils' so large that she feared they might 'endanger the bottoms of our trunks'.[22] This collection included 'the famous phosphorous of Bologna': 'I have got some of this phosphorous', Anna proudly declared in 1771, 'which one of the professors of the Instituto was so obliging to present me with, together with some crystallised petrified shells found in this country, remarkably curious'.[23] Discovered in 1602, the Bologna phosphorus was a translucent mineral (most likely barium sulphide). Once calcined it had the property of glowing in the dark after being exposed to sunlight.[24] This specimen, along with her 'crystalised petrified shells', would have captured the interest of Anna's salon guests when she held it up to the light and it glowed like the embers of a fire, or when she showed it to them in the dark and it glowed like a blue flame of burning sulphur.

In collecting such samples from the natural world throughout her travels and returning home with a large case of minerals and fossils, Anna sought to display her intellectual and experiential qualities to those who read her travel account and visited her salon. She did this by attaching herself to 'curiosity', an idea that pervaded the accounts of most eighteenth-century travellers, whether male or female. According to Nicholas Thomas, in his analysis of cultural conceptions of the artefacts from Cook's Pacific voyages, what was specific to the late eighteenth century was 'a field of meaning within which naming (the thing is a curiosity), adjectival characterisation (it is curious) and subject response (one's interest is passionately curious) were intimately connected'.[25] These associations implied 'a relationship between exotic object and knowing subject that was profoundly hermeneutic – a thing could not be considered a curiosity without reference to the knower's intellectual and experiential desire: discourses, inquiries and relations were curious, not just their objects'.[26]

However, while a spirit of enquiry might be thought to be irreproachable, its moral character was imperilled by some wider, hazardous associations with the notion of curiosity. Curiosity had been a morally slippery concept throughout the sixteenth and seventeenth centuries, but its ambiguity acquired a distinct salience in the second half of the eighteenth century in the shadow of debates about luxury, novelty and commercial society. Though the idea of legitimate inquisitiveness is often found in eighteenth-century literature, Thomas notes that 'there are many forceful statements in a variety of genres to the effect that curiosity was feminine, unstable, somehow tarnished, and licenced in the sense of licentiousness rather than that in authorisation'.[27] Burke's *Enquiry* (1757) infantilised curiosity and found the desire for novelties superficial and indiscriminate, possessing always the appearance of 'giddiness, restlessness and anxiety'.[28] Lord Kames noted that 'love of novelty ... prevails in children, in idlers and in men of shallow understanding'.[29] And so it was a fine line that separated curiosity as 'a desire and a passion: a desire to see, learn or possess rare, new, secret or remarkable things', from curiosity as a misguided desire for novelty and commodity.[30] A fine line also separated those curiosities found in the travel environment or gifted from those sold to tourists. Visitors to the English towns of Clifton, Keswick and Matlock, for instance, bought souvenir petrifactions (that is, objects mineralised and turned into stone) and spars (ornaments made from crystalline minerals) to remember their time at the Hotwells and the Lake and Peak Districts. Such curiosities were also sold in the Scottish Highlands, where the young Englishwoman Elizabeth Diggle was astonished by the 'amazingly cheap' prices.[31]

Throughout her account, Lady Anna Miller took care to note that her curiosities had been variously found or gifted, rather than bought, so avoiding her own curiosity as a travelling subject from being perceived as a desire for commodities. She did not, however, as easily traverse some of the other negative attributes of the idea.

Anna's surrender of self-government to drink the water at the hot springs and her surreptitious attempted robbery of the piece of cloth from the Vatican moved her enquiry from that of the scientific into the realm of addiction, a condition considered at the time to be morally problematic and associated with women. In her scientific collecting practices, as in her Grand Tour collecting practices described in Chapter 3, Anna thus never quite struck the right balance between the curious traveller, the scientist and the connoisseur.

Caroline Lybbe Powys took quite a different approach towards curiosity during her various journeys through England from 1756 to 1808. Rather than attempt to demonstrate her engagement with the more laudable aspects of curiosity, Caroline projected the negative feminised attributes of this morally slippery idea from herself onto male natural philosophers and natural historians as a means of questioning their authority over the natural and man-made worlds. Caroline was born in Beenham, Berkshire, in 1736, the daughter of the surgeon John Girle and his wife, Barbara.[32] In 1754, when she was eighteen years old, the family moved to Lincoln's Inn Fields, London. By 1761, at the age of fifty-nine, John retired and bought a house in the Circus in Bath, but sadly passed away just as the family were packing. Instead, Caroline moved to Caversham, Oxfordshire, with her mother. It was here, in 1762, at the age of twenty-six, that she married the twenty-eight-year-old Deputy Lieutenant of Oxon, Philip Lybbe Powys, so becoming mistress of Hardwick House, Whitchurch, which had been in her husband's family since 1526. The couple went on to have two sons and one daughter. At the behest of her father, Caroline started to keep a travel diary when she was twenty. Well off as the sole surviving child of her parents, in addition to marrying into a wealthy family, she had the opportunity to write of extensive travels to Bath, Shropshire, Norfolk, Hampshire, the Isle of Wight, Staffordshire, Kent and London. Caroline stopped writing only at the age of seventy-two, when rheumatism made it difficult. The resultant set of journals (1756–1808) have been dismissed in the *Oxford Dictionary of National Biography* as 'of little interest', except as a 'fascinating record of upper-class life'.[33] However, as we shall see, they are of great interest for considering one woman's self-positioning within scientific culture at the turn of the eighteenth century.

Throughout her various tours, Caroline, like many of her female and male counterparts, attended scientific lectures. In 1791, at the age of fifty-five, she saw a lecture on astronomy in Henley-On-Thames, Oxfordshire.[34] The lecture was presented by the inventor Adam Walker, who established a school in experimental philosophy in Manchester in 1762.[35] Walker was responsible for the introduction of the Eidouranion, a mechanical model of the Solar System that illustrated the relative positions and motions of the planets and moons, which he demonstrated and sold to eager audiences.[36] Three years earlier Caroline had also attended an evening exhibition of 'philosophical fireworks' in London: 'During the intervals, Mr. Cartwright performs on the musical glasses', she marvelled, 'whilst Mr. Dillon lights up an aerostatic branch suspended from the cupola of the saloon, in which light is produced in an instant of time, which Mr. Dillon carries at will, and extinguishes in an instant; wonderfully pretty'.[37] As the theatricality of these events indicate, in this age of amateur natural history and natural philosophy with few gainfully employed as professionals, the lines between science as an entertainment and science as a serious endeavour were far from clear.

Caroline not only attended lectures but also studied the sites that she visited and made her own empirical enquiries into them. In 1759, three years before her marriage to Philip, she visited 'that famous monument of antiquity on Salisbury Plain, call'd Stonehenge'.[38] Caroline made sure to read the antiquarian and physician William Stukeley's *Stonehenge: A Temple Restor'd to the British Druids* (1740) prior to her visit and included the following passage from it in her journal:

> 'Tis more than probable that it was a temple of the British Druids, and the chief cathedral (as it may be call'd), of all their temples in this island. 'Tis thought to be of an extraordinary antiquity, perhaps three thousand years old, executed not long after Cambyses' invasion of Egypt. When the Saxons and Danes came over, they wonder'd at Stonehenge then, and were at as great a loss about the founders and intent as we are now. Camden saw, with excellent judgment, 'twas neither Norman nor English. Inigo Jones endeavour'd to prove it the former; but whoever is acquaint'd with Roman architecture must be of a different opinion. After passing a circular ditch by which 'tis enclos'd, about 30 yards distant is the work itself, being 108 feet in diameter. On entering and casting your eyes around the yawning

ruins, you are struck with an ecstatic reverie. The temple was compos'd of two circles and two ovals, the whole number of stones 140; the great oval consisting of 10 uprights, the inner, with the altar, of 20; the great circle of 30; the inner of 40, and 5 imposts of the great oval; 30 of the great circle; 2 stones standing on the bank of the area, 2 others lying down, and one there seems to have been by the barrow nearest this place. The largest stones beyond controversy were brought from those called grey-wethers on Marlborough Downs, and a piece brought to the Royal Society, and examined with a micro-scope, 'tis found to be a composition of crystals, red, green, and white.[39]

While Caroline deferred to the greater learning of William Stukeley – because, in her words, 'I should be able of myself to give but a very incoherent account of this noble work' – she was encouraged to collect her own samples of red, green and white minerals from the ancient monument:

> Having spent some time in viewing this magnificent wonder, and endeavouring with some tools our servants had, to carry some pieces of it with us, which with great difficulty we at last accomplished, and have since had them polished; but in reading the above, altho' we were rather mortified, as 'tis his [William Stukeley's] sentiments that 'tis an absurd curiosity for people to wish the remains of this temple further ruinated, but, however, we have the comfort to think the very small bit we took could not greatly endanger the work and that, tho' our party were chiefly female, we had not more curiosity than the learn'd gentlemen of the Royal Society, who, it seems, with Dr. Stukeley, had some brought for their inspection thro' a microscope.[40]

Here Caroline (like Lady Anna Miller twelve years later) refers to the quality of 'curiosity'. However, she draws from the shifting and uncertain significance of this term to question the distinction between curiosity as an object/subject of reason, and curiosity as an object/subject of passion, commerce and luxury. By claiming that the 'absurd curiosity' of her party of polite women tourists was 'no more' than that of the Royal Society, Caroline is highlighting that such scientific institutions in fact sprung directly from the same passions and private interests as those of the polite woman travel collector. The group of women who took home their own pieces of Stonehenge were thus not 'absurd', or they were at least 'no more' absurd than the gentlemen of the Royal Society.

Later that year, Caroline again questioned the privileging of men's scientific collections when she went to see the antiquities and specimens of natural history displayed in the museum at Trinity College, Oxford:

> There may–, and no doubt there are many curiosities in this collection; but I must own some I should have thought too minute to be preserved by gentlemen of such a University; but ignorance ought always to be silent, and therefore I'll criticise no more! A present of Lady Pembroke's deserves mentioning, which is a magnet, the finest now in England, attracting a 200 pound weight. Then there is an ivory carved ball, enclosing three of the same sort, one within the other, all cut out of one piece, which I think is extremely curious, as is a band of paper prick'd by a young lady in imitation of lace; and many other things which would give entertainment could one be certain they really were what they now have, I fancy, only the same of; as, for instance, we were present'd with a view of the skull of Oliver Cromwell, when at the same time history informs us his body was never found; but his head indeed, for all I can tell, may have travelled to Oxford solo, and there lies among other curiosities, as the shield of Achilles, &c., &c.[41]

Caroline thus counters the period's trivialising of women's intellectual attainments, by querying why the gentlemen of Oxford would elevate 'minute' and possibly falsely attributed objects as specimens worthy of study. While she demurely follows this critique with a modest allusion to her own intellectual shortcomings as a woman ('but ignorance ought always to be silent, and therefore I'll criticise no more!'), Caroline here queries the processes by which particular and contingent forms of knowledge had been prioritised and abstracted within the museum setting. It is also worth noting that the two objects that she highlights as deserving of mention were both connected to women: one, 'a magnet, the finest in all England', having been given to the university by Elizabeth Herbert, the Countess of Pembroke, and the other, 'a band of paper prick'd by a young lady'. According to Caroline's assessment, then, there was no clear boundary between curiosities as objects/subjects of reason and curiosities as objects/subjects of passion, commerce and luxury – that is, no distinction other than that made by gentlemen of the college, whose reliability she found questionable.

Despite such efforts to critically engage with scientific collecting practices, throughout her many short tours of England, Caroline felt the inferiority of her polite female education on a number of occasions. One of these was in 1760 when, at twenty-four, she wanted to intellectually engage with the fortifications on Drake's Island, near Plymouth, Devon:

> After we had din'd, it then being the cool of the evening, we went to take a view of the citadel or garrison, a small but regular fortification over against the Isle of St. Nicholas. In my description of this place I fear (from not having a knowledge of that science), making a mistake; but that reason, I hope, will plead my excuse; but the terms of fortification are quite out of female knowledge; and what with many other things the men would perhaps say, we should not endeavour to understand; yet I must own 'tis my opinion that women might be made acquainted with various subjects they are now ignorant of, more for want of instruction than capacity, and what at first may appear intricate, after a quarter of an hour's converse might give entertainment. But is it anything surprising the sex should amuse themselves with trifles when these lords of creation will not give themselves the trouble (in my conscience, I believe for fear of being outshone), to enlarge our minds by making them capable to retain those of more importance?[42]

The frustration Caroline expressed at finding herself unable to properly describe the fortification 'from not having a knowledge of that science', and her fear of 'making a mistake' were not unusual for women travellers, who found themselves disadvantaged by their education when they had the opportunity to visit a barrow, church or ancient ruin. An ability to read Latin and an understanding of surveying and mathematics was necessary to conduct the research and fieldwork that such sites demanded. But while a reading knowledge of Latin was not uncommon among educated eighteenth-century women, it was comparatively uncommon, and surveying and mathematics were rarer still.[43] The familiarity with legal documents, charters and chronicles that many men gained in the course of managing an estate were likewise not within the skill sets of most women.[44] In this situation, as was the case with her visit to Stonehenge and the Trinity College museum, however, Caroline was not long perturbed. She moved beyond her regret to bring into question the very boundary that was being drawn between female and male scientific knowledge during the period by asserting that it was men's fear of women's potential for intellectual superiority that led them to exclude her sex from becoming scientific authorities.

Conclusion

This chapter has shown that it was in the world of the minute and microscopic that women saw an opportunity to assert their own unique experiential understandings of the landscapes through which they travelled. As Haywood's 'fair Columbus', they could take samples from the environment home that demonstrated their eyewitness expertise and so take part in the packaging and circulation of scientific knowledge. The shifting and uncertain significance of the idea of 'curiosity' in the late eighteenth century could work both for and against their scientific endeavours. Lady Anna Miller struggled to strike the right balance between curiosity as a laudable desire to seek knowledge and curiosity as a misinformed desire for personal gratification. Caroline Lybbe Powys, however, drew from these contrasting gendered meanings of the term to query the authority that the male scientific institutions from which they were excluded claimed through distinctions and modes of representation. This shows that women participated in scientific study and collection during a period when science as a discipline did not have a settled method and was in a state of flux. Whether they produced contributions that contain a valence relevant to modern research is irrelevant within the context of the agency they expressed in doing so. The next chapter explores more closely the scientific travel collecting practices of Dorothy Richardson. Born into an antiquarian family that encouraged women's education, she was able to participate in scientific study to a greater extent than Anna, Caroline and most other women.

Notes

1 Carl Linnaeus, *Systema Naturæ, Sive Regna Tria Naturæ Systematice Proposita per Classes, Ordines, Genera, & Species*, ed. J. A. Murray (Lugduni Batavorum: Haak, 1735); Denis Diderot and Jean le Rond d'Alembert, *Encyclopédie, ou dictionnaire raisonné des sciences, des*

arts et des métiers (Paris: André le Breton, Michel-Antoine David, Laurent Durand and Antoine-Claude Briasson, 1751–66).
2. Mary Louise Pratt, *Imperial Eyes: Travel Writing and Transculturation* (London: Routledge, 2008), 15.
3. Pratt, *Imperial Eyes*, 25.
4. Patricia Fara, 'The appliance of science: the Georgian British Museum', *History Today*, no. 8 (1997): 39–45.
5. Shelley Costa, 'The "Ladies' Diary": gender, mathematics, and civil society in early-eighteenth-century England', *Osiris, 2nd Series* 17 (2002): 49–73.
6. James A. Secord, 'Newton in the nursery: Tom Telescope and the philosophy of tops and balls, 1761–1838', *History of Science* 23, no. 2 (1985): 133.
7. Maria Edgeworth and Richard Lovell Edgeworth, *Practical Education* (London: J. Johnson, 1798).
8. Priscilla Wakefield, *Domestic Recreation; or, Dialogues Illustrative of Natural and Scientific Subjects* (London: Darton and Harvey, 1805).
9. Wakefield, 'Contents', *Domestic Recreation*.
10. Tiffany Jenkins, *Keeping Their Marbles: How the Treasures of the Past Ended Up in Museums – and Why They Should Stay There* (Oxford: Oxford University Press, 2016), 9.
11. Eliza Haywood, *The Female Spectator*, 5th edn (London: T. Gardiner, 1744–46), 88–9.
12. Andrew Thomas Gage and William Thomas Stearn, *A Bicentenary History of the Linnean Society of London* (London: Linnean Society of London, 1988), 85; Georgina Ferry, 'The exception and the rule: women and the Royal Society 1945–2010', *Notes and Records of the Royal Society* 64, no. 1 (2010): 163–72.
13. Lydia Carr, *Tessa Verney Wheeler: Women and Archaeology Before World War Two* (Oxford: Oxford University Press, 2012), 126.
14. Maria Elizabeth Jackson, *Botanical Dialogues, Between Hortensia and Her Four Children, Charles, Harriet, Juliette and Henry* (London: J. Johnson, 1797), 238.
15. Kristin M. Girten, 'Unsexed souls: natural philosophy as transformation in Eliza Haywood's Female Spectator', *Eighteenth-Century Studies* 43, no. 1 (2009): 67.
16. John Locke, *Some Thoughts Concerning Education* (London: A. & J. Churchill, 1693).
17. Pratt, *Imperial Eyes*, 26, 31.
18. Anna Riggs Miller, *Letters from Italy, Describing the Manners, Customs, Antiquities, Paintings, &c. of that Country, in the Years MDCCLXX and MDCCLXXI, to a Friend Residing in France* (Dublin: W. Watson, 1776), vol. 1, 22.

19 Miller, *Letters from Italy*, vol. 2, 219.
20 Ronald F. Dodson and Samuel P. Hammar, *Asbestos: Risk Assessment, Epidemiology, and Health Effects*, 2nd edn (Hoboken: CRC Press, 2011), 134.
21 Dodson and Hammar, *Asbestos*, 134.
22 Miller, *Letters from Italy*, vol. 1, 359.
23 Miller, *Letters from Italy*, vol. 1, 358.
24 Reuven Chen and Vasilis Pagonis, *Thermally and Optically Stimulated Luminescence: A Simulation Approach* (Hoboken: Wiley, 2011), 1.
25 Nicholas Thomas, 'Licenced curiosity: Cook's Pacific voyages', in *The Cultures of Collecting*, ed. John Elsner and Roger Cardinal (London: Reaktion Books, 1994), 122.
26 Thomas, 'Licenced curiosity', 122.
27 Thomas, 'Licenced curiosity', 123.
28 Quoted in Thomas, 'Licenced curiosity', 123.
29 Quoted in Thomas, 'Licenced curiosity', 123.
30 Kryzstof Pomian, *Collectors and Curiosities: Paris and Venice 1500–1800* (Cambridge: Polity Press, 1990), 58–9.
31 Quoted in Zoë Kinsley, *Women Writing the Home Tour, 1682–1812* (Aldershot: Ashgate, 2008), 142.
32 Stephen Powys Marks, 'Caroline Powys and her journals', *Powys Journal* 21 (2011).
33 Anne Pimlott Baker, 'Powys [née Girle], Caroline (1738–1817)', *Oxford Dictionary of National Biography*, last updated 23 September 2004, https://doi.org/10.1093/ref:odnb/68336. For the journals, see BL, Powys Diaries, Add. MS 42163, Caroline Lybbe Powys (née Girle), 'Norfolk Journal', 1756; Add. MS 42166, 'Shropshire Journal', 1770; Add. MS 42168, 'Journal of a Five days Tour in a Letter to a Friend', 1776; Add. MS 42169, 'Second Norfolk Tour', 1781; Add. MS 42170, 'Journal of a Tour a Tour to the Isle of Wight', 1792.
34 Caroline Lybbe Powys, *Passages from the Diaries of Mrs. Philip Lybbe Powys of Hardwick House, Oxon, 1756–1808*, ed. Emily J. Climenson (London: Longmans, Green, & Co., 1899), 253.
35 Adam Walker, *Analysis of a Course of Lectures on Natural and Experimental Philosophy: Viz. Astronomy, Use of the Globes, Pneumatics, Electricity, Magnetism, Chemistry, Mechanics, Hydrostatics, Hydraulics, Engineering, Fortification, Optics, &c.* (London: Adam Walker, 1790).
36 Ian Inkster, 'Advocates and audience: aspects of popular astronomy in England, 1750–1850', *Journal of the British Astronomical Association* 92, no. 3 (1982): 120.
37 Powys, *Passages from the Diaries*, 231–2.
38 BL, Powys Diaries, Add. MS 42164, Caroline Lybbe Powys (née Girle), 'Journal of a Tour to Oxford, Blenheim, &c.', 1759, fol. 20v°.

39 BL, Powys Diaries, Add. MS 42164, fols 20v°–21r°.
40 BL, Powys Diaries, Add. MS 42164, fols 22r°–20v°.
41 BL, Powys Diaries, Add. MS 42164, fol. 7r°.
42 BL, Powys Diaries, Add. MS 42165, Caroline Lybbe Powys (née Girle), 'Journal of a Tour to Plymouth Mount Edgcomb &c', 1760, fols 28r°–29r°.
43 Rosemary Sweet, *Antiquaries: The Discovery of the Past in Eighteenth-Century Britain* (London and New York: Hambledon and London, 2004), 71.
44 Sweet, *Antiquaries*, 71.

5

Dorothy Richardson's extensive knowledge

A single woman from a family with a tradition of scientific interests, Dorothy Richardson (1748–1819) used a combination of a picturesque aesthetic, empirical observation, antiquarian and natural history research to create her own unique scientific travel collection that had elements of the curiosity, the specimen and the souvenir. Dorothy was born in 1748 in Bierley Hall, Bradford – the renowned home of her grandfather, the physician and botanist Richard Richardson.[1] The garden at Bierley Hall was rich with the plants Richard Richardson had collected on his many travels through Britain and exchanged with botanists, including Samuel Brewer, Thomas Knowlton, Hans Sloane, Johann Friedrich Gronovius and James Petiver. Dorothy was the third child of Richard's third surviving son, Henry, the rector of Thornton, Craven, and his wife, Mary. She grew up with ready access to the Bierley Library (also established by her grandfather, and one of the best in England) and surrounded by a highly educated family; her father's eldest brother, Richard, was an avid collector of paintings and engravings, while Dorothy's other uncles, William and John, were members of the Society of Antiquaries. It is clear that the Richardson family encouraged female education, because the Bierley Library was left to Dorothy's niece, Frances Mary Richardson-Currer of Eshton Hall, along with the Currer family library. Since described as 'England's earliest female bibliophile', Frances would add to these libraries until they together amounted to some fifteen-to-twenty thousand volumes.[2]

This chapter analyses Dorothy's private study of the physical and natural world through observation, experiment and collection – that is, *her* science. I argue that Dorothy adopted and adapted forms of scientific knowledge and methods from which women were usually excluded to inform her personal reflections on the travel environment, so forming a collection of observations and objects that lay somewhere between curiosity, specimen and souvenir. In 1782 the founder of the Royal Society of Arts, William Shipley, urged the young gentlemen of England to visit 'important manufactures and trades, well-conducted systems of poor relief ... Abbeys, Roman Roads, Camps and Barrows', and at these sites to 'take perspective views of any Machines, Buildings, or Pieces of Antiquities'.[3] Over a period of forty years, from the ages of twelve to fifty-three, Dorothy adopted a similar programme to survey Yorkshire, Lancashire, Derbyshire, Nottinghamshire, Oxford, Bath and London, but hers was a private pursuit unattached to any institution.[4]

Dorothy was a painstaking observer and took delight in recording what she called 'minutes' of both natural and urban landscapes *in situ*, describing interior and exterior spaces. Following her travels, she would write these up in neat handwriting, supported with her wider reading of a range of aesthetic, antiquarian, history and natural history texts, which included William Camden's *Britannia* (1586); William Blackstone's *The Commentaries on the Laws of England* (1765–70); Thomas West's *A Guide to the Lakes* (1776); William Gilpin's various picturesque tours; and the Society of Antiquaries' *Archaeologia* (1770–1992). The resultant series of five highly structured manuscript journals were divided into Dorothy's various tours, with subheadings detailing the towns and sites visited. The same process was followed for each site, which she first observed as a whole, then separated into parts and then divided further into catalogues of contents.[5] Dorothy followed this practice from a young age and it became increasingly elaborate over the years. When she wrote of a day trip to Nostal Priory, near Crofton in West Yorkshire, at the age of thirteen in 1761, Dorothy observed that the Palladian house was 'built of Stone' with 'two Grand Fronts ... thirteen Windows in breadth, & three stories high'.[6] Following her entrance, she carefully described the 'Base Hall', before detailing the contents of each room:

> 1st A large Room hung with Crimson Flock Paper, with a handsome Marble Chimney Piece & Slab, the Furniture Crimson Silk Damask. Pictures the Beauties at Hampton Court; two Gentlemen; & over the Chimney Piece the two Mr Winns playing when they were Children.—

2nd The Dining Room; Stucco; a Large Marble Slab, & a most Elegant White Marble Chimney Piece supported by two White Marble statues of men. Pictures. 1st Over the Chimney Piece a View of Venice, 2nd Mr Rowland Winn a full length & 3rd Coll. Winn.—

3rd The Drawing Room; hung with Green Silk Damask.[7]

And the list continued as she walked through a further fifteen rooms. Here Dorothy shows the same organisational concern as the cartographer, the lexicographer or the encyclopaedist to convey the specificity of a place. Her order, however, was in relation to her own body and how she moved through the space (from a large room first, on to the dining room, to the drawing room and so on), and in relation to where her own vision happened to fall (first a view of Venice, then Mr Rowland Winn second). She supplemented such descriptions of the built and natural environment with detailed pen and ink drawings.

While this level of thoroughness and attention to detail is unusual, it was not uncommon for travellers (male and female) to try to organise their travel experiences through their journals. Most of the women that appear in this book expressed concerns about how to accurately recall the vast array of objects that constituted their travel experiences. For example, after exploring Oxford in 1791, Mary Morgan wrote of a mind 'much weighted down' by the 'infinite number of things that are passing before it', and went on to declare it 'filled with churches, colleges, libraries, statues, and pictures'.[8] As Zoë Kinsley has observed, while light-hearted, Mary's outline of such a range of objects suggested an 'accumulation' of travel experiences that had reached 'a point of excess' and were, therefore, difficult to recall.[9] Similarly, during her stay in Düsseldorf in 1783, Mary Berry despaired that the quantity of objects displayed in the electoral palace 'fatigues the mind more than it can be properly said either to entertain or improve it'.[10] Both women thus warned of the mental disarray the large jumble of objects which constituted their travel experiences could cause and hinted at the need for a means by which to properly process and recall them.

An empirical and aesthetic approach to writing as a sort of 'collecting' practice allowed male and female travellers to mentally organise the array of sights they encountered on their journeys. Instruction books outlined how to properly maintain a journal and to set order to one's recollections. Count Leopold Berchtold's *Essay to Direct and Extend the Enquiries of Patriotic Travellers* (1789) recommended a meticulous practice by which 'daily remarks ought to be copied from the pocket-book into the journal before the traveller goes to rest', and suggested a 'double journal' to prevent 'accidents'.[11] While this text was directed at a general audience, in 1778 Samuel Johnson advised that a woman specifically should:

> review her journal often, and set down what she finds herself to have omitted, that she may trust to memory as little as possible, for memory is soon confused by a quick succession of things; and she will grow every day less confident of the truth of her own narratives, unless she can recur to some written memorials.[12]

To prove the authenticity of her travel account, Lady Anna Miller claimed that she always took her 'notes upon the spot' and was, therefore, 'frequently obliged to write in my pocket-book standing, and at times supporting it on the pedestal of a statue, or the moulding of a surbase'.[13] Caroline Powys also recognised the importance of writing down her travel experiences when they occurred so that she could refer to them on future trips to the same site: 'As there's nothing so effectively empresses [sic] occurrences on the memory as the Pen and as in every Tour of pleasure one generally meets with many objects deserving observation', Caroline noted in her journal of her tour of Oxford and Blenheim in 1759,

> one ought I think (as an admired author says tis of infinite advantage to the style) to commit to writing each particular that gave pleasure at the time of seeing it, one having thereby an opportunity of a second view if I may so term it: and this only on paper the repeated sight is often not unpleasing.[14]

While Dorothy's practice of taking minutes *in situ* was quite typical of the travel writer, male or female, what is unusual is the level of research and writing-up she did upon her return home. Each of her five final volumes are paginated and (other than the fifth, which was left unfinished) are carefully indexed and cross-referenced with well-researched appendices referring the reader to other works of interest.[15] Dorothy's journals are thus a combination of personal narrative and rigorous scientific study. This quality is seen, for example, if we turn to the 1779 'Yorkshire' volume, which Dorothy wrote when she was thirty-one. This volume contains a carefully measured pen and ink diagram of the Halifax Gibbet – a sixteenth-century guillotine in West Yorkshire (figure 5.1). Dorothy's drawing supports her exhaustive written description of the machine and of the criminal laws of the Manor of Wakefield, where the lord of the manor had the authority to summarily execute petty criminals by decapitation, a practice that continued in Halifax until the mid-seventeenth century. Here she wrote in a careful and minute hand:

> in a place call'd Gibbet Lane where is yet seen a square platform of earth wall'd about & ascended by a flight of stone steps, on this were placed two upright pieces of timber, 5 yards in height joined at the top by a transverse beam; within these there was a square block of wood of the length of 4 feet and a ½, which rose up & down, between the uprights, by means of grooves: to the lower end of this sliding block an iron ax was fasten'd, which is yet in Halifax, it weighs 7 pound 12 ounces; is full 10 inches & a ½ long, 7 inches over at the top & very near at the bottom, its middle is about 7 inches & ½; & toward the top are two holes made to fasten it to the block; the ax was drawn up to the top by a cord & pully, & at the end of the cord was a pin, which being fix'd to the side of the Scaffold, or some other part below; kept it suspended, till either by pulling out the pin or cutting the cord, it was suffer'd to fall, & the criminals head was instantly separated from his body.[16]

It is evident that Dorothy measured every inch and ounce of the guillotine. She did this with historic sites throughout her travels, such as the prehistoric hillfort Danesfield Camp in Medmenham, Buckinghamshire, sometimes enlisting male relatives to step them out.[17] After this passage, Dorothy showed her growing self-assurance as a scholar by integrating and criticising multiple sources, including William Camden's *Britannia* (1586) and William Blackstone's *The Commentaries on the Laws of England* (1765–70), surmising that Camden's explanation 'seems the most probable'.[18] In the same volume, in her analysis of Bolton Abbey in Wharfedale, North Yorkshire, Dorothy expressed her frustration at being unable to reconcile the different accounts she found in Sir William Dugdale's *Monasticon Anglicanum* (1693) and Francis Grose's *The Antiquities of England and Wales* (1783–85); she would, she wrote, 'leave it to better antiquarians to resolve the differences'.[19] While this comment shows that Dorothy only had a modest opinion of her own abilities, her reference to 'better antiquarians' suggests that

thief escaped. Pamden says if the execution was
not done by a Bead, the bailiff or his servant cut the rope
this seems the most probable. Bentley mentions that
the bailiff, jurors, & the minister chosen by the Prisoner
were always on the scaffold with him, & Wright adds that
the 4th Psalm was play'd so and the Scaffold on the bag-
pipes, after which the Minister pray'd with him till
he underwent the fatal stroke —
The Gibbet Law at Halifax no doubt gave rise to
what is called the Beggars prayer —
From Hell Hull & Halifax, good Lord deliver us —
Watson thinks the custom did not belong to the Forest
of Hardwick as a Forest, for Halifax is not in it. but
that it was instituted to protect trade then in its
infancy, nor was it peculiar to Halifax: Cheshire
had the same privilege, & the Scottish Maiden at Eden-
-burgh is believ'd to have been copied from the Gibbet
at Halifax —

49 Persons
suffer'd between
the years 1541
& 1650 —

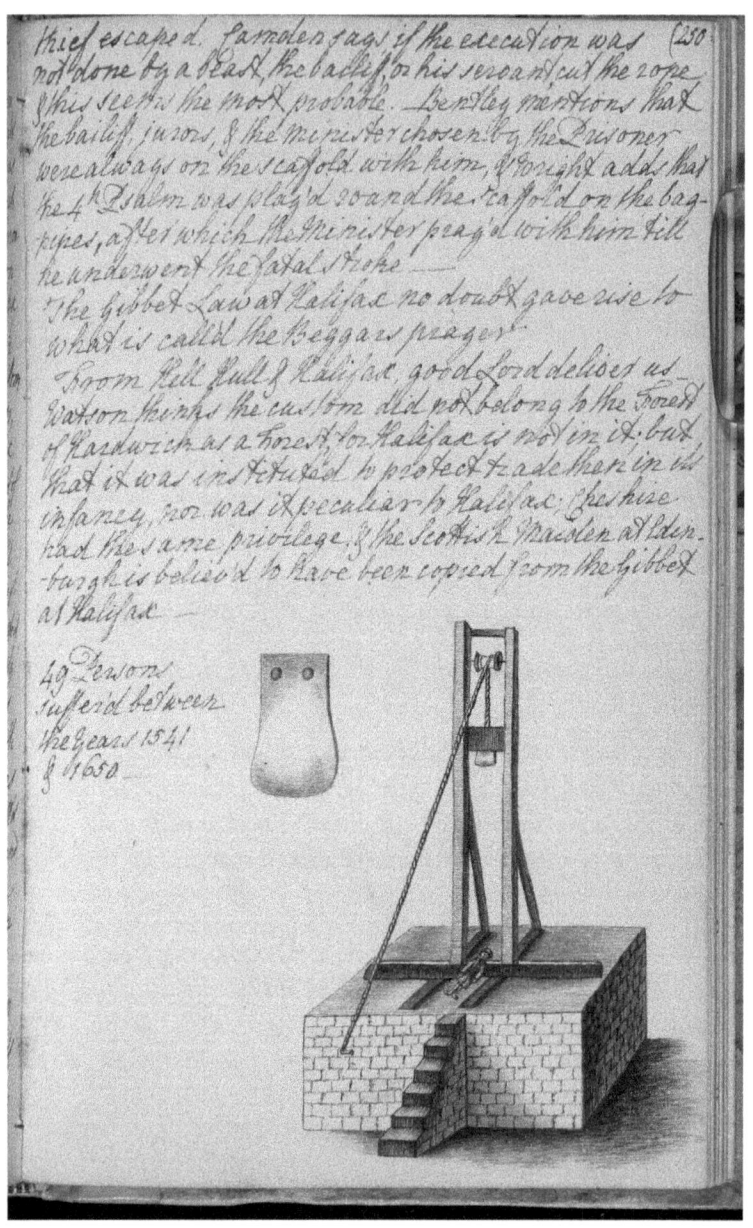

5.1 'Halifax Gibbet', in Dorothy Richardson, 'Travel Journal Yorkshire (North Riding) and Lancashire', 1779.

she (unlike Caroline) identified herself as a member of that largely male community.[20]

Yet, despite conceiving herself as a member of the scientific community, Dorothy understood the difference between a polite pursuit of science that was acceptable for a woman like herself, and the educated process of viewing and recording that was preserved for men, and moved from the first to the second with caution.[21] This is revealed by an incident in 1785 when she (at that time aged thirty-seven) visited a famous medical museum in London:

> In the morning we went to see Dr Hunter's Museum in Windmill Street. Dr Combe the Keeper, to whom we were introduced at Mr Bartlets, paid us the compliment to meet us there upon a private day; it being publically shown, I think, twice a week. The room is very large and was built by Dr Hunter. The top and sides are fine stone, and the floor is plasted. There is a gallery round three sides; I think, the forth, which has the fireplace in the centre, has not one, tho I am not quite certain. The iron rails of the galleries are hung full of various antiquities and natural curiosities as the horns of the mouse deer &c. but I am unable to give much account of this museum as we were joined by some of Dr Combe's learned friends, and I had not the courage to take out my pocket book to make minutes. In cases in the galleries adjoining the walls, but almost all of them closed, except a very few that were not disagreeable, are I am told the finest collection of anatomical preparations in the kingdom, perhaps in the world, but I was happy they were out of sight, indeed I made this enquiry of Dr Combe before I ventured.[22]

Instead of recording her observations in front of the learned gentlemen, Dorothy felt obliged to put her notebook away within the institutional space of the museum. She also restricted herself to viewing 'a very large collection of butterflies, moths, beetles', 'an extremely beautiful and valuable collection of shells' and an Egyptian mummy rather than the anatomical specimens.[23] As Marcia Pointon has argued, this shows that the public accumulation of knowledge through note-taking was considered unacceptable for a woman and that women could traverse some areas of science more freely than others.[24]

It is seldom that the first-person pronoun 'I' appears in Dorothy's rigorously empirical documentation of England's natural and urban history. When it does appear, however, she uses it to claim ownership of an object from the travel environment, revealing the personal preoccupation of the collector. Near Matlock, Derbyshire, in 1767, for example, nineteen-year-old Dorothy obtained a piece of ore from a lead mine:

> A little below the house we crossed the river in a boat, to a lead mine; having each taken a candle, we walked into the side of the hill with an arched rock over our heads, and over planks, under which ran a great quantity of water drawn out of the mine by the pumps, which are worked by prodigious large wheels, that go by water, and are a very curious piece of mechanism. The sides and top of the mine, made a most glistening appearance by candle light, being lead ore, spar and congealed water; I took a pick ax and helped myself to some ore.[25]

It is likely that Dorothy visited what is now known as Speedwell Cavern in Castleton. Operations to mine the lead at Speedwell began in proper four years after Dorothy's visit, in 1771, and continued for a further twenty years. Interest in this pioneering operation led to a steady stream of visitors who were given a tour of the cavern by boat while the mining continued around them. Tourism may have flourished, but the actual mining enterprise was a failure, with only £3,000 worth of lead taken from a mine which had cost £14,000 to establish and develop.[26] In this instance, Dorothy's was the private impassioned pursuit of the collector; she took pleasure in the exploratory act of entering a mine by candlelight and using an axe to break the stone and take some ore for herself.

Like many women tourists, Dorothy also collected specimens from the seaside towns that she visited throughout her travels. However, unlike many of her female counterparts, in these finds she prioritised science and economics over aesthetics. 'The rocks abound with the algae marian tho' little kelp is made here', Dorothy observed in 1775, during her stay in Heysham, Lancashire. 'I picked up a few shells, tho' none of any beauty, and gathered variety of sea weeds, which after having steeped in fresh water changing it often, I dried between pieces of flannels, opening every branch with the point of a needle'.[27] After noting her disinterest in the beauty of the oarweed, Dorothy dedicated several pages of her journal to exploring the scientific aspects and economic uses of this marine plant:

> The Alga Marina Fucus, or Oreweed, grows plentifully upon the rocks, which when the tide is out are uncovered. This useful plant is

Dorothy Richardson's extensive knowledge 131

food for cattle and when burnt till it turns into lumpish metal, or rather salt glass, is one principal ingredient in making glass, allum and soap, and is called kelp. It is made in June and July if the weather be dry. There are seven sorts of the Algae Marina, the glass bottle ore, which has hollow knobs or pustules in, is reckoned to make the best kelp. They lag it on the beach to dry, spread thin, turn it often, and when dry, if the weather is likely to be wet, cock it as hay, but in much less heaps. A circular shelving pit is made in the sand 7 feet diameter and 3 feet deep, and the sides lined with stones that, whilst they stir the oreweed, neither sand nor earth may mix with the kelp. Then putting a small bush o lighted fuzz into the bottom of the pit, some of the driest oreweed is laid lightly on the fire which being weak at first is nursed with great care, and fed with fresh oreweed, the smoke spreading itself like a thick mist with a most disagreeable scent. When the fire is strong the whole has the appearance of bright burnt embers; they then mix and stir it with iron rakes, till it begins to run, and when all the mass is melted, they let it settle and it consolidates into lumps in the bottom of the pit. When it is cold it is ready for sale and brings at an average price £1'2'6 a ton.[28]

It is evident from Dorothy's detailed description of the properties of Alga Marina Fucus and the processes used to turn it into kelp for the production of glass, alum and soap, she researched her specimens following her return home. She also took care to cite her source: William Borlase's *The Natural History of Cornwall* (1758). Dorothy thoughtfully combined Borlase's history with her own experiential understanding of the materiality of the oarweed, even to the point of describing the 'disagreeable scent' of the thick mist it produced when burnt. A Fellow of the Royal Society, Borlase also collected specimens and presented a large collection of mineral and metallic fossils from the rich copper works at Ludgvan to the Ashmolean Museum. In her actions here, Dorothy too displayed the detached mastery of a professional scientist employed to collect specimens for a museum or to study the economic feasibility of a particular industry, even to the point of giving the measurements of the pit in which the oarweed was burnt and its exact price on the market. However, no patrons or societies guided her pursuits.

We can directly contrast Dorothy's interests in collecting shells and seaweed with those of forty-two-year-old Mary Morgan on her journey to Milford Haven, Wales, where she travelled from Ely,

England, with her husband in 1791. 'There is nothing perhaps more curious than the shells and marine plants with which these shores are adorned', Mary noted in her journal:

> To a botanist and a collector of shells they would be an inexhaustible source of amusement and research. I regret that I know little of those pleasing sciences; yet I can trace the hand of the Deity in a pebble or a grain of sand; in the sea-weed, that strikes its tender fibres into the hard rock, or buoys itself up on the water by little bladders filled with air, as well as if I was perfectly acquainted with the class to which they belong.[29]

Here Mary placed emphasis on her own 'knowing' based on the attention she paid to the small details of the natural world: the pebble, grain of sand and the seaweed moving gently through the water. Hers was a more aesthetic form of observation and collection than the scientifically rigorous approach taken by Dorothy. Similarly, in her 1779 *Companion, and Useful Guide to the Beauties of Scotland*, Sarah Murray's interest lay in the picturesque and the sublime: 'My mind found wonders to contemplate; for those bare mountains, most of them being full of metals, when the sun-beams gild their huge sides, sparkle like gems; and from the walls on the road side, when I walked up the steep places, I picked numberless pieces of stones, filled (to an ignorant eye) with gold, silver, and all sorts of metallic substances', she wrote. 'The stones were so pretty I could not throw them away, though I knew they were neither uncommon, nor, to a mineralogist, worth a straw'.[30] This demonstrates that women approached the collection of samples from the natural environment in quite different ways depending on their upbringing, education and interests. Audience was also an important consideration, with Dorothy Richardson's account remaining in manuscript form while Mary Morgan's and Sarah Murray's were published as picturesque tours. It was more acceptable and easier for a woman to publish a picturesque tour than a scientific study, which required the support of male peers and exclusively male institutions. While Mary's aesthetic and poetic approach was more typical, the cases of Anna Miller and Caroline Powys (discussed in Chapter 4) show that many women also had an interest in studying the environment in a more scientifically rigorous manner, while Dorothy shows us that women could take this interest further under the right conditions.

Dorothy also empirically observed the working-class people she visited during her travels and took specimens from them. In this pursuit we see a combination of the personal preoccupation and passionate curiosity she showed in collecting the iron ore and the detached professionalism she showed in collecting the seaweed. In 1801, at the age of fifty-three, following a tour of St Roberts Chapel in Knaresborough, North Yorkshire, Dorothy visited the home of her tour guide. Here she found herself fascinated by the hair of one of the woman's sons, enquiring as to how its colour had changed with age and how it was cleaned and brushed:

> Our female guide conducted us to her cottage, which stands under the Rocks, where she has one room below and one above stairs, which holds herself, her Husband, and ten children. Garden ground surrounds their neat little cottage and many fruit trees are trained against the rocks, which even this scarce year bear plentifully, particularly the apricots, but the very greatest at this place is one of the woman's sons, a fine fair fresh boy about thirteen tho rather little of his age, with a very thick head of hair exactly resembling wool and of which the print gives a faithful idea. I got some of his hair which is now a light brown and has exactly the appearance of wool, but when he was younger his mother told me it was nearly white. His name is William Smith ... His hair is kept very clean, but as it curls amazingly his mother is necessitated once a week to wash it in soap and water and brush it dry. I asked her if any of hers or her husband's family had hair like it, she said no, but that her husband had dark curling hair, but not particularly thick.[31]

As Kinsey has noted, the social and economic position of this large working-class family allowed Dorothy to objectify them as 'curiosities', and by extension the boy's hair became one of her specimens to be included with her iron ore and seaweed.[32] In this instance, we can see that she inhabited the culturally displaced and morally ambiguous position of the colonial traveller.

Dorothy was not alone in taking up this position. Just as the male explorers on Cook's voyages collected evidence of Indigenous peoples practices, women tourists recorded their experiences of meeting people from different regionalities and classes, in Britain and Italy, and exchanging curiosities with them.[33] In 1803 (two years after Dorothy's encounter with the working-class boy), thirty-two-year-old Dorothy Wordsworth made some observations of the

Scottish Highlanders that centred on the exchange of curiosities. While staying in the mud home of her host, Mrs Macfarlane, Wordsworth reported meeting the woman's children, who she declared 'could not speak a word of English':

> they were very shy at first; but after I had caressed the eldest, and given her a red leather purse, with which she was delighted, she took hold of my hand and hung about me, changing her side-long looks for pretty smiles.[34]

This material interaction mirrors those of an explorer of the New World, who sought to induce progress through the introduction of manufactured articles to the people he encountered on his travels and to collect curiosities that informed larger investigations of human nature and civilisation. Indeed, later in her journal, Dorothy Wordsworth described obtaining her own specimen from her host:

> When we returned to the house she said she would show me what curious feathers they had in their country, and brought out a bunch carefully wrapped in paper. On my asking her what bird they came from, 'Oh!' she replied, 'it is a great beast.' We conjectured it was an eagle, and from her description of its ways, and the manner of destroying it, we knew it was so. She begged me to accept of some of the feathers, telling me that some ladies wore them in their heads. I was much pleased with the gift, which I shall preserve in memory of her kindness and simplicity of manners, and the Highland solitude where she lived.[35]

Here Wordsworth drew from voyage publications (which were extremely popular for their engravings of headdresses and other artefacts) to shape an image of Mrs Macfarlane as a quaint regional character who knew little of the world in comparison to Wordsworth herself, who was well read, although she had never travelled outside of Britain. Indeed, it is evident that Wordsworth had read of Captain James Cook's voyages, because she also drew a comparison between a Scottish Fog House and the semi-permanent domed wood and bark dwellings of the indigenous peoples of South America:

> We came to a pleasure-house, of which the little girl had the key; she said it was called the Foghouse, because it was lined with 'fog,' namely moss. On the outside it resembled some of the huts in the prints belonging to Captain Cook's Voyages.[36]

Dorothy Richardson's extensive knowledge   135

As Kinsey has explored, twelve years earlier, in 1791, Mary Morgan drew a similar comparison when she visited a miner's hut in Hook, Wales.[37] These huts were constructed of mud, road scrapings and stones, and thatched with straw. Once abandoned, they returned to the ground from whence they came:

> Though I had not the courage to descend a coal-pit, I ventured to crawl into a miner's hut; for you cannot enter any other way than on your hands and knees ... they eat in these huts, yet I saw no culinary utensils nor household furniture, nor even a bench of turf round the hovel to sit down upon. The miners sit on their hams, as the Indians do. In Byron's voyage there is a print of what he calls the whigwham or Indian hut, which will give you the perfect idea of these habitations; and the people, except that they are clothed, bear a strong resemblance to the natives of Terra del Fuego.[38]

The engraving Mary referred to here was from an account of Captain James Cook's *Endeavour* voyage of 1768–71 that appeared in the second volume of John Hawkesworth's *An Account of the Voyages Undertaken by the Order of His Present Majesty for Making Discoveries in the Southern Hemisphere* (1773).[39] Titled 'A View of the Indians of Tierra del Fuego in their Hut', the piece was the work of the engraver Francesco Bartolozzi, after the painter Giovanni Battista Cipriani (figure 5.2). Worked up for publication from a drawing taken at Tierra del Fuego by Joseph Banks's landscape and figure artist, Alexander Buchan, it depicted a group of semi-naked Fuegians seated in a hut made from stretched and dried skins.[40] Mary had likely read in *Voyages* that the Fuegians 'suffered nothing from the want of innumerable articles which we consider, not as the luxuries and conveniences only, but the necessities of life'.[41] According to her understanding, then, the miner's hut in Wales resembled the housing of the Yaghan people because it lacked the material culture of civilisation. Without utensils or furniture, the Welsh miners were curiosities to be gazed and wondered at, as were the Fuegians.

These examples of the exchange and collection of curiosities associated with the working classes of England, Wales and Scotland reveals that Dorothy and other women exploring Britain's interior were involved in the construction of the larger imperial discourse through their privileged access to people at its peripheries. There has been much debate around whether the writings of settler women

5.2 Francesco Bartolozzi (after Giovanni Battista Cipriani), *A View of the Indians of Terra del Fuego in Their Hut*, 1773, 208 mm × 280 mm, engraving.

show empathy with Indigenous women, or collusion in the imperial process.[42] Some have argued that settler women sympathised with Indigenous women under their common status as the colonised subjects of a patriarchal society.[43] According to Australian feminist scholar Dale Spender, 'they could see them as sisters in subordination – and in labour – and they portrayed them with sympathy and empathy'.[44] More recent scholarship has attempted a more nuanced exploration of the complex nature of colonial interaction. Writing of Australian settler women, Patricia Grimshaw and Julie Evans ask 'under what conditions was it possible for them to act? And, when they did so, where did they situate themselves within the male colonial enterprise?' In answering these questions, they argue that: 'While undeniably aligned to the colonists' value systems, the women challenged accepted wisdom to affirm aspects of Aboriginal lives and cultures', so offering 'fragmentary alternate readings that contested aspects of the dominant discourses and presented Aboriginal Women's lives in less negative ways'.[45]

From these few examples of women travelling to Britain's peripheries, we can see that because women's self-identities were so closely bound to sociability, household management and domesticity, they typically focused on these areas. It is this focus that has led to a perception of women as more empathetic and sympathetic than their male counterparts, but taking their collecting practices seriously shows that they too contributed to the development of imperialism. As historian Sara Mills has pointed out regarding colonial women in India in the nineteenth century:

> when women's activities are considered, it is clear that a wide range of activities that have been glossed by dominant discourses as fairly trivial serve as the supports for the imperial enterprise ... even relatively minor activities such as the British fashion and food industries and the move toward using Indian products were part of the maintenance of imperial rule.[46]

And, indeed, if we turn to earlier histories of the collection, display and exchange of objects between eighteenth-century tourists and the working-class people they met, we can see the social acceptability of the mindset that suggested imperialism.

Conclusion

Dorothy Richardson's sole publication was a memoir of her grandfather that appeared in John Nichols's *Illustrations of the Literary History of the Eighteenth Century* (1817) – the five travel volumes discussed here were never published. This in itself is not necessarily testimony to Dorothy's marginalisation from the possibilities of print publication as a woman writer, but it does suggest that a female-authored scientific study solicited a more private form of readership and circulation than a female-authored family history.[47] The only published hint we have of Dorothy's scientific contributions are in topographer Thomas Dunham Whitaker's *History and Antiquities of the Deanery of Craven, in the County of York* (1805). Here Thomas acknowledged Dorothy as

> a lady and friend, whom abundant leisure, and extensive knowledge, have enabled to procure more information, than any other person on the subject of this Work, and whose good wishes for its success have allowed her to withhold no efforts which could promote it.[48]

It was Dorothy's 'abundant leisure' that allowed her to develop her extensive scientific knowledge. Her unmarried status, in combination with the high level of education she received from a family supportive of her scientific pursuits, gave her the time, capability and confidence to conduct surveys of ancient man-made monuments that were outside of the realms of most other women. While she had 'knowledge of that science' that Caroline Powys regretted was 'quite outside of female knowledge', Dorothy felt pressure to hide her development of scientific knowledge from men in the public institution of the museum and dared not seek to gain any knowledge of the anatomical preparations. As with those discussed in Chapter 4, it was in the realm of the minute and microscopic that this woman's scientific knowledge could shine: in the small and delicate and detailed observations and sketches of her journals and the samples of ore, seaweeds and hair she took from the travel environment. It was also in the manuscript format that Dorothy could take her scientific knowledge the furthest among a small network of educated family and friends. While her gender and social position may have restricted her to this format, it was in it that she could reflect upon and revise her observations over time with further study and without the constraints imposed by the fixed print form.

What Dorothy's journals offer us, then, is a unique mode of collection that exploits the possibilities of the curiosity, the specimen and the souvenir – that is, the wonderful, the scientific and the personal. Dorothy's scientific travel collecting activities may or may not have provided new contributions to the field of science. What they do offer us is a window into the inner lives of eighteenth-century women, by displaying the private activity of one woman's knowledge-making in the eighteenth century, in contrast to men's public knowledge-making. By collecting specimens and noting down her observations during her travels, Dorothy formed a private space in which she could produce an understanding of science that was of her own making.

In the next chapter, we will turn to Lady Elizabeth Holland. While Elizabeth did not show the same meticulous written engagement with matters of science as Dorothy, as the heiress of a West Indian fortune she had the means to develop an immense cabinet of curiosities through which she claimed a privileged position in the social circulation of scientific knowledge.

Notes

1. W. P. Courtney and Peter Davis, 'Richardson, Richard (1663–1741)', *Oxford Dictionary of National Biography*, last updated 27 May 2010, https://doi.org/10.1093/ref:odnb/23576.
2. Colin Lee, 'Currer, Frances Mary Richardson (1785–1861)', *Oxford Dictionary of National Biography*, last updated 23 September 2004, https://doi.org/10.1093/ref:odnb/6951.
3. D. G. C. Allan, *William Shipley, Founder of the Royal Society of Arts: A Biography with Documents* (London: Hutchinson and Company, 1968), 24–5.
4. Marcia Pointon compares Dorothy's program with William Shipley's in her chapter on Dorothy Richardson in *Strategies for Showing: Women, Possession, and Representation in English Visual Culture, 1665–1800* (Oxford and New York: Oxford University Press, 1997), 98.
5. JRL, Dorothy Richardson Papers, GB 133 Eng MS 1122, Dorothy Richardson, 'Yorkshire (West Riding), Derbyshire, Nottinghamshire and Lancashire', 1761–75, fols 11–12.
6. For an examination of Dorothy and other women travellers' itinerary format, see Zoë Kinsley, *Women Writing the Home Tour, 1682–1812* (Aldershot: Ashgate, 2008), 35.
7. JRL, Dorothy Richardson Papers, GB 133 Eng MS 1122, fols 12–13.
8. Mary Morgan, *A Tour to Milford Haven, in the Year 1791* (London: John Stockdale, 1795), 51.
9. Zoë Kinsley, *Women Writing the Home Tour, 1682–1812* (Aldershot: Ashgate, 2008), 25.
10. Mary Berry, *Extracts from the journals and correspondence of Miss Berry: From the Year 1783 to 1852*, ed. Lady Theresa Lewis (London: Longmans Green, 1865), vol. 1, 21.
11. Count Leopold Berchtold, *An Essay to Direct and Extend the Inquiries of Patriotic Travellers* (London: Robinson, 1789), 43.
12. James Boswell, *The Life of Samuel Johnson* (London: Henry Baldwin and Charles Dilly, 1791), vol. 1, 270.
13. Anna Riggs Miller, *Letters from Italy, Describing the Manners, Customs, Antiquities, Paintings, &c. of that Country, in the Years MDCCLXX and MDCCLXXI, to a Friend Residing in France* (Dublin: W. Watson, 1776), vol. 1, 324.
14. BL, Powys Diaries, Add. MS 42164, Caroline Lybbe Powys (née Girle) 'Journal of a Tour to Oxford, Blenheim, &c.', 1759, fol. 1r°.
15. Kinsley, Zoë, "Considering the Manuscript Travelogue: The Journals of Dorothy Richardson (1761–1801)." *Prose Studies: History, Theory, Criticism* 26, no. 3 (2003): 423.

16 JRL, Dorothy Richardson Papers, GB 133 Eng MS 1125, Dorothy Richardson, 'Yorkshire (North Riding) and Lancashire', 1779, fols 246–50.
17 JRL, Dorothy Richardson Papers, GB 133 Eng MS 1125, fol. 155.
18 JRL, Dorothy Richardson Papers, GB 133 Eng MS 1125, fol. 250.
19 Quoted in Rosemary Sweet, *Antiquaries: The Discovery of the Past in Eighteenth-Century Britain* (London and New York: Hambledon and London, 2004), 76.
20 Sweet, *Antiquaries*, 76.
21 Marcia Pointon, *Strategies for Showing: Women, Possession, and Representation in English Visual Culture, 1665–1800* (Oxford and New York: Oxford University Press, 1997), 100.
22 JRL, Dorothy Richardson Papers, GB 133 Eng MS 1124, Dorothy Richardson, 'London', 1775 and 1785, fols 336–7. Dr Charles Combe was to become the executor and trustee of the museum following Dr William Hunter's death in 1783.
23 JRL, Dorothy Richardson Papers, GB 133 Eng MS 1124, fol. 337.
24 Marcia Pointon, *Strategies for Showing: Women, Possession, and Representation in English Visual Culture, 1665–1800* (Oxford and New York: Oxford University Press, 1997), 100.
25 JRL, Dorothy Richardson Papers, GB 133 Eng MS 1122, fol. 64.
26 Peter Naldrett, *Days Out Underground: 50 Subterranean Adventures beneath Britain* (London: Bloomsbury, 2019), 87.
27 JRL, Dorothy Richardson Papers, GB 133 Eng MS 1122, fol. 266.
28 JRL, Dorothy Richardson Papers, GB 133 Eng MS 1122, fols 260–3.
29 Morgan, *A Tour to Milford Haven*, 290–300.
30 Sarah Murray, *A Companion, and Useful Guide to the Beauties of Scotland* (London: George Nicol, 1799), 283–4.
31 JRL, Dorothy Richardson Papers, GB 133 Eng MS 1126, Dorothy Richardson, 'Yorkshire (East Riding)', 1801–2, fol. 9.
32 Zoë Kinsley, *Women Writing the Home Tour, 1682–1812* (Aldershot: Ashgate, 2008), 144.
33 This is explored in Tim Youngs, 'Buttons and souls: some thoughts on commodities and identity in women's travel writing', *Studies in Travel Writing* 1 (1997): 117–40; Zoë Kinsley, 'Travel and material culture: commodity, currency, and destabilised meaning in women's home tour writing', *Studies in Travel Writing* 10 (2006): 101–22.
34 Dorothy Wordsworth, *Recollections of a Tour Made in Scotland A.D. 1803*, ed. J. C. Shairp (New York: G. P. Putnam's Sons, 1874), 91.
35 Wordsworth, *Recollections of a Tour*, 94.
36 Wordsworth, *Recollections of a Tour*, 37.
37 For a full exploration of this incidence and the colonial meanings of Mary Morgan's engagement with material culture see Zoë Kinsley,

'Travel and material culture: commodity, currency, and destabilised meaning in women's home tour writing', *Studies in Travel Writing* 10 (2006): 107–110.
38 Morgan, *A Tour to Milford Haven*, 235–6.
39 John Hawkesworth, *An Account of the Voyages Undertaken by the Order of His Present Majesty for Making Discoveries in the Southern Hemisphere: And Successively Performed by Commodore Byron, Captain Wallis, Captain Carteret, and Captain Cook, in the Dolphin, the Swallow, and the Endeavor, Drawn Up from the Journals which Were Kept by the Several Commanders, and from the Papers of Joseph Banks, Esq*, vol. 2 (London: W. Strahan and T. Cadell, 1773).
40 Bernard William Smith, *European Vision and the South Pacific* (New Haven and London: Yale University Press, 1985), 16 and 40.
41 Hawkesworth, *An Account of the Voyages*, 59.
42 For the role that material culture played in Australian women's ethnographic pursuits, see Erica Kaye Izett, 'Breaking New Ground: Early Australian Ethnography in Colonial Women's Writing' (PhD thesis, University of Western Australia, 2014).
43 For an overview of relevant debates in the area of women and imperialism, see Ann Standish, *Australia through Women's Eyes* (Melbourne: Australian Scholarly Publishing, 2008), 19.
44 Dale Spender, *Writing a New World: Two Centuries of Australian Women Writers* (London: Pandora, 1988), xvi.
45 Patricia Grimshaw and Julie Evans, 'Colonial women on intercultural frontiers: Rosa Campbell Praed, Mary Bundock and Katie Langloh Parker', *Australian Historical Studies* 27 (1996): 81.
46 Sara Mills, 'Knowledge, gender and empire', in *Writing Women and Space: Colonial and Postcolonial Geographies*, ed. Alison Blunt and Gillian Rose (New York and London: Guilford Press, 1994), 32.
47 Zoë Kinsley, 'Dorothy Richardson's manuscript travel journals (1761–1801) and the possibilities of picturesque aesthetics', *Review of English Studies* 56, no. 226 (2005): 614. See also George L. Justice and Nathan Tinker, *Women's Writing and the Circulation of Ideas: Manuscript Publication in England, 1550–1800* (Cambridge: Cambridge University Press, 2002).
48 Thomas Dunham Whitaker, *The History and Antiquities of the Deanery of Craven, in the County of York*, 2nd edn (London: Nichols & Son, 1805), vi.

1 Johan Zoffany, *The Tribuna degli Uffizi*, 1772–78/9, 123.5 cm × 155 cm, oil on canvas.

2 W. Chambers, *The Townley Collection in the Dining Room at Park Street, Westminster*, 1794–95, 390 mm × 540 mm, watercolour on paper.

3 Pietro Fabris, *Kenneth Mackenzie, First Earl of Seaforth 1744–81, at Home in Naples: Concert Party*, 1771, 355 mm × 476 mm, oil on canvas.

4 Pietro Fabris, *Kenneth Mackenzie, First Earl of Seaforth 1744–81, at Home in Naples: Fencing Scene*, 1771, 355 mm × 476 mm, oil on canvas.

5 Sir Nathaniel Dance-Holland, *Portrait of Olive Craster*, 1762, 72.39 cm × 60.17 cm, oil on canvas.

6 Grand Tour fan, 1780, 275 mm (guardstick), leather (kid) leaf, ivory guards and sticks.

7 Lady Miller's monument, Bath Abbey.

8 Lady Miller's monument, Bath Abbey.

9 Unknown Italian artist, *Hester Lynch Piozzi (née Salusbury, later Mrs Thrale)*, 1785–86, 756 mm × 629 mm, oil on canvas.

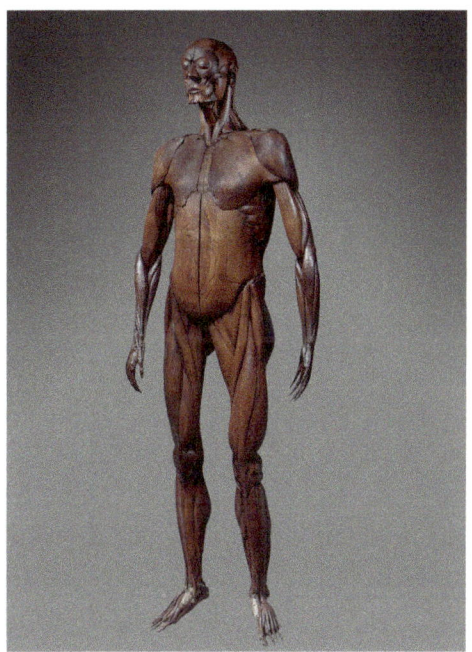

10 Felice Fontana, *Wooden Man*, 1799, 160 cm (height), wood and paper mâché, Musée de l'Histoire de la Médecine, Université René Descartes.

11 Felice Fontana, *Wooden Man*, 1799, 160 cm (height), wood and paper mâché, Musée de l'Histoire de la Médecine, Université René Descartes.

12 John Wykeham Archer, *Holland House*, 1857, 270 mm × 372 mm, watercolour over graphite.

13 Green leather case containing pencil and dance card, given by Queen Maria Carolina to Caroline Swinburne (front view).

14 Adrien Jean Maximilien Vachette, box; cameo, 1797–1815, 72 mm × 52 mm × 20 mm, gold and agate (front view).

15 Grigory Ugryumov, *Tsar Ivan IV Conquering Kazan in 1552*, 1799–1800, 1,075 cm × 875 cm, oil on canvas.

6

Lady Elizabeth Holland, the social orchestrator of science

Priest Noël Antoine Pluche's *Spectacle de la Nature* (1733–48) was one of the most widely translated polite scientific publications of the eighteenth century. In the nine-volume work a French countess is found eavesdropping on a male scientific society. After being discovered, the countess is permitted to join the gentlemen of the society, but soon finds that they 'don't expect much from me, and so I am not asked any questions'. To stimulate discussion, she retrieves a little box that she claims, 'will speak for me, as well as a fine Harangue'.[1] The box contains many specimens that the countess had 'collected and ranged, with the nicest Judgement and Propriety I was capable of', including 'butterflies covered with Plumage, or tinctured with a Variety of Colours'.[2] She provides the gentlemen of the society with a microscope to study her butterflies, and they marvel at the insect's wings, 'all the colours in Mother of Pearl ... Eyes that glow in a Peacock's Tail ... and Edges bordered with ... shining silks'.[3] As she establishes her authority through these specimens, the countess politely asks, 'Is it not one of the Maxims of their [men's] Politeness, to entertain us [women] with nothing but Trifles?'[4]

In this chapter I analyse how Lady Elizabeth Holland used the collection of specimens of natural history to establish a familiarity and ease among Europe's key scientists on her Grand Tour from 1791 to 1796. I then uncover how she developed this network following her return home, arguing that the exchange and display of an ever-increasing array of objects, stemming from her Grand Tour, was a key mechanism by which Elizabeth contributed to the social circulation of science. Born into immense New World wealth as the only child (and universal heiress) of Richard and Mary Vassall,

Lady Elizabeth Vassall Fox, Baroness Holland, like Pluche's fictional countess, had the economic clout to establish a name for herself as a scientific patron through travel collecting. All sources indicate that she did this because she had a genuine interest in science, which stemmed from its popularity at the time as an accessible polite pursuit for women, as discussed in Chapter 4, and also her imperial connections. Elizabeth's family's expropriation of land and natural resources from the West Indies provided her with the means to build a collection of objects from Europe and across the globe that in turn imbued her with a worldly air and cosmopolitanism appropriate to her status as an heiress and the wife of a major figure in Whig politics.

Elizabeth's grandfather Florentius Vassall was a prominent planter and slave owner in Jamaica, where he owned 8,357 acres.[5] It is unknown whether Elizabeth was born in Jamaica, but she was raised in Golden Square, London. Here, by her own account, she had a lonely childhood in which she was 'entirely left, not from system, but from fondness and inactivity, to follow my own bent'.[6] Elizabeth reflected in a letter to her son in 1828, at the age of fifty-two, that had she ever had 'advantages' such as the company and affection of a sibling or friend, and the entertainment of education,

> what a different & more amiable person I should *have* been. But I have few relations in the world, never had a young associate, and only a father and mother who did not always agree with each other, and never agreed about me. The warm, ingenuous affection of youth was never drawn out, but blunted and repressed; in that my adolescence and youth was gloomy, uncheered by any tender kindred feeling. I was solitary; and til thirteen years old, no mortal seemed to think of me beyond the necessaries of life.[7]

Her neighbour, the Whig politician and collector Anthony Morris Storer, provided her with some education, however.[8] According to Elizabeth, this 'old friend of my father's, struck by my good looks or my character, to a degree adopted me and became my tutor'.[9] Although her strained relationship with her son may have caused Elizabeth to exaggerate the educational barriers she faced in childhood, she clearly felt disadvantaged by her gender, having to rely on coincidence and family networks to shape her own learning. Under these restrictions, polite science was an area of learning more open to Elizabeth than others, particularly given her family background.

In 1786, at the age of fifteen, Elizabeth was married to Sir Godfrey Webster, fourth Baronet of Battle Abbey, Sussex. With Godfrey being more twenty years his bride's senior, it was not a happy match. Eleven years into their marriage, Elizabeth described her husband in her journal as a 'pompous coxcomb', who had 'squandered' her 'youth, beauty, and ... good disposition'.[10] The couple had five children together, two of whom died in infancy. Following the births of their first two children (Sir Godfrey Vassall Webster, fifth Baronet, born 6 October 1789, and a second son who was born in 1790 but unfortunately died later that year), Godfrey agreed to indulge Elizabeth's desire for foreign travel. Having satisfied the duty of birthing an heir, Elizabeth was granted more flexibility in her life and permitted to join her husband on a Grand Tour that lasted for nearly six years from 1791 to 1796 (figure 6.1).

It was on her fraught Tour with Godfrey that Elizabeth developed her scientific interests. 'I was left alone at twenty years old in a foreign country without a relation or any real friend', Elizabeth reflected of the commencement of her travels in Nice in 1791,

> yet some of the least miserable, I might add the most happy hours, of my life were passed there. I lived with great discretion, even to prudery. I never admitted any male visitors (except to numerous dinners), either in the morning or evening, with the exception only of two Dr. Drew [the physician William Drew], and a grave married man, a Mr. Cowper. Drew used to spend the whole eve. with me, and give me lectures on chemistry, natural history, philosophy, etc., etc.[11]

Elizabeth would go on to learn from many of Europe's greatest minds. During her stay in Turin, in 1792, for instance, she studied under physician and chemist Costanzo Benedetto Bonvicino.[12] At the time of Elizabeth's visit, Benedetto was a member of the Academy of Sciences of Turin and responsible for its laboratory which tested the waters used by dyers. Eight years later, in 1800, he would be made professor of pharmaceutical chemistry and the natural history of drugs at the University of Turin.[13] In the same year Elizabeth also travelled to Pavia, south-western Lombardy, to see 'the celebrated' Lazzaro Spallanzani, who she appreciatively described as 'a man who has made some filthy experiments upon digestion'.[14] A Catholic

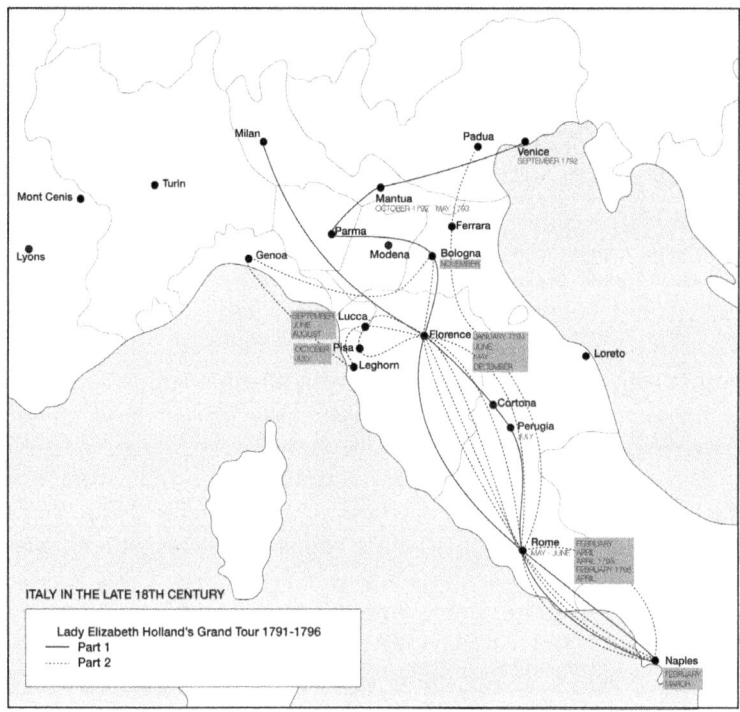

6.1 Map of Lady Elizabeth Holland's Grand Tour, 1791–96.

priest, biologist and physiologist, Spallanzani is now known for his research on biogenesis and his experimental demonstrations of *in vitro* fertilisation. When Elizabeth met the professor, he was well established at the University of Pavia and supportive of women scientists, having studied under the sponsorship of his cousin Laura Bassi at the University of Bologna.[15]

During her tour, Elizabeth inspected Europe's greatest collections and began to build her own. While in Milan in 1792, for instance, she visited Ermenegildo Pini, an Italian clergyman as well as a geologist who examined scientific ideas regarding geological phenomena and fossils with the aim of showing that they were consistent with the framework of Biblical Genesis.[16] 'Padre Pini, an old Barnabite monk, gave me many good specimens', Elizabeth noted, 'especially of his Adularia, a species of feldspar he has discovered'.[17] A few months after she was given this gift, Elizabeth obtained some specimens from another collector by quite different means: 'I have stolen some of the Baron's specimens of minerals', she wrote in her journal; 'my conscious smites me almost for the plunder'.[18] In her study of cabinets of curiosity, Marjorie Swann observed that during the early modern period collecting and travel were 'mutually sustainable activities' because 'not only was the experience of travel represented by the foreign objects in European collections of "rarities", but travel itself became predicated upon the very existence of such collections'.[19] In a display of the impassioned desire and licentiousness of the collector, Elizabeth had pillaged the curiosity cabinet of her host Baron d'Aviso in Valle d'Aosta, north-west Italy, just as Lady Miller attempted to steal the cloth from the Vatican and Caroline Powys pillaged Stonehenge (see Chapter 4).

The scientist who had the greatest influence on Elizabeth was the Italian physicist Felice Fontana, known for his discovery of the water–gas shift reaction and credited with launching modern toxicology.[20] When Elizabeth first met Fontana in 1792, he was the director of the Royal Museum of Physics and Natural History in the Palazzo Pitti, of which he took her on a private tour. Here she was delighted to find 'thirty-eight rooms filled with objects of every branch of Natural History, Philosophy, Physics, etc.'.[21] Both the museum's collections and its director clearly made a strong impression on Elizabeth, as she dedicated several pages of her journal to them, noting:

> The anatomical preparations in wax are very beautiful. The small representations of the ravages of the plague at Messina are admirably executed; the artist must have had a considerable portion of sombre in his imagination. I asked the real history of the tarantula, whether he [Fontana] thought there was any foundation for the stories they tell in Calabria of its producing such violent irritation that motion, such as dancing, relieves the patient. He says such a malady exists and is ascribed to the sting.[22]

Elizabeth also marvelled at 'an enormous snake called constrictor':

> Its mode of destroying its prey is by ingestion, it hides itself round the stem of a tree letting its head hang down which vibrates to and fro like the pendulum of a clock, it sieges its victim and curls itself around it, until it is squeezed and alarms. The natives catch him when

he is gorged, and eat him in their turn. His flesh is good and like a sturgeon. Fontana has made numberless experiments upon the poison of a viper. It is a glutinous mass in which he has never discovered the noxious ingredient; taken into the stomach, it is not prejudicial, it only acts upon the nerves. He has published in several quarto volumes his opinions on the subject. He entered into a long philosophical dissertation on the vital principle. He has worms or eels in which life is suspended, but he can bring them to existence. They came in diseased corn from the Morea. He has drawn conclusions from his experiments which prove too much for the Church to allow him to publish. He is an apostle in the cause of atheism and democracy, hence it is not likely he will make the world happier or wiser.[23]

Here Elizabeth's enjoyment of the theatre and exoticism of Fontana's experimental work is palatable. Her fascination in science was clearly the grand-scale interest of the patron, rather than the minute and methodical interest of Dorothy Richardson described in Chapter 5. This friendship between an English woman and a male Italian museum director was highly unusual. During the eighteenth century, men and women could be friends if they were related, but outside of these contexts friendship across gender lines was suspect.[24] Elizabeth's excessive wealth, however, put her in the unusual position of being able to patronise men. As a new director wanting to make his mark, Fontana would have been eager to please this young, keen and wealthy English woman and receive her patronage.

When he commenced his twenty-five years as director of the Royal Museum, Fontana promised that he would ensure it comprised 'everything that is most beautiful, most useful, and most ingenious that men have been able to find or imagine'. In the spirit of Enlightenment systematisation and public access, he also made sure that 'artefacts are displayed and explained precisely with that superior order, richness and means as is done in regular courses, so that it is enough to know how to read to understand firsthand the natural history of whatever is found in the Royal Museum'.[25] In particular, Fontana highlighted the beauty of the medical collection, which comprised 6 rooms containing 486 anatomical wax models; these ranged from iconic, three-quarter-size écorchés that demonstrated muscle and bone structures, to discrete organs and microscopic-scale studies.[26]

The central attraction of the museum was the *Anatomical Venus* (figure 6.2). It demonstrated the anatomy of the torso, from the

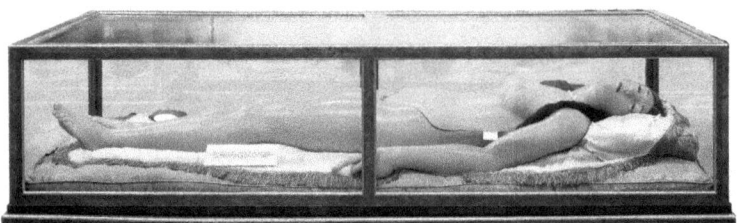

6.2 'Anatomical Venus', wax model with human hair and pearls in rosewood and Venetian glass case, 'La Specola' (Museo di Storia Naturale), Florence, Italy; probably modelled by Clemente Susini, around 1790.

surface musculature and glands of the breast, to the organs of the thoracic cavity and the lower abdomen (including a uterus and a foetus).[27] All of these components could be dismantled and held in the hand. These wax models were displayed to appeal to a male gaze. Grand Tourists visiting the *Anatomical Venus* would find her reclining evocatively on a silken bed in a state of passionate abandon. This aesthetic was not restricted to the goddess of beauty, desire and fertility. As Ludmilla Jordanova has observed, most anatomical models of women during the period were covered in flesh and decorated with soft hair and necklaces, while their faces often expressed the sexual and religious ecstasy of Bernini's Saint Theresa.[28] In comparison, male anatomical models typically stood upright with the layers of flesh removed to reveal their muscles, or were in the incomplete form of a torso.[29] When she visited the Royal Museum in 1839, Marguerite Gardiner, Countess of Blessington, found the 'nakedness and truth' of the anatomical wax specimens 'hideous and appalling', not only because of the visceral content but also because she was encountering them in the company of the opposite sex:

> I entered the Gabinetto Fisico today, and though I only remained a few minutes ... I carried away a sense of loathing that has not yet left me. Surely some restriction should exist to preclude men and women from examining these models together! ... It is meet that we should know that we are fearfully and wonderfully created; but not that we should witness the disgusting details of the animal economy in all its hideous and appalling nakedness and truth. What a lesson for personal vanity does this exhibition convey! ... I hold that its

fearful images will recur to my memory when I behold some creature, in the zenith of youth and beauty, who almost believes that she is not formed of the perilous stuff so shockingly delineated in the Gabinetto Fisico.[30]

Other women also reported an aversion to viewing anatomical specimens in the company of men.[31] For instance, Dorothy Richardson (see Chapter 5) noted that she was pleased that the 'finest collection of anatomical preparations in the kingdom' were not on display when she visited Hunter's museum with a party of men: 'I was happy they were out of sight, indeed I made this enquiry of Dr Combe before I ventured', she noted in her journal.[32] In comparison, Elizabeth's description of the 'anatomical preparations in wax' as 'very beautiful', not to mention her obvious enjoyment at describing the 'glutinous mass' of the boa constrictor, show a degree of comfort with such coarse subjects that was unusual for her sex and in which she appears to have taken some pride. Elizabeth's aristocratic status and wealth clearly gave her a licence to study objects that most women demurely forewent viewing. While the way it presents itself does not reconcile easily with our understanding of scientific rigour, Elizabeth's eager engagement with the anatomical collection at the Royal Museum shows that there was, in fact, a female presence in this aspect of science, typically viewed as off-limits for British women.

At the time of Elizabeth's second visit to the museum in 1793, Fontana had also just finished constructing a wooden male anatomical model, which she found 'astonishing':

> He [Fontana] showed me the details of his astonishing homme de bois [wooden man]. It is composed of 3000 pieces of wood that take off from the surface; beneath there are a variety of others which mark the veins, arteries, etc. In all there are 250,000 different pieces of wood.[33]

Fontana invented the *Wooden Man* (see plates 10 and 11) late in his career, when he was having second thoughts about wax's suitability for producing 'all the marvels of our animal machine'.[34] Consisting of three thousand removable body parts, the *Wooden Man*, unlike a wax model, offered the possibility of analysing and synthesising the entire body structure. Moreover, this model, Fontana claimed, could be refashioned to represent a male or female body as needed. 'It is impossible in a few words to give an accurate idea of a machine so composed', he admitted when designing the model, 'but it is easy to estimate the difficulties of the enterprise and its use for anatomy'.[35] In her history of cadavers, Katharine Park observes that, during the period, female cadavers

> emphasized the distance between the (male) anatomist and his (female) object and served to establish the author as the new empirical anatomist, who, with his own hands methodically disclosed and classified her strange and secret entrails, redolent symbols of the veiled truths of the human body and of Nature herself.[36]

The model's wooden construction and gender-neutral form, then, would not hamper Elizabeth with the repugnancy of deceased human flesh nor the sexual aesthetics of a female wax model based on canonical art. Instead, by touching and manipulating the *Wooden Man*, Elizabeth could herself become the anatomist and experience this relationship between each part and the whole. Her engagement with the *Wooden Man* shows a degree of female agency in the arena of anatomy that has not been recognised in the literature. Elizabeth's actions break the gender binary outlined by Katherine Park and others and show that a woman was, in fact, active in this space during this early period when scientific enquiry was still unstable.

In 1794–95, Elizabeth 'passed a delightful winter' in Naples, hosting dinners three times a week with Fontana; his rival, the chemist Giovanni Valentino Mattia Fabbroni; Lorenzo Pignotti, a physics professor from Pisa University; and the politicians Don Neri Corsini, Vittorio Fossombroni and Melchiore Delifico.[37] It was here that Elizabeth formed a relationship with twenty-one-year-old Grand Tourist Henry Richard Fox, third Baron Holland (and nephew of Whig statesman Charles James Fox). It is clear that Elizabeth's scientific aptitude was one of the qualities that attracted Henry to her, as evinced by the following poem he wrote to mark his lover's birthday:

> *To a Lady on her Birthday, 1795*
> When twice twelve times the rolling earth
> Brought back the period of her birth,
> Thus to the Genius of the day
> A certain Dame was heard to pray:
> Give me, indulgent Genius, give
> 'Midst learned cabinets to live,
> 'Midst curiosities, collections,
> Specimens, medals, and dissections,

With books of every tongue and land
All difficult to understand,
With instruments of various sorts,
Telescopes, air pumps, tubes, retorts,
With friends, fair wisdom to pursue,
Fontana, Macie, Blagden, Drew.

Such are thy wishes, but if kind
The Gods, and of a mortal's mind,
These sacrifices they will spare,
And long preserve you what you are
And when obdurate time besprinkles
Your head with grey, your face with wrinkles,
When sickness and when age shall come
And wither transient beauty's bloom,
Still shall the beauties of your mind,
By reading and by time refin'd,
Still shall thy wit and polish'd ease
In spite of fickle nature please;

And then th' enchanted world shall see
Rochefoucauld's laws belied in thee,
See female merit youth outlive,
And loveliness thy charms survive.
So when old Time's relentless page
At full threescore shall mark thy age,
With equal truth but better verse
Some Bard thy merits shall rehearse,
And like myself be proud to pay
A tribute to this happy day.[38]

The 'curiosities, collections, / Specimens, medals, and dissections' mentioned in this poem make visible the important role that material culture played in Elizabeth's cultivation and demonstration of an aptitude for science. Indeed, Elizabeth not only obtained specimens from Europe's great men of science but, like the women in the previous chapters, made her own empirical observations of the natural environment and collected specimens from it. Rather than marvelling at the beauty of Tivoli in 1793, for instance, she observed the reflection, refraction and dispersion of light within its rainbows:

> Rainbows are formed by a ray of light falling upon a sphere of a denser medium than air, by which means the ray of light is reflected towards the axis of this sphere and is decomposed into the original

colours; it is reflected in this sphere or drop of water, and lastly refracted again towards the original direction, by which the spherical appearance called rainbows is produced.[39]

In the same year, Elizabeth visited Montjovet, north-western Italy, which she knew was 'celebrated for fine steatites and garnets imbedded in quartz'. Here she 'obtained a few specimens'.[40]

Henry's poem also showed his appreciation of British women's promotion of science as a polite cultural pursuit by drawing a connection between Elizabeth's scientific engagement and her conversational abilities ('wit and polish'd ease'). Indeed, he flatteringly placed Elizabeth's scientific knowledge and artful conversation above her renowned beauty ('And wither transient beauty's bloom, / Still shall the beauties of your mind'). This shows that during the period scientific knowledge was not incompatible with femininity. Far from it – scientific knowledge could, in fact, support it.

Months after receiving the poem, Elizabeth refused to return to England with Godfrey, who promptly took her surname Vassall in order to succeed his father-in-law's West Indian estates. In 1796 (five years after she set out on her Grand Tour) Elizabeth returned to England with Henry and they had a child together. The following year, Godfrey divorced Elizabeth (resuming his previous surname but keeping her West Indian fortune of £7,000 per annum); a few months later, Elizabeth and Henry were married.[41] During her Grand Tour, Elizabeth negotiated social constraints and her own ideas of behaviour appropriate to her sex to explore knowledge-making and critical thinking. Like the elite male Grand Tourist, she returned home with a stronger understanding of herself and her identity, and she acted on that understanding by divorcing a husband who did not support her interests and marrying one who did. In taking this action, however, she would have been most aware that she would need to make a far greater social sacrifice than any man.

Following her divorce, Elizabeth was barred from court and ostracised by fashionable society. Her ignominy was increased by the public knowledge that, just prior to returning to England, she had staged a burial of her daughter in an attempt to keep her from Godfrey (this failed and the girl was returned to her father in 1799).[42] Even at the age of twelve, Henrietta Cavendish, daughter of Georgiana, Duchess of Devonshire, was aware of the cloud of infamy that followed Elizabeth. 'The first thing that struck our eyes was Lady Holland, seated in a box', she told her older sister after glimpsing the newly married couple at Astley's Circus in 1798. Georgiana continued:

> My aunt [Elizabeth's close friend Henrietta Ponsonby, Countess of Bessborough] moved all her *ten fingers* at once. Mr. and Mrs. Peterson [the housekeeper and butler] made signs, Lady Liz twisted her *shawls* with a forbidding glance, Caroline held up her head a little higher than usual, John reddened and I who did not know who she was, thought it rather strange that a poor lady looking so demure and quiet should cause such evident confusion.[43]

Despite this marginalisation, Elizabeth managed to reclaim a place in polite society as the formidable hostess of London's most famous political salon, Holland House (see plate 12). Inspired by her attendance at the Countess of Albany's *conversazioni* in Florence, which were 'crowded with strangers of all countries', she organised dinners for up to fifty guests at the couple's Jacobean mansion at Kensington (purchased by Henry's grandfather) that included some of the greatest names of the day.[44] Elizabeth's guests naturally included Whig politicians, such as Thomas Erskine and Richard Brinsley Sheridan, but these men were joined by Tory politicians, including Sir Walter Scott and Lord Eldon. The salon was also a centre for important writers and publishers like Lord Byron, Charles Dickens, Henry Luttrell, Thomas Macaulay and Thomas Moore, and for some of the period's key scientific figures, including the German geographer and explorer Alexander von Humboldt, the physicist who established the Royal Institution of Great Britain, Sir Benjamin Thompson, Count Rumford, and the founding father of palaeontology, Jean Léopold Nicolas Frédéric, Baron Cuvier.[45] As the diarist Charles Greville put it, although everyone who went to Holland House found 'something to abuse or to ridicule in the mistress of the house, or its ways, all, continue to go … It is the house of all Europe'.[46] This quote tells us something of the social stigma Elizabeth chose to endure for the pay-off of taking the curiosity of the traveller home and choosing self-actualisation over maintaining gender roles.

The cabinet of curiosities that Elizabeth began to build during her Grand Tour and, following it, continued to develop with Henry, played no small part in drawing such a diverse group of politicians, writers and scientists together. Those 'Ministers and Diplomats, men of learning and of science, historians, poets, artists, and wits' who had the privilege of dining with Elizabeth and Henry would enter the house via a Great Entrance Hall.[47] According to Thomas Faulkner's *History and Antiquities of Kensington* (1820), next to the Great Staircase they would see a 'great plan of London' and 'several curiosities', including:

> a wooden lance, a battle axe, a dart, and an arrow, a short pipe to throw against an enemy, and a fishing hook, all belonging to the savages of New Guinea. A mantle wove out of wool of different colours, which a princess, chief of a cast in South America, took from her person, and, as a mark of esteem, put it on Gen. Liniers [Santiago de Liniers, Count of Buenos Aires], the celebrated French adventurer.[48]

In the Hollands' dining room, these men would sit next to 'a sideboard rich and glittering with venerable family plate, a great looking-glass in which a merry party may have the satisfaction of finding itself repeated, and a gay china closet, filled mostly from the East'.[49] Inspired by Queen Mary's celebrated collection of white and blue porcelain at Kensington Palace, such closets were important components of the eighteenth-century interior that signified the taste and refinement of the hostess.[50]

As the men conversed about etymology, painting, oratory, botany and natural history, they would find 'many likenesses speaking to them from crimson damask walls', including Elizabeth's Grand Tour portrait by Robert Fagan.[51] This portrait depicted Elizabeth in a flowing ivory Grecian gown tied at the waist by a blue sash (figure 6.3). A hazy view of the Castel del'Ovo and Mount Vesuvius hinted at her love of Naples, where she first met Henry in 1794. 'I never in my life experienced the degree of happiness enjoyed', Elizabeth later reflected, 'it was the gratification of mind and sense'.[52] The steam rising from Vesuvius also reminded Elizabeth's guests that she had climbed the volcano. This was a popular activity for British women.[53] In 1784, for instance, Mary Berry enjoyed dining and socialising 'upon the very edge of the crater, where we could look down into the fiery gulf and enjoy the noble fireworks'.[54] In 1788 Ann Flaxman also climbed Vesuvius with her husband. She had trouble reaching the top but soldiered on after taking 'an additional

6.3 Charles Henry Jeens, after Robert Fagan, *Elizabeth Vassall Fox (née Vassall), Lady Holland (formerly Webster)*, 1874, 146 mm × 94 mm, line engraving.

draught of strong Beer' and 'brought up the rear most gallantly singing'.[55] Unlike Mary and Anne, however, Elizabeth's interest in Vesuvius was scientific. In her journal she carefully noted that the 'stratum of fresh lava' at Torre del Greco was 'of a peculiar texture, more charged with metallic particles than any of the other strata from Vesuvius, though not equal in specific gravity to that at Ischia', and that 'the density of the atmosphere marks the source of the lava'.[56] She would return home with a collection of the spoils of the mountain's volcanic eruptions, and also those of the islands of Lipari and Ischia.[57]

Immediately behind the Great Entrance Hall was the Hollands' journal room. Its glazed and black-stained mahogany bookcases were crowded not only with the printed journals of the Lords and

Commons but also 'a large collection of minerals, and a considerable number of stuffed birds and insects':

> Over the book-cases are placed ninety-six boxes of stuffed birds, small quadrupeds, and reptiles, chiefly from South America. Among which is the Ampelis Garrulus or Waxen Chatterer, killed in the grounds at Holland House, and the Phaeton Acthereas, or Tropical Bird, with many other rare and uncommon species. Here are also fourteen framed boxes, with butterflies and insects; amongst which are some very scarce, all from South America. A Cabinet with shells and marine productions, from the island of Mauritius. The collection of Minerals is extensive and valuable, consisting of many rare and beautiful specimens, the most remarkable of which is a large piece of gold ore, and another of silver ore, after having passed the first fire, and several others with and without the alloy. All these specimens, amounting to the many thousands, came from the mines of Mexico, and it is well known how jealous the Spanish court has always been of exhibiting such productions. A complete collection of the volcanic eruptions of Mount Vesuvius, and the correspondent volcanoes of Lipari and Ischia. Various gems from Brazil, amongst which are two small pieces of the stone called Eucluse by the naturalists, which are highly valued as rare and curious specimens.[58]

Alongside these cabinets stood pictures, casts and Chinese figures. 'Of the latter,' Thomas Faulkner noted, 'the most remarkable is a mandarin carved out of a root of a tree, and bought at Landsdown House sale in 1806'.[59] Elizabeth's dressing room too contained Chinese artefacts and porcelain figures, including 'two elegant Chinese pagodas, four feet two inches high, composed of mother of pearl, in high preservation', 'fourteen japanned cases' and 'Malaga figures representing Spanish costume, fandango dancers, bull fighters'.[60] As Stacy Sloboda has noted in her study of the Duchess of Portland's collection, Chinese artefacts, porcelain and specimens of natural history were complimentary materials in aristocratic women's curiosity cabinets, because they were all foreign and previously exoticised objects that had been domesticated through overseas networks, trade and collecting.[61] Elizabeth's display of the bulk of these objects in her dressing room reflects their association with a tasteful feminine aesthetic sensibility. This shows the acceptable intermingling of science and a cosmopolitan femininity in the eighteenth century.

It is clear that this cabinet largely reflected Elizabeth's interests. Henry was a Fellow of the Royal Society and had scientific family connections, including his cousin William Fox-Strangeways, Earl of Ilchester, who was a keen botanist and geologist, and his uncle William Petty, second Earl of Shelburne, who was a patron of Joseph Priestley and the Dutch chemist and biologist Jan Ingenhousz. However, his appointment to the Royal Society was a function of his position, and he rarely attended its meetings.[62] Excluded from that same institution, Elizabeth instead used the trade of specimens of natural history to develop a rich network of scientists, many of whom would become regular guests at her dinner parties.

Elizabeth developed her scientific network both for her social status and for her learning; the two are not mutually exclusive and, indeed, in the eighteenth century they were part and parcel of the same project of curiosity. Elizabeth's engagement with science throughout her travels indicates that she had a genuine interest in the subject and wanted to continue to learn more. At the same time, she enjoyed the social aspects and sought to use her scientific networks to prop up her place in society. In 1794, for instance, Elizabeth offered Reverend Laurent Joseph Murith, the botanist and canon of the choir of the St Bernard Hospice, Switzerland, a collection of volcanic rocks. In return, he enquired whether there were any alpine stones or gems that she would like to receive from him. In this manner, a reciprocal relationship was formed between Elizabeth and the Swiss botanist.[63] One year after her return to London, in 1797, William Drew sent Elizabeth 'Nine thousand nine hundred and ninety nine thanks',

> for I cannot afford the other so liberally given by great people in general to my dear good Lady Webster [Holland] for her charming Letter to me from Dresden. The topaz of Saxony from the Schnekenstein mine is precious, so are her observations on the Bohemian mountains and the turnpike roads in Austria. The story of the bug falling into the dripping pan and his miraculous escape from hence I cannot account for. – kiss pug three times for me and I will repay you with interest when we chance to meet – in heaven.[64]

The Schneckenstein (or 'Snail Stone') is a twenty-three-metre rock in Saxony that became known in the seventeenth century for its peculiar geological structure and yellowish topaz crystals on quartz.[65]

Elizabeth likely bought William's topaz from the Königskrone topaz mine, where it was extracted from 1734 to 1800. Providing William with these specimens evidently gave Elizabeth an opportunity to compare notes with him regarding the geology of Austria, although his remarks regarding the bug and the pug suggest that he did not find these 'precious' in a scholarly sense.

A constant flow of objects facilitated Elizabeth's networks, as collectors sent specimens in return for those from her Grand Tour and also asked her to pass others on to their acquaintances. In 1797 James Smithson ('Macie' from Henry's poem), the mineralogist and founding donor of the Smithsonian Institution whom Elizabeth had first met in Florence, ordered two sets of wooden models of crystals on her behalf from a mineralogist she had met in Saxony.[66] She kept one of the sets and sent the other to the Florentine botanist Antonio Targioni Tozzetti. Used to demonstrate the morphology of crystals, these models were very popular with scholars and mineral collectors for their pear wood construction, which allowed for smoother faces, sharper edges and more accurate dihedral angles than those of terracotta models.[67] Elizabeth's gift was thus very valuable. Smithson would go on to become one of the Hollands main mineral suppliers and assist in the arrangement of the Holland House curiosity cabinet. The fact that a scientist of Smithson's stature helped Elizabeth to obtain specimens and organise her cabinet further legitimised Elizabeth's position in the scientific realm.

In the same year that Elizabeth sent Targioni Tozzetti the wooden mineral models, she also received some specimens that she had requested from John Parker, Earl of Morley. He wrote from the Saltram estate in Devon:

> I have just received from my friend at Plymouth a list of the metallic specimens that had been sent to him from Cornwall, and which he proposes forwarding to London either by sea, or by the wagon. He seems to recommend the former method, and begs you to favour me with your orders that I may convey them to him and procure the arrival of the ores as speedily as possible.[68]

Such correspondence provides some indication of how the exchange of specimens from her Grand Tour allowed Elizabeth to weave a web of scholarly connection through which she could extend her own scientific interests. Further travels to Scotland (1798), Germany

(1800), Paris (1802), Spain (1805 and 1808–9) and Italy (1815) allowed her to draw together an even greater web of correspondence. Elizabeth and Henry's tour of Germany in 1800 led to a fresh flurry of letters. It was in the years shortly before and after the turn of the century that natural history and mining blossomed in Germany and geological research became recognised as an independent scientific discipline, with publications like Johann Carl Wilhelm Voigt's *Practische Gebirgskunde* (1792) and Franz Ambros Reuss's *Lehrbuch der Geognosie* (1805).[69]

Prior to Elizabeth's journey, the merchant Robert Gordon sent her a letter of introduction to the German geologist Johann Gottfried Schmeisser and a copy of his book *A System of Mineralogy* (1794) in the hope that she would find it useful and because 'it will be gratifying to the author to know you are acquainted with his system'.[70] Schmeisser lectured in London from 1786 to 1793 upon a recommendation from Joseph Banks. It was here that he befriended Robert Gordon, along with James Edward Smith (the founder of the Linnean Society) and the renowned Scottish surgeon John Hunter. At the time of Elizabeth's visit, Johann was working as a pharmacist for the merchant Caspar Reichsfreiherr von Voght in Altona, Hamburg.[71] Shortly after her return from Germany, Elizabeth also received 'a small box containing some of the productions of this neighbourhood' from James Smithson, who was, at the time, in Dover, Kent.[72] 'As there was space vacant within the box', James told her that he had taken 'the liberty to fill it also with a small parcel entertaining … for Gruber, the translator of Klaproth [the German chemist Martin Heinrich]. I flatter myself with the hope that you will send the contents to him'.[73] James had visited Germany a few years before the Hollands' tour. While it appears that he was unimpressed by the country and its inhabitants, having remarked that 'among twenty-six million people I found only one with common sense, that one being an unknown chemist', it is clear that he was still intent on building his mineral collections in a country that boasted some of the earliest mining academies in the world.[74]

It is difficult to trace women's influence, but there is some suggestion that Elizabeth had significant sway when it came to the scientific appointments of those men who came into her circle at a time when the majority of scientists did not hold full-time employment. In 1793, during a brief interlude from her tour of Italy, Elizabeth and her friend Georgiana Cavendish, Duchess of Devonshire, attended a lecture by Bryan Higgins at his newly established School of Chemistry in Greek Street, Soho.[75] Higgins was struggling to raise the capital required for a career of laboratory research and intended the school as a financial solution, 'wherein the pupils might have uncommon advantages, at the same time that my apparatus might be enlarged, and my experiments conducted at a common expense'.[76] Three years later, he would take up an appointment in Jamaica (1796–1801) to advise on the making of sugar and rum. Historians William Gibbs and Charles Mollan attribute this opportunity to Higgins's student William Lewis, who was the secretary of the Society of Rectifying Distillers.[77] Lewis himself was 'strongly attached to the politics' of the Hollands, so it is quite possible that Elizabeth, as heir of a wealthy Jamaican planter, played a significant role in his appointment.[78] Indeed, it was the Society of West India Planters and Merchants, of which Lord Holland was a member, who paid £1,400 a year for Higgins's expert knowledge.[79] Higgins's extensive suggestions culminated in *Observations and Advices for the Improvement of the Manufacture of Muscovado Sugar and Rum* (1797), which earned the once-struggling lecturer a bonus of £1,000 and early retirement in the countryside when he returned to England in 1801.

Elizabeth's influence is also suggested by the flattering correspondence she received from scientists vying for her favour.[80] In 1797, for instance, William Drew wrote Elizabeth a scathing letter about Jan Ingenhousz, the Dutch chemist and physician to the Austrian empress Maria Theresa. William asked, 'How do you rate him as a Philosopher?!!!!!! Mercy on me!' He complained that Ingenhousz was 'tiresome with his experiments which are childish to a degree beyond belief'. In comparison, he claimed that his own 'experiment on oxygen' was a 'revolution in medical knowledge'.[81] This correspondence makes it clear that William respected Elizabeth's ability to grasp and elucidate on a range of scientific advances and valued her opinion (and patronage).

There are no existing copies of Elizabeth's own letters to these scientists, but it appears that she did take the opportunity of exchanging specimens and correspondence to put forward her own informed opinions in respect of the natural history of the sites she visited or on contemporary scientific debates. In the same letter of November

1797, William addressed her questions regarding the solidity of comets:

> I assume your Ladyship expects to canter us poor country folk with Herschel's conjecture that comets are thin airy nothings. Newton and Halley have long since demonstrated that comets are solid bodies moving around the sun in very elliptical orbits. Their heat, their velocity and the periods of their revolutions have been calculated by astronomers. Objects placed beyond them have been seen through their penumbra or atmosphere especially their tails, but never till now have I heard that such bodies have been seen through the body or nucleus of the comet. If Herschel has really seen such bodies by his powerful glasses and it is not a mere optical delusion I shall endeavour to account, as well as I can, for this extraordinary circumstance. Then I will suppose in the comet that Mr Herschel has observed that there is an immense hole or perforation through the nucleus of the comet dug by nature (not by human hands as the French academician Maupertuis proposes to be done through our globe as a shorter route to Antipodes) now nature might have made this hole by the operation of two immense volcanoes situated exactly opposite to each other on the body of the comet. Thus volcano A digs up and throws out if its crater the materials in the direction of the line C. Volcano B does the same in the opposite direction till in process of time their operations meet and form a hole whose diameter will be equal to the diameters of the crater of each volcano. Thus Herschel may have seen through this perforation an object placed beyond the body of the comet. If this be the case (though I am not fond of prying into holes of comets) I should like to have a peep through this extraordinary hole! Or second to, I will suppose that this comet in its revolution round the sun has become vitrified and rendered transparent like glass by the solar heat. Now you may adopt either or both of these hypotheses for they are both at your service and will serve I think to tickle the sensorium of Mr Macie [James Smithson]. Comets cannot, must not, be mere vapour. They would never revolve in regular orbits and move with immense velocity. No their motions would be as various and uncertain as that ignis fatuus a lady's love wafted to and fro by every fluff of wind![82]

This letter shows that Elizabeth actively engaged in scientific debate. It was only three months before, in August 1797, that the German astronomer Caroline Herschel famously discovered her eighth and last comet; the only one she discovered without an optical aid.[83]

Here, however, William was referring to her brother William Herschel's speculations in 1795 that comets lacked any solid material. It was Herschel's conjecture that, within a comet, 'the matter of light may enter into combination with some other subtle fluid and become latent, circulate imperceptibly so as only to become visible again when it is decomposed in the sun'.[84] However, although William addressed Elizabeth's well-informed query regarding Herschel's new theory, his comparison of a comet with 'a lady's love wafted to and fro by every fluff of wind!' suggests that he took it lightly. His rival Jan Ingenhousz's response to Elizabeth's questions was equally droll:

> As Lady Holland interests herself laudably with the planetary world, and was pleased by being informed that the solidity of the last comet, as that of all the former ones observed by Dr Herschel, was of the same nature as is the French Jacobin's liberty, their happiness, prosperity, and liberty of the press, as was that liberty of the press also, which the independent and Presbyterian Jacobins of last century established here, and which the present Jacobins will establish after the overturn of the constitution (quid Deus avertat!) that is to say, that the solidity was a negative one.[85]

This shows that while women were not necessarily considered intellectually less capable of learning science by men, their social roles were defined differently, with their learning largely considered for the purposes of artful conversation. When women ventured outside of this arena, they would likely receive for their efforts merely a response appropriate to a lady that did not encourage advancement. Elizabeth's privileged position did not leave her immune to this contradictory encouragement and disdain for women's involvement in science even though she was able to influence the direction of scientific research with her collecting and patronage.

While the seeds of the Holland House curiosity cabinet were laid during Elizabeth's Grand Tour, the specimens within it were gathered from across the globe, including Mexico, South America, Mauritius and New Guinea. The bulk of the Hollands' mineral collection (amounting to several thousand specimens, including large pieces of gold and silver ore) were from Mexico.[86] These specimens were likely products of Elizabeth and Henry's close links with Spain.[87] The couple travelled to Spain during the Peninsular War (1807–14) and it was in Henry's position as Spain's unofficial ambassador that the couple may have received the mineral collection. Elizabeth herself was renowned for obtaining quite a different Mexican specimen: the dahlia. She grew her famous colourful pinwheels from 'exotic seeds' procured during her first tour of Spain in 1803.[88] Native to Central America, where the Aztecs knew it as Cocoxochitl (or 'water pipe flower', for its hollow stem), the dahlia was first described to Europeans by Francisco Hernández, Philip II's physician, when he visited Mexico in 1570.[89] It was not until 1789, however, that the dahlia was introduced to Europe when the director of the Royal Gardens of Madrid, Abbe Antonio José Cavanilles, received tubers from the director of the Botanical Garden at Mexico City, Vicente Cervantes.[90] In 1791 he named the species *Dahlia* for Anders Dahl, the Swedish botanist and pupil of Linnaeus.[91] Elizabeth received some tubers from Cavanilles and grew a new species, *Dahlia sambucifolia*.[92] 'Dahlia mania' quickly spread and by the end of the nineteenth century there existed over 1,500 different varieties.[93] Twenty years after their tour of Spain, Henry commemorated his wife's role in sparking this mania in a poem:

> The Dahlia you brought to our isle,
> Your praises for ever shall speak,
> 'Mid gardens as sweet as your smile,
> And in colours as bright as your cheek.[94]

The small Malaga figures that were displayed in the anteroom adjoining the Hollands' sitting room were also curiosities from Elizabeth's first tour of Spain.[95] The miniature fandango dancers mirrored the Spanish dancing Elizabeth enjoyed with the 'townspeople' of Elche, Baix Vinalopó, in April 1803, when she 'sent for musicians who played *boleros*, *seguidillas*, and *ye fandango*'.[96] Similarly, the miniature bull fighters reminded her of that 'national amusement' where the '*banderilleros* ... equipped in the richest and most perfect Spanish costume', and the picadors, with their 'large-brimmed, shallow white hat, leather breeches and gaiters, and ... brown coloured vest' turned 'the fury of the bull'.[97] Through her specimens of natural history and porcelain figures, Elizabeth expressed her understanding of both the Spanish people and Spain's colony.

The Hollands also had an immense collection of specimens from South America. These included 'ninety-six boxes of stuffed birds, small quadrupeds, and reptiles'; gems from Brazil (one of which was euclase, a beryllium aluminium hydroxide silicate mineral noted for its blue colour, ranging from pale to dark); and a wool mantle said to have been presented to Santiago de Liniers, Count of Buenos Aires, by a 'princess, chief of cast'.[98] Most of these also likely came from the Hollands' close contacts in Spain. Many of the birds, however, were gifts from Henry's cousin Henry Stephen Fox, who offered to supply 'some stuffed birds from Buenos Ayres, if your ancient fancy for them continues', when he was made first minister-plenipotentiary and envoy-extraordinary at Buenos Aires in 1828.[99]

The Hollands in turn exchanged their New World specimens with the scientists of their network. In 1801 James Smithson wrote to see if Elizabeth had received the minerals he had sent from Dover a few months prior. In return Smithson asked if Henry would procure him some samples of the red crystals found in the riverbeds of Ceylon (Sri Lanka), which the British formally established as a crown colony the following year:

> I sent Lady Holland just before leaving this place, about three weeks ago, on an excursion along the coast, a small box containing some of the mineral productions of this neighbourhood, but not having heard from her since I know not whether it has reached her.
>
> As I see that the island of Ceylon is to be retained by this country, I hope that you have not forgotten your very obliging offer of endeavouring to procure for me some crystals from thence. What I mean are small crystals of different kinds of stone, well known, I believe ... They are found in the beds of rivers and, I have been told, along the sea shore. They cannot be rare, since I have known of small barrels full of them being brought to Europe. Tho' many of them are gems, they have ... no commercial value. They are used by the Dutch, I have heard, as a substitute for emery. Their colour is mostly red.[100]

This exchange clearly displays the relationship between imperialism and science. The mineral Smithson was referring to here was corundum. Opaque and hard, common corundum is used as an abrasive emery, but its transparent crystals, tinted red by chromium, or blue by iron and titanium, are better known as ruby and sapphire. Freed by weathering from rocks, they wind up in the gummy gravels of riverbeds.[101]

As the sole heiress to substantial New World wealth, Elizabeth benefitted greatly from imperialism. 'It is sometimes argued that science justified imperial expansion', Nicholas Thomas notes in his study of the curiosities from Cook's Pacific voyages, 'but it would seem closer to the mark that imperialism legitimised science'.[102] Elizabeth channelled much of her wealth into building a cabinet of curiosities that demonstrated her mastery over the globe's natural resources and her place in Britain and Spain's larger imperial ambitions and colonial projects. The continual building of this cabinet acted as a nexus for relationships with Europe's most renowned scientists and intellects. Just as Eliza Haywood created the *Female Spectator* to envision an alternative public sphere that parodied Addison and Steele's *Spectator* (see Chapter 4), in the material culture of Holland House Elizabeth fostered an intriguing manifestation of the societies from which she was excluded.

Elizabeth formed this scientific hub at the same time that, according to Londa Schiebinger, 'the French Revolution sounded the death knell of the privilege that aristocratic women had known in science' as Hume's 'sovereigns of the empire of conversation'.[103] Following her death in 1845, Elizabeth's physician Sir Henry Holland (who, despite the name, was not a relation) reflected that 'she left a more marked impression of her individuality than any woman of her age'.[104] One of the last great salon hostesses, Lady Holland was a polymath, able and expected to grasp and elucidate on a range of scientific and other topics at ease with those who frequented her salon. When science professionalised and divided into disciplines in the succeeding decades, however, such a position became far more difficult to claim. Moving into formal educational institutes intended to train men for careers of increasing complexity, science became less accessible to amateur men and women alike, with women's social roles leaving them particularly excluded.

Conclusion

The 'learned cabinets ... curiosities, collections, specimens, medals, and dissections ... books of every tongue and land ... and instruments of various sorts, telescopes, air pumps, tubes, retorts' of science played a central role in the global systematising project of the Enlightenment.[105] Caroline Powys, Dorothy Richardson and Lady

Elizabeth Holland all enlisted the material culture of scientific travel in their own projects of intellectual self-fulfilment. All three women were more alert to the scientific associations of the places they visited than most due to family or friends who supported their learning and familiarised them with scientific subjects.

The varied productions of the women, however, reflect their own specific interests, abilities and experiences. Initially encouraged to keep a journal by her father (who was the Surgeon in Chief at St Thomas's and a member of the Royal Society), Caroline made the most of her privileged position within a wealthy and educated family to travel and write. However, she found herself excluded from scientific pursuits and explicitly articulated this exclusion through the conflicted idea of 'curiosity'. Informed by one of the best libraries and an encouraging intellectual family, Dorothy made the most of the freedom of singledom to turn her leisured travels into purposeful research, but hers was a private pursuit, shared only with close family and friends. Inheriting a unique level of wealth and with a (second) husband supportive of her interests, Elizabeth initially used the collection of specimens of natural history to establish a familiarity and ease among Europe's key scientists on her Grand Tour. She developed this network following her return home by developing a rich cabinet by which she could command the 'social circulation of science'. Her collection, display and exchange of these objects with scientists from across Europe drew from imperialism's expropriation of land and natural resources, as well as its appropriation of the skills, knowledge and labour of Indigenous peoples.

These three women each contributed to the dissemination, if not the construction, of scientific knowledge. I would suggest, however, that what they collected and contributed was rather less important than the scientific spaces they created. Their projects turned the consumption of the commodities of polite science expected of their sex into the production of a scientific culture. Looking at the scientific meanings that Caroline, Dorothy and Elizabeth brought to the objects they collected allows us to draw unexplored parallels between domestic tours of Britain, Continental tours and the Enlightenment exploration of the New World. It reveals links between domestic travel and travel abroad, which both built, sustained and reinforced Enlightenment science and imperialism.

Notes

1 Noël Antoine Pluche, *Spectacle de la Nature: Or, Nature Display'd: Being Discourses on Such Particulars of Natural History as Were Thought Most Proper to Excite the Curiosity, and Form the Minds of Youth*, ed. Samuel Humphreys (London: J. Pemberton, 1733), 50–1.
2 Pluche, *Spectacle de la Nature*, 67.
3 Pluche, *Spectacle de la Nature*, 67.
4 Pluche, *Spectacle de la Nature*, 41–2.
5 Florentius was a descendant of the builder and owner of the *Mayflower*, which transported the first English puritans from England to the New Word. His property in Jamaica included 2,700 acres in Saint James Parish, 3,714 in Westmoreland Parish and 1,943 in Saint Elizabeth Parish. See 'Florentius Vassall: Profile & Legacies Summary, 1689–1778', Centre for the Study of Legacies of British Slavery, University College London (n.d.), accessed 29 February 2020, www.ucl.ac.uk/lbs/person/view/2146651009.
6 Elizabeth Vassall Fox Holland, *The Journal of Elizabeth Lady Holland (1791–1811)*, ed. Giles Stephen Fox-Strangways Ilchester (London: Longmans Green, 1908), vol. 1, 158.
7 Elizabeth Vassall Fox Holland, *Elizabeth, Lady Holland, to Her Son, 1821–1845*, ed. Giles Stephen Fox-Strangways Ilchester (London: J. Murray, 1946), 85.
8 Sonia Keppel, *The Sovereign Lady: A Life of Elizabeth Vassall, Third Lady Holland, with Her Family* (London: Hamilton, 1974), 6; A. J. West, *The Shakespeare First Folio: The History of the Book – A New World Census of First Folios* (Oxford: Oxford University Press, 2003), 87.
9 Holland, *Lady Holland, to Her Son*, 85; Mary Berry, *Extracts from the Journals and Correspondence of Miss Berry: From the Year 1783 to 1852*, ed. Lady Theresa Lewis (London: Longmans Green, 1865), vol. 1, 7.
10 Holland, *Journal*, vol. 1, 159.
11 Holland, *Journal*, vol. 1, 5.
12 Holland, *Journal*, vol. 1, 7.
13 Giorgio Pedrocco, 'Bonvicino (also known as Bonvoisin or Buonvicino) Costanzo Benedetto', *Complete Dictionary of Scientific Biography*, Encyclopedia.com, accessed 15 March 2020, https://bit.ly/3mPwIFV.
14 Holland, *Journal*, vol. 1, 7, 9, 51.
15 M. Gacto, 'The bicentennial of a forgotten giant: Lazzaro Spallanzani (1729–1799)', *International Microbiology* 2, 4 (1999): 273–4.

16 Andrea Candela, 'Biblical deluge and Creationism in eighteenth century Italy: an overview of the geological theory of Ermenegildo Pini (1739–1825)', in *INHIGEO Annual Record*, no. 46, ed. Wolf Mayer (Canberra: International Commission on the History of Geological Sciences, 2014), 67–72; Agnese Visconti, 'The naturalistic explorations of the Milanese Barnabite Ermenegildo Pini (1739–1825) along the coast of Calabria: new observations and implications with regard to his views on the history of the Earth', *Proceedings of the California Academy of Sciences* 59, no. 4 (2008): 51–63.

17 BL, Holland House Papers, Add. MS 51927, Lady Elizabeth Holland, 'Journals, etc.', 13 May 1792, fol. 8r°.

18 Holland, *Journal*, vol. 1, 65.

19 Marjorie Swann, *Curiosities and Texts: The Culture of Collecting in Early Modern England* (Philadelphia: University of Pennsylvania Press, 2001), 23.

20 Felix (Felice) Fontana, *Treatise on the Venom of the Viper: On the American Poisons; and on the Cherry Laurel, and Some Other Vegetable Poisons*, trans. Joseph Skinner (London: John Cuthell, 1795).

21 BL, Holland House Papers, Add. MS 51927, 26 June 1793, fol. 66r°.

22 BL, Holland House Papers, Add. MS 51927, 26 June 1793, fols 66r°–66v°.

23 BL, Holland House Papers, Add. MS 51927, 26 June 1793, fol. 67r°.

24 David Garrioch, 'From Christian friendship to secular sentimentality: Enlightenment re-evaluations', in *Friendship: A History*, ed. Barbara Caine (London: Equinox, 2009), 195.

25 Felice Fontana, *Saggio del Real Gabinetto di Fisica e di Storia Naturale* (Roma: Giovanni Zempel, 1775), 2.

26 Rebecca Messbarger, 'The re-birth of Venus in Florence's Royal Museum of Physics and Natural History', *Journal of the History of Collections* 25, no. 2 (2013): 205.

27 Messbarger, 'The re-birth of Venus', 195.

28 Ludmilla Jordanova, *Sexual Visions: Images of Gender in Science and Medicine Between the Eighteenth and Twentieth Centuries* (Madison: University of Wisconsin Press, 1993), 43–65.

29 Jordanova, *Sexual Visions*, 45.

30 Marguerite Blessington, *The Idler in Italy by the Countess of Blessington* (Paris: Baudry's European Library, 1839), 215.

31 Francesco Paolo De Ceglia, 'Rotten corpses, a disembowelled woman, a flayed man. Images of the body from the end of the 17th to the beginning of the 19th century. Florentine wax models in the first-hand accounts of visitors', *Perspectives on Science* 14, no. 4 (2006): 417–56.

32 JRL, Dorothy Richardson Papers, GB 133 Eng MS 1124, Dorothy Richardson, 'London', 1775 and 1785, fols. 336–7.
33 Holland, *Journal*, vol. 1, 117.
34 Quoted in Joan B. Landes, 'Wax fibers, wax bodies, and moving figures', in *Ephemeral Bodies: Wax Sculpture and the Human Figure*, ed. Roberta Panzanelli (Los Angeles: Getty Research Institute, 2008), 52.
35 Quoted in Landes, 'Wax fibers, wax bodies, and moving figures', 58.
36 Katharine Park, *Secrets of Women: Gender, Generation, and the Origins of Human Dissection* (New York: Zone Books, 2006), 221.
37 Holland, *Journal*, vol. 1, 139.
38 Holland, *Journal*, vol. 2, 294–5.
39 BL, Holland House Papers, Add. MS 51927, 26 May 1793, fol. 58v^o.
40 Holland, *Journal*, vol. 1, 63–64.
41 They would go on to have a further five children (with one dying in infancy). Following Godfrey's suicide in 1800, Henry too assumed the name Vassall to protect his children's rights to Elizabeth's inheritance; see C. J. Wright, 'Fox, Elizabeth Vassall [née Elizabeth Vassall], Lady Holland [other married name Elizabeth Vassall Webster, Lady Webster] (1771?–1845)', *Oxford Dictionary of National Biography*, last updated 3 January 2008, https://doi.org/10.1093/ref:odnb/10028.
42 Wright, 'Fox, Elizabeth Vassall'.
43 Harriet Granville, *Hary-O: the letters of Lady Harriet Cavendish, 1796–1809*, ed. George Leveson-Gower and Iris Palmer (London: J. Murray, 1940), 7.
44 Giles Stephen Fox-Strangways Ilchester, *The Home of the Hollands 1605–1820* (London: John Murray, 1937), 136.
45 Susanne Schmid, *British Literary Salons of the Late Eighteenth and Early Nineteenth Centuries* (New York: Palgrave Macmillan, 2013), 99–100. For more detailed biographical sketches of Lady Holland's guests, see also Lloyd C. Sanders, *The Holland House Circle* (New York: B. Blom, 1969); BL, Holland House Papers, Add. MS 51827, Correspondence of Alexander von Humboldt to Lord Holland, 1813.
46 Charles Greville, *The Greville Memoirs: A Journal of the Reigns of King George IV and King William IV*, ed. Richard Henry Stoddard (New York: Scribner, Armstrong, 1875), 236.
47 Henry Holland, *Recollections of Past Life* (New York: D. Appleton, 1872), 228.
48 T. Faulkner and B. West, *History and Antiquities of Kensington* (London: T. Egerton, 1820), 95.
49 Marie Henriette Norberte Liechtenstein, *Holland House* (London: Macmillan, 1874), 244.

50 Stacey Sloboda, 'Displaying materials: porcelain and natural history in the Duchess of Portland's museum', *Eighteenth-Century Studies* 43, no. 4 (2010): 459.
51 C. J. Wright, 'Holland House and the fashionable pursuit of science: a nineteenth-century cabinet of curiosities', *Journal of the History of Collections* 1, no. 1 (1989): 101; Liechtenstein, *Holland House*, 244.
52 Holland, *Journal*, vol. 1, 26.
53 For more on women Grand Tourists and Vesuvius, see Emma Gleadhill, '"Upon the whole I expect he took me for an aventurière": eighteenth-century British women tourists' accounts of mountains and mountaineering', in *The Mountain and the Politics of Representation*, ed. Jenny Hall and Martin Hall (Liverpool: Liverpool University Press, forthcoming 2022).
54 Berry, *Extracts from the Journals and Correspondence*, vol. 1, 92.
55 Quoted in Rosemary Sweet, *Cities and the Grand Tour: The British in Italy, c.1690–1820* (Cambridge: Cambridge University Press, 2012), 55.
56 Holland, *Journal*, vol. 1, 143.
57 Faulkner and West, *History and Antiquities of Kensington*, 92.
58 Faulkner and West, *History and Antiquities of Kensington*, 92.
59 Faulkner and West, *History and Antiquities of Kensington*, 92.
60 Faulkner and West, *History and Antiquities of Kensington*, 112.
61 Sloboda, 'Displaying materials', 457.
62 Wright, 'Holland House and the fashionable pursuit of science', 100.
63 Frederick G. Meyer and Susanne Elsasser, 'The 19th century herbarium of Isaac C. Martindale', *Taxon* 22, no. 4 (1973): 390.
64 BL, Holland House Papers, Add. MS 51814, William Drew 'Letter to Lady Holland', 7 November 1797, fols 45r°–48r°.
65 Walter Schumann, *Gemstones of the World* (New York and London: Sterling, 2009), 118.
66 BL, Holland House Papers, Add. MS 51821, Correspondence of James Smithson to Lord Holland and Correspondence of John Ingenhousz to Lord and Lady Holland, 29 July 1797.
67 The first collections of crystal models were produced by the French mineralogist Jean-Baptiste Louis Romé de l'Isle, who offered sets of up to 448 models made of terracotta, measuring 3 cm, to stimulate sales of his expensive four-volume book *Cristallographie* (1783).
68 BL, Holland House Papers, Add. MS 51598, Correspondence of Lord Boringdon to Lady Holland, 2 March 1798, fol. 124.
69 Martin Guntau, 'The rise of geology as a science in Germany around 1800', in *The Making of the Geological Society*, ed. C. L. E. Lewis and S. J. Knell, 163–78 (Bath: Geological Society of London, 2009).

70 BL, Holland House Papers, Add. MS 51846, Robert Gordon, 'Letter to Lady Holland', 11 July 1800.
71 'Schmeisser, Johann Gottfried', in C. E. Waterston and A. Macmillan Shearer, *Former Fellows of The Royal Society of Edinburgh 1783 – 2002*, vol. 2 (Edinburgh: Royal Society of Edinburgh, 2006), 826.
72 BL, Holland House Papers, Add. MS 51846, Correspondence of Robert Gordon to Lady Holland and Correspondence of James Smithson to Lady Holland, 10 November 1801.
73 Holland House Papers, Add. MS 51846, 10 November 1801.
74 Heather Ewing, *The Lost World of James Smithson: Science, Revolution and the Birth of the Smithsonian* (London: Bloomsbury, 2010).
75 Holland, *Journal*, vol. 1, 97.
76 William Kirby Sullivan, *Memoir of Bryan Higgins, M. D. and of William Higgins, Professor of Chemistry to the Royal Dublin Society: With a Short Notice of Irish Chemists and the State of Chemistry in Ireland Before the Year 1800* (Dublin: Hodges & Smith, 1849), 19.
77 William Gibbs, 'Bryan Higgins and his circle', in *Chemistry in Britain*, ed. Royal Institute of Chemistry (London: Chemical Education Trust Fund, 1965), 60–5; Charles Mollan, *It's Part of What We Are*, vol. 1 (Dublin: Royal Dublin Society, 2007).
78 'Obituary, William Lewis', in Sylvanus Urban, *The Gentleman's Magazine and Historical Chronicle: From January to June, 1823*, vol. 133 (London: John Nichols, 1823), 185.
79 David Beck Ryden, "Sugar, spirits, and fodder: the London West India interest and the glut of 1807–15', *Atlantic Studies* 9, no. 1 (2012): n. 16.
80 BL, Holland House Papers, Add. MS 51845, Correspondence of C. H. Titius to Lady Holland, L. J. Murith to Lady Holland, Targioni Tozzetti to Lady Holland, 1792–98.
81 BL, Holland House Papers, Add. MS 51814, Correspondence of William Drew to Lady Holland, 7 November 1797, fol. 46v°.
82 BL, Holland House Papers, Add. MS 51814, 7 November 1797, fol. 46r°.
83 Michael Hoskin, *William and Caroline Herschel: Pioneers in Late 18th-Century Astronomy* (Dordrecht: Springer, 2013), 50.
84 Simon Schaffer, '"The great laboratories of the universe": William Herschel on matter theory and planetary life', *Journal for the History of Astronomy* 11 (1980): 93.
85 BL, Holland House Papers, Add. MS 51821, 24 December 1797.
86 Faulkner and West, *History and Antiquities of Kensington*, 92.
87 For more on the Holland House collection, including the Hollands' Spanish connection, see Emma Gleadhill, 'Performing travel: Lady

Holland's Grand Tour souvenirs and the "House of All Europe"', *eMaj (electronic Melbourne art journal)*, special issue 9.1, 'Cosmopolitan moments: instances of exchange in the long eighteenth century', ed. Jennifer Milam (December 2017).
88 Faulkner and West, *History and Antiquities of Kensington*, 124–5.
89 Claire Shaver Haughton, *Green Immigrants: The Plants That Transformed America* (New York: Harcourt, Brace, Jovanovich, 1978), 91.
90 Haughton, *Green Immigrants*, 77.
91 Haughton, *Green Immigrants*, 93–4.
92 William Nicholson, *A Journal of Natural Philosophy, Chemistry and the Arts*, vol. 22 (London: G. G. and J. Robinson, 1809), 228.
93 Twigs Way, *Virgins, Weeders and Queens: A History of Women in the Garden* (Cheltenham: History Press, 2013).
94 Liechtenstein, *Holland House*, 176.
95 Faulkner and West, *History and Antiquities of Kensington*, 112.
96 Elizabeth Vassall Fox Holland, *The Spanish Journal of Elizabeth Lady Holland*, ed. Giles Stephen Fox-Strangways Ilchester (London: Longmans, Green, 1910), 38.
97 Holland, *Spanish Journal*, 64.
98 Faulkner and West, *History and Antiquities of Kensington*, 92.
99 BL, Holland House Papers, Add. MS 51613, Correspondence of H. S. Fox to Lord Holland, 7 March 1828.
100 BL, Holland House Papers, Add. MS 51822, Correspondence of James Smithson to Lord Holland, 3 December 1801.
101 Frederick H. Pough and Roger T. Peterson, *Peterson First Guide to Rocks and Minerals* (Boston and New York: Houghton Mifflin, 1998), 60.
102 Nicholas Thomas, 'Licenced curiosity: Cook's Pacific Voyages', in *The Cultures of Collecting*, ed. John Elsner and Roger Cardinal (London: Reaktion Books, 1994), 116.
103 Londa Schiebinger, *The Mind Has No Sex?: Women in the Origins of Modern Science* (Cambridge, MA: Harvard University Press, 1991), 147.
104 John Fyvie, *Noble Dames and Notable Men of the Georgian Era* (New York: John Lane Company, 1911), 173.
105 Holland, *Journal*, vol. 2, 294–5.

Part III

Gendering friendship

7

From diplomatic gift to trifle from Tunbridge Wells

When Horace Walpole used the French term *souvenir* in his note to Anne Fitzpatrick, Countess of Upper Ossery, in 1775, he used it in the sense of a memory of friend's hospitality: 'You have always been so good to me, Madam, and I am so grateful that if all my *souvenirs* were marked with cups, there would be many more than mile stones from hence to Ampthill'.[1] By attaching the note to a cup, he also indicated that a souvenir was an object that could reduce the physical distance between friends.[2] Horace and Anne clearly had a close relationship, one that they had developed through fourteen years of correspondence between London and Bedfordshire, beginning in 1761 when Anne sent Horace a memory of her shadow in the form of a silhouette.[3]

In the following three decades, the word 'souvenir' was used in sentimental fiction to describe a memento given to a friend prior to (rather than following) a period of separation. In 1782 James Douglas's *Travelling Anecdotes* described a young country girl sobbingly asking a friend who was taking her leave 'if she was certain, that the little *souvenir* she gave her was safe in her pocket'.[4] In 1803 Maria Edgeworth attributed to one of her characters the desire to 'offer *souvenirs* to her English friends'.[5] The word 'keepsake' is dated to the same period and was used interchangeably. In 1794, for example, in Ann Radcliff's *The Mysteries of Udolpho*, the heroine's maidservant, Annette, referred to a 'beautiful new sequin, which Ludovico [another servant] gave me for a keep-sake', and which she 'would not part with ... for all St. Marco's Place'.[6] Whether termed a souvenir or a keepsake, the objects described in all of these instances were given as a means of resisting a physical separation, and the moment of exchange was laden with emotion.

In 1803 in a letter to her sister Harriet, Martha Wilmot wrote of exchanging keepsakes with her aunts and cousins during her journey to St Petersburg:

> A few mornings ago, Maria brought me a very elegant volume of the pleasures of memory with my name in it. To my great satisfaction, I had a fortunate opportunity of making a slight return by giving her a pair of *Limerick* gloves, but she vow'd to be *revenged*, and the next day I found on my Dressing Table, a beautiful necklace to match a garnet gown I had just got. Bell pop'd a pair of bracelets of her own workmanship into my *night cap*. Silena a little chain. Fanny got a most beauteous wreath of peach blossoms for my new hat. In short, at every *turn* I meet with fluttering proofs, of their friendship and attention for me, and (tho you know I have an unconquerable aversion to *presents*) I cannot help feeling highly gratified by the affection which these imply.[7]

Despite her 'unconquerable aversion to presents', the concatenation of the three obligations of giving, receiving and making a return gift once one has been accepted, bound Martha in a continuous process of exchanging keepsakes with other women throughout her travels.[8] A great deal of time and effort went into selecting or producing accoutrements intimately connected to the body of the giver or receiver. In 1804 Martha noted in her journal that she was fashioning a 'bracelet of my hair' with a female friend to send to her older sister Katherine, who would later join her in Russia. Here she meticulously recorded the processes involved in its creation, by which she 'counted 13 little locks of 40 hairs in each parcel', which her friend fastened to '13 different bobbins' and pinned to a large cushion, before further dividing and weaving them together.[9] This keepsake was time, labour and affection made concrete. It literally embodied something of Martha.

Both Martha and the women she exchanged keepsakes with expressed deep emotional attachments to these objects that they took care to memorialise in journals and letters. For instance, Martha noted in her journal that her host in Russia, the Princess Ekaterina Dashkova, kept a pair of her gloves, which she 'bath[ed] with tears' and 'kiss'd … a hundred times for my sake' during her absence. When Ekaterina later returned these gloves, Martha wrote, 'never will I wear them after all the affection, all the sentiment they have given rise to'; she would instead 'keep them as a *talisman* of affection'.[10]

The female giver and receiver's emotional written reflections on the moment of exchange fostered and intensified their relationships with both the objects themselves and with each other. Sentimental fiction (including the 'very elegant volume of the pleasures of memory with my name in it'), encouraged women like Martha to commit the personal meanings of their keepsakes to paper.

This chapter is about a shift that occurred in the eighteenth century towards the sentimentalisation of female–female relationships before, during and after travel, demonstrated through keepsakes. This period marked a transition from a formal mode of gift-giving, by which women travellers exchanged objects representing local manufacture with female acquaintances from their travels and female family and friends at home, to a sentimental mode of gift-giving, by which the means of production mattered less than the object's role as a surrogate for a person. In the pages that follow, I will trace the shift from a more detached form of gift exchange to sentimental keepsake exchange through the journals and letters of women travellers, and how this interwove with the development of sentimental travel literature and a tourist industry for mass-produced knick-knacks. The feminist conceptualisation of women's close relationships from the eighteenth to the early twentieth century as 'romantic friendships' has obscured the social, political and economic uses to which they put sentiment.[11] Rather than debating the character or meaning of eighteenth-century women's close relationships, I am interested in how the material expression of passionate commitment served them. I argue that women travellers amplified their female–female friendships through keepsake exchange to circumvent their social, political and economic dependence on men.

Exchanged between travelling nobles, officials, dignitaries and courts within strictly controlled ceremonies since biblical times, gifts have long functioned as mementos of visits and important occasions. In the eighteenth century, male and female royals took part in this activity on their Grand Tours. On his Tour of France, Spain and Italy from 1738 to 1740, Crown Prince Friedrich Christian of Saxony (later King of Poland), for example, was not only presented to Louis XIV at Versailles, but received precious gifts as part of their meeting that are registered in the Present du Roi.[12] Travelling in 1793, Georgiana Spencer, Duchess of Devonshire, received an antique stag's head from King Charles III when she visited the Royal Palace at Caserta.[13] In both of these cases it was royal status that first and foremost defined the relationship.

The exchange of items of local manufacture or significance and miniature portraits contributed to the cultivation of a certain trans-European class consciousness, an identification that linked the royals of Britain with their counterparts on the Continent and imposed a sense that they shared common rights and concerns.[14] Gifts usually took the form of art or rarities that were mined, grown or otherwise unique to a kingdom and represented the highest quality of artistry and workmanship, so symbolising the majesty and legitimacy of a ruler and their lands.[15] Popular gifts included guns, tapestries, clocks, snuff-boxes and porcelain. Another preferred gift was a portrait of a ruler, which took the form of either a pendant comprised of a painted miniature in a precious frame, or a portrait medal.

Noble and gentry women also travelled with gifts in Britain and Europe. Throughout the eighteenth century it was common, even expected, for women to exchange gifts with the women they met during their travels and to send gifts home to female family and friends. Gifts made between elite women served to strengthen ties of horizontal friendship by confirming gentility and sustaining acquaintance. The extreme inequality between the sexes during the period meant that gifts from their menfolk incorporated women into a vertical system of patronage, under which the top-down flow of property and status provided the foundations for social structures.[16] A woman giver and male receiver did not make sense within either the horizontal female–female and male–male friendship system or the male–female vertical relationship system, hence it was most common for women travellers to give gifts to other women.

One location from which women commonly bought gifts for each other was the English spa town of Tunbridge Wells, well known for its wooden wares. Tunbridge Wells, like other spa towns, was a largely homosocial environment.[17] Women travelled to spas with female friends and relatives and they expected to enjoy their company during their stay while being served by female staff. This tradition dated back to the late seventeenth century, when Katherine Percival travelled to France's celebrated mineral spas, accompanied by her daughters Helena and Katherine, her maid Betty Willis and housekeeper Deborah Fowler.[18] The baths themselves were sex-segregated spaces, shaped by rigidly prescribed rules.[19] In 1697 Celia Fiennes observed on her visit to Tunbridge Wells that there were 'such a number of Guides to each both of women to waite on ye ladyes, and of men to waite on the Gentlemen, and they keepe their due distance'.[20] She also observed the twenty to twenty-five shops on the town's main street offering visitors silver, ceramics, fine cloth, lace and a 'curious wooden ware which this place is noted for, the delicate neate and thin ware of wood both white and lignum vitae wood'.[21] These wooden wares included portable writing desks, tea caddies, workboxes, cups, casters and spice boxes and were popular gifts for women visitors to give to female friends and family throughout the eighteenth century.[22]

Women's letters from Tunbridge Wells in the show that its wooden wares served as part of a larger regular exchange of trinkets between women from the early eighteenth century. These wares and other trinkets were a form of relationship currency between women. For instance, in 1745 Lady Elizabeth Montagu sent her friend Margaret Cavendish Bentinck, the Duchess of Portland, some Tunbridge-ware. In the accompanying letter to Margaret, Elizabeth expressed her concern that 'in your magnificence you will despise, but I desire it may be sent to your Dairy, and there humbler thoughts will possess you, and churns of butter, prints, and skimming dishes will appear of consequence'.[23] As Helmuth Berking has noted of gift-giving in general, intimate knowledge of the other person involved in gift exchanges arouses 'expectations and expectations of expectations' that 'call for expression and demand satisfaction'. A receiver expects to receive a gift that is appropriate to their social status and the relationship they have with the giver. Further, 'the closer one is, the more chance there is of finding what is "just right" – but also the more risk of "putting one's foot in it"'.[24] The worry Elizabeth expressed over how Margaret – at that time the richest woman in Britain – would conceive her 'humble' wooden wares shows her care to precisely demarcate the status of the receiver and to select items appropriate to that status. By getting the gift right, Elizabeth confirmed her gentility and strengthened her friendship. This friendship was horizontal because both the giver and receiver were women, even if the Duchess outranked Elizabeth socially.

Those elite women who had the opportunity to undertake a Grand Tour also sent gifts to their female friends. Writing from Florence in February 1740, Henrietta Fermor, Countess of Pomfret, offered to supply her friend Frances Seymour, Countess of Hertford, 'from hence with alabaster vases, small brass statues, or marble and paste tables extremely fine and beautiful ... for I must have a representative in your grotto, where retired from company, I would sometimes steal your remembrance'.[25] Lady Hertford selected the alabaster vases for her grotto, writing in response:

> You confound me, dear madam, by requesting me to choose you a representative in my grotto: you will never want one in my heart; where your image is immovably fixed, with every amiable quality to adorn and secure its seat. But, if I am to have yet another proof of your generosity, I must prefer the alabaster vases, which may serve as a monument of the happiness I enjoy in your friendship; and I shall take care to place them so that an inscription can be put under them, that may perpetuate the memory of what I am so justly proud of.[26]

This gift formed part of a three-year exchange of letters between the two women from 1738, when Henrietta set out on a Grand Tour with her husband and two daughters. As Lizzie Rogers has noted, it cemented a friendship between the two women built on an epistolary exchange about discovery, learning and collecting.[27] Importantly, Frances took care to note the sentimental value of the vases, reflecting when they arrived that 'there being a mark of your friendship enhances their value to me even beyond their own merit'.[28]

Gifts between daughters and mothers were common and indicated familial affection in the face of physical separation. An early traveller who wrote of sending a gift of Tunbridge-ware home was twenty-seven-year-old Mary Delany, the daughter of Colonel Bernard Granville and Mary Westcombe, who would later become known for her botanic paper mosaics. In 1727 Mary sent a case of Tunbridge-ware to her sister Anne and mother with the following note attached:

> there is a little Tunbridge jewel box which Mrs. Tillier desires you to accept as her fairing and two Tunbridge voiders, which I hope mama will not think me saucy, if I desire the favour of her to make use of.[29]

The wooden wares would have been valued by Mary's mother and sister both in and of themselves and as material proof of a daughter and sibling's kind thoughts. Mary's reference to the jewel box as a 'fairing' from her female travelling companion suggests that she was following a social convention by sending Tunbridge-ware home and recognised the importance of material observance of that convention.

To the modern reader well accustomed to social conventions around sending family and friends souvenirs from one's travels, this exchange seems innocuous. For an early eighteenth-century woman, however, it reflected a modest level of female agency brought about by the ability to travel and to purchase gifts on one's travels. When business and commercial ventures took eighteenth-century husbands or fathers to towns, they would fulfil their wives' and daughters' commissions, rarely returning from such trips without an additional parcel of toys and novelties.[30] Travelling to Tunbridge Wells allowed Mary to instead fulfil this male patronage role. She disrupted a male-to-female flow of material goods with a gift between women. Gerald and Valerie Mars have written of this dynamic between the 1880s and 1950s, when working-class British daughters brought mass-produced ceramic ornaments home to their mothers from their seaside holidays in Blackpool, Lancashire. They argue that these gifts helped working-class women to 'short circuit' male control of household spending and build female gender links between generations, so contributing to 'gender-based conflict built into the north of England's working-class households'.[31] It was those elite women travelling in the early to mid-eighteenth century who began this practice, exercising their agency in the face of long-standing male–female benefaction.

Estranged mothers could also request forgiveness from their daughters with travel gifts. When she set out on her Grand Tour in 1785, Hester Piozzi wrote in her journal of her regret that her three daughters remained 'unreconciled to my choice [to marry their music teacher, Gabriel] (all at least except the eldest who parted with me cooly, not unkindly)'.[32] Throughout her travels she sent small accoutrements home to them in an attempt to salvage their relationship. In a 1785 letter to her friend Samuel Lysons, for instance, Hester remarked that her youngest daughters, Susan and Sophie, had recently 'thanked me for a little Box I sent them at the same Time as yours, with Female trifles in it'.[33] These gifts were typically items of local manufacture, like the samples of Calais lacework, which Hester referred to in her journal as 'some joys to send my younger daughters in England'.[34]

Such locally manufactured gifts could be enlisted to authenticate women's accounts of their travel experiences in their letters; the materiality of the objects proving that they had been to the locations described. The letters themselves sometimes fulfilled both the role of travel account and locally manufactured gift. 'Here is a manufactory of paper, of which you may yourself judge', Lady Anna Miller wrote to her mother from Bologna in 1770, 'as I have wrote many of my letters from hence upon what they esteem the first sort; the bluish cast is given by a sort of gum mixed with it when in a fluid state, as I understood from them'.[35] The material qualities of this letter authenticated Anna's account of her visit to the paper workshop by materially proving that she had witnessed the manufacturing process that she described.

These are some of the diverse meanings that women travellers could attach to the objects they gave female friends and family. But what of gifts from women to men? The unequal relationship between the sexes during the period rendered this difficult, but there are a few examples of women sending gifts home to their brothers or fathers. In 1804, for instance, Martha Wilmot sent the handle of a knife home to her brother Robert, and 'a top of a walking stick … which is precious' to her father.[36] In a society where a vertical gift-giving relationship typically operated in the opposite direction – that is, male family members would usually bring gifts home to female family members – it must have given Martha some satisfaction to reverse this arrangement. She was only able to do so because, unusually, she was not travelling with her menfolk and her host in Russia, the Princess Ekaterina Dashkova, inhabited such a position that she could provide Martha with expensive gifts to send home. The subtleties of the relationship between Martha and Ekaterina will be analysed further in Chapter 9.

Gift exchange between women and men who were unmarried and unrelated was even more problematic, with the inequality between the sexes rendering it liable to be interpreted in sexual terms. There are very few instances of women sending gifts to male friends. One of these is in 1785 when Hester sent a gift home to the antiquarian and engraver Samuel Lysons from Milan. She wrote to him:

> Young Bartolozzi, Son of our great Engraver: who is returning to England after visiting his Friends in Italy, and promised to take Care of your Fossills, and deliver them Safe into your own hand … My hope is that you will like your Petrefactions; they are Fish preserved in Slates very curious. Baron Cronthal the great Naturalist gave them to me, out of his own private Collection, with an account of whence they came, on the Paper that contains them.[37]

Hester's decision to give Samuel these specimens reflects the friends' shared interest in science. On a conceptual level, the choice of specimens as a gift also served to repudiate the dominant view, among both men and women, that men were rational while women were guided by their emotions, and that men were, therefore, capable of a 'true' friendship while women were only capable of love.[38] By giving Samuel some specimens, which she in turn had been given by another man, Hester was showing that the pair were fully capable of having a rational, intellectual friendship, rather than an affectionate relationship.

Always the exception due to her privileged position as a West Indian heiress, on her 1791 Grand Tour Lady Elizabeth Holland unusually bought a gift for her lover Thomas Pelham, second Earl of Chichester, who was also the political patron of her first husband. In her journal she wrote:

> I purchased a gun and a pair of pistols of the famous Kerkenruyter to make a present to Mr. Pelham. The maker stated he had sold to Col. Lennox the identical pair he used against the Duke of York. It was scarcely fair to use such sure weapons.[39]

Three years earlier Charles Lennox, fourth Duke of Richmond, had served as a colonel in the regiment of Prince Frederick, Duke of York and Albany. The pair had a duel after Frederick accused Charles of failing to respond to an insult in the manner of a gentleman. The tale of a duel between gentlemen was a fitting for a gift to a man with whom Elizabeth was having an affair. In return, Thomas sent Elizabeth a chemical laboratory.[40] With this gift exchange, Elizabeth went beyond Hester to completely reverse the broadly accepted ideas of male rationality and female emotionality. Elizabeth's gift to Thomas instead demonstrated the volatility of men's emotions, while his gift to her showed a respect for women's rational pursuits. This indicates the power of the travel gift as a narrative object that a woman in a privileged position of authority could use to put dominant views into question.

All the examples of gift exchange explored thus far occurred in the eighteenth century. It is clear that the women used their gifts to express affection. In general, however, the women's reactions to the moment of exchange were not overtly emotional and they did not long contemplate their connection to the person through the object.

The objects were gifts – for the receiver to value, but not to sentimentally cherish. There is one exception: Henrietta Fermor gave Frances Seymour the alabaster vases to represent herself in her friend's grotto. Frances wrote that she treasured the vases for their sentimental value and added an inscription to them to perpetuate the memory of the friendship. This indicates something of a cultural shift from gift to keepsake that was underway, but the language was still in formation because Frances called the vases a 'monument'. In the last decades of the century, women travellers increasingly wrote about the objects they exchanged with their friends in sentimental ways, more of their writings were published and the terms 'souvenir' and 'keepsake' entered the lexicon. By the early nineteenth century, the emotional attachments that the givers and receivers formed with the objects became as fraught with consequence as the emotional attachments that they had with each other.[41]

This sentimentality of female friendship and the accompanying rise of the keepsake was informed by the emergence of sensibility as a genteel virtue in the eighteenth century – sensibility indicated not only by the capacity to feel as others did but also, as a correspondent to London's *Monthly Magazine* put it in 1796, 'that peculiar structure, or habitude, of mind, which disposes man to be easily moved, and powerfully affected, by surrounding objects'.[42] If one were particularly sensitive one might react emotionally to objects that appear insignificant to another. This reactivity was considered an indication of a person's ability to perceive something intellectually or emotionally stirring in the world around them. It signalled their gentility.

Expressing sentiment about a gifted object, then, became an easy way to show one's sensibility, and by extension one's social status. This privileging emotional reactions to the material world was informed by the empiricist philosophy of John Locke. According to Locke, the 'conscious thinking thing', the self, was the summation of parts as small as one's 'little finger', all joined together by the same consciousness. He observed that if the little finger were to become separate and 'should this consciousness go along with the little Finger, and leave the rest of the Body, tis evident the little Finger would be the *Person*; the *same Person*; and Self then would have nothing to do with the rest of the Body'.[43] An object that had passed from the hand of one friend to another, then, was a potent vehicle for feeling. Gifted gloves, fans, hats, locks of hair, snuff-boxes and miniature portraits came to be seen as surrogates for individuals – that is, as keepsakes.

The transition from travel gift to keepsake in this period is perhaps most clearly spelt out in Laurence Sterne's *A Sentimental Journey* (1768). Sterne travelled through France and Italy in 1765, and after returning decided to describe his travels from the sentimental point of view of the character of the travelling parson Yorick. The novel was extremely popular and helped establish travel literature as the dominant genre of the second half of the eighteenth century. In one of the best-known scenes from the book, Yorick refuses to give alms to a monk and dismisses him as a parasite. The parson realises his fault later when he sees the monk talking to an attractive lady. Yorick offers the monk a tortoiseshell snuff-box to make amends and in return receives a less-valuable horn snuff-box. The monk thus gains the difference in value between the two snuff-boxes, while Yorick gains the sentiment. With the period's shift in emphasis from blood and breeding to refinement as the key source of social distinction, a man of feeling like Yorick did not need to have distinguished ancestors to be worthy of consideration. He could demonstrate his feeling (and social distinction) by placing sentimental value on otherwise mundane objects.

Sterne's travel tale was so popular that accounts exchanging snuff-boxes as keepsakes continued a decade later. In the *London Magazine* of 1782, a travelling gentleman correspondent wrote fondly of his snuff-box. The traveller's friend gave him the small wooden box when he departed for Margate. He swore that he would 'take it with me and whenever I take a pinch out of it, the remembrance of you will draw a pleasing veil of calmness over my breast, and soften the bitterness of separation'. Indeed, the traveller claimed that he would not 'take snuff as most people do – simply and purely for the sake of the said snuff – or as an amusement – or for the air of it – for that I absolutely despair; but for the sake of the sentiment that will accompany it'.[44] He termed this 'sentimental snuff-taking'. Formerly a diplomatic gift between royal families, valued for its liquidity, in the hands of the genteel the snuff-box had a sentimental value that trumped monetary worth.

While these examples are of male–male keepsake exchange, women – ostensibly emotional beings – were seen to exemplify sensibility.

In the late eighteenth and early nineteenth centuries there was a literary phenomenon of women writing novels about female characters weakening, fainting or having outpourings in reaction to an emotionally moving experience: 'I must, I will love you; and love you forever', women in these books told one another, 'I love you, as never woman loved another'.[45] In the second half of the twentieth century, feminist scholars reclaimed such open expressions of passionate emotional commitment between women from the likes of sexologists like Havelock Ellis, who they argued had invented the stereotype of 'the lesbian' to condemn close relationships between women. Rather, they termed these relationships and the expression of them 'romantic friendship' and claimed that their romantic character was widely recognised and accepted during the period.[46] I argue that this scholarly debate about the nature of the relationships between women from the eighteenth to the early twentieth century has caused historians to overlook how women used sentiment as a deliberately extreme narrative device to both express their gentility and to skirt their social, political and economic reliance on men. This is not to say that women did not experience these emotions, but the fact that an affected display of them became a key feature of women's (and, for a very short period, men's) writing suggests that they must have had a social, political and economic currency in late eighteenth and early nineteenth-century Britain.

In *Maria or the Wrongs of Women* (1798) Mary Wollstonecraft pointed to the ways in which women's subordination and their economic dependence on men for survival destroyed any sense of solidarity or friendship between them.[47] She did this through the sufferings of Maria, a woman who was incarcerated in an asylum by a dishonest husband. Yet, she also suggested that women could offer each other a kind of devotion and selfless love unknown to men through a cross-class friendship between Maria and Jemima, the asylum warden who helped her to escape.[48] Women romanticised female friendships to strengthen these horizontal bonds between themselves, to the point that they were stronger than the vertical bonds that tied them to their menfolk in an unequal relationship. The best way to do this was through the exchange of objects, their materiality giving substance to the relationship, and through travel because, as the saying goes, absence makes the heart grow fonder.

We see something of this empowering practice in Tunbridge Wells in the late eighteenth century. In 1779 the novelist Fanny Burney travelled to the Kent town with Hester Piozzi (at this time still married to her first husband, Henry Thrale). The pair spent their first evening at their friend Miss Streatfield's, who lived with her mother in Mount Ephraim.[49] On the second morning of their stay, Fanny and Hester were introduced to the ten-year-old niece of their acquaintance Mrs Pleydell: the 'sweet' Miss Birch, who sang for them over breakfast. Fanny was struck by the girl's voice, which she found 'charming – infinitely the most powerful, as well as sweet, I ever heard at her age'.[50] Fanny noted that

> Mrs Thrale was so much enchanted with her that she went on the Pantiles and bought her a very beautiful ink stand.
> 'I don't mean, Miss Birch' she said, when she gave it her, 'to present you this toy as to a child, but merely to beg you will do me the favour to accept something that may make you know and then remember us'.[51]

Unlike in the previous examples of Tunbridge-ware gift exchange from 1727 and 1745, this object was intended as a keepsake for Miss Birch to 'know and remember' Hester and her Bluestocking circle. Fanny reflected that Miss Birch was 'much delighted with this present and told me, in a whisper, that she should put a drawing of it in her journal'.[52] By giving the ink stand to the young female acquaintance, Hester materially supported her pursuit of singing (which she had the opportunity to practice), writing and drawing (which she promised to do in return for the keepsake). Hester thus supported the girl's intellectual pursuits and formed a friendship that extended the Bluestocking circle to the next generation.

Aristocratic women also used sentimental keepsake exchange to bolster friendships with women of their own social status, or to extend friendships to royal women that augmented their family's social status. Caroline Swinburne, the wife of Henry, third son of Sir John Swinburne, fourth Baronet of Capheaton Hall, Northumberland, enjoyed the company of Queen Maria Carolina during her time in Naples in 1776. In 1779 the couple returned to Naples and Caroline gave birth to a baby girl, with the Queen named as her godmother. Maria Carolina gifted her namesake a green leather case containing a pencil and dance card.[53] This gift was a keepsake, inscribed *souvenir* and decorated with a miniature portrait of the Queen and a lock of her hair adorned with diamonds (see plate 13 and figure 7.1). Such cases originated in France. In 1777 Marie Anne de Vichy-Chamrond, marquise du Deffand, wrote to Horace Walpole of an enamelled tablet for recording private sentiments which 'is called a *souvenir*'.

7.1 Leather case containing pencil and dance card, given by Queen Maria Carolina to Caroline Swinburne (back view).

She described it decorated with the receiver's monogram and a verse beginning '*Le souvenir est doux à l'homme heureux et sage*', or 'Memory is sweet to the man who is happy and wise'.[54] These precursors to a Filofax combined a textual inscription of the French word *souvenir* ('memory') with an object intended for the action of writing down a memory, or what we would today call 'a memo'. Horace received Marie Anne's description of this object two years after he used the term 'souvenir' for the first known time in English, but it shows that the French term had already been connected to a type of object that was circulating on the Continent.

In 1802 the Anglo-Irish noble Lady Margaret Mount Cashell spent six months in Paris. Here she entertained the Polish noblewoman Marie Countess Walewska. 'She [Walewska] has insisted on Lady Mount Cashell making her a present of a tree', Margaret's travelling companion Katherine Wilmot noted,

> which Lady Mount Cashell has, choosing an arbutus as being common in Ireland. She is to take it to Poland with her where she has a little plantation representative of her friends and favourites, each having given her the sort of tree most emblematic of their sentiment towards her, and in this place she walks, and imagines herself conversing with all she loves, and likes, in every corner of the world.[55]

Margaret had gifted Marie a native Irish strawberry tree (*Arbutus unedo*), known for its spherical and bumpy reddish-orange fruit and cream urn-shaped flowers. For the countess, this tree represented a friend's affection and country of origin, having come from its very soil. But according to Katherine's account of Marie imagining herself conversing with distant friends when walking among her trees, it also went beyond this as a proxy for Margaret and, by extension, her country. Marie's grove of trees, then, was an extraordinary collection of people and countries orchestrated by her that she had ultimate agency over. This circumvented the lack of agency that she had in life. Four years later Marie would meet Napoleon and become his mistress. Through the affair she sought to influence the Emperor to support Poland in its struggle to regain independence from Prussia. Thus, it was only through entering into an unequal sexual relationship with a man that Marie could exert agency on behalf of her country, but in the form of her keepsake trees she could organise her friends and, by extension, their countries of origin as she liked.[56]

As a form of moral superiority, sensibility could also be used by the nouveau riche to edge their way into the social elite. Covetous of upward mobility, Lady Anna Miller often used keepsake-giving in her published travel letters to indicate the gentility she had acquired through new friendships on the Continent. In Bologna in 1770 she wrote of receiving a pheasant, 'accompanied by a beautiful *bouquet* of three great carnations' from the 'Contessa Orsi'.[57] 'I am sure a large saucer would not cover the flower of any of them', she exclaimed, 'the bouquet and a note were tied with a rosette of rose-coloured ribbon to the pheasant's feet: how graceful these people in every trifle!'[58] While she happily accepted the pheasant, Anna rejected another keepsake of a curled and beribboned dog from 'Madama Aldrovandi'. She wrote:

> The breed of lap-dogs peculiar to this country, are extremely beautiful. Madama Aldrovandi was so very obliging as to send me one of the most perfect I ever saw, upon a magnificent velvet cushion, trimmed with gold fringe*; but I found myself under the necessity of refusing this pretty creature; my chief reason was, that I could not think of making my own dog uneasy, who has been my faithful companion and friend since I left, and she showed such a visible jealousy and disgust to this little stranger, that I determined not to vex her.[59]

By refusing to ruin her close relationship with her dog by taking on another, Anna showed that they had a close relationship as travel companions. Being well accustomed to the friendships between people and dogs, we might today view this as quite normal behaviour, but it was a relatively new practice in the eighteenth century that reflected the period's privileging of refined emotional sensibility as a measure of character and social status. Sarah Goldsmith has explored how male Grand Tourists' used servants and dogs as extensions of the self and emotional others.[60] According to Goldsmith, owner's accounts of their dogs reflected their characters. For instance, Horace Walpole rejected physical performances of endurance, so his accounts of his spaniel, Tory, are of a dog used to the sedate life and unsuited to harsh terrains. If we take this as a model, in this instance Anna may have been using her dog to demonstrate her own faithful and steadfast English character holding firm against the lures of Italian embellishment and frivolity. We know from Chapter 2 that Anna would be criticised for succumbing to these lures following her return home; perhaps this was something she anticipated with her account of her dog.

In seeking professional mobility, women travel writers described their published letters as keepsakes to mount a claim to authority with male travel writers, even a superiority. Glasgow-born Anne Grant – the only child of Duncan Macvicar, a Highlander in the 77th Regiment of Foot – imbued her published travel letters with a sentimental value that exceeded the value of the classical learning and objective non-personal points of view displayed in the male-authored Grand Tour accounts earlier in the century. In one of her letters, Anne asked why her female correspondent

> desire[d] me to burn your letters, while you so religiously preserve mine? You can have no motive for this, which I have not in a higher degree for keeping the pictures of your soul. I have cut all the leaves out of a great old goose of a book, and there I have placed those pretty pictures in regular succession; with Miss Ourry's and Mrs. Sprot's; cousin Jean's letters, which I value much for the vein of original humour that runs through them ... You can't think how diligently I peruse this good book.[61]

Anne thus framed her collection of letters as a keepsake that stood in for her friends; with their souls imprinted on the paper in ink. Other women whose letters were not published, but were still circulated widely, perfumed them to heighten their sentimental value. Martha Wilmot, for instance, asked her mother in one of her letters, 'Does this letter smell sweet? For I have perfumed it'.[62] This reference to smell imbued her letters with a sentimental value that exceeded any other, potentially including the value of the literary canon.

Seeing the cultural and social value of this practice, manufacturers and shopkeepers sought to monetise it. Prior to 1769, Shakespearian pilgrims would carve themselves a piece of the mulberry tree said to have been planted by the Bard in his garden at New Place, or a hunk of one the poet's alleged pieces of furniture. From 6 to 8 September 1769, however, David Garrick staged a jubilee to celebrate the playwright's birth. It led to the proliferation of keepsakes that helped to establish Shakespeare as *the* English poet. From the jubilee onwards, the pillaging activities of Shakespearian pilgrims were replaced by the purchasing activities of tourists, drawn to a growing array of commercially manufactured keepsakes, from mulberry-wood snuff-boxes to engravings of the birthplace and porcelain scent bottles modelled on Scheemakers's statue of Shakespeare.[63]

Until the turn of the nineteenth century, Tunbridge-ware had imitated Belgian Spa-ware, with much of it imported and sold by London traders who set up in the town for the summer season.[64] In the first decade of the nineteenth century, however, the material features of Tunbridge-ware began to reflect its status as a keepsake associated with that particular location. Intricate woodwork designs were replaced by topographical prints of key tourist sites, such as the Pantiles or the High Rocks, taken from guidebooks or produced by local artists. If Hester had given the young Miss Birch a Tunbridge ink stand in the early nineteenth century, it would have had a label affixed reading 'A Trifle from Tunbridge Wells' (figure 7.2). Knitting sheaths, pincushions and needle boxes had the same labels. A popular face-powder box was not just labelled as a keepsake, but specifically designed to function as one. The box contained a mirror and a label applied to the lid read: 'Within this Box You may see / The face of

7.2 Early wooden container for carrying ink, with a compartment for sand, stamped 'A trifle from Tunbridge Wells', 18th century.

7.3 Pincushion, 'A trifle from Brighton'.

one That's dear to me'.[65] When the receiver contemplated their own face mirrored inside this object, the text would also prompt them to contemplate the person who had given it to them. In this way the souvenir object was designed to prompt the receiver to create a performance out of the idea that love is about recognising something of yourself in another person.[66] The physical distance between the receiver who gazed in the mirror and the person who gave it to them increased the sentimental value of the face-powder box. Other spa and seaside towns, such as Brighton, quickly followed suit with similar goods, like pincushions inscribed 'A Trifle from Brighton'

7.4 Tunbridge-ware sewing clamp in the form of a castle, eighteenth century.

(figure 7.3), small cylinders holding panoramic views of the seafront and containers shaped like the domes of the Brighton Pavilion inscribed 'A present from Brighton' (figure 7.4).

Mary Morgan, wife of the Reverend Caesar Morgan, bought some keepsake gloves when she visited Woodstock, Oxfordshire, in 1791. Glove-making had been an important industry in Woodstock since the sixteenth century due to the demand for riding and hawking gloves among noble hunters lodging in the town.[67] In the seventeenth century, fashionably adorned and perfumed kid gloves were offered to royal visitors to the area.[68] In the late eighteenth century this practice was extended to genteel visitors, like Mary, keen to take part in a long-standing royal gift-giving ritual. In a note accompanying her gift, Mary wrote:

> As Woodstock is a place famous for its manufacture of gloves, such as Rosamond might have worn, and such as the duchess of Marlborough is painted graciously receiving from a Woodstock girl, I hope you will accept each a pair from me. But I beg you will not let your

ideas carry you back to the age of chivalry, and fancy that I mean to throw the gauntlet down. That, you know, was only one glove; but a pair is always emblematic of friendship: and as such, I hope, you will look upon this small token; and believe me, dear ladies, most sincerely yours.[69]

As a covering for that part of the body that can reach out in acceptance or, alternatively, be held back in rejection, a pair of gloves had long symbolised goodwill, love and loyalty.[70] By wearing these malleable fabric objects, it was Mary's hope that her friends would feel a sense of affection for her. But she also took care to specifically connect her gift to two of the most politically influential women of their time: Queen Anne's friend and confidant Sarah Churchill, the Duchess of Marlborough, and Rosamund Clifford, the mistress of King Henry II.[71] Henry II and Rosamond regularly frequented the royal manor in the park of Woodstock. Mary also linked the gloves to the 'Woodstock girl' who had made them. By 1809 it was noted that the local glove trade offered 'employment to the poor many miles round', with 1,400–1,500 women and girls earning 8–12 shillings per week sewing the gloves.[72] The gloves encouraged Mary's friends to physically express their relationship with her by putting their hands inside them. The travel narrative she attached to the gloves also encouraged her friends to express their relationship to the royal women who had worn the gloves throughout the town's history and the Woodstock girls who had produced them. Through her mass-produced gift, then, Anna encouraged her friends to reflect on and tell a history of the town that focused on royal women and supported women's industry.

Conclusion

In the last decades of the eighteenth century and first decades of the nineteenth century, the travel keepsake was popularised and monetised. This happened because elite women travellers of the eighteenth century had created a market for small, inexpensive gifts which recalled their travels. But when we put a price on our feelings, those feelings are rendered ingenuine and inauthentic. When bought at the market, a keepsake by its very nature loses its value because market value negates sentimental value. A cultural practice that at first brought agency to elite women travellers, when commodified, then began to devalue the woman consumer's feelings as fake and inauthentic. We can see this devaluation in 1827 when the poet Charles Heath sought contributions to a fledgling poetry annual he tentatively titled the *Keepsake*. The first editor of the annual, William Harrison Ainsworth, took issue with the title, worrying that it 'savour[ed] of a gift from Tunbridge Wells'.[73]

But, as we so often forget, eighteenth- and nineteenth-century women were both the targets and agents of consumption. While recognising the influence that the market had on women, it is also crucial to treat them as agents in their own lives whose actions were not solely determined by market structures. The purposes to which women put their keepsakes was increasingly mediated by designers and marketers in the nineteenth century, but they could still attach their own compelling relationship narratives to them. The degree to which individual women travellers could use these relationship narratives to exert agency under the right circumstances is the focus of the next two chapters.

Notes

1 Horace Walpole, *The Yale Edition of Horace Walpole's Correspondence*, ed. W. S. Lewis (New Haven: Yale University Press, 1965), vol. 34, 278.
2 Walpole, *Correspondence*, vol. 34, 278.
3 Matthew Kilburn, 'Fitzpatrick [née Liddell], Anne, Countess of Upper Ossory [other married name Anne FitzRoy, duchess of Grafton] (1737/8–1804)', *Oxford Dictionary of National Biography*, last updated 4 October 2008, https://doi.org/10.1093/ref:odnb/88658.
4 James Douglas, *Travelling Anecdotes Through Various Parts of Europe* (London: J. Debrett, 1786), 41.
5 Quoted in Judith Pascoe, 'Poetry as a souvenir: Mary Shelley in the annuals', in *Mary Shelley in Her Times*, ed. Betty Bennett and Stuart Curran (Baltimore: Johns Hopkins University Press, 2000), 174.
6 Ann Radcliffe, *The Mysteries of Udolpho: And a Sicilian Romance*, vol. 1 (London: J. Limbird, 1826 [1794]), 167.
7 Royal Irish Academy (hereafter RIA), Wilmot Papers, 12 L 24, Martha Bradford (née Wilmot), 'Letters from Russia (copied by her mother)', 31 May 1803, 20.

8 For the interlocking obligations of giving, receiving and reciprocating, see Pierre Bourdieu, *Outline of a Theory of Practice*, trans. Richard Nice (Cambridge: Cambridge University Press, 1977); Jacques Derrida, *Given Time: I. Counterfeit Money*, trans. Peggy Kamuf (Chicago: University of Chicago Press, 1992); Marcel Mauss, *The Gift: Forms and Functions of Exchange in Archaic Societies* (London: Routledge, 1989).
9 RIA, Wilmot Papers, 12 L 17–22, Martha Bradford (née Wilmot) 'Journal of stay in Russia', 1803–8, 6 vols, vol. 2, 187–9.
10 Wilmot Papers, 12 L 21, vol. 5, 223–4.
11 For a problematisation of the romantic friendship approach, see Liz Stanley, 'Romantic friendship? Some issues in researching lesbian history and biography', *Women's History Review* 1, no. 2 (1992).
12 Maureen Cassidy-Geiger, *Fragile Diplomacy: Meissen Porcelain for European Courts ca. 1710–63* (New Haven: Yale University Press, 2007), 8.
13 Brinsley Ford and John Ingamells, *A Dictionary of British and Irish Travellers in Italy, 1701–1800* (New Haven: Yale University Press, 1997), 296.
14 James Buzard, 'The Grand Tour and after (1660–1840)', in *The Cambridge Companion to Travel Writing*, ed. Peter Hulme and Tim Youngs (Cambridge: Cambridge University Press, 2002), 41.
15 See Michael Yonan, 'Portable dynasties: imperial gift-giving at the court of Vienna in the eighteenth century', *Court Historian* 14, no. 2 (2009).
16 Linda Zionkowski and Cynthia Klekar, *The Culture of the Gift in Eighteenth-Century England* (New York: Palgrave Macmillan, 2009), 3.
17 Amanda E. Herbert, 'Gender and the spa: space, sociability and self at British health spas, 1640–1714', *Journal of Social History* 43 (Winter 2009).
18 Cited by Herbert, 'Gender and the spa', 366.
19 Herbert, 'Gender and the spa', 365.
20 Celia Fiennes, *Through England on a Side Saddle: In the Time of William and Mary* (Cambridge: Cambridge University Press, 2010), 12.
21 Fiennes, *Through England on a Side Saddle*, 109–10.
22 Brian Austen, *Tunbridge Ware and Related European Decorative Woodwares: Killarney, Spa, Sorrento* (London: W. Foulsham Company, 1992), 47.
23 Elizabeth Montagu, *Elizabeth Montagu, the Queen of the Bluestockings: Her Correspondence from 1720 to 1761*, ed. Emily Jane Climenson, vol. 1 (London: John Murray, 1906), 213.
24 Helmuth Berking, *Sociology of Giving* (London: SAGE Publications, 1999), 5.

25 Frances Seymour Somerset and Henrietta Fermor Pomfret, *Correspondence between Frances, Countess of Hartford, (Afterwards Duchess of Somerset,) and Henrietta Louisa, Countess of Pomfret, between the Years 1738 and 1741*, 3 vols (London: Richard Phillips, 1805), vol. 1, 186–7.
26 Somerset and Pomfret, *Correspondence*, vol. 1, 196.
27 Lizzie Rogers, 'Conversing with collecting the world: elite female sociability and learning through objects in the age of Enlightenment', in *Women and the Art and Science of Collecting in Eighteenth-Century Europe*, ed. Arlene Leis and Kacie L. Wills (New York: Routledge, 2020), 93–107.
28 Somerset and Pomfret, *Correspondence*, vol. 2, 135
29 Mary Granville, *The Autobiography and Correspondence of Mary Granville, Mrs. Delany: With Interesting Reminiscences of King George the Third and Queen Charlotte*, ed. Lady Llanover, vol. 1 (London: Bentley, Richard, 1861), 135–6.
30 Amanda Vickery, *The Gentleman's Daughter: Women's Lives in Georgian England* (New Haven: Yale University Press, 1998), 167.
31 Gerald Mars and Valerie Mars, '"Souvenir-gifts" as tokens of filial esteem: the meanings of Blackpool souvenirs', in *Souvenirs: The Material Culture of Tourism*, ed. Michael Hitchcock and Ken Teague (Aldershot: Ashgate, 2000), 94.
32 JRL, Thrale-Piozzi Papers, GB 133 Eng MS 618, Hester Lynch Piozzi, 'Journals: Travels in Italy and Germany', 1784–1787, vol. 1, fol. 2r°.
33 Hester Lynch Piozzi, *The Piozzi Letters: Correspondence of Hester Lynch Piozzi (Formerly Mrs. Thrale)*, ed. Edward A. Bloom and Lillian D. Bloom, vol. 1, *1784–1791* (London: Associated University Presses, 1989), 141.
34 JRL, Thrale-Piozzi Papers, GB 133 Eng MS 618, vol. 1, fol. 3r°.
35 Anna Riggs Miller, *Letters from Italy, Describing the Manners, Customs, Antiquities, Paintings, &C. Of That Country, in the Years MDCCLXX and MDCCLXXI, to a Friend Residing in France* (Dublin: W. Watson, 1776), vol. 1, 356.
36 RIA, Wilmot Papers, 12 L 24, 28 March 1804, 194.
37 Piozzi, *The Piozzi Letters*, vol. 1, 128.
38 David Garrioch, 'Christian friendship to secular sentimentality: Enlightenment re-evaluations', in *Friendship: A History*, ed. Barbara Caine (London: Equinox, 2009), 174.
39 BL, Holland House Papers, Add MS 51927, Lady Elizabeth Holland, 'Journals, etc.', 3 July 1792, fol. 13v°.
40 Sonia Keppel, *The Sovereign Lady: A Life of Elizabeth Vassall, Third Lady Holland, with Her Family* (London: Hamilton, 1974), 17.

41 Deidre Lynch, 'Personal effects and sentimental fictions', *Eighteenth-Century Fiction* 12, no. 2–3 (2000): 345.
42 'Ought sensibility to be cherished or repressed?', *Monthly Magazine* 2 (October 1796): 706.
43 John Locke, *The Work*, vol. 1 (London: Printed for John Churchill and Sam Manship, 1714), 149.
44 Ansegise Clement, 'A trip to Margate, Chapter XI', in *London Magazine, Or, Gentleman's Monthly Intelligencer*, vol. 51 (London: Richard Baldwin, 1782).
45 Clarissa to Anne Howe, quoted in Garrioch, 'Christian friendship to secular sentimentality', 180.
46 For a critique of the concept of romantic friendship, see Stanley, 'Romantic friendship?', 196. Her critique is of Carroll Smith-Rosenberg, 'The female world of love and ritual: relations between women in nineteenth century America', *Signs* 1 (1975); Lillian Faderman, *Surpassing the Love of Men: Romantic Friendship and Love Between Women from the Renaissance to the Present* (London: Junction Books, 1979).
47 Mary Wollstonecraft, *Maria, or the Wrongs of Woman* (Paris: William Godwin, 1798).
48 Garrioch, 'Christian friendship to secular sentimentality'" 180.
49 Fanny Burney, *Diary and Letters of Madame d'Arblay*, ed. Charlotte Barrett, vol. 1 (London: Henry Colburn, 1842), 128.
50 Burney, *Diary and Letters*, 131.
51 Burney, *Diary and Letters*, 131.
52 Burney, *Diary and Letters*, 131.
53 Anne French, *Art Treasures in the North: Northern Families on the Grand Tour* (Norwich: Unicorn Press, 2009), 44–5.
54 Marie Anne de Vichy-Chamrond, *Letters of the Marquise Du Deffand to the Hon. Horace Walpole, Afterwards Earl of Orford, from the Year 1766 to the Year 1780. To which are Added Letters of Madame Du Deffand to Voltaire, from the Year 1759 to the Year 1775*, vol. 3 (London: Longman, Hurst, Rees and Orme, 1810), 236.
55 Katherine Wilmot, *The Grand Tours of Katherine Wilmot*, ed. Elizabeth Mavor (London: Weidenfeld and Nicolson, 1992), 43–4.
56 This practice continued to be followed by women into the twentieth century. In Australia, anthropologist and Aboriginal rights activist Olive Muriel Pink planted trees in honour of the government officials, missionaries and pastoralists who she lobbied to establish the Australian Arid Regions Native Flora Reserve in Alice Springs. Minister for the Territories Sir Paul Hasluck recalled that: 'Each tree bore the name of some prominent citizen and if that citizen fell out of favour with her she ceased to water it. So that if the leaves of "Mr Archer" were

drooping and the leaves of "Mr Marsh" were bright and green or "Mr Barclay" was growing vigorously one knew at once what had happened in the handling of her latest request. I visited her on several occasions and could never restrain a curious glance at my tree and felt suitably gratified if I saw that "Mr Hasluck" was being watered regularly'. Over a century on, Olive's practice is remarkably similar; her garden expressed a political agency that she was struggling to exert in real life; see Paul Hasluck, 'Miss Pink's love story', *Northern Territory Newsletter*, July 1975.

57 Miller, *Letters from Italy*, vol. 1, 359.
58 Miller, *Letters from Italy*, vol. 1, 360.
59 Miller, *Letters from Italy*, vol. 1, 357. In a footnote, Anna further described the fringe as being 'curled (*frifée*), and ornamented with rose-coloured ribbon round the neck and legs'.
60 Sarah Goldsmith, 'Dogs, servants and masculinities: writing about danger on the Grand Tour', *Journal for Eighteenth-Century Studies* 40, no. 1 (2017): 3–21.
61 Anne Grant, *Letters from the Mountains, Being the Real Correspondence of a Lady, between the Years 1773 and 1807*, vol. 2 (London: Longman, 1809), 51–2.
62 RIA, Wilmot Papers, 12 L 24, 5 September 1803, 106.
63 Michael Dobson *et al.* (eds), *The Oxford Companion to Shakespeare* (Oxford: Oxford University Press, 2015).
64 We know this from the records of the London dealers of wooden wares, like Mary Ferguson, who in the late seventeenth century petitioned customs officials to release the 'white wood boxes, Tunbridge deskes' that she had sent to 'Holland' to be lacquered and which the officials had impounded. As late as the 1790s John Robinson, a London perfumer and maker of Tunbridge-ware, was still only offering products in Tunbridge Wells during the spa season. See Brian Austen, 'English spa souvenirs: the Tunbridge ware industry to about 1830', *Magazine Antiques* 147, no. 6 (1995): 894.
65 Austen, 'English spa souvenirs', 899.
66 Marcia Pointon, '"Surrounded with brilliants": miniature portraits in eighteenth-century England', *Art Bulletin* 83, no. 1 (2001): 63.
67 William Hull, *The History of the Glove Trade: With the Customs Connected with the Glove: To which Are Annexed Some Observations on the Policy of the Trade between England and France, and its Operation on the Agricultural and Manufacturing Interests* (London: E. Wilson, 1834).
68 When James II opened the Ashmolean Museum at Oxford University in 1683, for instance, he was presented with 'a rich pair of gloves with

golden fring (as the fashion then was)', made in Woodstock, while his second wife, Mary of Modena, was given '12 pair of fine kid leather', and his daughter, Lady Anne, received '12 pair of the same, all valued (as they say) at 45li, and odd shillings' (T. E. Schulz, 'The Woodstock glove industry', *Oxoniensia* 3 (1938): 140).

69 Mary Morgan, *A Tour to Milford Haven, in the Year 1791* (London: John Stockdale, 1795), 87.

70 Hull, *The History of the Glove Trade*.

71 James Falkner, 'Churchill [née Jenyns], Sarah, duchess of Marlborough (1660–1744)', *Oxford Dictionary of National Biography*, last updated 3 January 2008, http://doi.org/10.1093.ref:odnb/5405; T. A. Archer, 'Clifford, Rosamund (b. before 1140?, d. 1175/6)', revised by Elizabeth Hallam, *Oxford Dictionary of National Biography*, last updated 23 September 2004, https://doi.org/10.1093/ref:odnb/5661.

72 Hull, *The History of the Glove Trade*.

73 Quoted in Pascoe, 'Poetry as a souvenir', 173.

8

A snuff-box and other Napoleonic keepsakes

The outbreak of the French Revolutionary Wars in 1793 made British travel to Europe difficult, if not impossible until the Treaty of Paris in 1815. Many scholars consider 1793 the natural conclusion of the Grand Tour, but while fewer Britons were travelling in Italy during this period, they were still present in large numbers for much of the 1790s. In 1802–3, there was a short armistice between Britain and France. At the commencement of the Peace of Amiens, British men and women raced across the Channel, eager to see the sites of the revolution and catch a glimpse of the First Consul, Napoleon Bonaparte.

Just over two years earlier, the young commander of the French army in Egypt had returned to France and overthrown the Directorial government in the *coup d'état* of 18 Brumaire (9 November), Year VIII (1799). Bonaparte formed a new consulate and named himself First Consul. In the spring of 1802, 3.6 million people (roughly 72 per cent of all possible voters) voted *oui* to the simple question, 'Should Napoleon Bonaparte be first consul for life?'[1] No alternative to the Life Consulate was provided for those who answered *non*. From this point forward, in the manner of royalty, Bonaparte took to using his first name, Napoleon. A shrewd visual strategist, he ensured his image triumphed everywhere, in the form of grand paintings of effortless conquest and public statues, but also the plaster busts, miniature portraits and medallions that decorated the homes of the bourgeois.

Rather than marking the conclusion of the Grand Tour, I argue that Napoleon's reign functioned as another event in an ongoing cultural struggle between sexes, classes and nations to control the meanings of travel. It was during this period that the British government

A snuff-box and other Napoleonic keepsakes 203

promoted domestic tours of Britain as a patriotic activity for both men and women, while Napoleon attempted to shift the Grand Tour's centre of gravity from Rome to Paris by transferring Italy's antiquities and artworks there. What it was to be a British subject and the nature of Britain's relation to France was hotly contested. Travel and souvenirs are significant but overlooked sites for this debate and for women's political expression.

This chapter will explore how Katherine Wilmot and Lady Elizabeth Holland used Napoleonic keepsakes during and after their travels to Paris to express their political opinions. Katherine vigorously rejected commercial Napoleonic keepsakes and the First Consul's attempts to transfer the centre-point of the Grand Tour from Italy to Paris, to voice both her rejection of his dictatorship and her unease at Ireland's place within Britain. Elizabeth Holland, meanwhile, amplified the sentimental value of bespoke Napoleonic keepsakes with a combination of effusive poetry and emotional outpourings to take part in social politics – that is, the management of people and social situations for political ends. I argue that, by enlarging our understanding of politics to include travel and souvenirs, we can see that women were significant political actors, albeit on a social stage rather than a parliamentary one.

Prior to the announcement of the Treaty of Amiens, Elizabeth and her husband, Henry, had intended to winter in Spain. The momentary peace made Paris an exciting place to begin their journey and the couple joined the party of Henry's uncle, the renowned Bonapartist Charles James Fox. In September 1802 they were presented to the First Consul and his wife. Following years of exclusion from court for her infidelity and divorce from Sir Godfrey Webster, this official reception in France must have somewhat assuaged Elizabeth's sense of marginalisation at home. A satirical print depicts Napoleon's reception of Charles James Fox and his party, with Elizabeth and Henry at the back (figure 8.1). It was intended to criticise Fox for bowing and paying court to a figure who had been Britain's enemy until a few months prior. Fox's title of Citizen Volpone indicated his duplicity with the new French regime; 'Citizen' pointing towards his French sympathy and 'Volpone' a play on his name, being Italian for 'big fox'.[2]

The print reflects a larger division in public opinion regarding France's new leader. With some noted exceptions, the British had

8.1 James Gillray, Introduction of Citizen Volpone and his suite, at Paris, 1802, 265 mm × 368 mm, hand-coloured etching.

generally welcomed the French constitutional monarchy from 1789 to 1792, but this was followed by a sharp turn against France with the massacres of September 1792 and the execution of the King in January 1793, at which point the government commenced a series of counter-revolutionary repressive measures.[3] At the time of the Hollands' travels the character of France's new leader was under debate. While Fox regretted the 'very bad beginning' that had brought Napoleon to power, he was convinced that the First Consul favoured peace to rebuild his country and strengthen his rule.[4] In July 1800 Fox had controversially claimed that Napoleon 'certainly has surpassed, in my judgement, Alexander & Caesar, not to mention the great advantage he has over them in the cause he fights in'.[5] In October 1801, when peace between Britain and France looked assured, Fox boldly admitted to future prime minister Charles Grey, second Earl Grey, 'the truth is, I am gone something further in hate to the English Government than perhaps you and the rest of my friends are, and certainly further than can with prudence be avowed. The triumph of the French Government over the English does in fact afford me a degree of pleasure which it is very difficult to disguise'.[6]

The Hollands did not go as far as Henry's uncle, but as members of the opposition they cautiously approved the new regime. In 1802 Henry wrote to his sister that while it was true the First Consul was a king in all but name, he was, at least, 'less likely to produce reaction, confusion and bloodshed than any Bourbon king would do'.[7] The revolutionary ambitions of merit-based careers, the equalisation of taxes and the removal of trade restrictions were, according to the Hollands, compatible with a strong government (even if it was arbitrary), but these gains would be squandered if the Bourbons returned.[8]

While she would later shape herself as a devotee of Napoleon, at this point Elizabeth did not express any strong personal attachment to him, observing to a female friend following their reception that the First Consul's head was

> out of proportion, being too large for his figure. It is well shaped; his ears are very neatly shaped and small, his teeth fine. The gracious smile he puts on is not in unison with the character of the upper part of his face; that is penetrating and severe and unbending.[9]

Scholars have referred to Elizabeth's negative reaction to Napoleon's oversized head and small body as a humorous aside to Fox's discussions with the First Consul, but it signals the important role that marketing and visual merchandise played in early nineteenth-century politics. Marketing and merchandise belonged in the social arena of politics where women wielded considerable power as consumers.

How much of Elizabeth's perception of Napoleon was informed by his actual appearance and how much was informed by both British and French visual propaganda is difficult to ascertain. From 1797, British caricatures depicted Napoleon as a grotesque monster with an oversized head and small body (figure 8.2). Perhaps, then, the British press had predisposed Elizabeth to view Napoleon as a disproportioned leader in real life, no matter his actual appearance. But equally, perhaps the British press were influenced by Elizabeth's impression of Napoleon and that of other women who saw him in Paris. On 1 January 1803 the renowned political caricaturist James Gillray created the character of 'Little Boney' (figure 8.3). From

8.2 George Cruikshank, *The Head of the Great Nation in a Queer Situation*, 1813, 250 mm × 350 mm, hand-coloured etching.

8.3 James Gillray, *Maniac-Ravings – or – little Boney in a Strong Fit –*, 1803, 262 mm × 353 mm, hand-coloured etching.

then on, almost every caricaturist then depicted the defenders of Britain in relative sizes against their tiny adversary. According to Alexandra Franklin, 'it was safer, seemingly, to encounter Bonaparte on a different scale of magnitude'.[10] Gillray's 'Little Boney' bears a strong resemblance to Elizabeth's written reflection on Napoleon's appearance.

While British propaganda enlarged Napoleon's head and reduced the size of his body, French propaganda duplicated his head to the point of saturation. 'We have not seen Bonaparte yet', Katherine Wilmot griped on her visit to Paris ten months earlier in December 1801,

> except adorning 'Reticules' (which are a species of little Workbag worn by the Ladies, containing snuff-boxes, Billet-doux, Purses, Handkerchiefs, Fans, Prayer-Books, Bon-bons, Visiting tickets, and all the machinery of existence). His image (in Plaster of Paris) reigns the Monarch of even every Gingerbread Stall, and you can not buy a bit of Barley sugar to cure your cold, without having 'le Premier Consul's' head, in all his heroic laurels, sent down your throat, doing the ignominious job of a Sweep chimney! So true it is, that push'd beyond certain bounds, compliment becomes an insult.[11]

The traveller from Glanmire, County Cork, was accompanying her neighbours Stephen Moore, second Earl of Mount Cashell, his wife, Margaret, and six 'Irish adventurers' on a Grand Tour. Her account of her first few days in Paris shows the rapid spread of Napoleon's profile through both official and unofficial iconography.

It is widely acknowledge that Napoleon mastered the use of visual and material culture to validate his empire and authority to lead, but he was not the only commissioner of his image and figure. From the fall of the monarchy in 1792, there was a 'democratisation' of paintings, statues and other representations of public figures in France. *Philosophes* and generals were celebrated not only in the form of artworks commissioned by the State but also in the form of cheap busts in bourgeois households, which took the place of kings and saints.[12] We see from Katherine's description of consumer spectacle how Napoleon harnessed this relatively new French bourgeois social practice of worshipping 'great men' on the street and in their homes. Commoditised sentiment was clearly a powerful political tool that Napoleon prized and, in recognising its political importance, we can see the significance of women's actions in accepting or rejecting it.

In placing consumerism at the centre of the promotion of his political ideology, Napoleon made women both the targets and agents of his politics. Popular culture, then, both perpetuated the image of Napoleon as an ideal leader and offered female audiences a (modest) platform to express their resistance to him.[13] Katherine took the latter option by claiming that the First Consul was quite literally pushing himself 'beyond certain bounds' by forcing his head (and his politics) down the throats of polite female consumers in the form of bon-bons. This was a reversal of a satirical print that would appear in 1803 depicting Napoleon with a grotesquely large head, about to swallow the world in his unceasing appetite for conquest (figure 8.4). Here it was Katherine, the female consumer, who decided that she did not want to swallow Napoleon's politics.

Unlike the Hollands, Katherine did not view Napoleon's rule as something quite set apart from that of the Bourbons. 'If I were to speak from what I have seen', she remarked during her time in Paris, 'I shou'd say the use the French Republicans have made of Liberty, is to create a universal choice of aristocracy'.[14] Like many of the Anglo-Irish elites, it seems that Katherine was doing some serious soul searching following the 1801 Act of Union, which was preceded by the Irish Rebellion of 1796 (triggered by the French expedition to Ireland).[15] The daughter of a port surveyor in Drogheda who had previously served as a captain in the 40th Regiment of Foot, Katherine was born into a wealthy and influential family. She travelled with the radical aristocrat Lady Margaret Mount Cashell. Margaret had been educated by Mary Wollstonecraft and was a close friend of the Irish nationalist Lord Edward Fitzgerald, who was killed while resisting arrest for treason.[16] While not a radical herself, Katherine was proud of her Irish heritage and throughout her travels made sure to separate herself from the English. When the diplomat Charles Maurice de Talleyrand-Périgord, for instance, mentioned to Katherine over dinner that he had 'been in England,- on the presumption of my being an English woman', she promptly corrected him, informing the diplomat that she 'was Irish, and the word seem'd to revive some remembrance of successful perfidy'.[17] It seems, however, that Katherine marginally preferred her country's lack of legislative independence within Britain to the possibility of being led by a man she viewed as a despot.

8.4 William Holland, *An Attempt to Swallow the World!!*, 1803, 327 mm × 250 mm, etching.

When Katherine finally had the chance to see Napoleon at a military demonstration in January 1802, like Elizabeth she found 'his person ... is remarkably small', but unlike Elizabeth, noted that it 'appears perfectly proportion'd'.[18] Clearly, British propaganda depicting Napoleon's large head and small body and French propaganda multiplying Napoleon's head reflected a growing public perception of his personage to such an extent that Katherine felt it necessary to make this qualification. Her descriptions of Napoleon as a spectacle of popular culture that was so dominating it threatened to turn the man himself into a caricature demonstrates the agency of the female consumer. The French and British markets were creating a multitude of competing impressions of Napoleon and it was up to the woman consumer to choose which of these she wanted to buy into, if any.

Elizabeth sought new adventures 'off the beaten track' following her stay in France. In September 1802, after spending three months in Paris enjoying the new society that had formed around the First Consul, the Hollands set out for Spain. While Henry sought material to write a biography of the great dramatist and poet Lope de Vega, Elizabeth was keenly interested in Spanish culture, visiting palaces, convents, libraries and attending a bullfight. From this trip, and another in 1808–9, she would acquire souvenirs to add to the Holland House collection. The small Malaga figures that were displayed in the anteroom adjoining the Hollands' sitting room, for example, captured the flamenco dancing and bullfighting that Elizabeth had experienced there.[19] Undertaken during the Peninsular War (1807–14), the Hollands' second tour of Spain saw them support the Spanish cause for liberty against the French. Upon their return, Henry and Elizabeth made Holland House a centre of hospitality for the representatives of various juntas seeking help from Britain.

The couple's stance towards Napoleon during this period was ambivalent. On the one hand, they welcomed his defeat in Spain, where the provisional government were nationalist and liberal; on the other, they were lukewarm about the allied victories in Germany, which pointed to the possibility of Napoleon's downfall and the restoration of the monarchy in France.[20] 'I cannot make out the consistency of their views', Lady Bessborough wrote to Lord Granville, 'they would defeat Buonaparte in Spain, and let him defeat the Allies in Germany. This is beyond my Politicks'.[21] Lady Bessborough's reference to 'their views', rather than Henry's, shows how Elizabeth's wealth and status, in combination with her intellect, allowed her to enjoy a horizontal friendship with her husband, rather than a vertical relationship. The pair worked together; her politics was his and his was hers. The political realms that they were able to work in, however, were informed by their sex; Henry took the lead in Parliament, while Elizabeth took the lead in the social realm.

It was only upon Napoleon's abdication on 6 April 1814 and subsequent exile to Elba that Henry carefully began to support Napoleon in Parliament and Elizabeth started to enlist Napoleonic keepsakes to elicit sympathy for the fallen emperor. In August 1814, twelve years after their audience with the newly proclaimed First Consul, the Hollands ventured to Paris once more. They joined hundreds of British travellers eager to gain access to a Continent from which they had been barred since the Peace of Amiens. The couple made sure to visit Fontainebleau, where Napoleon had signed his abdication just four months before. 'Alas! Alas! Why did he go to Russia and why was he so headstrong!' Elizabeth cried upon entering the 'fatal room'.[22] Such public outpourings of sympathy were a political device that Elizabeth used to shift public understandings of Napoleon from a proud despotic emperor to a fallen hero. By grieving over Napoleon's fate, Elizabeth also demonstrated her sensibility and by extension her gentility.

Two months later, from Florence, Elizabeth persuaded Colonel Campbell, the British commissioner in Elba, to take a bundle of English newspapers to Napoleon.[23] Knowing her interest in minerology, the former emperor sent Elizabeth some samples of iron ore from the island in return.[24] In Florence the Hollands commissioned a portrait of Napoleon.[25] In Rome they commissioned his bust from the Emperor's favourite Venetian sculptor Antonio Canova.[26] The bust was placed in the Holland House garden on a column of granite inscribed with the following four lines (in Greek) from Homer's *Odyssey* (figure 8.5):

> He is not dead, he breathes the air
> In lands beyond the deep,
> Some distant sea-girt island where
> Harsh men the hero keep.[27]

Alabaster busts in Napoleon's image had already sold out to eager British tourists visiting the Florentine shops by the time the Hollands had arrived in August. The Hollands separated themselves from these souvenir-hunters with their pricey commission and poetry. They were art patrons, like Lord John Russell, the future prime minister, who also commissioned a bust from Canova.[28]

8.5 Holland House, Dutch Garden, bust of Napoleon, reimagined by Gibon, classic art with a modern twist reimagined, 1889.

It was when they arrived in Naples that the Hollands heard news of Napoleon's escape from Elba on 26 February 1815. Again, Elizabeth made an excessive show of her emotions upon hearing of Napoleon's predicament. 'We are preparing for an excursion to Paestum', Henry wrote to his sister,

> but the escape of the *hero* has set Lady Holland's spirits in such a flurry of agitation that I suspect she will not be calm and sedate enough to enjoy the improving gravity of the Doric architecture.[29]

But this was more than just show. Elizabeth's gift of the newspapers may have played a role in Napoleon's escape, because it was upon reading a paragraph in the *Courier* that he learnt the allies were planning to move him following the Congress of Vienna.[30] The couple quickly set out for home, hearing of Napoleon's defeat at Waterloo just as they neared Koblenz, Germany. When they landed in England, Napoleon was waiting to be transported to St Helena.

In April 1816 Henry entered a protest against the British government's treatment of Napoleon on St Helena in the journal of the House of Lords: 'To consign to distant exile and imprisonment a foreign and captive Chief, who, after the abdication of his authority, relying on British generosity, had surrendered himself to us, in preference to his other enemies', Henry wrote, 'is unworthy the magnanimity of a great country'.[31] One year later, he moved in the House of Lords for papers connected with Napoleon's treatment.[32] By alerting the public to the fact that the decision of Napoleon's banishment had been made by the government without consulting Parliament, Henry, as leader of the opposition, put Britain's constitution and national character into question. Elizabeth's earlier emotional outpourings had helped to create a public image of Napoleon as a fallen hero that supported this claim.[33]

In parallel to Henry's political manoeuvres, Elizabeth sought to materially improve Napoleon's conditions on St Helena by soliciting his British supporters to send him over one thousand books, entertainments, delicacies and keepsakes, including sweetmeats, eau de cologne, a microscope, a glass locket with a portrait of the late empress Josephine, garden seeds and a machine to make ice.[34] This shows how women could use the affections of sympathy, compassion, benevolence and pity to advance political agendas, qualities that are particularly valued in female politicians today.

Napoleon died on 5 May 1821. According to Henry, the 'pruneaux pruno de Madame Holland were nearly the last article of food he ever asked for'.[35] In death Napoleon reciprocated Elizabeth's gifts by bequeathing her a cameo snuff-box. It was not uncommon for Napoleon to give snuff-boxes. He found them an irresistible form of self-promotion when decorated with his portrait and used them as bribes, gifts and rewards to those who served him.[36] Napoleon's will, however, shows that Elizabeth was one of the only people outside of his family to whom he bequeathed an object, rather than money:

> This 15th April, 1821, at Longwood, Island of St. Helena.
>
> This is my Testament, or act of my last will.
>
> II.
>
> 1. I bequeath to my son the boxes, orders, and other articles; such as my plate, field-beds, arms, saddles, spurs, chapel-plate, books, linen which I have been accustomed to wear and use, according to the list annexed (A). It is my wish that this slight bequest may he dear to him, as coming from a father of whom the whole world will remind him.
>
> 2. I bequeath to Lady Holland the antique Cameo which Pope Pius VI. gave me at Tolentino.[37]

The fact that Elizabeth was the second person listed on Napoleon's will, immediately below his son, suggests the significance of their relationship and the gifted item. It demonstrates her high status as a political actor.

The rectangular lid of the snuff-box was set with an oval agate cameo of Bacchus seated on a goat nibbling on a vine branch (see plate 14). The rest of the lid was covered with vine branches and Bacchic emblems, including a chalice and pan pipes. The image of Bacchus looks like a more youthful and innocent version of the scandalous sculpture of the satyr and the goat that Grand Tourists flocked to see the royal palace at Portici on the Bay of Naples (figure 8.6). Might Napoleon have meant it as a political statement about his legacy as a leader? About the new growth and rejuvenation that he had brought to France? And is there a playfulness here that says something about Napoleon? Was he trying to indicate a private self that lay behind the great military leader? To understand the meanings

8.6 *Il famoso Satyro colla Capra*, 1761, 138 mm × 126 mm, etching.

that the cameo held for Napoleon, we need to consider its history just prior to when he gave it to Elizabeth. Pope Pius VI gave the cameo to Napoleon on 19 February 1797 in Tolentino after they both signed the peace treaty between Revolutionary France and the Papacy. The gift of the precious antique cameo depicting the Roman god of agriculture, wine and fertility must have formed a fitting symbol for the handover of the Papal territories and cultural collections that occurred under the terms of the Treaty. For Napoleon, the cameo may have provided evidence of divine support of his mission. Its subsequent framing within an eighteenth-century snuff-box made in Paris could be considered a metaphor for Napoleon himself, signifying his rebirth as the new Roman emperor.[38] This object, then, was a valued souvenir for Napoleon from a significant event in his life that he wanted to leave to Elizabeth as a legacy.

Inside the box was a piece of playing card cut from a seven of diamonds. It was inscribed '*Lempereur Napoleon a Lady Holland temoignage de satisfaction et destime*' on one side and '*Camée antique donné par le Pape Pie VI a Tolentino en 1797*' on the other (figures 8.7 and 8.8). This playing card may have had any number of meanings. Napoleon did not like the medieval designs of the kings and queens on traditional playing cards. At the height of his victories in 1808 he commissioned new playing cards with classical Roman figures of 'extreme elegance and purity'.[39] Card players, however, rejected Napoleon's new playing cards, preferring the old medieval designs. It may then be that Napoleon used the cut-up playing card to express regret that his vision of the French empire had ultimately been rejected. Adding to the intrigue of this card are the predictions of the prophetess Marie Anne Le Normand. Marie Anne was one of Empress Josephine's closest confidantes and a cartomancer.[40] She is alleged to have successfully foreseen Robespierre's execution,

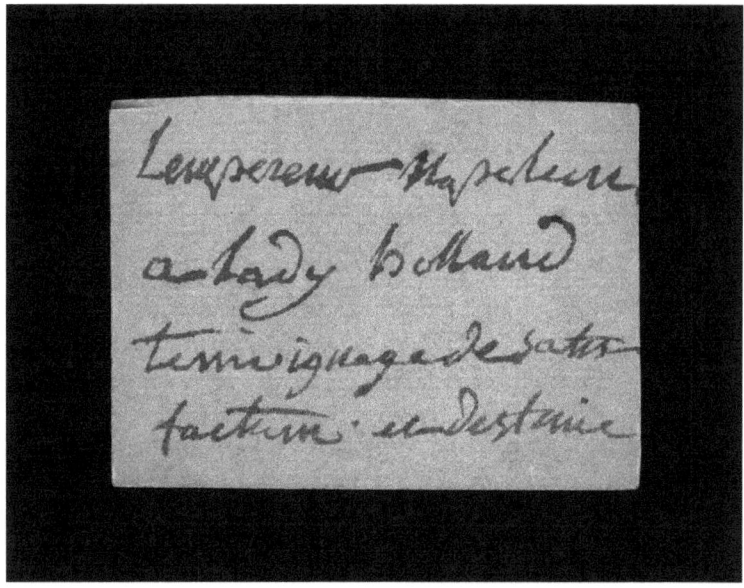

8.7 Adrien Jean Maximilien Vachette, box; cameo, 1797–1815, 72 mm × 52 mm × 20 mm, gold and agate (verso card insert).

A snuff-box and other Napoleonic keepsakes

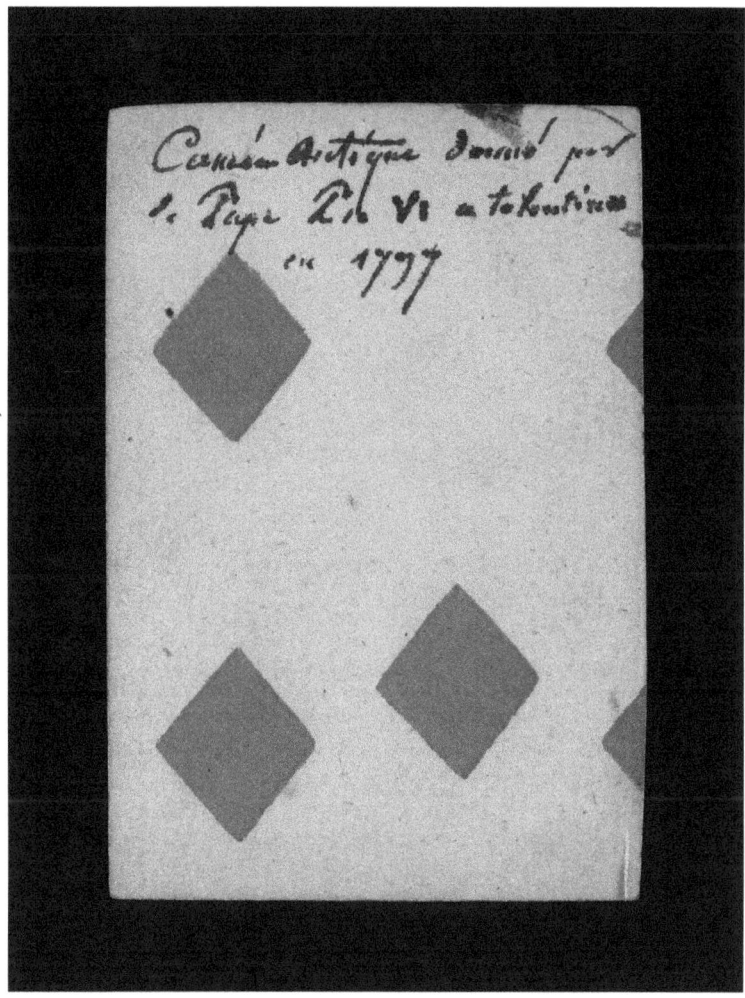

8.8 Adrien Jean Maximilien Vachette, box; cameo, 1797–1815, 72 mm × 52 mm × 20 mm, gold and agate (recto card insert).

Josephine's divorce from Napoleon, and Napoleon's eventual fall and the restoration of the Bourbons.[41] Napoleon may have used the cut-up card to refer back to her prediction. According to French cartomancy of the early nineteenth century, the seven of diamonds represented good news; cutting it in half may have indicated the opposite. While superstition is so often dismissed as a culpable feminine trait, Napoleon's inclusion of the playing card reminds us of the significant role it plays in politics.

No matter the possible meanings of the card that lay inside it, the history of the snuff-box's cameo top and the fact that Napoleon wrote a note indicate that he intended it as a keepsake of great communicative and emotive power. Elizabeth solicited poets to amplify the sentimental value of her snuff-box. Following her request, the Irish poet Thomas Moore presented her with a short poem celebrating her kindness to Napoleon during his isolation and her worthiness to receive the keepsake:

> Gift of the Hero, on his dying day,
> To her, whose pity watch'd, for ever nigh;
> Oh! Could he see the proud, the happy ray,
> This relic lights up on her generous eye,
> Sighing, he'd feel how easy 'tis to pay
> A friendship all his kingdoms could not buy.[42]

This quickly sparked a poetic debate when the Earl of Carlisle published another poem in the widely circulated *Gentleman's Magazine* begging Lady Holland to 'reject the gift' and presenting it as a Pandora's box of discord, slaughter and war:

> *Lines to Lady Holland on the Legacy of a Snuff-box*
> *Left her by Bonaparte*
> Lady, reject the gift, 'tis ting'd with gore!
> Those crimson spots a dreadful tale relate;
> It has been grasp'd by an infernal pow'r;
> And by that hand which seal'd young Enghien's fate.
>
> Lady reject the gift – beneath its lid
> Discord and slaughter, and relentless war,
> With every Plague to wretched man, lie hid:
> Let not these loose, to range the world afar.
>
> Say, what congenial to his heart of stone
> In thy soft bosom could the tyrant trace?
> When does the dove the eagle's friendship own,
> Or the wolf hold the lamb in pure embrace?
>
> Think of that pile, to Addison so dear,
> Where Sully feasted, and where Rogers' song
> Still adds sweet music to the perfum'd air,
> And gently leads each grace and muse along.

> Pollute not, then, these scenes – the gift destroy;
> 'Twill scare the Dryads from that lovely shade;
> With them will fly all rural peace and joy,
> And screaming fiends their verdant haunts invade.
>
> That mystic box hath magic pow'r to raise
> Spectres of myriads slain – a ghastly band!
> They'll vex thy slumbers, cloud thy sunny days,
> Starting from Moscow's snows or Egypt's sand.
>
> The warning muse no idle trifler deem;
> Plunge the curst mischief wide in ocean's flood,
> Or give it to our own majestic stream;
> The only stream he could not dye with blood.[43]

Here, Carlisle connected the keepsake to the continued political threat of Napoleon's relatives, and the Whig party's foreign policy towards France as an extension of their agenda in England. Posing a threat to the security of the nation, as a symbol of the bacchanal that had destroyed Rome, he claimed that Elizabeth's reception of the snuff-box would be unpatriotic. Elizabeth was not that easily defeated, however. She enlisted Lord Byron, another member of the Holland House circle, to parody Carlisle's poem. He simply advised:

> Lady, accept the box a hero wore,
> In spite of all this elegiac stuff:
> Let not seven stanzas written by a bore,
> Prevent your Ladyship from taking snuff![44]

By writing a short and simple four-line poem that told Elizabeth to use the box as a vehicle for tobacco, Byron moved the object from the realms of sentiment back into the realm of practicality. It ceased to be a 'mystic box' that 'hath magic pow'r to raise / Spectres of myriads slain', and became once more a snuff-box.

While Napoleon is known to have once said that women 'may dance and amuse themselves, but they shall not thrust their noses into politics', it was through amusing herself and men with Napoleon's own keepsake snuff-box that Elizabeth engaged in politics.[45] She did this by inviting a poetic form of political commentary. But Napoleon's reason for gifting the snuff-box to Elizabeth and the meanings he intended it to hold are less certain. Did he intend it as a sign of respect for Elizabeth's intelligence – as a complex puzzle that he knew she would enjoy solving? Or was it intended as an elaborate joke at her expense and also that of Josephine, Marie Anne Le Normand and all other women? Napoleon considered women to be less intelligent than men and thought that ultimately their place was in the home. 'I do not like women who make men of themselves, any more than I like effeminate men,' he observed. 'There is a proper part for every one to play in the world'.[46] His French Civil Code of 1804 placed legal control over women's lives and property firmly in the hands of fathers or husbands, so reversing the gains in the liberty and equality of women brought by the revolution.[47]

An extremely wealthy, intelligent and tenacious political salon hostess, unlike most women during the period, Elizabeth enjoyed an equal partnership with her husband. In a highly patriarchal society, however, this was viewed as a reversal of gender norms, as is perhaps best seen in a caricature of Elizabeth and Henry sneaking Napoleon into the treasury building (figure 8.9). She wears trousers in the caricature, while he wears a skirt. Elizabeth courted scandal, having divorced her first husband to marry Henry, with a child born out of wedlock in the process. She was in every way the opposite of Napoleon's ideal woman; 'A husband who suffers himself to be led by his wife always ranks very low in my estimation', he once quipped.[48] Perhaps, then, the Emperor knew that in Elizabeth's hands his keepsake would make for another scandal and in fact this was his very intention: to thrust her nose into politics to show that ultimately it had no place there.

Conclusion

By marketing himself through visual merchandise, Napoleon came to rely on women's consumer decisions during his reign. Women used Napoleonic keepsakes to show their political affiliation. A rejection of such keepsakes showed the opposite.

Ultimately, in death, Napoleon relied heavily on the sentiment of women to prolong his legacy. Following the bequest of the snuff-box, Elizabeth received other keepsakes from Napoleon's female family and friends. In November 1821 Albine de Montholon – who

A snuff-box and other Napoleonic keepsakes 221

8.9 Samuel de Wilde, *Sketch for a Prime Minister or How to Purchase a Peace*, 1811, 235 mm × 195 mm, etching and aquatint.

accompanied Napoleon on St Helena with her husband, Napoleon's trusted general Charles Tristan, Marquis de Montholon – delivered a crystal locket, containing a thin strand of Napoleon's hair, tied with faded tricolour string. Countess Françoise-Elisabeth Bertrand – the wife of Henri-Gatien, comte Bertrand and a relation of Josephine Bonaparte – followed this keepsake with a gift of Napoleon's gold ring, together with one of his socks worn at time of his death.[49] Such small and mundane objects rendered extraordinary through their association with the Emperor, have played just as significant a role in prolonging his legacy as grand history paintings and sculptures.

Elizabeth exerted her agency as a wealthy and intelligent woman to enjoy an equal relationship with her husband and a warm friendship with an Emperor. It was through a combination of emotional display, keepsake exchange and soliciting poetry that she engaged in politics. It is by recognising the legitimacy of these personal avenues for political expression and examining the cultural and social context in which they operated that we can better understand the complexities of eighteenth-century women's involvement in social politics.

Notes

1 Martyn Lyons, *Napoleon Bonaparte and the Legacy of the French Revolution* (London: Macmillan, 1994), 113.
2 In using the term 'Volpone' the print drew from the popular Jacobean-era satire of greed and lust by the English playwright Ben Johnson.
3 Kari E. Lokke and Adriana Craciun, *Rebellious Hearts: British Women Writers and the French Revolution* (New York: State University of New York Press, 2001), 10–11.
4 Letter to Henry Holland, dated 23 November 1799, in John Russell, *Memorials and Correspondence of Charles James Fox*, vol. 3 (London: Richard Bentley, 1854), 167.
5 Letter to Dennis O'Bryen, dated 16 July 1800, in *Putnam's Magazine: Original Papers on Literature, Science, Art, and National Interests* (New York: G. P. Putnam & Son, 1868), 692.
6 Letter to Charles Grey, dated 22 October 1801, in Russell, *Memorials and Correspondence of Charles James Fox*, 349.
7 Quoted in Linda Kelly, *Holland House: A History of London's Most Celebrated Salon* (London: I. B. Tauris, 2013), 38.
8 Kelly, *Holland House: A History of London's Most Celebrated Salon*, 38.
9 Edward V. R. Powys, 'Napoleon and Lady Holland', *Spectator* (8 November 1913): 17.

10 Alexandra Franklin, 'John Bull in a dream: fear and fantasy in the visual satires of 1803', in *Resisting Napoleon: The British Response to the Threat of Invasion, 1797–1815*, ed. Mark Philp (Burlington: Ashgate, 2006), 134.
11 Katherine Wilmot, *An Irish Peer on the Continent 1801–1803: Being a Narrative of the Tour of Stephen, Earl Mount Cashell*, ed. Thomas Sadleir (London: Williams and Norgate, 1920), 21.
12 For more on Napoleon and popular culture, see Philip Dwyer, *Napoleon: The Path to Power 1769–1799* (London: Bloomsbury, 2014).
13 For more on women's engagement with the French Revolution through consumer culture, see Pamela Buck, 'The Things She Carried: Nationalism, Commerce, and the Souvenir in British Romantic Women's Writing on the French Revolution' (PhD thesis, Tufts University, 2008), 85–122. Buck is currently working on a book on how women writers used souvenirs to circulate political ideas tentatively titled "Objects of Liberty: Romantic Women Writers and Revolutionary Souvenirs".
14 Wilmot, *An Irish Peer on the Continent*, 29.
15 Raphaël Ingelbien, *Irish Cultures of Travel: Writing on the Continent, 1829–1914* (London: Palgrave Macmillan, 2016), 22.
16 Peter Thorold, *The British in France: Visitors and Residents since the Revolution* (London: Bloomsbury, 2008), 6.
17 Wilmot, *An Irish Peer on the Continent*, 47.
18 Wilmot, *An Irish Peer on the Continent*, 36.
19 T. Faulkner and B. West, *History and Antiquities of Kensington* (London: T. Egerton, 1820), 112.
20 Kelly, *Holland House: A History of London's Most Celebrated Salon*, 81.
21 Granville Leveson-Gower, *The Private Correspondence of Lord Granville Leveson-Gower, First Earl Granville*, ed. Castalia Rosalind Campbell Leveson-Gower, vol. 2 (London: J. Murray, 1916), 495.
22 Quoted in Sonia Keppel, *The Sovereign Lady: A Life of Elizabeth Vassall, Third Lady Holland, with Her Family* (London: Hamilton, 1974), 205.
23 Katharine Macdonogh, 'A sympathetic ear: Napoleon, Elba and the British', *History Today* 44, no. 2 (February 1994), 32; Desmond Gregory, *Napoleon's Jailer: Lt. Gen. Sir Hudson Lowe: A Life* (London: Fairleigh Dickinson University Press, 1996), 121–2.
24 Faulkner and West, *History and Antiquities of Kensington*, 118.
25 Faulkner and West, *History and Antiquities of Kensington*, 117.
26 C. J. Wright, 'Fox, Elizabeth Vassall [née Elizabeth Vassall], Lady Holland [other married name Elizabeth Vassall Webster, Lady Webster] (1771?–1845)', *Oxford Dictionary of National Biography*, last updated 3 January 2008, https://doi.org/10.1093/ref:odnb/10028.

27 Marie Henriette Norberte Liechtenstein, *Holland House* (London: Macmillan, 1874), 121.
28 Macdonogh, 'A sympathetic ear: Napoleon, Elba and the British', 30.
29 Leslie Mitchell, *Holland House* (London: Duckworth, 1980), 258.
30 Macdonogh, 'A sympathetic ear: Napoleon, Elba and the British', 32; Gregory, *Napoleon's Jailer*, 121–2.
31 Henry Richard Vassall Holland, 'Protest to the second part of Bonaparte's Detention Bill', *National Register* 1, no. 15 (1816): 240.
32 Keppel, *The Sovereign Lady*, 223.
33 Stuart Semmel, 'British Uses for Napoleon', *MLN* 120, no. 4 (2005).
34 Letter from Lady Elizabeth Holland to Sir Hudson Lowe, 29 July 1820 in Liechtenstein, *Holland House*, 152; see also, Kelly, *Holland House: A History of London's Most Celebrated Salon*, 93.
35 Keppel, *The Sovereign Lady*, 225–6; Henry Richard Vassall Holland, *Foreign Reminiscences*, ed. Henry Edward Fox, 2nd edn (London: Longman, Brown, Green, and Longmans, 1851), 196–7.
36 Nancy du Tertre, *The Art of the Limoges Box* (New York: Harry N. Abrams Inc., 2003), 41.
37 'Buonaparte's last will and testament', Appendix 12 of Walter Scott, *The Life of Napoleon, Emperor of the French: With a Preliminary View of the French Revolution*, vol. 2 (Exeter: J. & B. Williams, 1836), lvi.
38 The maker's mark of a cock between two grains and the inscription 'AV' indicate that the box was made in Paris by Adrien Jean Maximilien Vachette, the celebrated goldsmith and box-maker of the Napoleonic Empire.
39 Catherine Perry Hargrave, *A History of Playing Cards and a Bibliography of Cards and Gaming* (New York: Dover Publications, 2000), 50.
40 Marie Anne Le Normand, *Historical and Secret Memoirs of the Empress Josephine (Marie Rose Tascher de la Pagerie): First Wife of Napoleon Bonaparte*, trans. Jacob M. Howard, vol. 1 (Philadelphia: Carey and Hart, 1848).
41 *Remarkable Women of Different Nations and Ages* (Boston: John P. Jewett, 1858), 211–13.
42 Thomas Moore, *The Poetical Works of Thomas Moore* (London: Longman, Orme, Brown, Green, and Longmans, 1841), 398.
43 Earl of Carlisle, 'To Lady Holland, on the legacy of a snuff-box, left to her by Buonaparte', *The Gentleman's Magazine: And Historical Chronicle. From July to December 1821*, vol. 91 (1821): 457–8.
44 Thomas Medwin, *Conversations of Lord Byron: Noted During a Residence with His Lordship at Pina, in the Years 1821 and 1822* (London: Colburn, 1824), 362.

45 Louis Antoine Fauvelet de Bourrienne, *The Life of Napoleon Bonaparte* (Philadelphia: Carey & Lee, 1832), 196.
46 Bourrienne, *The Life of Napoleon Bonaparte*, 196.
47 George Spence, *The Code Napoleon, or, the French Civil Code. Literally Translated from the Original and Official Edition, Published at Paris, in 1804. By a Barrister of the Inner Temple* (London: Charles Hunter, 1824).
48 Armand Augustin Louis de Caulaincourt, *Recollections of Caulaincourt, Duke of Vicenza*, vol. 1 (London, 1838), 135.
49 Keppel, *The Sovereign Lady*, 254.

9

Princess Ekaterina Dashkova's gifts to Martha Wilmot

In 1803, towards the end of her life, Ekaterina Romanovna Dashkova welcomed twenty-eight-year-old Martha Wilmot to her rural estate of Troitskoe, around 60 miles west of Moscow. Exiled from court and finding herself alone and forgotten, Ekaterina hoped that Martha, the Anglo-Irish niece of her old travelling companion Katherine Hamilton, would be a source of companionship. The closest female friend of Catherine the Great and the only female head of the St Petersburg Academy of Sciences and the Russian Academy, Ekaterina must have cut an impressive figure in the eyes of her young visitor from County Cork. Martha remained as her guest for five years. Waited upon by two hundred servants and three thousand serfs in the surrounds of Ekaterina's immense collection of artworks and natural history specimens, she was given paintings, books, precious stones, sables, shawls and keepsakes in the form of jewellery, miniatures and personal accoutrements connected with significant people and events from the life of the sixty-year-old princess.[1] Martha returned home with these objects and others that captured something of her experience of Russian culture, including traditional dresses and transcripts of Russian songs and folklore.[2]

This chapter explores Ekaterina's strategic gift-giving to Martha that had the aim of sealing a friendship with an impression of both herself and of her country. The second-eldest daughter of Captain Edward Wilmot and his wife, Martha (née Moore), of Glanmire, Ireland, Martha came from a wealthy and well-connected family but was overwhelmed by Ekaterina's status in a country where 'every woman has the right over her own fortune totally independent of her husband'.[3] As the daughter of the influential noble Vorontsov family, Ekaterina owned multiple estates in Russia and Poland. A defining part of her identity were her nearly two decades of travel in Britain and Europe, and her academic positions. I argue that these three factors – the ownership of property, travel and the inhabitation of positions usually reserved for men – gave Ekaterina an unusual degree of flexibility in relation to gender norms. She used a combination of sentiment and patronage to form a friendship with Martha and to inspire immense loyalty in her Anglo-Irish guest. She also used femininity and masculinity in her gifts to narrate aspects of Russian history and culture in which her personal and political lives intersected. The maternal bonds developed through Ekaterina's keepsakes would lead Martha to dedicate her life to the woman she came to call her 'Russian mother'. These objects led to a female-oriented story of Russian culture that combined the grand with the commonplace.[4]

When Martha first arrived at Ekaterina's white stucco mansion in Troitskoe on 24 April 1803, she found 'the Princess Ds reception of me kind, indeed affectionately so', and upon first entering her room was delighted to discover 'two trunks, containing different sorts of things, which all mark attention and kindness in the Princess towards me'.[5] This generous gift was succeeded by many more. By 8 November Martha was missing her family: 'I am woefully disappointed at not receiving letters', she lamented in her journal, but in the next sentence happily remarked that Ekaterina 'offered one of her boxes of treasures and curiosities to amuse us'.[6] The box contained 'a multitude of snuffboxes', '40 different stones from all parts of the world' and 'curiosities taken from the ruins of Herculaneum'.[7] Martha's journals and letters home are laden with exclamations of 'the princess presented me' and 'the princess gave me'. The following excerpts from her journal entries between January and February 1804 are typical:

10 January, 'This morning Princess D came to my room and brought me a most elegant pearl necklace';

18 January, 'Princess D presented me with a most elegant ornament for my head, an opal, set in diamonds';

24 January, 'The princess presented me with a very pretty Russ truswell gown, and a piece of ditto to send to England';

1 February, 'The princess sent to my room this morn a rose tree in full bloom';

23 February, 'Yesterday Gent Harring sent the Princess a string of black amber and a cross, which she gave to me';

27 February, 'the princess sent me some beads &c to send to Ireland to my sisters by Mr Wilson'.[8]

With each gift, Martha's sense of affection and gratitude increased correspondingly. By 30 March the sentiment required to match Ekaterina's excess of gifts had overwhelmed Martha. She wrote:

Today the Princess gave me her writing case de voyage and talked to me on the subject of arranging a plan to make me at ease in my circumstances in case of her sudden death. This conversation affected me more than she supposed, not that I think her ill, at least seriously so, but her affection and consideration for me, have a tenderness in them, that at times goes to my very heart – it makes me too, fear to look forward – gratitude is a strong chain and my feelings acknowledge its force, my affection too, is not I hope less sincere, than the Princess – yet, alone, separated from every relation – with new circumstances, people, dispositions, to deal with, there are moments when I feel deeply my own insufficiency.[9]

Here, Martha refers to her gratitude as a 'strong chain' that bound her to Ekaterina with 'force'. She fretted that her sincerity and affection were insufficient in comparison to those of the Princess, stretched as she was between Ekaterina and her family at home. Martha likely truly felt these emotions for her friend, but this does not stop them, at the same time, from reflecting the social necessity of sentimentality in the late eighteenth and early nineteenth centuries. When Lady Louisa Stuart, for instance, read Henry Mackenzie's novel *The Man of Feeling* (1771) at the age of fourteen, she was 'secretly afraid lest she should not cry enough to gain the credit of proper sensibility'.[10] By fretting over the level of her affection in comparison to Ekaterina, Martha was also subconsciously fretting over the level of her sensibility in comparison to that of the Princess.

When Katherine joined her younger sister in Russia in 1805 and saw the extravagant presents loaded upon her, she exclaimed in a letter to her sister in-law Anna Chetwood:

Tis all *a Chance* when she gets really valuable things. For whether it is a *diamond*, or a *Flower*, I think the Princess seems to know no difference, & wd not give it, if she thought there was any other value attached, than what her affection insures.[11]

While on the surface this statement seems to support the sentimental value of the objects as keepsakes, Katherine only noted Ekaterina's inability to distinguish their monetary worth because Martha and her family, as the receivers, appreciated the difference between a diamond and a flower. Indeed, in her journals and letters to family and friends, Martha took note of financially valuable items, such as 'a Siberian amethyst set in the *best* brilliants, & very large', which she feared 'has cost a world of money'; a picture 'which has cost a mint'; and snuff-boxes, 'set in gold' and decorated with mosaic lids and precious stones.[12] Martha and her family clearly valued Ekaterina's keepsakes because their social status was enhanced by the precious materials they were made from and the technological skills required to create them.

A conflict between the financial value of the objects themselves and the value of Ekaterina's affection, however, is evidenced by Martha's frequent qualifications. In a letter to her father in August 1803, for instance, Martha asserted that the Princess's gifts indicated 'a good nature and attention that is of a thousand times more value than the things themselves'.[13] In a letter to her mother in February 1804, Martha described Ekaterina's affection for her as 'really and truly boundless', noting that it 'occupies more than half her life and literally animates every action'.[14] The financial value of the keepsakes thus remained carefully unacknowledged by Martha because she understood that articulating this would undermine their sentimental value and, by extension, her relationship with the Princess.

It was through bestowing expensive gifts steeped in sentimental value that Ekaterina was able to establish a hierarchical relationship with Martha and her family. In January 1805 Martha wrote in her journal that she wished the Princess 'would be less generous, as I cannot bear the idea of causing her so much expense, but there's no stopping her noble nature, when she wishes to give pleasure, or to ornament a person who is fortunate enough to possess her affection'.[15] Ekaterina lightly reinforced this vertical patronage relationship if Martha failed to appropriately display her gratitude, for example when she 'jokingly ask'd' Katherine 'what punishment she should inflict!' on her sister for not taking snuff, 'as she had seven or eight Imperial boxes'. Katherine suggested that the Princess 'shou'd serve Matty's *nose*, as she does her favourite trees, in the shrubbery – *crop it*, till as many *noses sprung up in a copse*, as she had *gorgeous*

Snuff Boxes – The Princess look'd ready to cry, & thought us both no better than Butchers – she instantly turn'd the conversation!'[16] This humorous aside from Katherine appears harmless enough, but it reveals the nature of the relationship between the three women. Ekaterina clearly sought to instil some small guilt in Martha for not using her snuff-boxes when she had so many. While this was Martha's first time travelling, Katherine had come to Russia from her travels through Revolutionary France and Italy. As the more worldly and forthright older sister, Katherine often took issue with Ekaterina's proprietorship of Martha. In this case, she argued that the excessive number of snuff-boxes rendered her younger sister incapable of using them for the functional purpose of storing tobacco. Katherine then upset Ekaterina by alluding to the true purpose of the snuff-boxes – that is, as vessels for the Princess to exert her power over Martha by instilling in her an excess of gratitude. Like a topiary shrub, the more Ekaterina trimmed Martha, the more her will to please grew, so that the Princess could mould her into any shape she desired. This aside, then, indicates the power that a woman could hold over another when she was in the unusual position of being able to combine sentiment and patronage.

Ekaterina was able to exert this authority for four distinct reasons: the first was her ability, as a Russian woman, to own property; the second, her widow status (her husband had passed away in 1764); third, her worldliness for having travelled; and finally, the leadership positions she had held under Catherine the Great, ordinarily given to men. Between 1769 and 1771, and again from 1775 to 1782, Ekaterina had lived abroad, travelling to Germany, France, England, Scotland, Italy, Switzerland and Holland. While in Ferney, Paris and Edinburgh, she built a network around personal acquaintances with François-Marie Arouet (known by his nom de plume, Voltaire), Denis Diderot, Benjamin Franklin and leading members of the Scottish Enlightenment such as William Robertson, Adam Smith, Hugh Blair and Adam Ferguson. In 1783 the Princess retuned to Russia to take up a position as director of the Imperial Academy of Arts and Sciences. In the following year she was named the first president of the newly created Russian Academy, which claimed some of Russia's greatest minds as its members, including the poets Gavriil Derzhavin, Mikhail Kheraskov, Nikolay Lvov and Aleksei Rzhevsky; the playwrights Denis Fonvizin and Yakov Knyazhnin; and the historians

Ivan Boltin and Mikhailo Shcherbatov.[17] Knowing Ekaterina to be well versed in Enlightenment arts and sciences and well connected (she was already a member of the American Philosophical Society, St Peterburg Economic Society and Royal Irish, Berlin and Stockholm academies at the time of her appointment), Catherine the Great deliberately chose her for these positions to send a message to her subjects about women's capabilities.[18]

At the time, State positions were usually reserved for men, meaning the Princess had to carefully display masculine attributes to inhabit the positions. But Ekaterina's travels had given her worldly knowledge and connections. This combination is seen in a portrait painted by the court painter Dmitry Levitsky a year after Ekaterina's appointment to the role of director. Instead of representing herself in the midst of her intellectual and administrative pursuits, Ekaterina chose to be shown as a faithful servant. In the portrait (figure 9.1), she was dressed as a lady-in-waiting and decorated with a sash of the order of St Catherine, which she received as a sign of gratitude from Catherine the Great for helping to organise the 1762 coup that put the latter on the throne. This painting demonstrated the feminine subservience of the Princess. At the same time, however, it took a playful attitude towards gender that elevated Ekaterina to a position closer to her monarch. Catherine the Great is known for using the stereotypes and iconography relating to gender in flexible ways. Like her predecessor, Elizabeth Petrovna (who also wore armour and hunted), Catherine 'exemplified male as well as female qualities, both prowess and graciousness'.[19] Here, Ekaterina sought to use the male feature of a flat chest and her military style outfit to make an argument for her suitability as director of the academy. The Princess acknowledged the need for this gender shift to Catherine the Great, wondering 'whether I ought to thank you for this mark of your good opinion of me, or whether, on the contrary, I ought not rather to condole with you for this strange and unheard-of creation, in making a woman the director of an academy of science'.[20]

Publicly, viewers interpreted the painting according to Ekaterina's intention. In his collection of poetry published in 1790, the highly renowned poet and statesman Gavriil Derzhavin wrote in a poem accompanying the printed version of the portrait:

> Her companion she was,
> When from heaven Astrea

9.1 Dmitry Grigorievich Levitsky, *Portrait of Yekaterina Vorontsova-Dashkova*, 1784, 59.6 cm × 49.5 cm, oil on canvas.

> Went forth to mount the throne;
> But now – she is Apollo.[21]

Here Derzhavin connected Ekaterina's early position to that of the celestial virgin, who lived with humans before ascending to heaven to become the constellation Virgo. Legend had it that Astrea would one day come back to earth, bringing the return of a utopian Golden

Age.²² Instead, Derzhavin had Ekaterina return as male – the son of Zeus, god of sun, archery, music, dance, poetry, truth, prophecy and healing. Privately, however, the assessment was crude. Derzhavin wrote 'To the portrait of a Hermaphrodite', circulated among his friends and found in his manuscripts following his death in 1816:

> This physiognomy:
> Both a she and a he.
> These features:
> Both a bird's and a geezer's.
> This phizog:
> Both bitch and dog.
> This physique:
> Both *baba* and *muzhik*.²³

While the public poem lauded Ekaterina's combination of masculine and feminine attributes, the private couplet painted it as something lewd (as indicated by Georgina' Barker's translation above). In Chapter 8 we saw that Elizabeth Holland's expression of an equal relationship with her husband was represented in a caricature as a gender reversal in which she wore trousers while her husband wore a skirt. Here Ekaterina's exertion of an equal relationship with men of her same rank by inhabiting the position of director was represented as hermaphroditism. Yet, Ekaterina had to combine femininity and masculinity in all aspects of her life in order to maintain her position. By questioning her sex, Derzhavin and others sought to undermine her authority at a fundamental level.

How Ekaterina used gendered iconography to form a binding friendship with Martha is perhaps most clearly seen in their exchange of portraits. One of the first keepsakes Ekaterina gave Martha was a bracelet containing a miniature portrait of the Princess. In a letter to her mother in September 1803, Martha wrote that it was intended to be worn on the left arm and was 'literally call'd a *sentiment*'. 'You may be sure', she continued, 'this same bracelet is a more agreeable testimony of Ekaterina's affection than anything else cou'd be'.²⁴ Three months later, Martha described her 'favourite room' to her mother. It was her study, which contained 'a most elegant Bureau where all my writing implements are arranged in the compleatest order. Over the Bureau hangs the Princess's picture'.²⁵ Through these gifts, the Princess ensured that Martha's body publicly displayed their relationship and that Martha looked at her face whenever she sat down to write.

In giving Martha the portraits, Ekaterina combined a horizontal female–female romantic friendship with a monarchal/patriarchal vertical patronage relationship. As discussed in Chapter 7, to express their sensibility and gentility, women regularly exchanged keepsakes with one another, including miniature portrait objects. In 1759 Louisa Connolly, for instance, similarly used a miniature portrait as a motif to express her close friendship with her sister Emily Lennox. She declared in a letter to Emily, 'You have no notion, my dearest sister, how happy I am to have so sweet a picture of you as I have to wear constantly; its [sic] the greatest pleasure almost I have, to look at it so constantly as I do'.[26] Worn on the body as jewellery, exhibited in specially constructed rooms, placed on top of snuff-boxes and memorandum cases, or concealed in a woman's dressing table, the miniature portrait was, according to Susan Stabile, 'the most personal form of portraiture'.[27] Ekaterina's portrait gifts, then, expressed a sentimental horizontal female–female friendship between her and Martha by encouraging affectionate private remembrance of the Princess.

On another level, however, Ekaterina's portraits were diplomatic gifts with political import. Ambassadors and loyal subjects carried miniature portraits of their monarchs on their bodies. These usually took the form of either a pendant comprised of a painted miniature in a precious frame or a portrait medal. The hand-painted miniature emphasised physical characteristics and indicated a closeness between the recipient and the monarch.[28] During her time at court, Martha observed that Grigory Grigoryevich Orlov – who led the palace coup that placed Catherine the Great on the throne and was her virtual co-ruler – wore 'the Empress' picture, which is covered with a single diamond, instead of glass'.[29] According to Martha, 'Princess Dashkaw was also adorned with her red ribbon, and order of St Katherine, her magnificent portrait set round and crowned with most magnificent diamonds &c &c'.[30] By accepting the sentiment and wearing it, then, Martha was engaging in a political practice that showed her loyalty to Ekaterina and the influence the Princess had at court.

At home the portraits placed Ekaterina in the position of a father or husband in relation to Martha. In the second half of the eighteenth

9.2 Portrait of Martha Wilmot, in *The Russian Journals of Martha and Katherine Wilmot 1803–1808*, 1934 (inside front cover).

century it was common practice to have miniature portrait objects depicting men reinscribed onto larger-scale portraits of their wives.[31] These representations were usually hung from a ribbon, worn as part of a parure (a set of matching jewellery), or mounted on a pearl bracelet. They suggested allegiance to a spouse who had legal rights over his wife's person but also a financial obligation to her. Ekaterina's age and status allowed her to claim this vertical patronage role in relation to her young Anglo-Irish guest. As the reigning monarch of her household, Ekaterina also commissioned many portraits of Martha (figure 9.2). These included one large oil as the 'principal object in her drawing room at Moscow' and a second in her bedchamber. Again, in this arena the Princess overwhelmed Martha with her largesse. On 9 January 1804 Martha wrote to her sister-in-law:

> I give you twenty guesses to find out what I am going to do – you cannot – well I'll tell you – to sit for four pictures – only think – The Princess will have a miniature of this ridiculous face of mine, in a

snuff box – a second miniature she intends to send to my mother – is not that amiable and affectionate? The two others are to be large painted in oyles – I am confronted beyond measure – and the notion of so many shadows appearing in the noon day – but what can I do?[32]

Much of Martha's time over the coming months was spent in 'that stupid and most disagreeable occupation' of sitting for her picture.[33] When she joined Martha in 1805, Katherine was surprised that Ekaterina found her unremarkable sister 'a *perfect beauty*', worthy of so many portraits, and exclaimed in a letter to Anna Chetwood in September 1804:

> To doubt this is heresy! And as all the varieties are not expressed in one single picture I have no doubt that before she stops a dozen will be drawn! In fact this is so establish'd an idea that without hazarding an investigation Anna Petrovna and I (neither of whom Lord help us have perform'd any metamorphosis since our birth) take her on the grounds of a Venus de Medicis! I solemnly protest, I do not exaggerate an iota![34]

In the eighteenth and early nineteenth centuries artists were often commissioned to paint portraits of women about to be married, or recently wed. The women were typically painted in the guise of goddesses or virtues easily identified by symbolic attributes, such as Diana, Hebe, the Muses, pastoral figures or seasons. Men were seldom portrayed at the moment of this rite of passage: their portraits would instead celebrate their Grand Tour or, later in life, some moment of civil or military achievement.[35] While Martha was not marrying Ekaterina, the social and age dynamic between the two made it appropriate for the Princess to commission portraits of herself as an individual and portraits of her guest as a mythological beauty.

Unlike young, unmarried and untravelled Martha, the Princess had participated in the Grand Tour and in several moments of military and civil achievement during her lifetime. On 28 June 1762 she had played a central role in the coup that overthrew her godfather, Peter III, and brought his thirty-three-year-old wife to power. When Catherine was proclaimed empress on 28 June 1762, the two women symbolically donned the green-and-red Preobrazhenskii Regiment uniform, unpopularly abolished by Peter III, to lead troops from the Winter Palace to Peterhof Palace.[36] While she was an academic director, the

Princess participated in scholarly pedagogical and publishing activities, oversaw research projects and instituted courses and public lectures. Her writings appeared in various journals, including translations of Enlightenment philosophers Claude Helvétius, David Hume and Voltaire, and articles on agriculture, education and morality.[37] Two key projects were the publication of Mikhail Lomonosov's complete works and the creation of a six-volume dictionary of the Russian languages.[38] She was thus in the unusual position of having the status and means to take control of her own portraits, while Martha, like most elite British women, was not. Ekaterina's agency was reflected in the degree to which she was able to shape both her own image and that of other women.

Unwell, aged and having found herself removed from the Russian court, it was Ekaterina's intention to form this binding multidimensional relationship with Martha in order to ensure a legacy. As Katherine put it, she was acting, 'precisely as if she was already Dead' by giving her young Anglo-Irish guest 'monuments of her esteem'.[39] Catherine the Great died in 1796 and was succeeded by her son Paul. A capricious leader with a passion for military order, Paul imposed tight censorship on travel abroad and prohibited foreign books, fashion and music. He forced the Princess to give up her directorship and move to her son's property in the village of Korotovo in the northern regions of Novgorod Province, where she was expected to 'recollect the epoch of 1762'.[40] Paul's reign was short, however: he was murdered by conspirators from the upper society of St Petersburg in 1801. When his son Alexander took the throne, Russia was at odds with most of Europe. The new monarch quickly shifted this dynamic by making peace with France and Britain and restoring normal relations with Austria. Alexander also allowed Ekaterina to return to her white stucco mansion in Troitskoe to which she invited Martha and Katherine Wilmot to stay.[41] Alexander's reign began a new period in which the ageing princess turned her gift-giving towards leaving a history of herself, and of the vision of Russia she had promoted under Catherine the Great.

Sociologists and anthropologists have noted that histories create 'inalienability'.[42] The inalienable gift is never fully transferred to the receiver, but is instead lent as a repository of genealogies, origin myths, sacred ancestors or gods. Ekaterina frequently gave Martha items that had obtained inalienability from a female lineage. In November 1805, for instance, Ekaterina presented Martha with a keepsake originally given to her by Catherine the Great. Martha wrote in her journal:

> But a few days ago she gave me a gage d'amitie which she prized to such a degree that she told me she had intended to have it buried with her, and that in changing that intention in order to give it to me, I might judge of her tenderness and affection for, it was the first present she ever received from Katherine the second, and certainly served to recall the most interesting period of a friendship, which then existed assuredly ... it is a beautiful fan; which the princess happening to admire in Katherine's hand, was requested by the Empress to accept as a memorandum of her affections. This happened just before the Princess D's marriage. I think I shall get it most elegantly framed, and consider it as one of the most valuable memorandums of friendship which I possess.[43]

Catherine the Great must have given Ekaterina the fan in 1758, one year before the Princess's marriage to Prince Mikhail Dashkov. This was the first time the women met and in the figure of the future empress, Ekaterina found a model of intelligence and achievement.[44] Following Catherine's succession, however, the pair fell out, in part because Ekaterina disproved of her monarch's increasingly conservative policies and tendency to let her romantic attachments to men influence her politics. After her husband's death in 1764, Ekaterina's life assumed a pattern of exile and return until her academic appointment of 1783. This fan was an heirloom of the most important person in Ekaterina's life and a moment of affection they had shared before growing apart. By giving the fan to Martha the Princess was guaranteeing remembrance of their personal connection.

A few days after giving Martha the fan, Ekaterina presented her with a keepsake from another significant woman in her life. Martha wrote in her journal:

> This evening the Princess presented me with a most exquisitely beautiful box of arborized agate, set in gold with as much taste as if it had been the fashion of today, it is rendered a still more valuable present from the assurance which she gave me, of her attaching an idea of sentiment to it, quite peculiar, as it had belonged to her *mother*, for whose memory, her respect was unbounded, and that box, is one of the only memorandums of her which she ever possessed.[45]

Martha valued this gift for its tasteful design of arborised agate set in gold, which remained in fashion despite its age. Its chief value, however, lay in the remembrance it encouraged of its original owner, Ekaterina's mother, Marfa Surmina, who died when she was just two. With these two keepsakes Ekaterina connected Martha to the two most important women in her life: her birth mother and Catherine the Great. She so incorporated Martha into a long and powerful chain of female lineage that was both personal and political.

In 1806 Ekaterina gave Martha her largest monument (and one she was, in the end, unable to take home because of its size).[46] This was a copy of a painting the classical history painter Grigory Ugriumov created for Paul's resurrection hall in the Mikhailovsky palace.[47] The original *The Conquest of Kazan by Ivan the Terrible* sat within a set of six paintings that all portrayed historical Russian conquests like *The Victory of Dmitry Donskoi over Tatars* and *Peter the Great's Victory in Poltava*.[48] The Emperor's first act after his ascension was to sign a decree that prevented women from ruling Russia. These paintings helped to remove women's leadership from history by celebrating the role that male leadership in war played in the creation of strong state.

They connected Paul I to a long tradition of male rulers lasting almost a millennium to obscure the previous centuries' empresses (Catherine I, Anna Ioannovna, Elizabeth I and Catherine II).[49] Each painting instead portrayed women as subordinate characters or victims. In the painting that Ekaterina chose to copy, the women were symbols of the three types of femininity valued by a patriarchal society: the innocent virgin, represented by the girl looking down; the whore, represented by the sexually active young woman; and lastly, the mother, represented by the woman with the baby (see plate 15).

At first impression, it seems strange that the Princess went to the effort of commissioning a copy of a painting that blatantly celebrated male leadership and obscured female power. It is probable that, on a personal level, Ekaterina used this painting to draw parallels between the three women's suffering and her own under forced retirement. But more broadly, displaying the copy in a new context provided an opportunity to reject Paul I's promotion of male leadership in war. In the context of the Princess's house, which was predominantly decorated with images of powerful independent women and peaceful landscapes, the message of dominant masculinity at the centre of the painting was replaced by a focus on the plea of the three women at its centre.[50] Ekaterina thus effectively subverted the painting's original intention to contest the tyranny of emperors. She so transformed the focus of the painting from the monumental and magnificent to the sentimental and personal, from masculine to feminine, and from the promotion of war into the promotion of peace.

Ekaterina sent many keepsakes back to Martha's family in Ireland. One of these, a steel and brass fireplace (figure 9.3), made similar links between the monumental and the intimate, and between war and peace. Martha's parents and sisters must have been puzzled when they received this gift in 1806 without instruction. It could not serve its practical purpose of warming a room, because anyone attempting to light it would have found themselves burnt by its red-hot steel. Martha revealed the gift's true purpose in a later letter. 'Have you found out that the Curiosity from Tula is a Machine for perfuming the rooms?' she asked in December 1806, before going on to provide further explanation: 'Charcoal is placed in it & perfumes burn'd which *fume* through Suites of Apartments as the little machine is whisk'd about ... Its office I now suppose will be to lie quietly on the steel chimney peice'.[51]

Sent to the Wilmots one year after Russia and Britain had joined the Third Coalition against Revolutionary France, this fireplace had a sentimental symbolic application rather than a practical one. It was manufactured in Russia's Imperial Armoury Factory at Tula, which had, since 1712, produced both practical and diplomatic weapons. By having a fireplace, which sits at the heart of the home, manufactured at Tula, rather than guns and weapons, which signify the home's destruction, Ekaterina sought to demonstrate the larger reconciliation of Britain and Russia, whose relationship had been tumultuous over the preceding decade. To join the Third Coalition, Russia had agreed to receive £1.25 million a year from Britain for every hundred thousand troops the country put up against Napoleon.[52] Made using the same techniques and materials that were used to produce weapons, the fireplace thus embodied Russia's defence of the home hearth that lay at the very heart of the British Empire.[53] In the form of the fireplace, Ekaterina again cleverly connected the personal and the political to display a friendship of two families and also two empires.

Ekaterina Dashkova's gifts to Martha Wilmot 241

9.3 Fireplace, *c.*1800, Russian Imperial Arms Factory, Tula, forged, blued and cut steel with facetted steel and gilt brass ornaments.

One of the most valuable keepsakes that Ekaterina gave Martha was 'three most interesting Volumes of a Description of all the Nations submitted to Russia', containing 'full of colour'd Prints of the Costumes of Each'.[54] On a personal level, Ekaterina attempted to use this book to establish a familial chain of connection. On the inner cover she wrote, 'This Book is offered to my Darling child Martha Romanovna Wilmot'. Martha took up this invitation into the Princess's family years later when she added to the inscription with one of her own: 'By her beloved Russian Mother, Princess Daschkaw, Who wrote the above lines – M. Wilmot (Moscow)'. After returning to Ireland in 1807, Martha married the rector William Bradford and, in 1813, gave birth to a daughter. The couple christened the baby Catherine Daschkaw and Martha bequeathed her the book, further adding to the inscription: 'I now offer these volumes to my dear child Catherine Daschkaw Bradford – named after the dear Princess. M. Bradford (Storrington, 25 Nov 1837)'.[55] Ekaterina's gift-giving so ensured her place as the matriarch in a familial chain of women offshore.

Brimming with expensive hand-coloured plates, the volumes formed the first ever attempt to give a comprehensive picture of the peoples of the Russian Empire through their traditional dress (figure 9.4). The author Johann Gottlieb Georgi's expeditions to Altai, Baikal, Zabaikalye and Povolzhye to conduct ethnographic research were sponsored by Catherine the Great and it was she who funded the book's publication.[56] The Empress often complained that Russian history was written by foreigners, who reported fables instead of facts.[57] The book formed part of her larger efforts to remedy this, while at the same time supporting her imperial mission to create a record of people and landscapes that were (or soon would be) tamed, domesticated and subservient to the Russian Empire.[58] As was the case with Ekaterina's other gifts, this gift thus combined the personal and the political to paint a picture of Catherine the Great as a 'protector' of the people while simultaneously promoting her wartime gains.

It is significant that Ekaterina only gave Martha the first three of Georgi's four volumes. The missing fourth volume, published in German in 1780 and in Russian in 1799, was solely dedicated to the 'Russians'.[59] This volume was outmoded by the time that Ekaterina gave Martha the other three, because it represented Russians through their costume, rather than their songs. In 1805 Nikolay Lvov – a Russian follower of German philosopher Johann Gottfried von Herder, who had promoted an interest in folklore as a source of information about each nation's early stages of development – argued that peasant songs were the key to understanding the Russian people.[60] Martha, therefore, returned to Ireland with notebooks filled with Russian folk songs that she had written up in the original Russian

9.4 'Eine Finnin im Feyertags Kleide', in *Description de toutes les nations de l'Empire de Russie*, St. Petersbourg, 1776–7.

and also translated into English, French and Italian.[61] Ekaterina's omission of the final volume coupled with Martha's collection of Russian songs signified their desire to quite literally give the Russian people a voice.

Unfortunately, peace between Britain and Russia was short-lived. Relations between the two countries soured again one year after Ekaterina sent the fireplace to Ireland, when Napoleon defeated the Russians at the Battle of Friedland and Alexander I signed the Treaties of Tilsit (1807). The terms obliged Russia to cease her maritime trade with Britain, leading to the Anglo-Russian War (1807–12). Faced by increasing danger, Katherine Wilmot fled Russia in 1807, with Martha following one year later. The Princess was devastated by the loss of her Anglo-Irish guests. 'The theatre is closed', she lamented in a letter to Martha in October 1809. 'I have not had a single performance; the pianoforte continues silent; the femmes de chambre have ceased to sing. Everything paints your absence and my sorrow'.[62] She died on 15 January 1810, just two years after Martha's forced departure.

Ekaterina's project to create a legacy through her bestowal of keepsakes was a success. After their trip, Martha's ties to Ekaterina became an integral part of her status as the self-proclaimed 'adopted child' of Russia.[63] Once resettled in Ireland, the sisters embarked on a series of excursions throughout the country, entertaining their hosts with excerpts from their travel journals, followed by tasters of Russian song and dance.[64] Martha and Katherine quickly became known for their travel accounts, Russian talents and keepsakes, as evidenced by Sarah Martha Holroyd's admiration of a 'Miss Wilmot' who 'sings Russ very sweetly and knows a hundred languages, and is as gentle and humble as if she knew nothing. She landed with most valuable presents, curious as well as rich, and was left 18,000l'.[65] Although they remained in manuscript form, it is clear that the sisters' travel journals and letters were doing the rounds, with Mrs Elizabeth Morgan noting in a letter to Martha, dated 19 February 1810, that her friends Miss Smyth and Mrs Tighe were 'employed at Barbavilla, in reading Miss Wilmot's Letters from the South of Europe, with great delight'. Morgan herself hoped 'to enjoy the same pleasure', and also looked forward to 'the treat, will it be, when you have ... transcrib[ed] into one Volume, those incomparable Letters from Russia, of which I read only two or three'.[66] The writings and souvenirs were a valuable form of cultural capital that represented Martha's experience of an exotic country few British people had visited and her friendship with an important figure there.

On 30 May 1814 the Treaty of Paris was signed, ending the war between France and the Sixth Coalition. The Congress of Vienna was then held from November 1814 to June 1815 to provide a long-term peace plan for Europe. Britain and Russia played a major cooperative role.[67] From 1819 to 1829, Martha and William lived in Vienna, where Reverend Bradford had been appointed chaplain to the British Embassy. Here she became known for her brilliant necklace showcasing 'the most magnificent cross you ever beheld'.

The Austrian court jeweller fashioned this cross from Martha's various Russian keepsakes, including the diamonds that had once surrounded her miniature portrait 'sentiment' bracelet.[68] Upon the completion of her new cross and other jewellery, Martha proclaimed her joy at 'gaining two beautiful (indeed three) beautiful and useful ornaments for the picture setting which you know I never wore'.[69] She wore the cross for her presentation to the Austrian imperial family and other occasions at court.[70]

It might be assumed that any alterations Martha made to her gifts dishonoured her relationship with Ekaterina. However, as an item of jewellery, the sentiment bracelet was located in the domain of luxury and fashionable display, and Martha's comment upon seeing her new cross shows that it was outmoded. By using parts of the bracelet to form her new cross, she ensured that the object still fulfilled its intended function as an item of fashionable adornment, which, in turn, served to encourage her remembrance of the Princess.[71] In the form of her new cross, Martha's remembrance of Ekaterina combined with her remembrance of other women throughout Russian history. The opal forming its centre had previously formed the clasp of a 'very elegant necklace of pearl' that Ekaterina had given Martha. She recorded the necklace's history in her journal in August 1808:

> *Christine Queen of Sweden!* had once upon a time a very beautiful opal ring, set round with very miserable little rubys, this ring, she gave to one of the Lords of her Court, who gave it to his Son. Count Pannin, being Ambassador at Stockholm from the Court of Russia, & an Amateur of raritys, saw this ring, & finding the stone of very uncommon beauty, exchang'd a *Solitaire* of the same size, against it. Return'd to Russia the Princess Dashkaw saw & admired it, Count P. her uncle gave it to her, & a year ago she had it magnificently set in diamonds as a clasp for a necklace, & gave it to me![72]

Martha's new cross, then, wrote her body into a timeless narrative by connecting it to both Ekaterina and this long line of royalty. As Marcia Pointon puts it, it is jewellery's 'capacity for transformation – this lending itself to stand as both material and immaterial, to be malleable and changeable while representing permanence', that gives it inalienable value.[73] Refashioned by the court jewellers, the cross now also took on Martha's own history as a figure in the Viennese court.

Conclusion

While on one level Ekaterina's keepsakes reduced Martha's agency to the level of a loyal subject, on another the stories they told of Russia's female leaders and herself were empowering. The objects would lead Martha to spread abroad a vivid picture of Catherine the Great, Ekaterina and Russian folk culture. In 1840, thirty years after Ekaterina's death, Martha published the Princess's memoirs, which she and Katherine had recorded and translated during their stay in Russia. Then, in 1859, at the age of eighty-four, Martha sat down with her daughter to compile an album of watercolours. The pair painted 'each bibelot, snuff-box, etc.' that Ekaterina had given Martha, accompanied by careful records of the 'exact history of each object'.[74] The album opened with an autograph signature of the Princess, followed by a portrait of her aged fifteen (her age when she first met Catherine the Great), wearing the order of St Catherine and garlanding a marble bust of her friend and monarch. Alongside Martha's various keepsakes, the album included illustrations of some of the characters Martha described in her journals and letters home, such as the elderly firelighter who shuffled into her room each morning to light the stove, dancing Cossacks and slave girls, and merchants' wives with bright clothing and jewels. This album and the collection of objects and writings Martha brought home were *souvenirs* in the French sense of the word – that is, memories – for they captured her recollections of a person with whom she had formed a close friendship in another country and also her first-hand experiences of the peoples of that country and its history.

Notes

1 Diana Scarisbrick, 'Companion to a Russian princess: Martha Wilmot's green book', *Country Life* (8 January 1981), 77.
2 Sections of the gift analysis in this chapter appeared in Emma Gleadhill and Ekaterina Heath, 'Giving women history: a history of Ekaterina Dashkova through her gifts to Catherine the Great and others', *Women's History Review*, published online 19 April 2021, https://doi.org/10.1080/09612025.2021.1912269. The research and analysis of the Grigory Ugriumov painting was conducted by Dr Heath and is her contribution.

On the souvenirs from a literary perspective see Buck, Pamela. "From Russia with Love: Souvenirs and Political Alliance in Martha Wilmot's *the Russian Journals*." In *Eighteenth-Century Thing Theory in a Global Context*, edited by Ileana Baird and Christina Ionescu, 133–48. Burlington: Ashgate, 2014.

3 Lorna Sage, Germaine Greer, and Elaine Showalter, *The Cambridge Guide to Women's Writing in English* (Cambridge: Cambridge University Press, 1999), 669.

4 RIA Wilmot Papers, 12 L 22, Martha Bradford (née Wilmot), 'Journal of stay in Russia', vol. 6, 17 October 1808, 165. Martha also referred to her 'Russian mother' in the preface to, Ekaterina Romanovna Dashkova, *Memoirs of the Princess Daschkaw, Lady of Honour to Catherine II, Empress of All the Russians*, vol. 1, ed. Martha Wilmot (London: Henry Colburn, 1840), xix.

5 RIA, Wilmot Papers, 12 L 17, vol. 1, 25 August 1803, 114–15.

6 RIA, Wilmot Papers, 12 L 17, vol. 1, 8 November 1803, 143.

7 RIA, Wilmot Papers, 12 L 17, vol. 1, 8 November 1803, 144.

8 RIA, Wilmot Papers, 12 L 18, vol. 2, 10 January–27 February 1804, 10–73.

9 RIA, Wilmot Papers, 12 L 18, vol. 2, 30 March 1804, 100.

10 Quoted in William J. Burling, 'A "sickly sort of refinement": the problem of sentimentalism in Mackenzie's *The Man of Feeling*', *Studies in Scottish Literature* 23, no. 1 (1988): 137.

11 RIA, Wilmot Papers, 12 L 30, Katherine Wilmot, 'Copies of Letters from Russia', 24 September 1805, 41.

12 RIA, Wilmot Papers, 12 L 19, vol. 3, 27 January 1805, 6 and 129; 12 L 24, Martha Bradford (née Wilmot), 'Letters from Russia (Copied by her mother)', 1 December 1805, 194.

13 Martha Wilmot and Katherine Wilmot, *The Russian Journals of Martha and Katherine Wilmot 1803–1808*, ed. The Marchioness of Londonderry and H. M. Hyde (London: Macmillan and Co., 1934), 45.

14 Wilmot and Wilmot, *Russian Journals*, 79–80.

15 Wilmot Papers, 12 L 19, vol. 3, 27 January 1805, 6.

16 Katherine Wilmot, *The Grand Tours of Katherine Wilmot*, ed. Elizabeth Mavor (London: Weidenfeld and Nicolson, 1992), 142.

17 A. Woronzoff-Dashkoff, 'Princess E. R. Dashkova: first woman member of the American Philosophical Society', *Proceedings of the American Philosophical Society* 140, no. 3 (1996): 411.

18 On the gendered epistolary strategies Catherine II used to convince Ekaterina to take the position, see Kelsey Rubin-Detlev, *The Epistolary Art of Catherine the Great*, Oxford Studies in the Enlightenment (Liverpool: Liverpool University Press, 2019), 106–7.

19 Richard Wortman, *Scenarios of Power: Myth and Ceremony in Russian Monarchy from Peter the Great to the Abdication of Nicholas II* (Princeton: Princeton University Press, 2013), 53. See also Brenda Meehan-Waters, 'Catherine the Great and the problem of female rule', *Russian Review* 34, no. 3 (1975): 293–307.
20 Dashkova, *Memoirs of the Princess Daschkaw*, 300.
21 Gavriil Romanovich Derzhavin, 'To the Portrait of Princess Ekaterina Romanovna Dashkova, During her Presidency of the Academy of Sciences', in *Sochineniia Derzhavina*, trans. from Russian by Georgina Barker in *Princess Dashkova, the Woman who Shook the World: Accounts of her Extraordinary Life* (Edinburgh: University of Edinburgh, 2018), 36.
22 Catherine the Great promoted herself as Astrea at the beginning of her reign. See Vera Proskurina, *Creating the Empress: Politics and Poetry in the Age of Catherine II* (Brighton, MA: Academic Studies Press, 2011).
23 Gavriil Romanovich Derzhavin, 'To the Portrait of a Hermaphrodite', in *Sochineniia Derzhavina*, trans. from Russian by Georgina Barker in *Princess Dashkova, the Woman who Shook the World*.
24 RIA, Wilmot Papers, 12 L 24, 5 September 1803, 37.
25 RIA, Wilmot Papers, 12 L 24, 18 December 1803, 131
26 Louisa Connolly, quoted in Stella Tillyard, *Aristocrats: Caroline, Emily, Louisa and Sarah Lennox 1740–1832* (London: Vintage, 1995), 108.
27 Susan Stabile, *Memory's Daughters: The Material Culture of Remembrance in Eighteenth-Century America* (New York: Cornell University Press, 2004), 164.
28 Michael Yonan, 'Portable dynasties: imperial gift-giving at the court of Vienna in the eighteenth century', *Court Historian* 14, no. 2 (2009): 183.
29 RIA, Wilmot Papers, 12 L 18, vol. 2, 23 December 1803, 8.
30 RIA, Wilmot Papers, 12 L 18, vol. 2, 23 December 1803, 8–9.
31 Marcia Pointon, '"Surrounded with brilliants": miniature portraits in eighteenth-century England', *Art Bulletin* 83, no. 1 (2001): 51.
32 RIA, Wilmot Papers, 12 L 24, 9 January 1804, 159–60.
33 RIA, Wilmot Papers, 12 L 18, vol. 2, 13 February 1804, 59.
34 RIA, Wilmot Papers, 12 L 30, 24 September 1805, 29–30.
35 Marcia Pointon, *Strategies for Showing: Women, Possession, and Representation in English Visual Culture, 1665–1800* (Oxford and New York: Oxford University Press, 1997), 59.
36 Dashkova, *Memoirs of the Princess Daschkaw*, 82. See also Victoria Ivleva, 'Catherine II: uniform dresses and regional uniforms', *Costume* 53, no. 2 (2019): 207–30.

37 Woronzoff-Dashkoff, 'Princess E. R. Dashkova: first woman member of the American Philosophical Society', 410.
38 On Ekaterina's tenure at the academy see Michael D. Gordin, 'Arduous and delicate task: Ekaterina Dashkova, the Academy of Sciences, and the taming of natural philosophy', in *The Princess and the Patriot: Ekaterina Dashkova, Benjamin Franklin, and the Age of Enlightenment*, ed. Sue Ann Prince, 3–22 (Philadelphia: American Philosophical Society, 2006). On her library see A. Woronzoff-Dashkoff, 'Princess E. R. Dashkova's Moscow library', *Slavonic and East European Review* 72, no. 1 (1994): 60–71.
39 Katherine Wilmot to Anne Latham, 15 May 1807, in Wilmot and Wilmot, *Russian Journals*, 246.
40 Dashkova, *Memoirs of the Princess Daschkaw*, 387.
41 Alexander Woronzoff-Dashkoff, *Ekaterina Dashkova. Zhizn vo vlasti i v opale* (Moscow: Molodaya gvardiya, 2010), 265–7.
42 See Marcel Mauss, *The Gift: Forms and Functions of Exchange in Archaic Societies* (London: Routledge, 1989); Annette Weiner, *Inalienable Possessions: The Paradox of Keeping-While-Giving* (Berkeley: University of California Press, 1992).
43 Wilmot Papers, 12 L 19, vol. 3, 27 January 1805, 129–30.
44 In 1762 Ekaterina expressed her enthusiasm for Catherine II in a short poem; 'Nature in bringing You into the world / Bestowed all of its gifts on You alone. By granting all to You, it granted all to us / And elevated You to the majesty of the throne'. Ekaterina Romanovna Dashkova, 'Inscription to a Portrait of Catherine II', *Conversational Companion of the Lovers of the Russian Word* 1 (1783).
45 RIA, Wilmot Papers, 12 L 19, vol. 3, 27 January 1805, 129–30
46 E. Petrova and S. Moiseeva, *Grigoriy Ugryumov* (St Petersburg: Palace editions, 2014), 24.
47 Grigory Ugryumov, *The Conquest of Kazan by Ivan Grozny*, 2 October 1552, State Russian Museum, oil on canvas, 1799, ZH 5053. See also Z. T. Zonova, *Grigory Ivanovich Ugriumov* (Moscow: Iskusstvo, 1966), 41–2.
48 Nikolay Shilder, *Imperator Pavel Perviy* (St Petersburg: Izdaniye A. S. Suvorina, 1901), 430.
49 Paul I installed a new succession law according to the principle of primogeniture, no. 17906 'Ucherezhdeniye ob Imperatorskoi Familii', in *Polnoye Sobraniye Zakonov Rossiyskoi Imperii (PSZ)*, ed. Georgiy Savich (St Petersburg: Tip. II otd., 1830), 525–69.
50 Ekaterina Romanova Dashkova, *Zapiski. Pisma sester M. i K. Vilmot iz Rossii* (Moscow: Moscow University, 1987), 296–9; RGADA (Rossiyskiy Gosudarstvenniy Arkhiv Drevnykh Aktov), 'Reestr kartinam ostavshimsya

posle pokoinoi knyagini Ekateriny Romanovny Dashkovoi', fol. 1261 op. 2 ed.khr. 915, l. 11–12. For a list of the paintings that decorated her house see P. I. Shukina, 'Opis kartin i knig pokoinoi kn. E.R. Dashkovoy', in *Sbornik Starinnykh Bumag, Khranyashikhsya v Muzee* (Moscow: Tov. Tip. A.I. Mamontova, 1901), 85–89.

51 Letter to Edward Wilmot, dated 13 December 1806, in Wilmot and Wilmot, *Russian Journals*, 273.

52 'Treaty of Concert between His Majesty and the Emperor of all the Russians, signed at St. Petersburg, the 11th April, 1805', in *Cobbett's Parliamentary Debates, During the Fourth Session of the Second Parliament of the United Kingdom of Great Britain and Ireland, and of the Kingdom of Great Britain the Nineteenth, Comprising the Period Between the 21st of January and the 6th of May, 1806*, vol. 4 (London: R. Bagshaw, 1806), Appendix, iii–iv.

53 Indeed, at the time Russians preferred to use stoves over fireplaces, so it is clear that this gift was manufactured specifically for export to Britain.

54 Letter to Edward Wilmot, dated 13 December 1806, in Wilmot and Wilmot, *Russian Journals*, 274.

55 RIA, Wilmot Papers, 12 L 26–8, *Description de toutes les nations de l'Empire de Russie. St. Petersbourg, 1776–7*, 3 vols, vol. 1, first page inscription.

56 Elena Vishlenkova, *Vizualnoye Narodovedeniye Imperii* (Moscow: Novoye Literaturnoye Obozreniye, 2011), 61–2; Nathalie Bondil, *Catherine the Great: Art for Empire: Masterpieces from the State Hermitage Museum, Russia* (Montreal: Montréal Museum of Fine Arts, 2005), 307.

57 Vishlenkova, *Vizualnoye Narodovedeniye Imperii*, 63–7; Bondil, *Catherine the Great*, 307.

58 Finland, for example, was included in the first edition, but would not be conquered by Russia until the beginning of the nineteenth century. On imperialism and costume see Joe Snader, 'The masquerade of colonial identity in Frances Brooke's *Emily Montague* (1769)', in *The Clothes That Wear Us: Essays on Dressing and Transgressing in Eighteenth-Century Culture*, ed. Jessica Munns and Penny Richards (Newark: University of Delaware Press, 1999), 119–42.

59 Johann Gottlieb Georgi, *Beschreibung aller Nationen des russischen Reichs: ihrer Lebensart, Religion, Gebräuche, Wohnungen, Kleidungen und übrigen Merkwürdigkeiten*, vol. 4 (St. Petersburg: Carl Wilhelm Muller, 1780). Catherine the Great considered Russians to be a mixture of Slavic people, Tatars and Sarmatians, hence the volume on Russians was only published after her death.

60 Vishlenkova, *Vizualnoye Narodovedeniye Imperii*, 119.
61 RIA, Wilmot Papers, 12 L 29, Martha Bradford (née Wilmot) and Katherine Wilmot, 'Letters. Include Russian poems and verses with translations into English, French and Italian', *c*.1806–8.
62 Dashkova, *Memoirs of the Princess Daschkaw*, 54–5.
63 'I have never for a moment felt otherwise, than as an adopted child of Russia, by the great kindness and maternal affection of the Princess Daschkaw. I would not for any consideration withhold from the public, a narrative so eminently qualified to add lustre to her character & her name, & for which I hold myself responsible to her memory' (RIA, Wilmot Papers, 12 M 16, correspondence from travelling writing case, Martha Wilmot to the Countess of Pembroke, 31 May 1838).
64 Martha Wilmot, *More Letters from Martha Wilmot: Impressions of Vienna, 1819–1829*, ed. The Marchioness of Londonderry and H. M. Hyde (London: Macmillan, 1935), xx; RIA, Wilmot Papers, 12 L 25, Martha Bradford (née Wilmot) and Princess Ekaterina Romanovna Daskova, 'Poems and miscellaneous notes', late nineteenth century; Wilmot Papers, 12 L 29.
65 Maria Josepha Holroyd to her niece Lady Maria Josepha Stanley, 17 February 1812, in Maria Josepha Holroyd, *The Girlhood of Maria Josepha Holroyd (Lady Stanley of Alderley) Recorded in Letters of a Hundred Years Ago: From 1776–1796*, ed. Jane Henrietta Adeane (London: Longmans, Green, 1897), 332.
66 RIA, Wilmot Papers, 12 M 18, Correspondence from red chamois travelling writing case, Mrs Elizabeth Morgan to Martha Wilmot, 19 February 1810.
67 Brian E. Vick, *The Congress of Vienna* (Cambridge, MA: Harvard University Press, 2014).
68 Letter to Alicia Wilmot, dated 8 December 1819, in Wilmot, *More Letters from Martha Wilmot*, 32.
69 Martha Wilmot to Catherine, Countess of Pembroke, 31 May 1839, quoted in Wilmot, *More Letters from Martha Wilmot*, 33.
70 Martha Wilmot describes her presentation to Alicia in a letter dated 21 December 1819, in Wilmot, *More Letters from Martha Wilmot*, 44.
71 Letter to Alicia dated 21 December 1819, in Wilmot, *More Letters from Martha Wilmot*, 33.
72 RIA, Wilmot Papers, 12 L 22, vol. 6, 17 October 1808, 103.
73 Marcia Pointon, 'Women and their jewels', in *Women and Material Culture, 1660–1830*, ed. Jennie Batchelor and Cora Kaplan (Basingstoke: Palgrave Macmillan, 2007), 23.
74 Wilmot, *More Letters from Martha Wilmot*, xlvi.

Conclusion: remembering the souvenir

Taking Travel Home has exposed the gendered nature of the souvenir. By viewing the souvenir through a gendered lens, we see how women of the past challenged and subverted gender norms in the pursuit of their own subjectivity. Part I showed that women Grand Tourists of the late eighteenth century used souvenirs to form spaces in which they could produce their own understandings of taste, virtue and connoisseurship. Part II explored how scientifically minded British women tourists travelling both domestically and on the Continent combined the symbolic meanings of the souvenir with their curiosity and specimen collecting to transform their leisured travels into knowledge-finding pursuits. In both connoisseurship and science, women carved out agency by creating their own travel narratives and attaching them to readily available objects, whether small household objects, personal effects or samples from nature. Late eighteenth-century women imbued these mundane items with the spirit of their travel narratives. The souvenir was the exclusive possession of the traveller, for only she had experienced the travel tales that gave the object its extraordinary association.

The final part of this book showed that the growing desire of all travellers from the 1790s to the 1830s to give, receive and collect their own keepsakes resulted from the actions of the women tourists of the preceding decades, who privileged the small and personal to represent the value of travel, rather than the large and magnificent. They led a cultural shift whereby the objects brought home from one's travels, or given to others, moved from having a public significance to having a more personal significance, and where the term *souvenir* shifted from a concept to an object. This was the birth of the souvenir as we know it today – that is, a small memento taken from the travel environment that memorialises a past experience, past identity or past state of mind.

Modern theorists and anthropologists have downplayed the value of the souvenir in recognition of its association with commodified sentiment. These scholars consider the souvenir to be an object that creates inauthentic and manufactured feeling divorced from the means of production. Similar opinions are common among historians, eliding the female-driven origins of the souvenir. The souvenir only became popular and monetised in the late eighteenth and early nineteenth centuries because women had created a market for small, inexpensive objects which recalled their travels. Men merely magnified and marketed a practice that elite women travellers of the second half of the eighteenth century had created. The women profiled in this book, known and unknown, were thus trailblazers in the literal and figurative sense. They took control of the souvenir and moulded it to suit their unique desires. It is through the souvenir that we can understand how women of the past reworked their memories of their travels to better understand what they wanted from the future.

Bibliography

Archival primary sources

British Library. Holland House Papers. Add. MS 51613. Correspondence of Henry Stephen Fox to Lord Holland, 1812–38.

———. Holland House Papers. Add. MS 51598. Correspondence of Lord Boringdon to Lady Holland, 1797–1842.

———. Holland House Papers. Add. MS 51814. Correspondence of William Drew to Lady Holland, 7 November 1797.

———. Holland House Papers. Add. MS 51821. Correspondence of James Smithson to Lord Holland and Correspondence of John Ingenhousz to Lord and Lady Holland, 1797.

———. Holland House Papers. Add. MS 51822. Correspondence of James Smithson to Lord Holland, 1801.

———. Holland House Papers. Add. MS 51827. Correspondence of Alexander von Humboldt to Lord Holland, 1813.

———. Holland House Papers. Add. MS 51845. Correspondence of C. H. Titius to Lady Holland. L. J. Murith to Lady Holland. Targioni Tozzetti to Lady Holland, 1792–98.

———. Holland House Papers. Add. MS 51846. Correspondence of Robert Gordon to Lady Holland and Correspondence of James Smithson to Lady Holland, 1800–2.

———. Holland House Papers. Add. MS 52000. Caroline Fox, 'A Catalogue of the Books at Little Holland House', 1809–42.

———. Powys Diaries. Add. MS 42163. Caroline Lybbe Powys (née Girle), 'Norfolk Journal', 1756.

———. Powys Diaries. Add. MS 42164. Caroline Lybbe Powys (née Girle), 'Journal of a Tour to Oxford, Blenheim, &c.', 1759.

———. Powys Diaries. Add. MS 42165. Caroline Lybbe Powys (née Girle), 'Journal of a Tour to Plymouth Mount Edgcomb &c', 1760.

———. Powys Diaries. Add. MS 42166. Caroline Lybbe Powys (née Girle), 'Shropshire Journal', 1770.

———. Powys Diaries. Add. MS 42168. Caroline Lybbe Powys (née Girle), 'Journal of a Five days Tour in a Letter to a Friend', 1776.
———. Powys Diaries. Add. MS 42169. Caroline Lybbe Powys (née Girle), 'Second Norfolk Tour', 1781.
———. Powys Diaries. Add. MS 42170. Caroline Lybbe Powys (née Girle), 'Journal of a Tour a Tour to the Isle of Wight', 1792.
———. Holland House Papers, Add. MS 51927. Lady Elizabeth Holland, 'Journal', June 1791 – 6 July 1797.
John Rylands Library. Thrale-Piozzi Papers. GB 133 Eng MS 617. Hester Lynch Piozzi, 'Journal: Travels in France', 15 September 1775 – 11 November 1775.
———. GB 133 Eng MS 618. Hester Lynch Piozzi, 'Journals: Travels in Italy and Germany', 1784–87, 2 vols.
———. Thrale-Piozzi Papers. GB 133 Eng MS 619. Hester Lynch Piozzi, 'Draft: Observations and reflections collected from the diary of Hester Lynch Piozzi', c.1788, 7 vols.
———. Thrale-Piozzi Papers. GB 133 Eng MS 620-2. Hester Lynch Piozzi, 'Hester Piozzi's final draft: Observations and reflections made in the course of a journey through France, Italy, and Germany', c.1788, 3 vols.
———. Thrale-Piozzi Papers. GB 133 Eng MS 623. Hester Lynch Piozzi, 'Journal: Travels in the North of England, etc.', 1789.
———. Dorothy Richardson Papers, Travel Journals. GB 133 Eng MS 1122. Dorothy Richardson, 'Yorkshire (West Riding), Derbyshire, Nottinghamshire and Lancashire', 1761–75.
———. Dorothy Richardson Papers, Travel Journals. GB 133 Eng MS 1123. Dorothy Richardson, 'Oxford and Bath', 1770.
———. Dorothy Richardson Papers, Travel Journals. GB 133 Eng MS 1124. Dorothy Richardson, 'London', 1775 and 1785.
———. Dorothy Richardson Papers, Travel Journals. GB 133 Eng MS 1125. Dorothy Richardson, 'Yorkshire (North Riding) and Lancashire', 1779.
———. Dorothy Richardson Papers, Travel Journals. GB 133 Eng MS 1126. Dorothy Richardson, 'Yorkshire (East Riding)', 1801–2.
Royal Irish Academy. Wilmot Papers. 12 L 17–22. Martha Bradford (née Wilmot), 'Journal of stay in Russia', 1803–8, 6 vols.
———. Wilmot Papers. 12 L 23. Martha Bradford (née Wilmot), 'Journal of a year spent in Italy', 1821–22.
———. Wilmot Papers. 12 L 24. Martha Bradford (née Wilmot), 'Letters from Russia (Copied by her mother)', April 1803 – October 1806.
———. Wilmot Papers. 12 L 25. Martha Bradford (née Wilmot) and Princess Ekaterina Romanovna Daskova, 'Poems and miscellaneous notes', early nineteenth century.

———. Wilmot Papers. 12 L 26–8. *Description de toutes les nations de l'Empire de Russie. St. Petersbourg, 1776–7*, 3 vols. Given to Martha Bradford (née Wilmot) by her Russian mother, Princess Ekaterina Romanovna Daschkova, 1743–1810.

———. Wilmot Papers. 12 L 29. Martha Bradford (née Wilmot) and Katherine Wilmot, 'Letters. Include Russian poems and verses with translations into English, French and Italian', *c*.1806–8.

———. Wilmot Papers. 12 L 30. Katherine Wilmot, 'Copies of Letters from Russia', 1805–7.

———. Wilmot Papers. 12 L 31. Katherine Wilmot, 'Journal in Russia', 1806–7.

———. Wilmot Papers. 12 L 32. Katherine Wilmot, 'Letters from France-Italy', 1801–3. Copied by Martha Bradford (née Wilmot), Moscow, 1805.

———. Wilmot Papers. 12 L 33. Katherine Wilmot, 'Letters in English from Russia', 1805–7.

———. Wilmot Papers. 12 L 34. Katherine Wilmot, 'Moscow Notebook. Includes letters and poems, notes of books read, extracts in French from books', 1806.

———. Wilmot Papers. 12 M 16. Correspondence from travelling writing case.

———. Wilmot Papers. 12 M 18. Correspondence from red chamois travelling writing case with embroidered motifs in metal thread with an abacus and a secret drawer in the base.

Sir John Soane's Museum Library and Archive. Anna Riggs Miller. *Letters from Italy, Describing the Manners, Customs, Antiquities, Paintings, &c. of that Country, in the Years MDCCLXX and MDCCLXXI*, vol. 2. London: Edward and Charles Dilly, 1777. Annotated by Sir John Soane During his Travels.

Printed primary sources

It is thanks to the Gale database, Eighteenth Century Collections Online (ECCO) and the non-profit digital library the Internet Archive that I have been able to access many of these printed primary sources. ECCO contains every significant English-language and foreign-language title printed in the United Kingdom between the years 1701 and 1800. The Internet Archive contains twenty-eight billion books and texts. These digital resources have allowed me to explore this topic in greater depth and breadth than has been possible in the past.

Andrews, John. *Remarks on the French and English Ladies*. Dublin: Walker, Beatty, Burton, White and Doyle, 1783.

Barker, Georgina. *Princess Dashkova, the Woman who Shook the World: Accounts of her Extraordinary Life.* Edinburgh: University of Edinburgh, 2018.

Berchtold, Count Leopold. *An Essay to Direct and Extend the Inquiries of Patriotic Travellers.* London: Robinson, 1789.

Berry, Mary. *Extracts from the Journals and Correspondence of Miss Berry: From the Year 1783 to 1852*, edited by Lady Theresa Lewis. 2 vols. London: Longmans Green, 1865.

Billington, Elizabeth. *Memoirs of Mrs. Billington, from Her Birth: Containing a Variety of Matter, Ludicrous, Theatrical, Musical, and with Copies of Several Original Letters, Now in the Possession of the Publisher, Written by Mrs. Billington, to Her Mother, the Late Mrs. Weichsel.* London: James Ridgway, 1792.

Blessington, Marguerite. *The Idler in Italy by the Countess of Blessington.* Paris: Baudry's European Library, 1839.

Boswell, James. *The Life of Samuel Johnson.* 2 vols. London: Henry Baldwin and Charles Dilly, 1791.

Bourrienne, Louis Antoine Fauvelet de. *The Life of Napoleon Bonaparte.* Philadelphia: Carey & Lee, 1832.

Burney, Charles. *The Present State of Music in France and Italy: Or, the Journal of a Tour through Those Countries, Undertaken to Collect Materials for a General History of Music,* vol. 1. London: T. Becket, 1771.

Burney, Fanny. *Diary and Letters of Madame D'Arblay,* vol. 1. Edited by Charlotte Barrett. London: Henry Colburn, 1842.

Carlisle, Earl of. 'To Lady Holland, on the legacy of a snuff-box, left to her by Buonaparte'. *The Gentleman's Magazine: And Historical Chronicle. From July to December, 1821,* vol. 91 (1821): 457–8.

Cobbett's Parliamentary Debates, During the Fourth Session of the Second Parliament of the United Kingdom of Great Britain and Ireland, and of the Kingdom of Great Britain the Nineteenth, Comprising the Period Between the 21st of January and the 6th of May, 1806, vol. 4. London: R. Bagshaw, 1806.

Coke, Mary. *The Letters and Journals of Lady Mary Coke,* vol. 2. Edited by James Archibald Home. Bath: Kingsmead Bookshops, 1970.

'Copy of a Doggrel letter to his friend from Bath'. *The Hibernian Magazine, Or, Compendium of Entertaining Knowledge* (January 1781).

Dashkova, Ekaterina Romanovna. 'Inscription to a portrait of Catherine II'. *Conversational Companion of the Lovers of the Russian Word* 1 (1783).

———. *Memoirs of the Princess Daschkaw, Lady of Honour to Catherine II, Empress of All the Russians,* vol. 1. Edited by Martha Wilmot. London: Henry Colburn, 1840.

258 Bibliography

Diderot, Denis, and Jean le Rond d'Alembert. *Encyclopédie, ou dictionnaire raisonné des sciences, des arts et des métiers.* Paris: André le Breton, Michel-Antoine David, Laurent Durand and Antoine-Claude Briasson, 1751–66.

Douglas, James. *Travelling Anecdotes through Various Parts of Europe.* London: J. Debrett, 1786.

Edgeworth, Maria, and Richard Lovell Edgeworth. *Practical Education.* London: J. Johnson, 1798.

Farington, Joseph. *The Farington Diary,* vol. 3. Edited by James Greig. London: Hutchinson, 1924.

Faulkner, T., and B. West. *History and Antiquities of Kensington.* London: T. Egerton, 1820.

Fiennes, Celia. *Through England on a Side Saddle: In the Time of William and Mary.* Cambridge: Cambridge University Press, 2010.

Fontana, Felice. *Saggio del Real Gabinetto di Fisica e di Storia Naturale.* Roma: Giovanni Zempel, 1775.

Fontana, Felix [Felice]. *Treatise on the Venom of the Viper: On the American Poisons; and on the Cherry Laurel, and Some Other Vegetable Poisons.* Translated by Joseph Skinner. London: John Cuthell, 1795.

Fyvie, John. *Noble Dames and Notable Men of the Georgian Era.* New York: John Lane Company, 1911.

Georgi, Johann Gottlieb. *Beschreibung aller Nationen des russischen Reichs: ihrer Lebensart, Religion, Gebräuche, Wohnungen, Kleidungen und übrigen Merkwürdigkeiten,* vol. 4. St Petersburg: Carl Wilhelm Muller, 1780.

Gilpin, William. *Observations on the River Wye and Several Parts of South Wales Relative Chiefly to Picturesque Beauty Made in the Summer of the Year of 1770.* London: R. Blamire, 1789.

Grant, Anne. *Letters from the Mountains, Being the Real Correspondence of a Lady, between the Years 1773 and 1807,* vol. 2. London: Longman, 1809.

Granville, Harriet. *Hary-O: The Letters of Lady Harriet Cavendish, 1796–1809.* Edited by George Leveson-Gower and Iris Palmer. London: J. Murray, 1940.

Granville, Mary. *The Autobiography and Correspondence of Mary Granville, Mrs. Delany: With Interesting Reminiscences of King George the Third and Queen Charlotte,* vol. 1. Edited by Lady Llanover. London: Bentley, Richard, 1861.

Graves, Richard. *The Triflers: Consisting of Trifling Essays, Trifling Anecdotes, and a Few Poetical Trifles.* London: H. D. Symonds, 1805.

Greville, Charles. *The Greville Memoirs: A Journal of the Reigns of King George IV and King William IV.* Edited by Richard Henry Stoddard. New York: Scribner, Armstrong, 1875.

Hawkesworth, John. *An Account of the Voyages Undertaken by the Order of His Present Majesty for Making Discoveries in the Southern Hemisphere: And Successively Performed by Commodore Byron, Captain Wallis, Captain Carteret, and Captain Cook, in the Dolphin, the Swallow, and the Endeavor, Drawn up from the Journals Which Were Kept by the Several Commanders, and from the Papers of Joseph Banks, Esq*, vol. 2. London: W. Strahan and T. Cadell, 1773.

Hayley, William. *Memoirs of the Life and Writings of William Hayley, Esq: The Friend and Biographer of Cowper*, vol. 1. London: H. Colburn and Co., 1823.

Haywood, Eliza. *The Female Spectator*. 5th edn. London: T. Gardiner, 1744–46.

Hesselgrave, Ruth Avaline. *Lady Miller and the Batheaston Literary Circle*. New Haven: Yale University Press, 1927.

Holland, Elizabeth Vassall Fox. *Elizabeth, Lady Holland, to Her Son, 1821–1845*. Edited by Giles Stephen Fox-Strangways Ilchester. Edited by Giles Stephen Fox-Strangways Ilchester. London: J. Murray, 1946.

———. *The Journal of Elizabeth Lady Holland (1791–1811)*. Edited by Giles Stephen Fox-Strangways Ilchester. 2 vols. London: Longmans Green, 1908.

———. *The Spanish Journal of Elizabeth Lady Holland*. Edited by Giles Stephen Fox-Strangways Ilchester. London: Longmans, Green, 1910.

Holland, Henry. *Recollections of Past Life*. New York: D. Appleton, 1872.

Holland, Henry Richard Vassall. *Foreign Reminiscences*. Edited by Henry Edward Fox. 2nd edn. London: Longman, Brown, Green, and Longmans, 1851.

———. 'Protest to the second part of Bonaparte's Detention Bill'. *National Register* 1, no. 15 (1816): 240.

Holroyd, Maria Josepha. *The Girlhood of Maria Josepha Holroyd (Lady Stanley of Alderley) Recorded in Letters of a Hundred Years Ago: From 1776–1796*. Edited by Jane Henrietta Adeane. London: Longmans, Green, 1897.

Hull, William. *The History of the Glove Trade: With the Customs Connected with the Glove: To Which Are Annexed Some Observations on the Policy of the Trade between England and France, and Its Operation on the Agricultural and Manufacturing Interests*. London: E. Wilson, 1834.

Ilchester, Giles Stephen Fox-Strangways. *The Home of the Hollands 1605–1820*. London: John Murray, 1937.

Jackson, Maria Elizabeth. *Botanical Dialogues, between Hortensia and Her Four Children, Charles, Harriet, Juliette and Henry*. London: J. Johnson, 1797.

Lassels, Richard. 'A preface to the reader concerning travelling'. In *The Voyage of Italy, or a Compleat Journey through Italy. In Two Parts*. London: John Starkey, 1670.

Le Normand, Marie Anne. *Historical and Secret Memoirs of the Empress Josephine (Marie Rose Tascher De La Pagerie): First Wife of Napoleon Bonaparte*, vol. 1. Translated by Jacob M. Howard. Philadelphia: Carey and Hart, 1848.

Leveson-Gower, Granville. *The Private Correspondence of Lord Granville Leveson-Gower, First Earl Granville*, vol. 2. Edited by Castalia Rosalind Campbell Leveson-Gower. London: J. Murray, 1916.

Liechtenstein, Marie Henriette Norberte. *Holland House*. London: Macmillan, 1874.

Linnaeus, Carl. *Systema Naturæ, Sive Regna Tria Naturæ Systematice Proposita Per Classes, Ordines, Genera, & Species*. Edited by J. A. Murray. Lugduni Batavorum: Haak, 1735.

Loci, Genius. *Bath Anecdotes and Characters*. London: Dodsley, 1782.

Locke, John. *Some Thoughts Concerning Education*. London: A. & J. Churchill, 1693.

———. *The Work*, vol. 1. London: Printed for John Churchill and Sam Manship, 1714.

London Magazine: Or, Gentleman's Monthly Intelligencer, vol. 51. London: R. Baldwin, 1782.

Louis de Caulaincourt, Armand Augustin. *Recollections of Caulaincourt, Duke of Vicenza*, vol. 1. London: n.p., 1838.

Louis, Dutens. *Memoirs of a Traveller, Now in Retirement*. 5 vols. Vol. 2. (London: R. Phillips), 1806, 100–1.

Medwin, Thomas. *Conversations of Lord Byron: Noted During a Residence with His Lordship at Pina, in the Years 1821 and 1822*. London: Colburn, 1824.

Miller, Anna Riggs. *Letters from Italy, Describing the Manners, Customs, Antiquities, Paintings, &C. of that Country, in the Years MDCCLXX and MDCCLXXI, to a Friend Residing in France*. 2 vols. Dublin: W. Watson, 1776.

———. *Poetical Amusements at a Villa near Bath*, vol. 1. London: Edward and Charles Dilly, 1776.

Montagu, Elizabeth. *Elizabeth Montagu, the Queen of the Bluestockings: Her Correspondence from 1720 to 1761*, vol. 1. Edited by Emily Jane Climenson. London: John Murray, 1906.

Montagu, Lady Mary Wortley. *Lady M. W. Montagu's Letters from France and Italy*. The British Prose Writers, vol. 8. London: John Sharpe, 1821.

Moore, John. *A View of Society and Manners in Italy: With Anecdotes Relating to Some Eminent Characters*, vol. 2. London: A. Strahan and T. Cadell, 1781.

Moore, Thomas. *The Poetical Works of Thomas Moore*. London: Longman, Orme, Brown, Green, and Longmans, 1841.

Morgan, Mary. *A Tour to Milford Haven, in the Year 1791*. London: John Stockdale, 1795.
Morritt, John Bacon Sawrey. *The Letters of John B. S. Morritt of Rokeby Descriptive of Journeys in Europe and Asia Minor in the Years 1794–1796*. London: John Murray, 1914.
Murray, Sarah. *A Companion, and Useful Guide to the Beauties of Scotland*. London: George Nicol, 1799.
The New Annual Register, or General Repository of History, Politics, and Literature, for the Year 1785. London: G. G. and J. Robinson, 1786.
Nicholson, William. *A Journal of Natural Philosophy, Chemistry and the Arts*, vol. 22. London: G. G. and J. Robinson, 1809.
The Original Bath Guide: Considerably Enlarged and Improved; Comprehending Every Species of Information That Can Be Required by the Visitor and Inhabitant. Bath: J. Savage; Meyler and Son, 1811.
Ostervald, Frédéric-Samuel. *Description des montagnes et des vallées qui font partie de la Principauté de Neuchatel et Valangin*. Neuchatel: Samuel Fauche, 1766.
'Ought sensibility to be cherished or repressed?'. *Monthly Magazine* 2 (October 1796): 706–9.
Oxford, Members of the University of. *The Oxford Magazine: Or, Universal Museum*, vol. 4. London, Cambridge, Dublin and York: Bladon, Coote, Fletcher, Hodson, Smith and Etherington, 1770.
Patterson, M. W. *Sir Francis Burdett and His Times (1770–1844)*. London: Macmillan, 1931.
Pembroke, Henry Herbert. *Henry, Elizabeth and George (1734–80): Letters and Diaries of Henry, Tenth Earl of Pembroke, and His Circle*. Edited by Sidney Charles Herbert. London: J. Cape, 1939.
Piozzi, Hester Lynch. *Autobiography, Letters and Literary Remains of Mrs Piozzi (Thrale): With Notes and an Introductory Account of Her Life and Writings*, vol. 2. Edited by Abraham Hayward. Cambridge: Cambridge University Press, 2013.

———. *Observations and Reflections Made in the Course of a Journey through France, Italy, and Germany*. 2 vols. London: A. Strahan and T. Cadell, 1789.

———. *The Piozzi Letters: Correspondence of Hester Lynch Piozzi, 1784–1821 (Formerly Mrs. Thrale)*. Edited by Edward A. Bloom and Lillian D. Bloom. 6 vols. London: Associated University Presses, 1989–2002.

———. *Retrospection: Or: A Review of the Most Striking and Important Events, Characters, Situations, and Their Consequences, Which the Last Eighteen Hundred Years Have Presented to the View of Mankind*. London: J. Stockdale, 1801.

———. *Streatham Park, Surrey: A Catalogue of the Excellent and Genuine Household Furniture*. London: Mr. Squibb, 1816.

———. *Thraliana: The Diary of Mrs Hester Lynch Thrale (Later Mrs Piozzi), 1776–1809*. 2nd edn. Oxford: Clarendon Press, 1951.

Pluche, Noël Antoine. *Spectacle De La Nature: Or, Nature Display'd: Being Discourses on Such Particulars of Natural History as Were Thought Most Proper to Excite the Curiosity, and Form the Minds of Youth*. Edited by Samuel Humphreys. London: J. Pemberton, 1733.

Plumptre, James. *The Lakers: A Comic Opera, in Three Acts*. London: W. Clarke, 1798.

Powys, Caroline Lybbe. *Passages from the Diaries of Mrs. Philip Lybbe Powys of Hardwick House, Oxon, 1756–1808*. Edited by Emily J. Climenson. London: Longmans, Green, & Co., 1899.

Powys, Edward V. R. 'Napoleon and Lady Holland'. *Spectator* (8 November 1913): 17.

Putnam's Magazine: Original Papers on Literature, Science, Art, and National Interests. New York: G. P. Putnam & Son, 1868.

Radcliffe, Ann. *The Mysteries of Udolpho: And a Sicilian Romance*, vol. 1. London: J. Limbird, 1826 [1794].

Remarkable Women of Different Nations and Ages. Boston: John P. Jewett, 1858.

Russell, John. *Memorials and Correspondence of Charles James Fox*, vol. 3. London: Richard Bentley, 1854.

Sarnelli, Pompeo. *La guida de' forestieri curiosi di vedere, e di riconoscere le cose più memorabili di Pozzuoli, Baja, Cuma, Miseno, Gaeta, ed altri luoghi circonvicini*. Naples: Saverio Rossi, 1768.

Scott, Walter. *Complete Works: With a Biography, and His Last Additions and Illustrations*. Philadelphia: A. Hart, 1853.

———. *The Life of Napoleon, Emperor of the French: With a Preliminary View of the French Revolution*, vol. 2. Exeter: J. & B. Williams, 1836.

Ségur, Louis-Philippe de. *Oeuvres complètes de M. le comte de Ségur*. Paris: Alexis Eymery, 1825.

Seward, Anna. *The Poetical Works of Anna Seward: With Extracts from Her Literary Correspondence*, vol. 2. Edited by Walter Scott. Edinburgh: J. Ballantyne, 1810.

Shelley, Mary Wollstonecraft. *The Last Man*, vol. 1. Philadelphia: Carey, Lea and Blanchard, 1833.

Smollett, Tobias. *The Miscellaneous Works of Tobias Smollett, M.D.*, vol. 6. Edinburgh: David Ramsay, 1790.

Somerset, Frances Seymour, and Henrietta Fermor Pomfret. *Correspondence between Frances, Countess of Hartford, (Afterwards Duchess of Somerset,) and Henrietta Louisa, Countess of Pomfret, between the Years 1738 and 1741*. 3 vols. London: Richard Phillips, 1805.

Spence, George. *The Code Napoleon, or, the French Civil Code. Literally Translated from the Original and Official Edition, Published at Paris, in 1804. By a Barrister of the Inner Temple*. London: Charles Hunter, 1824.

Spence, Joseph. *Joseph Spence: Letters from the Grand Tour*. Edited by Slava Klima. Montreal; London: McGill-Queen's University Press, 1975.

Sullivan, William Kirby. *Memoir of Bryan Higgins, M. D. And of William Higgins, Professor of Chemistry to the Royal Dublin Society: With a Short Notice of Irish Chemists and the State of Chemistry in Ireland before the Year 1800*. Dublin: Hodges & Smith, 1849.

Thicknesse, Philip. *The New Prose Bath Guide: For the Year 1778*. London and Bath: Dodsley, Brown and Wood, 1778.

Tickell, Richard. *The Wreath of Fashion: Or, the Art of Sentimental Poetry*. London: T. Becket, 1778.

Urban, Sylvanus. *The Gentleman's Magazine and Historical Chronicle: From January to June, 1823*, vol. 133. London: John Nichols, 1823.

——. 'Poetical essays; December 1764'. In *The Gentleman's Magazine and Historical Chronicle*. London: D. Henry and R. Cave, 1764.

Vichy-Chamrond, Marie Anne de. *Letters of the Marquise Du Deffand to the Hon. Horace Walpole, Afterwards Earl of Orford, from the Year 1766 to the Year 1780. To Which Are Added Letters of Madame Du Deffand to Voltaire, from the Year 1759 to the Year 1775*, vol. 3. London: Longman, Hurst, Rees and Orme, 1810.

Wakefield, Priscilla. *Domestic Recreation; or, Dialogues Illustrative of Natural and Scientific Subjects*. London: Darton and Harvey, 1805.

Walker, Adam. *Analysis of a Course of Lectures on Natural and Experimental Philosophy: Viz. Astronomy, Use of the Globes, Pneumatics, Electricity, Magnetism, Chemistry, Mechanics, Hydrostatics, Hydraulics, Engineering, Fortification, Optics, &C*. London: Adam Walker, 1790.

Walpole, Horace. *The Yale Edition of Horace Walpole's Correspondence*. Edited by W. S. Lewis. 48 vols. New Haven: Yale University Press, 1937–83.

Whalley, Thomas Sedgewick. *Journals and Correspondence of Thomas Sedgewick Whalley, D.D.*, vol. 2. Edited by Hill Wickham. London: Richard Bentley, 1863.

Whitaker, Thomas Dunham. *The History and Antiquities of the Deanery of Craven, in the County of York*. 2nd edn. London: Nichols & Son, 1805.

Wilmot, Katherine. *The Grand Tours of Katherine Wilmot*. Edited by Elizabeth Mavor. London: Weidenfeld and Nicolson, 1992.

——. *An Irish Peer on the Continent 1801–1803: Being a Narrative of the Tour of Stephen, Earl Mount Cashell*. Edited by Thomas Sadleir. London: Williams and Norgate, 1920.

Wilmot, Martha. *More Letters from Martha Wilmot: Impressions of Vienna 1819–1829*. Edited by The Marchioness of Londonderry and H. M. Hyde. London: Macmillan, 1935.

Wilmot, Martha, and Katherine Wilmot. *The Russian Journals of Martha and Katherine Wilmot 1803–1808*. Edited by The Marchioness of Londonderry and H. M. Hyde. London: Macmillan and Co., 1934.

Wollstonecraft, Mary. *Maria, or the Wrongs of Woman*. Paris: William Godwin, 1798.

Wordsworth, Dorothy. *Recollections of a Tour Made in Scotland A.D. 1803*. Edited by J. C. Shairp. New York: G. P. Putnam's Sons, 1874.

Secondary sources

Alexander, Helene. *Fans*. Oxford: Shire Publications, 2002.

Allan, D. G. C. *William Shipley, Founder of the Royal Society of Arts: A Biography with Documents*. London: Hutchinson and Company, 1968.

Anderson, Luella F., and Mary A. Littrell. 'Group profiles of women as tourists and purchasers of souvenirs'. *Family and Consumer Sciences Research Journal* 25, no. 1 (1996): 28–56.

———. 'Souvenir-purchase behavior of women tourists'. *Annals of Tourism Research* 22, no. 2 (1995): 328–48.

Archer, T. A. 'Clifford, Rosamund (b. before 1140?, d. 1175/6).' Revised by Elizabeth Hallam. *Oxford Dictionary of National Biography*, last updated 23 September 2004, https://doi.org/10.1093/ref:odnb/5661.

Auslander, Leora. 'Beyond words'. *American Historical Review* 110, no. 4 (2005): 1015–45.

Austen, Brian. 'English spa souvenirs: the Tunbridge ware industry to about 1830'. *Magazine Antiques* 147, no. 6 (1995): 894.

———. *Tunbridge Ware and Related European Decorative Woodwares: Killarney, Spa, Sorrento*. London: W. Foulsham Company, 1992.

Baird, Ileana, and Christina Ionescu. *Eighteenth-Century Thing Theory in a Global Context*. Farnham and Burlington: Ashgate, 2014.

Baker, Anne Pimlott. 'Powys [née Girle], Caroline (1738–1817)." *Oxford Dictionary of National Biography*, last updated 23 September 2004, https://doi.org/10.1093/ref:odnb/68336.

Barker, Nicolas, Mark Jones, and P. T. Craddock. *Fake?: The Art of Deception*. Berkeley: University of California Press, 1990.

Baudino, Isabelle. *Les voyageuses britanniques au XVIIIe siècle: l'étape lyonnaise dans l'itinéraire du Grand Tour*. Paris: L'Harmattan, 2015.

Beck Ryden, David. 'Sugar, spirits, and fodder: the London West India interest and the glut of 1807–15'. *Atlantic Studies* 9, no. 1 (2012): 41–64.

Benjamin, Walter. *Walter Benjamin: Selected Writings, 1938–1940*. Edited by Michael William Jennings and Howard Eiland, vol. 4. Cambridge, MA, and London: Belknap Press of Harvard University Press, 2003.

Berking, Helmuth. *Sociology of Giving*. London: SAGE Publications, 1999.

Berry, Helen. 'Polite consumption: shopping in eighteenth-century England'. *Transactions of the Royal Historical Society* 12 (2002): 375–94.

Bignamini, Ilaria, and Clare Hornsby. *Digging and Dealing in Eighteenth-Century Rome*, vol. 1. New Haven: Yale University Press, 2010.

Black, Jeremy. *The British Abroad: The Grand Tour in the Eighteenth Century*. New York: St. Martin's Press, 1992.

———. *Italy and the Grand Tour*. New Haven: Yale University Press, 2003.

Blackwell, Mark. *The Secret Life of Things: Animals, Objects and It-Narratives in Eighteenth-Century England*. Lewisburg: Bucknell University Press, 2007.

Bohls, Elizabeth A. *Women Travel Writers and the Language of Aesthetics, 1716–1818*. Cambridge: Cambridge University Press, 1995.

Bondil, Nathalie. *Catherine the Great: Art for Empire: Masterpieces from the State Hermitage Museum, Russia*. Montreal: Montréal Museum of Fine Arts, 2005.

Bourdieu, Pierre. *Outline of a Theory of Practice*. Translated by Richard Nice. Cambridge: Cambridge University Press, 1977.

Brewer, John. *The Pleasures of the Imagination: English Culture in the Eighteenth Century*. London: HarperCollins, 1997.

Bryant, Mary. *The Museum by the Park: 14 Queen Anne's Gate from Charles Townley to Axel Johnson*. London: Paul Holberton Publishing, 2017.

Buchli, Victor. *The Material Culture Reader*. Oxford and New York: Berg, 2002.

Buck, Pamela. 'The Things She Carried: Nationalism, Commerce, and the Souvenir in British Romantic Women's Writing on the French Revolution'. PhD thesis, Tufts University, 2008.

Burling, William J. 'A "sickly sort of refinement": the problem of sentimentalism in Mackenzie's *The Man of Feeling*'. *Studies in Scottish Literature* 23, no. 1 (1988): 136–49.

Buzard, James. 'The Grand Tour and after (1660–1840).' In *The Cambridge Companion to Travel Writing*, edited by Peter Hulme and Tim Youngs, 37–52. Cambridge: Cambridge University Press, 2002.

Candela, Andrea. 'Biblical deluge and creationism in eighteenth century Italy: an overview of the geological theory of Ermenegildo Pini (1739–1825).' In *INHIGEO Annual Record*, no. 46, edited by Wolf Mayer, 67–72. Canberra: International Commission on the History of Geological Sciences, 2014.

Carr, Lydia. *Tessa Verney Wheeler: Women and Archaeology before World War Two*. Oxford: Oxford University Press, 2012.

Cassidy-Geiger, Maureen. *Fragile Diplomacy: Meissen Porcelain for European Courts Ca. 1710–63*. New Haven: Yale University Press, 2007.

Chaney, Edward. *The Evolution of the Grand Tour: Anglo-Italian Cultural Relations since the Renaissance*. London: Frank Cass, 1998.

Chard, Chloe. *Pleasure and Guilt on the Grand Tour: Travel Writing and Imaginative Geography, 1600–1830*. Manchester: Manchester University Press, 1999.

Chen, Reuven, and Vasilis Pagonis. *Thermally and Optically Stimulated Luminescence: A Simulation Approach*. Hoboken: Wiley, 2011.

Clifford, James L., and Margaret Anne Doody. *Hester Lynch Piozzi (Mrs. Thrale)*. 2nd edn. Oxford and New York: Oxford University Press, 1986.

Cohen, Erik. 'A phenomenology of tourist experiences'. *Sociology* 13 (1979): 179–201.

Cohen, Michèle. *Fashioning Masculinity: National Identity and Language in the Eighteenth Century*. New York: Routledge, 1996.

———. 'The Grand Tour: constructing the English gentleman in eighteenth-century France'. *History of Education* 21, no. 3 (1992): 241–57.

———. 'The Grand Tour: language, national identity and masculinity'. *Changing English* 8, no. 2 (2001): 129–41.

———. 'Manliness, effeminacy and the French: gender and the construction of national character in eighteenth-century England'. In *English Masculinities, 1660–1800*, edited by Tim Hitchcock and Michèle Cohen, 44–62. London: Longman, 1999.

———. '"Manners" make the man: politeness, chivalry, and the construction of masculinity, 1750–1830'. *Journal of British Studies* 44, no. 2 (2005): 312–29.

Colley, Linda. *Britons: Forging the Nation, 1707–1837*. New Haven and London: Yale University Press, 1992.

Coltman, Viccy. *Classical Sculpture and the Culture of Collecting in Britain since 1760*. Oxford and New York: Oxford University Press, 2009.

———. *Fabricating the Antique: Neoclassicism in Britain, 1760–1800*. 1st edn. Chicago; London: University of Chicago Press, 2006.

———. 'Representation, replication and collecting in Charles Townley's late eighteenth-century library'. *Art History* 29, no. 2 (2006): 304–24.

Costa, Shelley. 'The "ladies' diary": gender, mathematics, and civil society in early-eighteenth-century England'. *Osiris, 2nd Series* 17 (2002): 49–73.

Courtney, W. P., and Peter Davis. 'Richardson, Richard (1663–1741).' *Oxford Dictionary of National Biography*, last updated 27 May 2010, https://doi.org/10.1093/ref:odnb/23576.

'Cumae (Napoli, Italy)'. In *International Dictionary of Historic Places: Southern Europe*, edited by Adele Hast et al., 176–9. Chicago and London: Fitzroy Dearborn, 1994.

Dashkova, Ekaterina. *Zapiski. Pisma Sester M. I K. Vilmont Iz Rossii*. Moscow: Moscow University, 1987.

D'Ezio, Marianna. 'The advantages of "demi-naturalization": mutual perceptions of Britain and Italy in Hester Lynch Piozzi's *Observations and Reflections Made in the Course of a Journey through France, Italy and Germany*.' *Journal for Eighteenth-Century Studies* 33, no. 2 (2010): 165–80.

De Ceglia, Francesco Paolo. 'Rotten corpses, a disembowelled woman, a flayed man. Images of the body from the end of the 17th to the beginning of the 19th century. Florentine wax models in the first-hand accounts of visitors'. *Perspectives on Science* 14, no. 4 (2006): 417–56.

Derrida, Jacques. *Given Time: I. Counterfeit Money*. Translated by Peggy Kamuf. Chicago: University of Chicago Press, 1992.

Dobson, Michael, Stanley Wells, Will Sharpe, and Erin Sullivan (eds). *The Oxford Companion to Shakespeare*. Oxford: Oxford University Press, 2015.

Dodson, Ronald F., and Samuel P. Hammar. *Asbestos: Risk Assessment, Epidemiology, and Health Effects*. 2nd edn. Hoboken: CRC Press, 2011.

Dolan, Brian. *Ladies of the Grand Tour*. London: HarperCollins, 2001.

Dorfles, Gillo, and John McHale. *Kitsch: An Anthology of Bad Taste*. London: Studio Vista, 1969.

Downes, Stephanie, Sally Holloway, and Sarah Randles. *Feeling Things: Objects and Emotions Through History*. Oxford: Oxford University Press, 2018.

Du Prey, Pierre de la Ruffinière. *John Soane: The Making of an Architect*. Chicago: University of Chicago Press, 1982.

Du Tertre, Nancy. *The Art of the Limoges Box*. New York: Harry N. Abrams Inc., 2003.

Dwyer, Philip. *Napoleon: The Path to Power 1769–1799*. London: Bloomsbury, 2014.

Earle, Rebecca. *Epistolary Selves: Letters and Letter-Writers, 1600–1945*. Aldershot: Ashgate, 1999.

Edwards, Elizabeth. '"Place makes a great difference": Hester Piozzi's Welsh independence'. *Wales Arts Review*, 28 August 2014, accessed 8 March 2020, www.walesartsreview.org/the-gregynog-papers-7-place-makes-a-great-difference-hester-piozzis-welsh-independence/.

Eger, Elizabeth. 'Luxury, industry and charity: Bluestocking culture displayed'. In *Luxury in the Eighteenth Century: Debates, Desires and Delectable Goods*, edited by Maxine Berg and Elizabeth Eger, 190–204. New York: Palgrave Macmillan, 2003.

Ewing, Heather. *The Lost World of James Smithson: Science, Revolution and the Birth of the Smithsonian*. London: Bloomsbury, 2010.

Faderman, Lillian. *Surpassing the Love of Men: Romantic Friendship and Love between Women from the Renaissance to the Present*. London: Junction Books, 1979.

Falkner, James. 'Churchill [née Jenyns], Sarah, Duchess of Marlborough (1660–1744).' *Oxford Dictionary of National Biography*, last updated 3 January 2008, http://doi.org/10.1093.ref:odnb/5405.

Fara, Patricia. 'The appliance of science: the Georgian British Museum'. *History Today*, no. 8 (1997): 39–45.

Ferry, Georgina. 'The exception and the rule: women and the Royal Society 1945–2010'. *Notes and Records of the Royal Society* 64, no. 1 (2010): 163–72.

Findlen, Paula. *Early Modern Things: Objects and Their Histories, 1500–1800*. London and New York: Routledge, 2012.

Finn, Margot. 'Men's things: masculine possession in the consumer revolution'. *Social History* 25, no. 2 (2000): 133–55.

'Florentius Vassall: Profile & Legacies Summary, 1689–1778'. Centre for the Study of Legacies of British Slavery, University College London (n.d.), accessed 29 February, 2020, www.ucl.ac.uk/lbs/person/view/2146651009.

Ford, Brinsley, and John Ingamells. *A Dictionary of British and Irish Travellers in Italy, 1701–1800*. New Haven: Yale University Press, 1997.

Franklin, Alexandra. 'John Bull in a dream: fear and fantasy in the visual satires of 1803'. In *Resisting Napoleon: The British Response to the Threat of Invasion, 1797–1815*, edited by Mark Philp, 125–39. Burlington: Ashgate, 2006.

Franklin, Michael J. 'Piozzi [née Salusbury; other married name Thrale], Hester Lynch (1741–1821).' *Oxford Dictionary of National Biography*, last updated 23 September 2004, https://doi.org/10.1093/ref:odnb/22309.

French, Anne. *Art Treasures in the North: Northern Families on the Grand Tour*. Norwich: Unicorn Press, 2009.

French, Henry, and Mark Rothery. '"Upon your entry into the world": masculine values and the threshold of adulthood among landed elites in England, 1680–1800'. *Social History* 33, no. 4 (2008): 402–22.

Gacto, M. 'The bicentennial of a forgotten giant: Lazzaro Spallanzani (1729–1799)'. *International Microbiology* 2, 4 (1999): 273–4.

Gage, Andrew Thomas, and William Thomas Stearn. *A Bicentenary History of the Linnean Society of London*. London: Linnean Society of London, 1988.

Garrioch, David. 'From Christian friendship to secular sentimentality: Enlightenment re-evaluations'. In *Friendship: A History*, edited by Barbara Caine, 165–214. London: Equinox, 2009.

Gerritsen, Anne, and Giorgio Riello. *Writing Material Culture History*. London: Bloomsbury, 2014.

Gibbs, William. 'Bryan Higgins and his circle'. In *Chemistry in Britain*, edited by Royal Institute of Chemistry, 60–65. London: Chemical Education Trust Fund, 1965.

Giesz, Ludwig. *Phänomenologie des Kitsches: ein Beitrag zur anthropologischen Ästhetik*. Heidelberg: Rothe, 1960.

Girten, Kristin M. 'Unsexed souls: natural philosophy as transformation in Eliza Haywood's *Female Spectator*'. *Eighteenth-Century Studies* 43, no. 1 (2009): 55–74.

Glazebrook, Charles Field. 'Brynbella'. In *Brynbella, Tremeirchion, St. Asaph, Clwyd, the Contents Including an Important Collection of Modern British Paintings and Other British Paintings, Furniture, Clocks, Silver, Carpets, Ceramics and Glass, Works of Art, Books, Garden Statuary and Household Items*, 8–13. London: Sotheby's, 1994.

Gleadhill, Emma. '"For I asked him men's questions": late eighteenth-century British women tourists' contributions to scientific inquiry'. *Eighteenth-Century Life* 45, no. 3 (2021): 158–77. https://doi.org/10.1215/00982601-9273034.

———. 'Improving upon birth, marriage and divorce: the cultural capital of three late eighteenth-century female Grand Tourists'. *Journal of Tourism History*, published online 28 March 2018. https://doi.org/10.1080/1755182X.2018.1449904.

———. '"Let her now set her thoughts down as she can recollect them": late eighteenth-century British women tourist's literary souvenirs'. In *Microtravel: Confinement, Deceleration, Proximity*, edited by Charles Forsdick, Zoë Kinsley and Kate Walchester. New York: Anthem Press, forthcoming 2022.

———. 'Performing travel: Lady Holland's Grand Tour souvenirs and the "House of All Europe"'. *eMaj (electronic Melbourne art journal)*, special issue 9.1, 'Cosmopolitan moments: instances of exchange in the long eighteenth century', edited by Jennifer Milam (December 2017).

———. '"Upon the whole I expect he took me for an aventurière": eighteenth-century British women tourists' accounts of mountains and mountaineering'. In *The Mountain and the Politics of Representation*, edited by Jenny Hall and Martin Hall. Liverpool: Liverpool University Press, forthcoming 2022.

Gleadhill, Emma, and Ekaterina Heath. 'Giving women history: a history of Ekaterina Dashkova through her gifts to Catherine the Great and others'. *Women's History Review*, published online 19 April 2021. https://doi.org/10.1080/09612025.2021.1912269.

Glover, Katharine. *Elite Women and Polite Society in Eighteenth-Century Scotland*. Woodbridge: Boydell Press, 2011.
Goldsmith, Sarah. 'Dogs, servants and masculinities: writing about danger on the Grand Tour'. *Journal for Eighteenth-Century Studies* 40, no. 1 (2017): 3–21.
———. *Masculinity on the Grand Tour*. London: University of London Press, 2020.
———. 'Nostalgia, homesickness and emotional formation on the eighteenth-century Grand Tour'. *Cultural and Social History* 15, no. 3 (2018): 333–60.
Gordin, Michael D. 'Arduous and delicate task: Ekaterina Dashkova, the Academy of Sciences, and the taming of natural philosophy'. In *The Princess and the Patriot: Ekaterina Dashkova, Benjamin Franklin, and the Age of Enlightenment*, edited by Sue Ann Prince, 3–22. Philadelphia: American Philosophical Society, 2006.
Gordon, Beverly. 'The souvenir: messenger of the extraordinary'. *Journal of Popular Culture* 20, no. 3 (1986): 135–46.
Gowrley, Freya. 'Craft(ing) narratives'. *Eighteenth-Century Fiction* 31, no. 1 (2018): 77–97.
———. *Domestic Space in Britain, 1750–1840: Materiality, Sociability and Emotion*. London: Bloomsbury, 2021.
Graburn, Nelson. *Ethnic and Tourist Arts: Cultural Expressions from the Fourth World*. Berkeley: University of California Press, 1976.
Graburn, Nelson H. H. 'Tourism: the sacred journey'. In *Hosts and Guests: The Anthropology of Tourism*, edited by Valene L. Smith, 21–36. Philadelphia: University of Pennsylvania Press, 1989.
Gregory, Desmond. *Napoleon's Jailer: Lt. Gen. Sir Hudson Lowe: A Life*. London: Fairleigh Dickinson University Press, 1996.
Grimshaw, Patricia, and Julie Evans. 'Colonial women on intercultural frontiers: Rosa Campbell Praed, Mary Bundock and Katie Langloh Parker'. *Australian Historical Studies* 27 (1996).
Guntau, Martin. 'The rise of geology as a science in Germany around 1800'. In *The Making of the Geological Society*, edited by C. L. E. Lewis and S. J. Knell, 163–78. Bath: Geological Society of London, 2009.
Hagglund, Elizabeth. 'Tourists and Travellers: Women's Non-Fictional Writing About Scotland 1770–1830'. PhD thesis, University of Birmingham, 2000.
Haldane Grenier, Katherine. *Tourism and Identity in Scotland, 1770–1914: Creating Caledonia*. Aldershot: Ashgate, 2005.
Hamling, Tara, and Catherine Richardson. *Everyday Objects: Medieval and Early Modern Material Culture and Its Meanings*. London: Routledge, 2016.
Hargrave, Catherine Perry. *A History of Playing Cards and a Bibliography of Cards and Gaming*. New York: Dover Publications, 2000.

Harvey, Karen. *History and Material Culture: A Student's Guide to Approaching Alternative Sources*. London and New York: Routledge, 2013.
Hasluck, Paul. 'Miss Pink's love story.' *Northern Territory Newsletter*, July 1975, 4–9.
Haughton, Claire Shaver. *Green Immigrants: The Plants That Transformed America*. New York: Harcourt, Brace, Jovanovich, 1978.
Hayward, Abraham. *A Selection from the Correspondence of Abraham Hayward, Q.C., from 1834 to 1884: With an Account of His Early Life*. Edited by Henry E. Carlisle. 2 vols. Vol. 2. London: John Murray, 1886, 49.
Herbert, Amanda E. 'Gender and the spa: space, sociability and self at British health spas, 1640–1714.' *Journal of Social History* 43 (Winter 2009): 361–83.
Hibbert, Christopher. *The Grand Tour*. London: Hamlyn Publishing Group, 1974.
Hornsby, Clare. *The Impact of Italy: The Grand Tour and Beyond*. London: British School at Rome, 2000.
Hoskin, Michael. *William and Caroline Herschel: Pioneers in Late 18th-Century Astronomy*. Dordrecht: Springer, 2013.
Ingamells, John. *National Portrait Gallery Mid-Georgian Portraits 1760–1790*. London: National Portrait Gallery, 2004.
Ingelbien, Raphaël. *Irish Cultures of Travel: Writing on the Continent, 1829–1914*. London: Palgrave Macmillan, 2016.
Inkster, Ian. 'Advocates and audience: aspects of popular astronomy in England, 1750–1850'. *Journal of the British Astronomical Association* 92, no. 3 (1982): 119–23.
Ivleva, Victoria. 'Catherine II: uniform dresses and regional uniforms'. *Costume* 53, no. 2 (2019): 207–30.
Izett, Erica Kaye. 'Breaking New Ground: Early Australian Ethnography in Colonial Women's Writing'. PhD thesis, University of Western Australia, 2014.
Jenkins, Tiffany. *Keeping Their Marbles: How the Treasures of the Past Ended up in Museums – and Why They Should Stay There*. Oxford: Oxford University Press, 2016.
Jordanova, Ludmilla. *Sexual Visions: Images of Gender in Science and Medicine between the Eighteenth and Twentieth Centuries*. Madison: University of Wisconsin Press, 1993.
Justice, George L., and Nathan Tinker. *Women's Writing and the Circulation of Ideas: Manuscript Publication in England, 1550–1800*. Cambridge: Cambridge University Press, 2002.
Kairoff, Claudia. *Anna Seward and the End of the Eighteenth Century*. Baltimore: Johns Hopkins University Press, 2011.

Kelly, Jason M. *The Society of Dilettanti: Archaeology and Identity in the British Enlightenment*. New Haven: Yale University Press, 2009.

Kelly, Linda. *Holland House: A History of London's Most Celebrated Salon*. London: I. B. Tauris, 2013.

Keppel, Sonia. *The Sovereign Lady: A Life of Elizabeth Vassall, Third Lady Holland, with Her Family*. London: Hamilton, 1974.

Kilburn, Matthew. 'Fitzpatrick [née Liddell], Anne, Countess of Upper Ossory [other married name Anne Fitzroy, Duchess of Grafton] (1737/8–1804).' *Oxford Dictionary of National Biography*, last updated 4 October 2008, https://doi.org/10.1093/ref:odnb/88658.

Kinsley, Zoë. 'Considering the Manuscript Travelogue: The Journals of Dorothy Richardson (1761–1801).' *Prose Studies: History, Theory, Criticism* 26, no. 3 (2003): 414–31.

———. 'Dorothy Richardson's manuscript travel journals (1761–1801) and the possibilities of picturesque aesthetics'. *Review of English Studies* 56, no. 226 (2005): 611–31.

———. 'Travel and material culture: commodity, currency, and destabilised meaning in women's home tour writing'. *Studies in Travel Writing* 10 (2006): 101–22.

———. *Women Writing the Home Tour, 1682–1812*. Aldershot: Ashgate, 2008.

Kugel, Alexis. *Piqué: Gold, Tortoiseshell and Mother-of-Pearl at the Court of Naples*. Paris: Milano Mondadori Electa, 2018.

Lamb, Susan. *Bringing Travel Home to England: Tourism, Gender, and Imaginative Literature in the Eighteenth Century*. Newark, DE: University of Delaware Press, 2009.

Landes, Joan B. 'Wax fibers, wax bodies, and moving figures'. In *Ephemeral Bodies: Wax Sculpture and the Human Figure*, edited by Roberta Panzanelli, 41–66. Los Angeles: Getty Research Institute, 2008.

Latour, Bruno. *Pandora's Hope: Essays on the Reality of Science Studies*. Cambridge; London: Harvard University Press, 1999.

Le Corbeiller, Clare. *Eighteenth-Century Italian Porcelain*. New York: Metropolitan Museum of Art, 1985.

Lee, Colin. 'Currer, Frances Mary Richardson (1785–1861).' *Oxford Dictionary of National Biography*, last updated 23 September 2004, https://doi.org/10.1093/ref:odnb/6951.

Lee, Elizabeth. 'Miller [née Riggs], Lady Anna (1741–1781).' Revised by Rebecca Mills. *Oxford Dictionary of National Biography*, last updated 23 September 2004, https://doi.org/10.1093/ref:odnb/18720.

Lokke, Kari E., and Adriana Craciun. *Rebellious Hearts: British Women Writers and the French Revolution*. New York: State University of New York Press, 2001.

Lynch, Deidre. 'Personal effects and sentimental fictions'. *Eighteenth-Century Fiction* 12, no. 2–3 (2000): 345–68.

Lyons, Martyn. *Napoleon Bonaparte and the Legacy of the French Revolution*. London: Macmillan, 1994.

Macdonogh, Katharine. 'A sympathetic ear: Napoleon, Elba and the British'. *History Today* 44, no. 2 (February 1994): 29–35.

'Madeleine de Scudéry'. *Stanford Encyclopedia of Philosophy* [website], Stanford University, updated 22 August 2019, accessed 7 February 2020, https://plato.stanford.edu/entries/madeleine-scudery/.

Marks, Stephen Powys. 'Caroline Powys and her journals'. *Powys Journal* 21 (2011): 183–201.

Mars, Gerald, and Valerie Mars. '"Souvenir-gifts" as tokens of filial esteem: the meanings of Blackpool souvenirs'. In *Souvenirs: The Material Culture of Tourism*, edited by Michael Hitchcock and Ken Teague, 91–111. Aldershot: Ashgate, 2000.

Marshall, David Ryley, Susan May Russell, and Karin Elizabeth Wolfe. *Roma Britannica: Art Patronage and Cultural Exchange in Eighteenth-Century Rome*. London: British School at Rome, 2011.

Mauss, Marcel. *The Gift: Forms and Functions of Exchange in Archaic Societies*. London: Routledge, 1989.

Meehan-Waters, Brenda. 'Catherine the Great and the problem of female rule'. *Russian Review* 34, no. 3 (1975): 293–307.

Messbarger, Rebecca. 'The re-birth of Venus in Florence's Royal Museum of Physics and Natural History'. *Journal of the History of Collections* 25, no. 2 (2013): 195–215.

Meyer, Frederick G., and Susanne Elsasser. 'The 19th century herbarium of Isaac C. Martindale'. *Taxon* 22, no. 4 (1973): 375–404.

Mills, Sara. 'Knowledge, gender and empire'. In *Writing Women and Space: Colonial and Postcolonial Geographies*, edited by Alison Blunt and Gillian Rose, 29–50. New York and London: Guilford Press, 1994.

Mitchell, Leslie. *Holland House*. London: Duckworth, 1980.

Moir, Esther. *The Discovery of Britain: The English Tourists 1540–1840*. London: Routledge, 1964.

Mollan, Charles. *It's Part of What We Are*, vol. 1. Dublin: Royal Dublin Society, 2007.

Moore, Susan. 'The virtuosic tortoiseshell workers of 18th-century Naples'. *Apollo: The International Art Magazine*, 11 September 2018, accessed 21 January 2020, www.apollo-magazine.com/the-virtuosic-tortoiseshell-workers-of-18th-century-naples/.

Mori, Jennifer. 'Hosting the Grand Tour: civility, enlightenment and culture, c.1740–1790'. In *Educating the Child in Enlightenment Britain: Beliefs, Cultures, Practices*, edited by Jill Shefrin and Mary Hilton, 117–30. London: Routledge, 2016.

Mount, Harry. 'The monkey with the magnifying glass: constructions of the connoisseur in eighteenth-century Britain'. *Oxford Art Journal* 29, no. 2 (2006): 169–84.

Naddeo, Barbara Ann. 'Cultural capitals and cosmopolitanism in eighteenth-century Italy: the historiography of Italy and the Grand Tour'. *Journal of Modern Italian Studies* 10, no. 2 (2005): 183–99.

Naldrett, Peter. *Days out Underground: 50 Subterranean Adventures beneath Britain*. London: Bloomsbury, 2019.

Newman, Gerald. *The Rise of English Nationalism: A Cultural History 1740–1830*. New York: St. Martin's Press, 1987.

Olcelli, Laura. 'Lady Anna Riggs Miller: the "modest" selfexposure of the female Grand Tourist'. *Studies in Travel Writing* 19, no. 4 (2015): 312–23.

Ousby, Ian. *The Englishman's England: Taste, Travel and the Rise of Tourism*. Cambridge: Cambridge University Press, 1990.

Park, Julie. *The Self and It: Novel Objects in Eighteenth-Century England*. Stanford: Stanford University Press, 2010.

Park, Katharine. *Secrets of Women: Gender, Generation, and the Origins of Human Dissection*. New York: Zone Books, 2006.

Pascoe, Judith. 'Poetry as a souvenir: Mary Shelley in the annuals'. In *Mary Shelley in Her Times*, edited by Betty Bennett and Stuart Curran, 176–84. Baltimore: Johns Hopkins University Press, 2000.

Pearce, Susan. *Visions of Antiquity: The Society of Antiquaries of London 1707–2007*. London: Society of Antiquaries of London, 2007.

Pedrocco, Giorgio. 'Bonvicino (also known as Bonvoisin or Buonvicino) Costanzo Benedetto'. *Complete Dictionary of Scientific Biography*, Encyclopedia.com, accessed 15 March 2020, https://bit.ly/3mPwIFV.

Petrova E., and S. Moiseeva, *Grigory Ugryumov*. St Petersburg: Palace editions, 2014.

Pointon, Marcia. *Strategies for Showing: Women, Possession, and Representation in English Visual Culture, 1665–1800*. Oxford and New York: Oxford University Press, 1997.

———. '"Surrounded with brilliants": miniature portraits in eighteenth-century England'. *Art Bulletin* 83, no. 1 (2001): 48–71.

———. 'Women and their jewels'. In *Women and Material Culture, 1660–1830*, edited by Jennie Batchelor and Cora Kaplan, 11–30. Basingstoke: Palgrave Macmillan, 2007.

Pomian, Kryzstof. *Collectors and Curiosities: Paris and Venice 1500–1800*. Cambridge: Polity Press, 1990.

Pough, Frederick H., and Roger T. Peterson. *Peterson First Guide to Rocks and Minerals*. Boston and New York: Houghton Mifflin, 1998.

Pratt, Mary Louise. *Imperial Eyes: Travel Writing and Transculturation*. London: Routledge, 2008.

Proskurina, Vera. *Creating the Empress: Politics and Poetry in the Age of Catherine II*. Brighton, MA: Academic Studies Press, 2011.

Purdue, A. W. 'John and Harriet Carr: a brother and sister from the north-east on a Grand Tour'. *Northern History* 30 (1994): 122–38.

Rauser, Amelia. 'Hair, authenticity, and the self-made macaroni'. *Eighteenth-Century Studies* 38, no. 1 (2004): 101–17.

Redford, Bruce. *Venice and the Grand Tour*. New Haven: Yale University Press, 1996.

RGADA (Rossiyskiy Gosudarstvenniy Arkhiv Drevnykh Aktov, Moscow), fol. 1261, op. 2 ed.khr. 915. 'Reestr kartinam ostavshimsya posle pokoinoi knyagini Ekateriny Romanovny Dashkovoi'.

Ribeiro, Aileen. *The Gallery of Fashion*. London: National Portrait Gallery, 2000.

Roberts, Charlotte. 'Living with the Ancient Romans: past and present in eighteenth-century encounters with Herculaneum and Pompeii'. *Huntington Library Quarterly* 78, no. 1 (2015): 61–85.

Robinson, Jane. *Unsuitable for Ladies: An Anthology of Women Travellers*. Oxford and New York: Oxford University Press, 1994.

———. *Wayward Women: A Guide to Women Travellers*. New York: Oxford University Press, 1990.

Rogers, Lizzie. 'Conversing with collecting the world: elite female sociability and learning through objects in the age of Enlightenment'. In *Women and the Art and Science of Collecting in Eighteenth-Century Europe*, edited by Arlene Leis and Kacie L. Wills, 93–107. New York: Routledge, 2020.

Rubin-Detlev, Kelsey. *The Epistolary Art of Catherine the Great*. Oxford Studies in the Enlightenment. Liverpool: Liverpool University Press, 2019.

Russell, Mary. *The Blessings of a Good Thick Skirt*. London: Collins, 1986.

Sage, Lorna, Germaine Greer, and Elaine Showalter. *The Cambridge Guide to Women's Writing in English*. Cambridge: Cambridge University Press, 1999.

Sanders, Lloyd C. *The Holland House Circle*. New York: B. Blom, 1969.

Saunders, Nicholas. *Trench Art: Materialities and Memories of War*. Oxford: Berg Publishers, 2003.

Scarisbrick, Diana. 'Companion to a Russian princess: Martha Wilmot's green book'. *Country Life*, 8 January 1981.

Schaffer, Simon. '"The great laboratories of the universe": William Herschel on matter theory and planetary life'. *Journal for the History of Astronomy* 11 (1980): 81–110.

Schiebinger, Londa. *The Mind Has No Sex?: Women in the Origins of Modern Science*. Cambridge, MA: Harvard University Press, 1991.

Schmid, Susanne. *British Literary Salons of the Late Eighteenth and Early Nineteenth Centuries*. New York: Palgrave Macmillan, 2013.

Schulz, T. E. 'The Woodstock glove industry', *Oxoniensia* 3 (1938): 139–52.
Schumann, Walter. *Gemstones of the World*. New York and London: Sterling, 2009.
Scott, Jonathan. *The Pleasures of Antiquity: British Collectors of Greece and Rome*. New Haven: Yale University Press, 2003.
Secord, James A. 'Newton in the nursery: Tom Telescope and the philosophy of tops and balls, 1761–1838'. *History of Science* 23, no. 2 (1985): 127–51.
Semmel, Stuart. 'British uses for Napoleon'. *MLN* 120, no. 4 (2005): 733–46.
Shilder, Nikolay. *Imperator Pavel Perviy*. St Petersburg: Izdaniye A. S. Suvorina, 1901.
Shukina, P. I. 'Opis Kartin I Knig Pokoinoi Kn. E.R. Dashkovoy'. In *Sbornik Starinnykh Bumag, Khranyashikhsya V Muzee*, 85–9. Moscow: Tov. Tip. A.I. Mamontova, 1901.
Sloboda, Stacey. 'Displaying materials: porcelain and natural history in the Duchess of Portland's museum'. *Eighteenth-Century Studies* 43, no. 4 (2010): 455–72.
Smith-Rosenberg, Carroll. 'The female world of love and ritual: relations between women in nineteenth century America'. *Signs* 1 (1975): 1–29.
Smith, Bernard William. *European Vision and the South Pacific*. New Haven and London: Yale University Press, 1985.
Snader, Joe. 'The masquerade of colonial identity in Frances Brooke's Emily Montague (1769)'. In *The Clothes That Wear Us: Essays on Dressing and Transgressing in Eighteenth-Century Culture*, edited by Jessica Munns and Penny Richards, 119–42. Newark: University of Delaware Press, 1999.
Spender, Dale. *Writing a New World: Two Centuries of Australian Women Writers*. London: Pandora, 1988.
Stabile, Susan. *Memory's Daughters: The Material Culture of Remembrance in Eighteenth-Century America*. New York: Cornell University Press, 2004.
Standish, Ann. *Australia through Women's Eyes*. Melbourne: Australian Scholarly Publishing, 2008.
Stanley, Liz. 'Romantic friendship? Some issues in researching lesbian history and biography.' *Women's History Review* 1, no. 2 (1992): 193–216.
Staves, Susan. '"Books without which I cannot write": how did eighteenth-century women writers get the books they read?'. In *Women and Material Culture, 1660–1830*, edited by Jennie Batchelor and Cora Kaplan, 192–211. Basingstoke and New York: Palgrave Macmillan, 2007.
Stewart, Susan. *On Longing: Narratives of the Miniature, the Gigantic, the Souvenir, the Collection*. Baltimore: Johns Hopkins University Press, 1984.
Sturge, Martin. 'Lady Miller of Batheaston'. Public lecture, University of Bath, Claverton Down, 23 November 2009.
Swann, Marjorie. *Curiosities and Texts: The Culture of Collecting in Early Modern England*. Philadelphia: University of Pennsylvania Press, 2001.

Sweet, Rosemary. 'Antiquaries and antiquities in eighteenth-century England'. *Eighteenth-Century Studies* 34, no. 2 (Winter 2001): 181–206.

———. *Antiquaries: The Discovery of the Past in Eighteenth-Century Britain*. London and New York: Hambledon and London, 2004.

———. *Cities and the Grand Tour: The British in Italy, c.1690–1820*. Cambridge: Cambridge University Press, 2012.

Sweet, Rosemary, Gerrit Verhoeven, and Sarah Goldsmith. *Beyond the Grand Tour: Northern Metropolises and Early Modern Travel Behaviour*. London and New York: Routledge, 2017.

Tames, Richard. *Josiah Wedgwood: An Illustrated Life of Josiah Wedgwood 1730–1795*. Aylesbury: Shire Publications, 1984.

Thomas, Nicholas. 'Licenced curiosity: Cook's Pacific voyages'. In *The Cultures of Collecting*, edited by John Elsner and Roger Cardinal, 116–36. London: Reaktion Books, 1994.

Thorold, Peter. *The British in France: Visitors and Residents since the Revolution*. London: Bloomsbury, 2008.

Thurgood, J. E. 'Swinburne, Henry (1743–1803).' *Oxford Dictionary of National Biography*, last updated 3 October 2013, https://doi.org/10.1093/ref:odnb/26837.

Tillyard, Stella. *Aristocrats: Caroline, Emily, Louisa and Sarah Lennox 1740–1832*. London: Vintage, 1995.

Towner, John. 'The Grand Tour: A Key Phase in the History of Tourism'. *Annals of Tourism Research* 12 (1985): 297–333, 312.

Trivellato, Francesca. 'The exchange of Mediterranean coral and Indian diamonds'. In *The Familiarity of Strangers: The Sephardic Diaspora, Livorno, and Cross-Cultural Trade in the Early Modern Period*, 224–50. New Haven: Yale University Press, 2009.

Turner, Katherine. *British Travel Writers in Europe, 1750–1800: Authorship, Gender, and National Identity*. Aldershot; Burlington: Ashgate, 2001.

'Ucherezhdeniye ob Imperatorskoi Familii'. In *Polnoye Sobraniye Zakonov Rossiyskoi Imperii (PSZ)*, edited by Georgiy Savich, 525–69. St Petersburg: Tip. II otd., 1830.

Uglow, Jenny. 'Vase mania'. In *Luxury in the Eighteenth-Century: Debates, Desires and Delectable Goods*, edited by Maxine Berg and Elizabeth Eger, 151–62. New York: Palgrave Macmillan, 2003.

Van Buren, E. Douglas. 'The Scorpion in Mesopotamian Art and Religion'. *Archiv für Orientforschung* 12 (1937): 1–28.

Vick, Brian E. *The Congress of Vienna*. Cambridge, MA: Harvard University Press, 2014.

Vickery, Amanda. *Behind Closed Doors*. New Haven: Yale University Press, 2009.

———. *The Gentleman's Daughter: Women's Lives in Georgian England.* New Haven: Yale University Press, 1998.

———. 'His and hers: gender consumption and household accounting in eighteenth-century England'. *Past and Present* Supplement 1 (2006).

Vishlenkova, Elena. *Vizualnoye Narodovedeniye Imperii.* Moscow: Novoye Literaturnoye Obozreniye, 2011.

Visconti, Agnese. 'The naturalistic explorations of the Milanese Barnabite Ermenegildo Pini (1739–1825) along the coast of Calabria: new observations and implications with regard to his views on the history of the Earth'. *Proceedings of the California Academy of Sciences* 59, no. 4 (2008): 51–63.

Walchester, Kathryn. *Our Own Fair Italy: Nineteenth Century Women's Travel Writing and Italy 1800–1844.* Oxford: Peter Lang, 2007.

Walvin, James. *Beside the Seaside: A Social History of the Popular Seaside Holiday.* London: Penguin, 1978.

Waterston, C. E., and A. Macmillan Shearer. *Former Fellows of the Royal Society of Edinburgh 1783 – 2002*, vol. 2. Edinburgh: Royal Society of Edinburgh, 2006.

Way, Twigs. *Virgins, Weeders and Queens: A History of Women in the Garden.* Cheltenham: History Press, 2013.

Weiner, Annette. *Inalienable Possessions: The Paradox of Keeping-While-Giving.* Berkeley: University of California Press, 1992.

West, A. J. *The Shakespeare First Folio: The History of the Book – A New World Census of First Folios.* Oxford: Oxford University Press, 2003.

Whyman, Susan. 'Letter-writing, reading, and literary culture: the Johnson family and Anna Miller'. In *The Pen and the People: English Letter Writers 1660–1800*, 191–217. Oxford: Oxford University Press, 2009.

Wilkins, Hugh. 'Souvenirs: what and why we buy'. *Journal of Travel Research* 50, no. 3 (2010): 239–47.

Wilson, Ellen. 'A Shropshire lady in Bath, 1794–1807'. *Bath History* 4 (1992): 95–123.

Wilton-Ely, John. 'Classic ground: Britain, Italy, and the Grand Tour' (book review). *Eighteenth-Century Life* 28, no. 1 (2004): 136–65.

Wilton, Andrew. *The Swagger Portrait: Grand Manner Portraiture in Britain from Van Dyck to Augustus John, 1630–1930.* London: Tate Gallery, 1992.

Wilton, Andrew, and Ilaria Bignamini. *Grand Tour: The Lure of Italy in the Eighteenth Century.* London: Tate Gallery Publishing, 1996.

Withey, Lynne. *Grand Tours and Cooks' Tours: A History of Leisure Travel, 1750–1915.* 1st edn. New York: W. Morrow, 1997.

Woronzoff-Dashkoff, A. *Ekaterina Dashkova. Zhizn vo vlasti i v opale.* Moscow: Molodaya gvardiya, 2010.

———. 'Princess E. R. Dashkova: first woman member of the American Philosophical Society'. *Proceedings of the American Philosophical Society* 140, no. 3 (1996): 406–17.

———. 'Princess E. R. Dashkova's Moscow library'. *Slavonic and East European Review* 72, no. 1 (1994): 60–71.

Wortman, Richard. *Scenarios of Power: Myth and Ceremony in Russian Monarchy from Peter the Great to the Abdication of Nicholas II.* Princeton: Princeton University Press, 2013.

Wright, C. J. 'Fox, Elizabeth Vassall [née Elizabeth Vassall], Lady Holland [other married name Elizabeth Vassall Webster, Lady Webster] (1771?–1845).' *Oxford Dictionary of National Biography*, last updated 3 January 2008, https://doi.org/10.1093/ref:odnb/10028.

———. 'Holland House and the fashionable pursuit of science: a nineteenth-century cabinet of curiosities'. *Journal of the History of Collections* 1, no. 1 (1989): 97–102.

Yonan, Michael. 'Portable dynasties: imperial gift-giving at the court of Vienna in the eighteenth century'. *Court Historian* 14, no. 2 (2009): 177–88.

Youngs, Tim. 'Buttons and souls: some thoughts on commodities and identity in women's travel writing'. *Studies in Travel Writing* 1 (1997): 117–40.

Zionkowski, Linda, and Cynthia Klekar. *The Culture of the Gift in Eighteenth-Century England.* New York: Palgrave Macmillan, 2009.

Zonova, Z. T. *Grigory Ivanovich Ugriumov.* Moscow: Iskusstvo, 1966.

Zuelow, Eric. *A History of Modern Tourism.* London and New York: Palgrave Macmillan, 2015.

Index

Note: 'n' after a page number indicates the number of a note on that page; 'f' indicates a figure on that page

Addison, Joseph 79, 165, 218
adolescence 33, 35, 49–50, 143
Aix-en-Provence 5, 110–11
anatomical models 129, 138, 147–9
Anatomical Venus 147–8, 148f6.2
antiquarian pursuits 9, 119, 123, 124, 127
Antoniani, Pietro 63
Arouet, François-Marie *see* Voltaire
Australian settler women 135–6

Banks, Joseph 108, 109, 135, 159
Baron Holland *see* Fox, Henry Richard (third Baron Holland)
Bartolozzi, Francesco 135, 136f5.2
Bassano, Jacopo 96
Batheaston *see* Miller, Lady Anna
Batoni, Pompeo 36, 38f1.3, 42, 52n16, 60
Benjamin, Walter 1, 13, 14
Bentham, Sarah 40
Bentinck, Margaret Cavendish (Duchess of Portland) 109, 179
Berry, Agnes 5, 9–10

Berry, Mary 5, 9–10, 41, 58–9, 60, 61–2, 65, 125, 154
Berry, Robert 5, 9
Bertrand, Countess Françoise-Elisabeth 221–2
Berwick, Baroness Anna 39
Bianchi, Giuseppe Francesco 40
Billington, Elizabeth 40
Blackpool souvenirs 19, 181
Blackstone, William 124, 127
Bluestocking circle 84, 85, 89, 90, 187
Bluestocking Society 85
Bonaparte, Napoleon *see* Napoleon
Bonvicino, Costanzo Benedetto 144
Borlase, William 131
Bradford, Catherine Daschkaw 242
Bradford, William 242, 244
Brighton keepsakes 193, 193f7.3, 194, 194f7.4
British Museum 107–8
Bruce, Miss 46, 88
Brudenell-Bruce, Charles (Marquess of Ailesbury) 39

Buchan, Alexander 135
Burney, Fanny 81, 83, 87, 187
Byres, James 39, 56–7
Byron, Lord 91, 135, 153, 219

Cades, Giuseppe 42, 43f1.4
Camden, William 115, 124, 127
Canaletto 63, 95–6
caricatures 88, 205, 207, 210, 220, 233
Carlisle, Earl of 81, 218–19
Carolina, Queen Maria 187–8
Carr, Harriet 7, 8
Catherine the Great 226, 230, 231, 234, 236, 237, 238, 239, 242, 246, 248n22, 249n44, 250n59
Cavendish, Elizabeth Christiana 57
Cavendish, Georgiana (Duchess of Devonshire) 40, 152, 160
Cavendish, Henrietta 152–3
Chambers, W. viii, plate 2, 48
Chappelow, Reverend Leonard 91
Chetwood, Anna 228, 236
Child, Richard (first Earl of Tylney) 34
Chinese artefacts 156
Churchill, Sarah (Duchess of Marlborough) 195
Cipriani, Giovanni Battista 93, 135, 136f5.2
Claude glass 63
Clifford, Rosamund 194, 195
colliery families 4, 7, 36, 46, 98
Coltman, Viccy 17
Combe, Dr Charles 129, 149
combs 10, 60, 64–5, 65f2.1
commercially manufactured keepsakes 191–3, 195, 203
connoisseurship 2, 10, 11, 12, 20, 41–2, 44, 46, 47, 50, 57, 59, 64, 72, 84, 97–8, 252
Connolly, Louisa 234
consumer culture 13, 86, 223n13

consumption practices 13, 36, 57, 58, 62, 64, 65, 67, 72, 166, 196
contemporary paintings 8, 59, 92, 97
Cook, Captain James 84, 108, 112, 133, 134–5, 165
coral 56, 59, 69, 81, 109
Correggio (artist) 41, 67
Coutts, Mrs Betty 45, 88
coverture, laws of 10, 67
Craster, Olive plate 5, 6, 58–9, 60
crystals 116, 157, 158, 164, 170n67, 221
curiosity 21, 108, 111, 112–13, 114, 116, 119, 123, 124, 133, 138, 153, 157, 166, 252
curiosity cabinet 21–2, 72, 108, 109, 138, 146, 153, 156, 157, 158, 162, 165, 166

Damer, Anne Seymour 41
Dance-Holland, Sir Nathaniel viii, plate 5, 60
Dashkova, Princess Ekaterina
 female–female friendships 234
 friendship with Martha Wilmot 176, 182, 227, 228, 229, 242, 246, 247n4
 gift-giving to Martha Wilmot 23, 226–30, 238–42, 244–5
 hierarchical relationship with Martha 229
 masculine attributes 231, 232, 233
 portrait by Dmitry Levitsky 231, 232f9.1
 portrait gifts 233–4
 portraits of Martha 235, 235f9.2, 236
 published writings 237
 Russian Academy 226, 230
 sentimental value of objects 229
 Troitskoe 226

daughter–mother gift exchange 180–1
Dawe, Philip 37
debauchery 35, 49
Delane, Solomon 63
Delany, Mary 180, 181
Derzhavin, Gavriil 230, 231, 232, 233
de Scudéry, Madeleine 84
Dickens, Charles 88, 153
Diderot, Denis 107, 230
Discobolus (sculpture) 48, 58n59
  see also Townley Collection at Park Street Gallery
Doccia factory 62
domestic tours of Britain 3, 5, 6, 11, 85, 166, 202–3
Drew, William 144, 151, 157, 158, 160, 161
Drusilla, Livia 65–6
Durno, James 59

Earle, Margaret 39
Edgeworth, Maria 109, 175
effeminacy 36
elite male Grand Tourists
  consumption practices on Tours 34, 35, 56, 57, 58, 68, 72
  Grand Tour as a rite of passage 3, 4, 33, 44, 48, 49, 97, 236
  homosocial comradery on Tour 34
  idealised elite male tourist 36, 39, 47, 56
  social status gained following a Tour 34, 35, 36
  style of male Tour travel accounts 86, 90
elite women 3, 11, 16, 18, 20, 41, 48, 57, 62, 178, 179, 181, 195, 196, 237, 253
empowering travel experiences 2, 15, 19, 186–7, 246
Etruscan borders on combs 10, 64, 81

Etruscan vase 1, 56, 81–2, 83, 86, 87, 93
Evans, Maria Lathbury 110

Fabris, Pietro viii, plate 3, plate 4
Fagan, Robert 154, 155f6.3
fans viii, plate 6, 9, 20, 60, 64, 65–6
Farnese Hercules sculpture 45
female agency xiv, 3, 15, 19, 20, 22, 119, 150, 181, 189, 196, 210, 222, 237, 246, 252
female–female friendships 23, 83, 176, 177, 178, 179, 180, 181, 182, 184, 186, 191, 234
  see also Dashkova, Princess Ekaterina; Wilmot, Martha
female–female keepsake exchange 22, 134, 135, 176, 177, 179, 180, 181, 183, 184, 186, 187, 233, 234
  see also Dashkova, Princess Ekaterina; Wilmot, Martha
female–male keepsake exchange 178, 182
Female Spectator 109, 165
femininity 3, 10, 12, 21, 22, 39, 46, 57, 64, 79, 152, 156, 227, 233, 239
Fermor, Henrietta (Countess of Pomfret) 179–80, 184
Fitzgerald, Lord Edward 208
Fitzpatrick, Anne (Countess of Upper Ossery) 13, 175
Flaxman, Ann 154–5
Fontana, Felice
  anatomical models 148, 149
  friendship with Lady Elizabeth Holland 146–7, 149, 250
  Wooden Man xv, plate 10, plate 11, 149, 150
Forbes, Anne 28n52, 40–1

Index

fossils 1, 21, 112, 131, 145
Fox, Charles James 6, 150, 203, 204, 204f8.1, 205
Fox, Henry Richard (third Baron Holland) 6, 150–1, 152, 153, 154, 157, 158, 159, 162–3, 164, 169n41, 203–5, 210–11, 213–14, 220
see also Holland, Lady Elizabeth
Fox, Lady Caroline 41
Fox-Strangeways, William (Earl of Ilchester) 157
French Revolution 5, 36, 94, 165, 202, 223n13

Gardiner, Marguerite (Countess of Blessington) 148
Garrick, David 83, 191
Gascoigne, Sir Thomas (eighth Baronet) 36, 37, 38f1.3, 39, 52n16
gems 8, 60, 68, 70, 97, 132, 156, 159, 163–4
gentility 178, 179, 184, 186, 190, 211, 234
Giles of Eastcourt, Wiltshire 39
Gillray, James 204f8.1, 205, 206f8.3, 207
see also Little Boney
Gilpin, William 7, 63, 124
Ginori, Marchese Carlo 62
gloves as keepsakes 60, 176, 185, 194, 195, 200n68
Gordon, Beverly 14–15
Grant, Anne 191
Grey, Charles (second Earl Grey) 40, 204

hair combs *see* combs
Halifax Gibbet 127, 128f5.1
Hamilton, Gavin 41, 42, 43f1.4, 59
Hamilton, Sir William 34, 51n7, 56

Hardwick House 1, 114
Hare-Naylor, Georgiana 40
Hayley, Elizabeth 83
Haywood, Eliza 109–10, 119, 165
Herculaneum 56, 62, 67, 227
Herschel, Caroline 161
Herschel, William 161, 162
Hewetson, Christopher 39
Higgins, Bryan 160
Hoare I, Henry 34
Holland, Lady Elizabeth
anatomical models 149, 150
caricature of Elizabeth and Henry 220, 221f8.9, 233
Chinese artefacts 156
curiosities from Spain 163
curiosity cabinet 22, 153–4, 156–7, 158, 162, 166
dahlia specimens 163
educational barriers in childhood 143
engagement in politics 210, 211, 219, 220, 222
Fontana's *Wooden Man* 149, 150
friendship with Felice Fontana 146–7, 149, 150
Grand Tour map (1791–96) 145f6.1
Grand Tour portrait, 1793 9
Henry's poem for Elizabeth's birthday 150–1
Italy tour with Sir Godfrey Webster (1791) 6
mineral collection 156, 158, 162, 163, 164
Mount Vesuvius 154, 155
Napoleon
ambivalence towards Napoleon 210
Napoleonic keepsakes 23, 203, 211, 218, 219, 220, 221, 222
Napoleon's physical appearance 205, 207

Napoleon's will 214
snuff-box bequeathed to Lady Elizabeth Holland 214, 215–19
New World specimens 163–4
Nice trip (1791) 144
ore, samples of 156, 158, 162, 211
Paris trip (1814) 211
polite science 143, 166
portrait by Robert Fagan 154, 155f6.3
Royal Museum of Physics and Natural History visit (1792) 146, 149
Saltram House, Devon visit (1799) 48
scientific knowledge and femininity 152
Turin trip (1792) 144
West Indian fortune 6, 138, 152, 183
see also Fox, Henry Richard (third Baron Holland); Holland House; Webster, Sir Godfrey
Holland, Sir Henry 165
Holland House 8, 16, 153, 154, 155–6, 158, 162, 165, 210, 211, 212f8.5, 219, 220
homosocial society 34, 44, 49, 178
horizontal friendships 178, 179, 186, 210, 234
Hotwells, Bristol 87, 113
Hunter, Dr William 129, 149

identity formation 3, 10, 12, 14, 15, 17, 24, 50, 64, 90, 91, 92, 152, 226, 253
imperialism and science 164–5, 166
inalienability 237–8, 245
Indigenous women 136
Ingenhousz, Jan 157, 160, 162

Johnson, Samuel 33, 51n4, 89–90, 94, 126

keepsake exchange for social advancement 142, 158, 164, 166, 175, 222
King Charles III 57, 177
King Frederick II (King of Prussia) 71
King Henry II 195
Knight, Lady Phillipina 40

Lady Holland *see* Holland, Lady Elizabeth
Lady Webster *see* Holland, Lady Elizabeth
Lake District 5, 9, 113
landscape paintings 8, 59, 62–3, 93, 124, 135, 240
Lassels, Richard 3
Latin education 33, 39, 41, 46, 118
Latour, Bruno 21
Leda and the Swan (painting) 44
Lennox, Emily 234
letters, sentimental value of 176, 177, 180, 181–2, 187, 191
letters as keepsakes 181–2, 187, 191
Levitsky, Dmitry 231, 232f9.1
Lewis, William 160
Linnaean Society 110
Linnaeus, Carl 107, 163
Little Boney 205, 206f8.3, 207
Livorno coral 59
Locke, John 16, 109, 110, 184–5
Louis XIV 177
Lvov, Nikolay 230, 242
Lysons, Samuel 95, 181, 182–3

Macaroni phenomenon 36
Macie *see* Smithson, James
Mackenzie, Kenneth (First Earl of Seaforth) plate 3, plate 4, 56

Index

male–female friendships 39, 178, 182, 183, 186, 210
male–female keepsake exchange 181, 182
male Grand Tourist *see* elite male Grand Tourist
male–male exchange of objects 123, 185
male–male friendship 178
male political elite 19, 87
Malmesbury, Lady Harriet Maria 42, 63
Mann, Sir Horace 42, 46
marketing and visual merchandise 205, 220
masculinity 12, 21, 36, 227, 233, 240
material culture 1, 2, 12, 16, 17–18, 21, 135, 140n36, 151, 165, 166, 207
Medici, Francesco de 34, 92
medicinal qualities of thermal springs 110–11
Mengs, Anton Raphael 57
merchant families 4, 7, 8, 9, 36, 46, 98
Miller, Lady Anna
   Aix-en-Provence visit (1770) 110–11
   Bath Abbey plate 7, plate 8, 87
   Batheaston 6, 77, 78, 79–80, 80f3.2, 82f3.3, 84, 85, 88
   Bologna phosphorus 112
   bouts-rimés 83
   Cicero's villa 1, 93
   criticism
      of Bath 85
      of the Etruscan vase 86, 87
      from Horace Walpole 84
      from John Moore 45
      from London's literary elite 85, 86, 97
      from Richard Tickell 86
      from Sir John Soane 45
   crystallised petrified shells 112
   curiosity 111, 112, 119
   Etruscan vase 1, 81, 82f3.3, 83, 86, 87, 93
   Farnese Hercules sculpture 45
   fossil collection 1, 112
   hair comb 10, 64, 65f2.1
   her dog 190–1
   jasper intaglio from Sibyl's Cave 70, 81
   Lady Miller's monument viii, plate 7, plate 8
   Letters from Italy 1, 45, 79
   literary salon 81, 83, 84, 112
   medicinal qualities of thermal springs 110–11, 114
   memorial and epitaph 87–8
   minerals 112
   myrtle wreaths 83, 86, 87
   Naples trip (1771) 1, 69–70
   Piranesi, prints of Rome 1, 81
   poems 83, 84
   Poetical Amusements at a Villa Near Bath 84
   Portici museum visit (1771) 62
   Sibyl's Cave, Naples 69–70
   Temple of Clitumnus 80–1
   Vatican's asbestos shroud 111–12, 114
Miller, Sir John 78, 80, 84, 98n3
millocracy families 36, 46, 98
minerals 21, 112, 113, 116, 131, 146, 156, 158, 159, 162, 163, 164
miniature portraits 178, 185, 188, 202, 233, 234, 235, 245
Miss Bruce *see* Bruce, Miss
Moir, Patrick 57
Montagu, Lady Elizabeth 85, 90, 179
Montholon, Albine de 220–1
Moore, John 44, 45
Moore, Stephen 7, 207
   see also Mount Cashell, Lady Margaret
Moore, Thomas 153, 218
More, Jacob 59

Morgan, Mary 6, 125, 131, 132, 135, 194
Morgan, Reverend Caesar 6, 194
Morritt, John Bacon Sawrey 67
Mount Cashell, Lady Margaret 7, 189, 207, 208
Mount Cashell, second Earl of *see* Moore, Stephen
Mount Vesuvius *see* Vesuvius, Mount
Murillo 8, 93
Murray, Sarah 6–7, 9, 132

naked figures 44, 45, 46, 88, 135, 148
Napoleon
  British caricatures 205, 207, 210, 220, 221f8.9
  consumerism 207, 208
  escape from Elba 213
  friendship with Henry Richard Fox 203–5
  friendship with Lady Elizabeth Holland 23, 203, 205, 207, 210, 211, 214, 215–19, 220, 221, 222
  Little Boney 205, 206f8.3, 207
  marketing and visual merchandise 205, 220
  move to Helena 213
  Napoleon's physical appearance 205, 207, 209
  Napoleon's will 214
  Peace of Amiens 202, 211
  playing cards 216
  reception of Charles James Fox 203, 204f8.1
  relationship with Marie Countess Walewska 189
  snuff-box bequeathed to Lady Elizabeth Holland
    Bacchus cameo 214–15, 216f8.7, 218
    playing card 216–17, 217f8.8, 218

  Pope Pius VI 214
  superstition 217–18
  Napoleonic keepsakes 203, 211, 218, 219, 220, 221, 222
Napoleonic Wars 5, 7, 19
natural and man-made phenomena 20–1, 114
natural history and natural philosophy 108, 109, 114, 115
natural history specimens 21, 70, 107, 108, 112, 117, 119, 132, 142, 156, 157, 163, 166, 226
Normand, Marie Anne Le 216, 220
nouveau riche 4, 7, 8, 36, 88, 98, 190
novelty 113

ore, samples of 130, 131, 133, 138, 156, 158, 162, 211

Parker II, John (Earl of Morley) 48, 158
  see also Saltram House, Devon
Parmigianino (artist) 67
Parminter, Elizabeth 68
Parminter, Jane 68, 68f2.2
Parminter, Mary 68, 68f2.2
Parry, William 56
Patch, Thomas 34, 56
Peak District 5, 113
Pelham, Thomas 183
Percival, Katherine 178
Percy, Lady Elizabeth (Duchess of Northumberland) 7, 8, 70, 81
  see also Smithson, Hugh; Vilet, Jean
Percy estates, Northumberland 7, 8, 70
personality 2, 77, 92, 96
Petty, William (second Earl of Shelburne) 157
Pini, Ermenegildo 145

Piozzi, Gabriel 6, 89, 92, 93, 94–5, 181
Piozzi, Hester Lynch
  Bluestocking salon 89
  Brynbella 77, 89, 94–5, 95f3.4, 96
  Cotton, Sir Robert 89
  decorated fans 65–6
  demi-naturalised persona 90, 91–2, 94, 97
  Exmouth trip (1788) 91
  friendship with Fanny Burney 187
  friendship with Samuel Lysons 95, 181, 182–3
  honeymoon with Gabriel 6
  map of Hester's Grand Tour (1784–86) 78f3.1
  Miss Birch gift exchange 187, 192
  mother–daughter gift exchange 181
  Observations and Reflections 15, 90, 91
  portrait (1785–86) plate 9
  Queeny 89, 94
  Retrospection 96
  Salusbury family 89
  self-portraits 92
  social exclusion 90
  Streatham Park 89, 92, 93, 94
  Thraliana 15, 91, 93–4
  Townley Collection at Park Street Gallery 47–8
  Tunbridge Wells trip (1779) 187, 192
  Venice trip (1784) 58, 59
  Welsh–Italian identity 90, 97
  see also Bluestocking circle; Chappelow, Reverend Leonard; Johnson, Samuel; Thrale, Henry
Pitt, Anne 42
Pluche, Noël Antoine 142, 143
Plumptre, James *see The Lakers* (comic opera, 1798)

Pointon, Marcia 17, 129, 245
Portici museum 44, 62
Portici royal palace 214
Powys, Caroline 1, 114, 115, 116, 117, 118, 119, 125, 126, 132, 138, 146, 165
Powys, Philip Libbe 114, 115
Pratt, Mary Louise 107
precious stones *see* stones
Priestley, Joseph 109, 157

Queen Anne 195
Queen Charlotte 34, 65
Queen Maria Carolina plate 13, 187–8, 188f7.1
Queen Mary 154

Redford, Bruce 4, 24n7
regionality 2, 77, 88
Reni, Guido 41, 56, 95
Renaissance paintings 8, 56, 59, 67, 92, 97
Reynolds, Joshua 34, 35f1.1, 48
Richardson, Dorothy
  Alga Marina Fucus 130–1
  attention to detail in journals 124, 125, 126
  Bierley Hall 9, 123
  Danesfield Camp, Medmenham 127
  Dr Hunter's Museum visit (1785) 129, 149
  East Riding of Yorkshire visit (1801) 7
  Halifax Gibbet 127, 128f5.1
  iron ore 133, 138
  minute taking 124, 126
  Nostal Priory visit (1761) 124
  seaweed specimens 10, 130, 131, 133, 138
  shell collecting 130, 131
  specimens from working-class people 133, 135

Speedwell Cavern, Castleton
 visit (1767) 130
 see also Richardson, Henry;
 Richardson, Richard
Richardson, Henry 9
Richardson, Richard 9, 123
Richardson-Currer, Frances Mary 123
Robinson, George 109
Robinson, Hugh 57
romantic friendships 177, 186, 197n11, 199n46, 234
Royal Museum of Physics and Natural History 146, 147, 148, 149
 see also Anatomical Venus; Fontana, Felice
Royal Society 9, 109, 110, 116, 131, 157, 166
Royal Society of Arts 124
royalty and gift exchange 177–8, 185, 187, 194, 195

salon hostesses 47, 57, 77, 84, 88, 89, 153, 154, 165, 220
salons 1, 8, 20, 22, 77, 81, 83, 84, 88, 89, 112, 153, 165, 220
 see also Bluestocking circle
Saltram House, Devon 48, 49f1.6, 158
satires against female artists 63–4
Say, William 35
Schmeisser, Johann Gottfried 159
scientific debates 160, 161
scientific institutions 108, 110, 116, 119
scientific knowledge 21, 110, 118, 119, 123, 126, 129, 130, 132, 137, 138, 143, 149, 150, 152, 157, 158, 161, 162, 164–5, 166
scientific travel collecting 21, 22, 114, 117, 119, 123, 138
Scott, Sir Walter 84, 153
self-identity *see* identity formation

sentimental fiction 16, 175, 177
sentimentalisation of friendships 22, 23, 177, 184, 234
sentimental value of objects 16, 22, 23, 68, 88, 177, 180, 184, 185, 187, 191, 193, 195, 203, 218, 228, 229, 234, 240
Seward, Anna 83, 84, 87–8
Seymour, Algernon (seventh Duke of Somerset) 70
Seymour, Frances (Countess of Hertford) 180, 184
Shakespeare, William 47, 191, 192
Shelley, Mary 70
shells 68, 69, 81, 109, 112, 129, 130, 131–2, 186
Shipley, William 124
shopping as a pastime 58, 62, 72
sketches 8, 42, 63, 64, 138
Smithson, Hugh 7, 70, 75n54
Smithson, James 151, 158, 159, 161, 164
snuff-boxes 16, 60, 178, 185, 192, 207, 214, 215–16, 218, 219, 220, 227, 229, 230, 234, 236, 246
Soane, Sir John 45, 80
social circulation of science 142, 158, 164, 166, 175
social elite 3, 11, 18, 36, 47, 50, 88, 97, 190
social politics 203, 222
social status 7, 34, 77, 85, 86, 88, 96, 157, 179, 184, 187, 190, 229
Society of Antiquaries 56, 72, 73n2, 110, 123, 124
Society of Dilettanti 34, 35f1.1, 51n7, 56, 72
Somerset, Elizabeth (Duchess of Beaufort) 40, 41, 42, 56
Spallanzani, Lazzaro 144–5
specimens 22
Speedwell Cavern, Castleton 130

Spencer, Georgiana (Duchess of Devonshire) 57, 177
Sterne, Laurence 185
Stewart, Susan 1, 14, 15, 71
Stonehenge 1, 115, 116, 118, 146
stones 1, 60, 116, 132, 156, 157, 226, 227, 229
Storer, Anthony Morris 143
Stuart, Mary 4–5
Stukeley, William 115, 116
Swinburne, Caroline plate 13, 187, 188f7.1
Swinburne, Henry 6, 37, 42, 52n16, 187
Swinburne, Martha 6, 37, 38–9, 52n16

Taylor, Sir John (first Baronet) 34
The Ladies Diary 108–9
The Lady's Magazine 109
The Lakers (comic opera, 1798) 64
thermal springs 110–11
thing theory 16–17
Thomas, Nicholas 112–13, 164–5
Thrale, Henry 89, 187
Tipper, John 108
Titian 41, 93
Townley, Charles plate 2, 47, 48
Townley Collection at Park Street Gallery plate 2, 47–8
see also *Discobolus* (sculpture)
Tozzetti, Antonio Targioni 158
traveller versus tourist identity 14
Tresham, Henry 42, 43f1.5, 59
Tristan, Charles (Marquis de Montholon) 221
Tunbridge-ware 20, 179, 180, 187, 192, 192f7.2, 194f7.4, 200n64
Tunbridge Wells 5, 178–9, 181, 187, 192, 196, 200n64

Vachette, Adrien Jean Maximilien plate 14, 216f8.7, 217f8.8, 224n38

Vassall, Elizabeth see Holland, Lady Elizabeth
Vassall, Florentius 143, 167n5
Vassall, Godfrey see Webster, Sir Godfrey
vertical relationships 178, 182, 186, 210, 229, 234, 235
Vesey, Elizabeth 84, 85
Vesuvius, Mount 40, 63, 154–5, 156
Vichy-Chamrond, Marie Anne de 188–9
Vilet, Jean 7, 71
Virgil (poet) 41, 70
Voltaire 71, 230, 237

Wakefield, Priscilla 109
Walewska, Marie Countess 189
Walker, Adam 115
Walpole, Horace (fourth Earl of Orford) 9, 13, 34, 79, 84, 175, 188, 190
Webster, Elizabeth Vassall see Holland, Lady Elizabeth
Webster, Sir Godfrey 6, 144, 152, 169n41, 203
Wedgwood, Josiah 86
Whig political salon see Holland House
Whig politics 6, 8, 143, 153, 219
Wilmot, Katherine
 audience with Pope Pius VI 7, 10
 bracelet of hair from Martha 176
 condemnation of Napoleon 23, 208
 Ekaterina's hold over Martha 229–30
 Ekaterina's memoirs 246
 Grand Tour 1801 7
 Irish heritage 208
 Napoleonic keepsakes 203
 Napoleon's physical appearance 209–10
 Paris trip (1801) 207

Paris trip (1802) with Lady
  Margaret Mount Cashell
  189
Troitskoe visit (1803) 237
Wilmot, Martha
  friendship with Ekaterina
    Dashkova
    album of watercolours 246
    Ekaterina's memoirs 246
    female–female keepsake
      exchange 176
    hierarchical relationship with
      Ekaterina 229
    level of sensibility 228
    portraits of Martha 235,
      235f9.2, 236
    Russian mother 227, 242,
      247n4
  Troitskoe 226
  gift-giving to men 182
  gifts from Ekaterina Dashkova
    arborised agate from
      Ekaterina's mother 238–9
    fan from Catherine the Great
      238
    financial value of gifts 228,
      229
    fireplace for the Wilmot
      family 240, 241f9.3
    necklace created from
      sentiment bracelet 244–5

painting plate 15, 239–40
Russian book with three
  volumes 241–2
sentimental value of objects
  23, 229
sentiment bracelet 233–4,
  245
snuff-boxes 229–30
value of Ekaterina's affection
  229
volume of gifts 227
letter to Anna Chetwood 228,
  236
sentimental value of letters
  191
travel journals 176, 227–8,
  229, 238, 244, 245, 246
Wollstonecraft, Mary 186, 208
Woodstock gloves 194, 195,
  200n68
Wordsworth, Dorothy 133–4
working-class people 19, 133, 137,
  181
Worsley, Sir Richard 39–40
Wortley Montagu, Lady Mary
  4–5
Wykeham Archer, John ix, plate
  12

Zampieri, Domenico 93, 95
Zoffany, Johan viii, plate 1, 34

EU authorised representative for GPSR:
Easy Access System Europe, Mustamäe tee 50,
10621 Tallinn, Estonia
gpsr.requests@easproject.com

www.ingramcontent.com/pod-product-compliance
Lightning Source LLC
Chambersburg PA
CBHW050925240426
43668CB00021B/2435